BOOKS BY STEVEN RAICHLEN

DINING IN BOSTON COOKBOOK

STEVEN RAICHLEN'S GUIDE TO
BOSTON RESTAURANTS

A TASTE OF THE MOUNTAINS
COOKING SCHOOL COOKBOOK

BOSTON'S BEST RESTAURANTS

STEVEN RAICHLEN

POSEIDON PRESS

New York   London   Toronto   Sydney   Tokyo

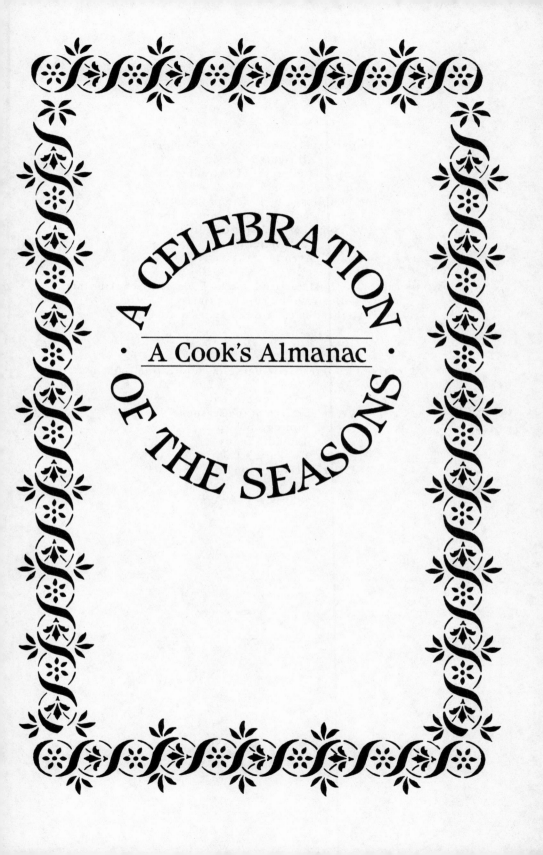

A CELEBRATION
OF THE SEASONS

· A Cook's Almanac ·

Published by Poseidon Press
A Division of Simon & Schuster Inc.
Simon & Schuster Building
Rockefeller Center
1230 Avenue of the Americas
New York, NY 10020
POSEIDON PRESS is a registered trademark of Simon & Schuster Inc.
Designed by Karolina Harris
Manufactured in the United States of America

1   3   5   7   9   10   8   6   4   2

Library of Congress Cataloging-in-Publication Data

Raichlen, Steven.
A celebration of the seasons.
Bibliography: p.
Includes index.
1. Cookery.   I. Title.
TX715.R12   1988   641.5   88-4049

ISBN 0-671-62498-9

To Barbara
with love

ACKNOWLEDGMENTS

WRITING A book is like making a movie. This one involved the proverbial cast of thousands.

First and foremost, I would like to thank Marcia Walsh, assistant extraordinaire, researcher, editor, recipe tester, and fine cook, many of whose recipes grace these pages. The book quite literally could not have been written without her.

Margaret Crane, Andrea Panella, and Denise Iozo provided logistical support. Janet Meakin came to my rescue, typing the manuscript at the eleventh hour. Chris Kauth and Rick Spencer were congenial cooking companions, developing many fine recipes. Dick and Laura Chasin furnished me with a spectacular place to write. Norman Martel kept my computer humming smoothly. Philip Helfaer, Ildri Ginn, and Norman Moss provided sorely needed spiritual support.

Many friends rallied around me to help with proofreading: Kathy Hawley, Katherine Kenny, Joe Kropp, Cindy Levine, Darryl Pomicter, and Ted and Carol Spach. Liz Lowe catered the proofreading party and helped with recipe testing.

Recipe testers included Holly Collins, Sonya Deitman, Laura Dennison, Laurie Fallon, Joanne Lennon, Lisa Lipton, Kernan Manion, Joan McConologue, Ellie Merson, Debby Pearse, Sybil Stone, Nancy Theriault, Jean and John Wiecha, and Nancy Young. And thanks to those great gals from Glen Ellyn, Jean True, Julie Wolsky, and Darlene Peterson for recipe R and D.

I would like to thank my agent, Meg Ruley, who inspired the book; my editor, Pat Capon, who cut an 839-page manuscript down to manageable size; my copy editor, Andrée Pagès; and my parents and grandparents for being there—now as then. I had the privilege of training with many fine chefs, including Fernand

Chambrette, Albert Jorant, Louis LeRoy, Claude Vauguet, and Anne Willan.

This book was written on a Kaypro computer in Cambridge, Massachussetts; Chappaquiddick, Massachussetts; and Glen, New Hampshire.

CONTENTS

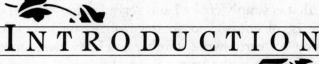

INTRODUCTION

F O R all human history, save the last hundred years, people have feasted on seasonal provender. Spring was a time for lamb, because the baby sheep had reached eating size. Summertime meant berries, for the bushes in the forest were laden. In the fall, people enjoyed shellfish that had been unpalatable during the summer months of spawning. In the winter, they ate gourds and root vegetables, for these alone could survive the long, dark months without refrigeration. The human diet was infinitely varied and in harmony with the natural cycles. True, there were occasional famines, and months when some superabundant foods grew monotonous. But in general, whatever people ate was at its freshest, ripest, and seasonal best.

Modern man has taken a somewhat different approach. The invention of canning in the mid–nineteenth century and freezing in the twentieth made it possible to prolong for months and years the shelf life of perishable foods. Modern agriculture bequeathed us the hothouse tomato; modern industry, the frozen fish stick. Unfortunately, freezing destroys the delicate texture of seafood, and hothouse fruits are about as appetizing as cotton balls.

Happily, the march of progress has not completely eliminated the pleasures of seasonal provender. If anything, seasonal cooking is undergoing a resurgence. A new generation of American chefs has taught us to seek our ingredients not in France, but in our own backyards. Airfreight has made it possible for Bostonians to sample the year's first asparagus within hours of its harvest in California. Progressive greengrocers stock their shelves with arugula, morels, and starfruit; our local supermarkets have begun to sell local fish and garden-grown herbs. As a nation— the most technological in the world—we have come to understand a fundamental truth recognized by untold generations of cooks—that no amount of culinary artifice can rival a fresh ingredient that is simply cooked and served at its seasonal best.

There is, of course, no shortage of seasonal cookbooks in print. Why on earth write another one? My main motive for writing this book is the very nature of seasonal cooking itself. The foods we cook and the way we cook them are continuously evolving. Modern-day cooks use a host of ingredients unavailable (or at least uncommon) ten years ago: hazelnut oil, goat cheese, ancho chilies, dried tomatoes, and fresh herbs, just to name a few. The food processor and microwave oven have revolutionized our cooking methods—so have the wok, steamer, and nonstick frying pan. Our tastebuds are more international than ever before: Thai soups or French pâtés are as much a part of the new "American" cuisine as Texas chili or Indian pudding. Finally, with today's hectic pace, few of us have the time to spend hours in the kitchen. We still love food and want to eat well, but we want to do it fast. Thus, the need for an up-to-date seasonal cookbook is as great now as it was when Grimod de la Reynière wrote his *Almanac des Gourmands* in the early nineteenth century. Each new generation reinvents seasonal cooking, and it shouldn't be any other way.

There are three types of seasonal foods covered in this cookbook. The first are the truly seasonal foods, like soft-shell crabs or chestnuts, which are available only a few weeks a year. The second includes ingredients like salmon and asparagus, which, though available year-round, are decidedly better in some months than in others. You will notice that many of my recipes call for canned tomatoes, and this may seem contrary to the spirit of seasonal cooking. But a good canned tomato has infinitely more flavor than a wintertime hothouse fruit. The third type of seasonal foods are those associated with holidays, like matzoh at Passover or turkey for Thanksgiving. Some traditions are so binding that even in our jet-set era it would seem a sacrilege to let them fall by the wayside.

The United States is a vast country. What is seasonal in one region may not be in another. Blueberries ripen in New Jersey two months before they appear in Maine. Bluefish take four months to complete their migration from Florida to Massachusetts and back again, and they are fished at every point along the way. By its very nature, seasonality is tied to geography, and it is impossible for a writer, much less a book, to be everywhere at once. I live in Massachusetts, and while portions of this book were researched in California, Florida, and the Midwest, it is written from the perspective of a New Englander.

At the same time, however, we live in an age of shrinking distances and increased global awareness. The airplane has eliminated the traditional boundaries of time, place, and nationality. Thanks to airfreight, the first Italian chestnuts or Florida stone crabs arrive at market in most American cities within days, if not hours, of being gathered. The chances are that wherever you live, you will probably be able to enjoy fresh fennel or seckel pears at the same time that I do. If not, they will certainly be available in your area soon enough.

HOW TO USE THIS BOOK

A CELEBRATION OF THE SEASONS is divided into fourteen chapters—one for each month of the year, plus one for miscellaneous recipes and one for basic recipes. Each monthly chapter profiles five or six seasonal foods, with recipes for how to use them. I discuss the food's natural and social history, and offer practical tips for its purchase, storage, and preparation.

The best guide to seasonal food is the market. That is how I do my menu planning—I buy what looks fresh, and figure out what to do with it once I get home. This book is designed to eliminate some of the guesswork. But let the spirit of seasonal shopping be your guide.

Cooking is not a fixed science but an ever-evolving art. Recipes are the guidelines. There is no definitive text. The recipes in this book represent a point in time, but undoubtedly they will continue evolving. I invite you to modify my recipes to suit the ingredients you have on hand and your tastes.

In keeping with contemporary lifestyles, I have tried to create recipes that are interesting and quick to prepare—most can be cooked in thirty minutes or less. Anyone wishing to know more about my particular techniques and theories of cooking should consult my book *A Taste of the Mountains Cooking School Cookbook* (also published by Poseidon Press).

To everything there is a season,
And a time for every purpose under heaven

—*E C C L E S I A S T E S*

JANUARY

Then came old January, wrapped well
In many weeds to keep the cold away;
Yet did he quake and quiver like to quell,
And blow his nails to warm them if he may;
For they were numbed with holding all the day
An hatchet keen with which he felled wood.

E D M U N D   S P E N S E R

J A N U A R Y is the month of new beginnings. Appropriately, it was sacred to Janus, the Roman god of doors and gateways. (*Janua* is the Latin word for "door.") The Romans prayed to him at the start of each month and year, and before undertaking a new enterprise. Janus was portrayed as a god with two faces, one looking forward, the other, back. One hand held a staff, a symbol of his power; in the other hand was a key, representing his right to open and close all things.

In many places January is the coldest month of the year. The Anglo-Saxons called it *Wulf-Monath,* "wolf's month," for in this season starving wolves would leave the forests, invade small villages, and prey on human beings. In the Middle Ages, January was portrayed as a woodsman, carrying an ax, gathering firewood, and blowing on his fingers because of the cold. In the French Revolutionary calendar it corresponded to parts of the months *Nivose* ("month of snow") and *Pluvoise* ("month of rain").

The most important holiday in January is New Year's Day. In England it was customary to clean house on January 1, a practice that survives metaphorically in our "cleaning the slate" to make New Year's resolutions. Janunary 2 is sacred to St. Macarius, the patron saint of pastry cooks. Other January holidays include Twelfth Night (January 5), which marks the end of the Christmas festivities, and Epiphany (January 6), which honors the visit the Wise Men from the East made to Christ. In rural England on Epiphany Eve, an Apple Howling would take place: revelers would gather in an orchard, drink toasts of hard cider, and beat their favorite tree with sticks, hoping to bully the tree into bearing more fruit in the coming year.

January has been called "the blackest month of the year." True, it is a time of darkness and unhospitable weather. That's all the more reason to spend one's time in a warm, bright, cheery kitchen! Hearty soups, homemade breads, and robust stews help take the chill off winter. Braising is my favorite cold-weather cooking method: the long, slow, moist heat produces exceptionally tender meats, and has the advantage of warming up the kitchen! January produce is limited to sturdy root vegetables and winter squashes. Fresh fruits are scarce, but this is an ideal time of year to enjoy dried fruits, like figs, and all manner of dried beans, the only foods available to our thrifty ancestors. Another food I associate with January is blue cheese: there are few things more comforting than sitting by the fire, sipping port, and nibbling Stilton cheese.

So let the winds blow and the temperature plummet—below are some heartwarming recipes for winter.

BLUE CHEESE

"I should no more want Stilton on a hot August day, than boiled silverside and dumplings," observed a nineteenth-century English journalist, Sir John Squire. Hyperbole, perhaps, but it does point out that this blue cheese is supremely satisfying in winter—especially when partaken with a glass of port or Sauternes in front of a blazing fire. The closest many people get to blue cheese is salad dressing, which is unfortunate, because the blues include three of the world's greatest cheeses: Stilton, Gorgonzola, and Roquefort.

"The noble word comes as easily to an Englishman's tongue as the word Shakespeare, and a touch of pride accompanies both." So wrote Edward Bunyard about Britain's celebrated Stilton. This suave blue cheese originated in Leicestershire in the eighteenth cenutry; a Mrs. Orton, housekeeper in Quenby Hall, is credited with its discovery. Today, its production is limited to three counties in central England: Rutland, Leicestershire, and Huntington.

Made from cows' milk, Stilton comes in cylinders the size and shape of a sugar canister. The rind is wrinkled like that of a melon; the inside is ivory-colored, darkening to amber at the edges. Stilton's texture is creamy; its flavor, buttery and mellow. It is the mildest member of the blue cheese aristocracy. It's not without reason that the English refer to Roquefort as a Stilton lacking a college education.

Gorgonzola is Italy's answer to Stilton. Since the ninth century, it has been made in the Po Valley, near Milan. The first Gorgonzola, so the story goes, was an unveined cheese that shepherds would swap for wine at a local tavern. The tavern basement filled with these uneaten cheeses; the cool, damp environment gave birth to the distinctive green mold. The very mention of Gorgonzola is enough to curl the toes of anyone who has experienced tasting a mature one.

Like Stilton, Gorgonzola is made from cows' milk, and like Roquefort, it is aged in caves. Unlike either, its veining is green. Its assertive aroma is unsettlingly reminiscent of a gym locker. Gorgonzola is the creamiest of the blues, especially when ripe, but eiderdown softness hides a pungency that could almost wake the dead. It is often served in polenta or pasta; a classic dessert combination is Gorgonzola and figs.

Roquefort began, legend holds, as a cheese sandwich discarded by a shepherd in a cave. The place was a town in south central France, and since Roman times, its blue-veined cheese has been favored around the world. Unlike other blue cheeses, Roquefort is made from sheep's milk, which produces its distinctive tang. But the cool limestone caves in which the cheese must be aged in order to be called Roquefort are equally responsible for the salty, prickly flavor that makes this cheese unique.

The town of Roquefort clings to the side of Mount Combalou, a three-thousand-foot-high, sparsely vegetated mass that's as rocky as a lunar landscape. (The town's name comes from the French words *roc,* "rock," and *fort,* "strong.") On the surface, Roquefort is a sleepy French town, for all the activity takes place deep underground. The mountain is honeycombed with cavelike fissures—twenty-five acres' worth—which surface a mile away from the town. Made of porous limestone, the caves are a unique cooling system, with an unwavering temperature of around 45 degrees and 95 percent humidity.

Roquefort is among the most expensive of the world's blues, but given the time and effort that goes into it, it's surprising that it doesn't cost more. It takes twelve days' worth of milk from one ewe to make a single six-pound cheese. Each cheese is salted, turned, and wrapped by hand, and aged for a minimum of four months in one of the twenty-five caves under the city. The mold is grown in the caves on specially baked loaves of rye bread and injected into the cheese with stainless steel needles.

BUYING BLUE CHEESES

BLUE cheeses are usually sold in wedges. Avoid those with oozing brown spots or incrustations of salt. A whole Stilton, swaddled in a cloth napkin, makes an elegant centerpiece for a buffet. Avoid Stiltons with waxed rinds—unable to "breathe," they do not ripen properly.

SERVING BLUE CHEESES

PORT wine and Stilton is a heaven-made marriage, but to hollow the center of a cheese and fill it with wine is to ruin a good morsel by drowning. Enjoy Stilton with biscuits and sip the port separately—preferably on a winter's day in front of a crackling fire. Gorgonzola should be eaten with crusty bread; figs and red wine are the traditional accompaniments. Roquefort is eaten on buttered bread in France (use unsalted butter). The traditional wine is Sauternes: the sweetness of this rich dessert wine balances the saltiness of the cheese. Like most cheeses, the blues taste best at room temperature.

Stilton *Crostini*

MAKES 16 TOASTS

THIS dish has a dual heritage. *Crostini* are butter-baked toast points from Italy (they can also be brushed with oil) and Stilton is a blue cheese from England. Alternatively, you could use Gorgonzola or Roquefort. Stilton crostini are excellent for cocktail parties: the salt makes people thirsty!

For the crostini:
 1 loaf French bread
 4 tablespoons butter, melted

For the topping:
 4 tablespoons unsalted butter, at room temperature
 ¼ pound Stilton cheese, at room temperature
 3 tablespoons heavy cream
 1 egg yolk
   Plenty of fresh black pepper

(1) Make the crostini. Preheat the oven to 400 degrees. Cut the bread into diagonal, 1/2-inch slices. Lightly brush each slice on both sides with the melted butter. Bake the toasts in the oven for 5 to 10 minutes per side, or until golden brown. Transfer the crostini to a cake rack to cool.

(2) Meanwhile, prepare the topping. Cream the butter in a food processor or in a large bowl with a whisk or wooden spoon.

Mash the cheese with a fork and beat it into the butter. Gradually beat in the remaining ingredients—the mixture should be soft but not runny. Spread it liberally atop the cool toasts.

(3) Just before serving, bake the crostini in a preheated 500-degree oven for 3 to 4 minutes (under a broiler for 1 to 2 minutes) or until the topping is bubbly and browned. Serve at once.

Roquefort-Leek Soufflé

SERVES 4

ROQUEFORT-LEEK tart is a specialty of the main hotel in the village of Roquefort. Some years ago, I decided to try this felicitous combination as a flavoring for a soufflé. Soufflés are a cinch to make, but there are three important watchpoints. First, carefully butter the bottom, sides, and rim of the soufflé dish so the soufflé can rise without obstruction. Second, beat the egg whites stiff but not dry, adding pinches of salt and cream of tartar to stabilize the whites. Finally, have your base mixture piping hot when you fold in the whites—this partially cooks the whites and helps prevent them from deflating.

> 3–4 ounces Roquefort cheese
> 2–3 leeks (¾ cup chopped)
>   5 tablespoons butter
>   ⅓ cup bread crumbs or finely chopped nuts (for lining the soufflé dish)
>   4 tablespoons flour
>   1 cup milk
>   4 egg yolks
>   Salt, fresh black pepper, cayenne pepper, and freshly grated nutmeg
>   6 egg whites
>   Pinch of cream of tartar
>
>   1 5-cup soufflé dish or 4 1-cup ramekins

(1) Crumble the Roquefort cheese and reserve. Wash the leeks and finely chop. Melt the butter in a heavy, 1-quart saucepan. Brush the bottom, sides, and rim of the soufflé dish or ramekins with melted butter, chill for 30 minutes, and brush again. Coat the inside of the dish or ramekins with the bread crumbs or chopped nuts.

(2) You should have about 3 tablespoons melted butter remaining in the saucepan. Add the leeks and cook over low heat for 3 to 4 minutes, or until tender. Stir in the flour and cook over medium heat for 1 minute to make a roux. Whisk in the milk off the heat, return the pan to the heat, and boil the sauce for 2 to 3 minutes, stirring constantly—the mixture should thicken. Lower the heat and beat in the egg yolks, one by one. Remove the pan from the heat as soon as the mixture thickens. Stir in the crumbled Roquefort and seasonings, but go easy on the salt, for the cheese is quite salty.

(3) Meanwhile, beat the egg whites until stiff, adding a pinch of salt and of cream of tartar after 15 seconds. Stir one-quarter of the whites into the *hot* cheese mixture (reheat it if necessary). Fold the lightened cheese mixture back into the eggs, working as gently as possible—overfolding will deflate the soufflé. Don't worry about stray clumps of white. Spoon the soufflé mixture into the soufflé dish or ramekins and smooth the top with a wet spatula. Note: if the base mixture was hot and the whites were stiffly beaten, the soufflé can be prepared several hours ahead.

(4) Preheat the oven to 400 degrees. Run your thumbs around the inside of the soufflé dish to clear the edges, and wipe any spills off the sides of the dish—they'll be hard to remove when baked. Bake the soufflé for 20 to 30 minutes (10 to 15 minutes for individual soufflés) or until puffed and cooked to taste—I like my soufflés a little runny in the center. Guests wait for soufflés, not the other way around: serve at once. A full-bodied Chardonnay would be an appropriate wine, or for an interesting contrast, try a Sauternes.

Polenta with Gorgonzola

SERVES 8

POLENTA is a cross between cornbread and grits. This sturdy starch is popular in northern Italy, where it is often served with Gorgonzola sauce. *Parmigiano-reggiano* from Emilia-Romagna is the best Italian grating cheese. Unless these words are stamped into the rind, you have not bought the real McCoy. The polenta requires constant attention and stirring—don't make it when you're feeling fatigued! Our thanks to Maurie Warren, of the Il Capriccio restaurant in Waltham, Massachussetts, for the recipe.

For the polenta:
  2 teaspoons salt
  2 cups coarse-grain cornmeal

For the Gorgonzola sauce:
  3 cups heavy cream
  ½ pound Italian Gorgonzola, or to taste
  ½ cup grated Parmigiano-reggiano
    Freshly ground white pepper

  1 jelly roll pan or baking sheet, lined with plastic wrap or foil and oiled
  1 12-inch baking dish suitable for serving, heavily buttered

(1) Bring 6½ cups water and the salt to a boil in a large saucepan and slowly whisk in the cornmeal. Reduce the heat and gently simmer the mixture, stirring frequently with a wooden spoon, until it stiffens and starts to come away from the side of the pan. Do not be discouraged: it may take 20 to 30 minutes for the polenta to reach this critical point. You don't have to stir every single minute, but you should watch the pan closely. (*Note:* Italian gourmet shops sell electric polenta machines, which do the arduous stirring for you.) Pour the polenta into the prepared jelly roll pan, smooth the top with a spatula, and let it cool to room temperature.

(2) When cooled, cut the polenta into 2-inch circles, using a plain or fluted cookie cutter. You should wind up with 16 circles. Alternatively, to save time, you can cut the polenta with a knife into rectangles or squares. The scraps can be recombined. The recipe can be prepared up to a day ahead at this point, provided the polenta is tightly wrapped and refrigerated.

(3) Now make the sauce. Place the cream in a heavy saucepan, and simmer, stirring frequently, until the liquid is reduced to 2 cups. Cut the Gorgonzola into ½-inch pieces. Reduce the heat and whisk in the cheese, a few chunks at a time, until the sauce is sufficiently cheesy. Continue whisking until the sauce is smooth. Remove the pan from the heat and whisk in two-thirds of the Parmesan and pepper to taste. The sauce can be prepared ahead of time, but don't let it boil when reheating it.

(4) Preheat the oven to 450 degrees. Just before serving, arrange the polenta circles in the prepared baking dish, each overlapping the next. Spoon the Gorgonzola sauce on top, sprinkle with the remaining Parmesan, and bake for 10 minutes, or until the polenta is thoroughly heated and the sauce is bubbling and golden. Serve with a gutsy red wine, like an Amarone or Taurasi from Italy.

BEEF

WE Americans are no longer the nation of beef-eaters we once were—before we were made aware of the dangers of cholesterol and cancer. The stereotypical meat-and-potatoes man is headed the way of the vacuum tube and Indian-head nickel.

During these cold, lean months, however, let us pause to reconsider. A steaming roast or hearty beef stew is just the thing for fortifying you against the rigors of winter. The oven warms up your kitchen; the richness of meat makes you feel not just nourished, but nurtured.

My favorite winter meat is beef—not sirloin or tenderloin, but the inexpensive cuts that are loaded with connective tissue. The best way to prepare them is by a moist, low-heat cooking method called braising. The universality of this method attests to its popularity: the Italians have their *osso bucco*; the French, their *boeuf à la mode*; New Englanders, Yankee pot roast. The word comes from the French *braises,* "embers," for in the days before gas and electricity, roasts would be cooked in a Dutch oven set on the embers, with more glowing coals placed in the hollow of the cover.

The theory of braising is simple. The meat is seared on all sides in hot fat to seal in the juices, then baked on a bed of aromatic vegetables with a little liquid in a tightly sealed pan. The low, moist heat melts the connective tissue; the steam generated from the pan juices penetrates the muscle fibers, tenderizing the meat. A low temperature is essential, because if the meat boils, it will toughen. It is also important to use a pan just large enough to hold the roast, and with a tight-fitting lid, to confine the steam. Beef can be braised over a low flame on top of the stove or in the oven. The latter has the advantage of requiring less attention. Braising is well suited to inexpensive cuts of beef, like blade steak, shoulder, or chuck. There's no need to buy prime, as the cooking method will tenderize the meat. Figure on one-half to three-quarters of a pound per person.

Below are three classic European beef dishes: German sauerbraten, French boeuf à la mode, and Belgian *carbonnade*. Any would warm the cockles of your heart on a winter night.

Sauerbraten

SERVES 6 TO 8

SAUERBRATEN is Germany's answer to the pot roast, and a splendid version it is. The roast owes its tenderness, not to mention its "sourish" tang to a spicy marinade of wine and vinegar in which it soaks for up to a week. The best sauerbraten I ever had was in Nuremberg, where the local gingerbread *Lebkuchen* ("love cakes," literally) is crumbled into the sauce. In this country similar results can be obtained by using crumbled gingersnap cookies. For extra flavor the sauce is puréed with the braising vegetables, then enriched with sour cream.

2 eyes of the round of beef (about 4 pounds)

For the marinade:
1 onion
1 carrot
1 branch celery
2 cloves garlic
2 cups dry red wine
½ cup red wine vinegar
20 black peppercorns
5 cloves
2 sticks cinnamon
10 juniper berries, or ½ cup gin
5 bay leaves
Generous pinch of thyme

For cooking the beef:
3 tablespoons butter
3 tablespoons oil
2 tablespoons brown sugar
Bouquet garni (see recipe on page 471)

To finish the sauce:
½ cup crumbled gingersnap cookies
½ cup sour cream
1 tablespoon flour

(1) Finely chop the vegetables and garlic. In a saucepan, combine them with the rest of the ingredients for the marinade and bring to a rapid boil. Remove pan from heat and allow the marinade to cool completely. Place the meat in a crock or glass bowl just large enough to hold it. Pour the marinade over the meat and marinate in the refrigerator for 3 to 5 days, turning the meat twice a day so all sides are exposed to marinade.

(2) Preheat the oven to 300 degrees. Strain the marinade from the meat and vegetables and reserve it. Remove the whole spices from the vegetables. Blot the meat and vegetables dry with paper towels. Heat half the butter and oil in a casserole just large enough to hold both pieces of meat. When the foam subsides, brown both pieces of meat on all sides in hot fat. Do not crowd the pan: it may be necessary to brown the meat in two batches. Transfer the meat to a platter and discard the fat from the casserole.

(3) Heat the remaining fat and cook the vegetables from the marinade over medium heat for 3 minutes. Add the sugar and cook a few minutes longer or until the vegetables are soft, but do not let them brown. Lay the browned roasts on top of the vegetables and add the reserved marinade and bouquet garni. Press a piece of foil over the top of the beef to make a tent, and tightly cover the pot. Bake the sauerbraten for 2 hours. Add the gingersnaps, and continue baking 30 to 45 minutes, or until the roasts are tender enough to be easily pierced with a skewer.

(4) To serve, cut the roasts into ½-inch slices and arrange them on a platter. Cover to keep warm. Discard the bouquet garni, and purée the pan juices and vegetables as finely as possible in a blender. In a separate bowl, whisk the sour cream with the flour. Bring the puréed sauce to a boil in a saucepan. Whisk in the sour cream and simmer for 3 minutes. Correct the sauce for seasoning, adding salt, pepper, sugar, even vinegar—it should be spicy and sweet and sour.

Sauerbraten demands a wine of tremendous power—a California Zinfandel, or perhaps a Crozes-Hermitage from the Rhône.

Beef *Mode*

SERVES 4 TO 6

BEEF *mode* (pot roast in wine) is as central to French home cooking as *gedempte fleisch* is to Jewish. The dish has a curious history. Once a year in nineteenth-century Paris, the meat merchants would parade their largest steer, garlanded with flowers, through streets lined with cheering crowds. This practice gave rise to a restaurant, the Boeuf à la Mode, whose sign portrayed a steer decked out in the latest fashion (*mode*). Actually, this hearty dish has been around for centuries. Our recipe has been adapted from one in Pierre de la Lune's *Le Cuisinier* ("The Cook"), published in 1659.

1 4-pound chuck roast
  Salt and fresh black pepper
3 tablespoons butter or bacon fat
3 tablespoons oil
1 onion
1 carrot
1 branch celery
1 clove garlic
3 strips bacon
3 cups dry red wine
  Bouquet garni (see recipe on page 471)

For the garnish:
3 carrots
3 new potatoes
3 turnips
3 small leeks, green leaves and roots discarded
3 tablespoons finely chopped fresh parsley

(1) Season the beef with salt and pepper. Heat half the butter and oil in a casserole pan just large enough to hold the beef and all the vegetables. Brown the beef thoroughly on all sides and transfer to a platter. Discard the fat. Meanwhile, finely chop the vegetables and mince the garlic.

(2) Preheat the oven to 325 degrees. Heat the remaining fat in the pan and cook the chopped vegetables over medium heat for 3 to 4 minutes, or until soft. Return the beef to the pan, drape the bacon strips over the top, and add the wine and bouquet garni. Bring the mixture to a gentle boil, press a tent of foil over the beef, and tightly cover the pan. Bake the beef in the oven for 1 hour.

(3) Meanwhile, prepare the vegetable garnish. Peel the carrots, potatoes, and turnips. Cut them into 2-inch pieces, and, if you are feeling ambitious, carve them into olive shapes. Cut the leeks in half lengthwise and wash. Add the vegetables to the beef *mode* and continue cooking for 1½ hours, or until the beef and vegetables are very tender.

(4) To serve, carve the beef into ½-inch slices and arrange them on a platter or plates surrounded by the vegetables. Discard the bouquet garni, and skim off any fat that has risen to the surface of the sauce. Purée the sauce in a blender and correct the seasoning. Pour the sauce on top of the meat and sprinkle with the parsley. (*Note:* If the sauce is too thin, you may wish to thicken it with a little cornstarch. Dissolve 1 teaspoon cornstarch in 1 tablespoon Madeira. Stir this mixture into the sauce and simmer for 1 minute.)

Beef *mode* cries out for a robust red wine: a Chambertin or Côte de Beaune from Burgundy, a Cahors from the southwest of France, or a Pinot Noir from Oregon.

Carbonnade de Boeuf
(Beef Braised in Beer)

SERVES 6

CARBONNADE is a specialty of northeast France, where the common beverage is beer, not wine. Not surprisingly, when people make pot roast here, the preferred cooking liquid is beer. Carbonnade and other roasts were traditionally cooked in a pot surrounded by glowing coals. The French word for coal is *char-bon,* whence the name of the dish.

> 1 3 to 4-pound blade steak or chuck steak
>   Salt and fresh black pepper
> 3 tablespoons butter
> 3 tablespoons oil
> 1½ pounds onions, thinly sliced
> 2 cloves garlic, minced
> 1 14-ounce can imported plum tomatoes, peeled, seeded, and
>   coarsely chopped
> 3 tablespoons flour
> 2 bottles French beer or other light, "hopsy" beer (about 2 cups),
>   plus extra if needed
> 1 cup veal or beef stock
> 1 tablespoon tomato paste
>   Bouquet garni (see recipe on page 471)
> ¼ cup chopped fresh parsley

(1) Preheat the oven to 350 degrees. Sprinkle the meat with salt and fresh black pepper. Heat half the butter and oil in a large casserole, and thoroughly brown the meat on all sides. Set aside and discard the fat from the pan.

(2) Heat the remaining fat in the pan, and cook the onions and garlic over medium heat for 4 to 5 minutes, or until soft and golden brown. Add the tomatoes, increase the heat to high, and cook for 2 to 3 minutes to evaporate some of the excess liquid. Stir in the flour and cook for 1 minute. Stir in 2 cups beer, the stock, and the tomato paste. Return the beef to the pan with the bouquet garni, and spoon some of the vegetables over the meat. Cover tightly.

(3) Place the pan in the oven and bake for 2–3 hours, or until the meat is soft and tender enough to be easily pierced with a fork. Add more beer if the liquid level falls too low; if there is too much liquid, leave the pan uncovered during the last half-hour of cooking. All told, there should be 2 cups sauce. To serve, slice the roast and arrange it on a platter. Remove the bouquet garni, correct the seasoning, and spoon the sauce and vegetables on top. Serve carbonnade with mustard and the same beer you used for cooking.

LEGUMES

LEGUMES are seeds that come in a pod (the word comes from the Latin *legere,* "to gather"). While some species, like peas, are enjoyed fresh, most are dried for use during the winter months, when fresh vegetables are scarce. Legumes are good for you; these hardy seeds contain twice as much protein as grains do, and substantial doses of the B vitamins and iron.

Societies have been mixed in their attitudes toward legumes. The Romans esteemed them—so highly that four prominent families were named for legumes: Piso from the pea, Lentulus from the lentil, Fabius from the fava bean, and Cicero from the chick-pea. The church fathers of the Middle Ages found them offensive: St. Augustine saw the flatulence they caused as one of the signs of man's fall from grace. By a twist of logic peculiar to Jews, legumes were served at medieval weddings: being associated with mourning, they would "trick" the evil eye into bothering more fortunate victims.

In this country, legumes have been the traditional food of the poor: the blacks of the South ate black-eyed peas, backwoods New Englanders doted on baked beans. Fortunately, our interest in regional American cooking has helped rehabilitate these nutritious seeds.

The advantage of dried peas and beans is that they are available when fresh vegetables aren't. Nonetheless, legumes that have sat around too long become overly dry and will be tough, no matter how long they are cooked. I try to buy legumes in bulk from an ethnic market or health food store that has a rapid turnover. Choose beans that are clean and of even size. Avoid any with tiny holes: they may be infested with bugs.

Pick through dried peas or beans to remove woody stems or

small pebbles. Legumes should be soaked in water to cover before cooking: this not only shortens the cooking time, but also helps prevent the beans from splitting. You need only soak them for 2 to 3 hours (or overnight in the refrigerator). Oversoaked beans begin to ferment, which makes them extra flatulent.

The starting point for most legume recipes is cooking the beans in water (use the soaking water) with aromatic vegetables (onions, carrots, leeks, and garlic) and herbs and spices (bay leaves, thyme, parsley, peppercorns, cloves, and allspice). Adding the salt toward the end helps prevent the skins from splitting.

Tarasco (Pinto Bean Soup)

SERVES 8 TO 10

TARASCO, pinto bean soup, is a specialty of Michoacan, a state in central Mexico. We picked up the recipe at a wonderful, family-run restaurant in San Antonio called El Mirador.

Pinto beans are speckled, kidney-shaped beans similar to red (kidney) beans. They lose their speckles when cooked but not their flavor. In the Southwest ripe tomatoes are available in the winter. If unavailable in your area, use good canned tomatoes. The *pasilla* is a large dried chili with a wrinkled black skin. Its smoky, bitter flavor tastes uncannily like chocolate. Assorted dried chilies are generally available at specialty shops, but if you can't find pasillas, substitute one ounce of unsweetened chocolate and a fresh or pickled jalapeño pepper instead. (Melt the chocolate in the soup—don't attempt to fry it.)

> 1 pound pinto beans, soaked as described above
> 6 fresh tomatoes, or 1 32-ounce can imported plum tomatoes
> 2 small onions, peeled
> 5 cloves garlic, peeled
> 4 tablespoons oil
> 3 pasilla chilies
> 3–4 cups chicken stock (see recipe on page 472)
> Salt and fresh black pepper

For the garnish:
  4 corn tortillas
  ⅔ cup oil for frying
  ¾ pound Monterey Jack cheese, finely grated
  1 cup sour cream
  ½ cup chopped scallions

(1) Place the beans in a large, heavy pot, with water to cover (4 to 6 cups). Bring the water to a boil, reduce the heat slightly, and briskly simmer the beans for 1 hour, or until quite soft. Add water as necessary to keep the beans wet.

(2) Meanwhile, roast the fresh tomatoes, onions, and garlic on a preheated grill or under the broiler. (The canned tomatoes don't need to be roasted.) The vegetables should be nicely browned. Heat half the oil in a heavy, four-quart pan. Crumble the chilies (see Note below) and fry them over medium heat for 1 to 2 minutes, or until lightly toasted. Purée the vegetables and chilies in the food processor.

(3) Heat the remaining oil in the pan you used for frying the chilies. Add the vegetable purée, and bring it to a boil over high heat, stirring with a wooden spoon. Purée the beans with their cooking liquid in a blender or food processor. Stir this purée into the vegetable mixture. Stir in enough chicken stock to obtain a soup the consistency of heavy cream. Add salt and pepper to taste. The soup can be prepared to this stage up to 24 hours before serving.

(4) Prepare the garnish. Cut the tortillas into ½-inch strips. Heat the oil in a small frying pan. Fry the tortillas over high heat for 1 to 2 minutes, or until crisp and lightly browned. Transfer the strips to paper towels to drain. Just before serving, arrange the tortilla strips and grated cheese in the bottoms of soup bowls or a tureen. Heat the soup and ladle it into the bowls or the tureen. Spoon the sour cream in the center and sprinkle the chopped scallions on top.

NOTE: Some people react more to hot peppers than others. I recommend wearing rubber gloves when handling chilies. The seeds are the hottest part of the chili, so if you don't like spicy food you may wish to discard them. Be sure to wash your hands afterwards, and be careful not to touch your eyes, nose, or privates until you have washed.

Black-eyes and Rice

SERVES 8 TO 10

THIS colorful seed isn't really a pea, but a bean related to the mung bean. It was brought to the U.S. by African slaves, along with okra and peanuts. Southern aristocrats called it a cowpea, because it was thought to be fit only for cattle. Today, it is a regional favorite—beloved by blacks and whites alike. Black-eyed peas with ham hocks are a traditional Southern New Year's repast. This recipe comes from Margaret Wilkinson, a native of Grenada and longtime friend of my assistant Marcia Walsh.

    1 2 to 3-ounce piece of salt pork
    ½ pound black-eyed peas, soaked as described above
    1 medium onion, cut in half and stuck with 2 cloves
    1 cup long-grain rice
    1 tablespoon vegetable oil
    1 tablespoon sugar
    Fresh black pepper
    Salt (optional)

(1) Rinse the salt pork and cut it into ¼-inch dice. Place the pork in a small saucepan with cold water to cover, bring to a boil, and simmer for 1 minute. (This blanching helps remove the excess salt.) Drain the pork and rinse under cold water.

(2) Place the salt pork, peas, and onion in a large saucepan with 3 to 3½ cups water. Bring the peas to a rolling boil and simmer over a medium-high flame for 20 minutes, or until the peas are almost cooked—they should still have a slight crunch

and firm, opaque white center. Cooking time varies, so test the black-eyes after 15 minutes. Discard the onion.

(3) Add the rice, oil, sugar, and pepper to the peas and salt pork. Stir in an additional cup of water, cover, and simmer for 15 minutes, or until the rice is cooked and all the liquid has evaporated from the pan. The timing is tricky: if you overcook the peas, you will end up with a sticky mess. Ideally, you will wind up with fluffy white rice and tender black-eyed peas.

(4) Taste the black-eyes and rice, adding salt and pepper to taste. Serve this dish right out of the pan in which you cooked it. It is even better the next day, reheated in the oven or on top of the stove; the rice at the bottom browns to a delicious salty crisp.

Lentil Salad with Smoked Mozzarella and Smithfield Ham

SERVES 6

THE ancient Greeks believed that lentils softened the temper and disposed the mind to study. Lentils gave their name (*lenticula* in Latin) to that Renaissance vision aid, the lens. Lentils are usually eaten as soups or stews, but they are also delicious in salads. The following recipe features a cumin–sour cream dressing.

For the lentils:
   ½ **pound brown or green lentils**
   1 **medium onion**
   1 **medium carrot**
   1 **rib celery**
   1 **clove garlic**
      Bouquet garni (see recipe on page 471)
      Salt and fresh black pepper

For the garnish:
    4 ounces Smithfield or baked ham — *proscuitto*
    2 tablespoons vegetable oil
    4 ounces smoked mozzarella
    2 scallions
    4 tablespoons chopped parsley

For the dressing:
    3 tablespoons sour cream
    2 tablespoons red wine vinegar
    2 tablespoons extra-virgin olive oil
    1 tablespoon Dijon-style mustard
    Juice of ½ lemon or lime
    1 teaspoon cumin seed, or ½ teaspoon ground cumin
    Pinch of cayenne pepper

3–4 tablespoons sour cream and a few sprigs parsley for decoration

(1) Pick through the lentils, removing any pebbles or stems, and wash. Cut the vegetables in quarters. Place the lentils, vegetables, bouquet garni, and seasonings in a large pot with plenty of cold water to cover. Simmer the lentils for 20 to 30 minutes, or until tender, but do not overcook. Pour the lentils into a strainer, refresh under cold water, and drain. Discard the vegetables and bouquet garni.

(2) Cut the ham into ¼-inch dice. In a small saucepan, boil it for 1 minute, then drain. Heat the oil in a small frying pan and sauté the ham for 1 minute, or until crisp, and set aside. Cut the cheese into ¼-inch dice. Discard the roots of the scallions and finely chop the stalks. Chop the parsley.

(3) Combine the ingredients for the dressing in a large bowl and whisk until smooth. Mix in the lentils, ham, cheese, scallions, and parsley. Correct the seasoning, adding salt, pepper, or vinegar to taste—the salad should be highly seasoned. Spoon the salad into a bowl and decorate with rosettes of sour cream and sprigs of parsley.

WINTER ROOTS

The parsnip, children, I repeat
Is merely an anemic beet.
Some people say the parsnip's edible.
Myself, I find that claim incredible.

OGDEN NASH

"FAIR words butter no parsnips." Nor turnips, nor rutabagas. These sturdy roots are the drudges of the vegetable kingdom. Kids detest them; grown-ups push them to the edge of their plate; even canines have been known to reject them.

Reviled as they are, I raise my voice in their favor. In my kitchen turnips turn up a lot. The rotund rutabaga has rounded out many a meal, and I would actually go out of my way to eat what Ogden Nash called "an anemic beet"—the parsnip. These humble roots are remarkable for their full, earthy flavor, not to mention their excellent keeping properties in winter. During World War II, they saved countless Europeans from starvation.

"It was as true . . . as turnips is. It was as true . . . as taxes is. And nothing's truer than them." This keen observation was made by a character in Dickens' *David Copperfield.* A true turnip is easily recognizable by its round white body and purple crown. Its flesh is as white as mother-of-pearl; its earthy flavor is faintly pungent, like radish. These root vegetables are welcome friends in winter. For a special treat, look for tiny new turnips in the spring. Nor should we forget the leaves of the turnip, which turn up at farm stands in autumn. Turnip greens have a hotness reminiscent of watercress; the flavor mellows when cooked. Turnip greens are rich in calcium; I like to serve them in soup.

The rutabaga, sometimes called Swede turnip, is often mistaken for a turnip. Its appearance is really quite different. It looks like a giant turnip but it is yellow rather than white. The rutabaga was developed in the Middle Ages, a cross between wild cabbage and turnip. It is usually waxed to prevent it from drying out. Rutabagas are sweeter, though harder, than turnips: they are often served puréed or sautéed.

Sweeter still is the parsnip, particularly when it has been left in the ground after the first frost—the cold helps convert the starches in the root to sugars. Along with carrot, celery, parsley, and fennel, this elongated root is a member of the Umbelliferae family—it looks like a swell-headed blond carrot.

The parsnip has a checkered past. In second-century England, it was thought to cause delirium and madness. In medieval Europe its sweetness made it a favored foil for salt fish. Before the arrival of the potato in Europe, parsnips were the most common vegetable starch. Modern food writers have maintained that the ancients ate wild parsnips but never cultivated them. Etymology suggests otherwise: our word parsnip comes from the Latin *pastinare,* "to dig and trench the ground."

When buying these root vegetables, look for firm, unblemished specimens, avoiding any with brown spots or splits. Do not buy turnips or rutabagas with leafy sprouts: these grow at the expense of the natural sugars.

The Romans seasoned turnips with cumin, honey, and vinegar. There's no reason for all the camouflage. All three roots are delectable boiled and glazed with butter. My Aunt Anette adds parsnips to her broth, and her chicken soup is the acknowledged best in town. Like all vegetables that grow below-ground, turnips, parsnips, and rutabagas should be started in cold water when boiled.

Parsnip Pancakes

MAKES 16 TO 20 3-INCH PANCAKES—
ENOUGH TO SERVE 4 TO 6

THE recipe was inspired by one I found in a Colonial American cookbook. The original was flavored with sherry and sugar, however, and served for dessert. This version makes an unusual vegetable side dish and is guaranteed to please even people who swear they hate parsnips.

> 1 pound parsnips
> 2 eggs
> ½ cup flour
> ½ teaspoon baking powder
>   Salt, fresh white pepper, and freshly grated nutmeg
> 3 tablespoons butter
> 3 tablespoons oil

(1) Peel the parsnips and cut into ½-inch slices. Cook the parsnips in a steamer for 5 minutes, or until soft, and drain. Purée the cooked parsnips in a food processor, gradually adding the eggs, flour, baking powder, and seasonings. The mixture should be highly seasoned.

(2) Heat half the butter and oil in a skillet or griddle over medium heat. Ladle the batter into the pan in 3-tablespoon batches to make 3-inch pancakes. Cook the pancakes for 1 to 2 minutes per side, or until golden brown. Use the remaining butter and oil as you cook the rest of the batter. Serve at once.

Parsnip and Pear Soup

WHEN nouvelle cuisine was in its heyday, purées of vegetables and fruit were all the rage. The perfumed flavor of pears is
a perfect match for the natural sweetness of parsnips.

1 small carrot
1 pound parsnips
1 rib celery, washed
1 leek, furry root and dark green leaves discarded
3 ripe pears
3 tablespoons butter
1 quart chicken or light veal stock
  Bouquet garni (see recipe on page 471)
  Salt and fresh black pepper
1 cup heavy cream
  Pinch of cayenne
  Freshly grated nutmeg
  Chopped chives or scallions for garnish

(1) Peel and finely chop the carrot, parsnips, and celery.
Wash and chop the leek (see page 123). Peel, core, and dice 2 of
the pears. Melt the butter in a large saucepan. Add the vegetables
and the 2 pears, and cook for 10 minutes, or until tender. Add
the stock, bouquet garni, and salt and pepper to taste, and simmer the soup for another 15 to 20 minutes, or until the vegetables are soft.

(2) Meanwhile, core and dice the remaining pear. Purée the
soup in a food processor or blender and return it to the pan,
adding the cream. The recipe can be prepared ahead to this stage.

(3) Just before serving, reheat the soup and correct the seasoning with salt, black pepper, cayenne, and fresh nutmeg to
taste—it should be both spicy and a little sweet. Ladle the soup
into warm bowls, and garnish with the diced pear and chives or
scallions.

Turnips *au Jus*

SERVES 4

ALEXANDER Dumas is best known for such swashbuckling novels as *The Three Musketeers* and *The Count of Monte Cristo*. All in all he "sired" more than four hundred works. His last book was inspired by his lifelong love of food: a *Grande Dictionnaire de Cuisine* that ran 750,000 words. English food authority Alan Davidson recently published an excellent translation called *Dumas on Food*. Here is Dumas' recipe for glazed turnips with stock, an excellent accompaniment to roasts.

> 1 **pound small turnips, or large turnips cut in quarters, or even rutabagas**
> **Salt**
> 3 **tablespoons butter**
> 1½ **tablespoons sugar**
> ½–1 **cup brown stock (see recipe on page 473)**
> 1 **stick cinnamon**
> **Fresh white pepper**

(1) Peel the turnips and cut off the ends. Place them in a pan just large enough to hold them in a single layer, and add cold, lightly salted water to cover. Bring the turnips to a boil, refresh under cold water, and drain. Return the turnips to the pan with the butter and sugar, and cook over high heat, stirring steadily, for 3 to 5 minutes, or until the turnips are golden brown.

(2) Add the stock and cinnamon stick, press a piece of buttered parchment paper or foil on top of the turnips, and cover the pan. Cook the turnips over low heat or in a 350-degree oven for 10 to 15 minutes, or until crispy-tender, adding stock as necessary to keep the vegetables moist. Increase the heat to high and boil off all but a few tablespoons liquid; it should become thick and syrupy, like a glaze. Add salt and pepper to taste.

Punchnap

PUNCHNAP is a Welsh dish, a buttery purée of potatoes and turnips. In the recipe below we use rutabaga, but you could also make it with parsnips or turnips.

1 1-pound rutabaga
1 pound potatoes
4 tablespoons butter
  Salt and fresh black pepper
4 tablespoons heavy cream

(1) Peel the rutabaga and potatoes and cut each into ½-inch chunks. Place each in a separate pan with salt and cold water to cover, and slowly bring each to a boil. Cook the vegetables until soft: 3 to 5 minutes for the potatoes, 4 to 6 minutes for the rutabaga. Purée the vegetables through a food mill or in a processor, and beat in the butter, and salt and pepper to taste. The recipe can be prepared up to 4 hours ahead to this stage.

(2) To serve, spoon the purée into a warm serving dish. Make several holes in the purée, using the end of a wooden spoon. Pour the cream in the holes and serve at once.

FIGS

Let the world slide, let the world go;
A fig for care, and a fig for woe!
If I can't pay, why I can owe,
And death makes equal the high and low.

JOHN HEYWOOD

JANUARY is an unreliable month for fresh fruit. But dried fruit is a delicacy in its own right—especially my favorite, dried figs. Figs originated in the Near East, where they have been popular for at least five thousand years. The fig was the only tree in the Garden of Eden mentioned by name (its leaf an emblem of modesty ever since), and it is said that the great Buddha acquired his wisdom while sitting under a fig tree. It's not without reason that figs have been extolled as the "manna of the Mediterranean."

The ancient Greeks were so fond of figs, they passed laws forbidding their export. The inspectors charged with finding smugglers were called *syko phantes,* "fig showers," literally, and to this day we use the word *sycophant* to describe an informer or a person who uses flattery to curry favor. The Greeks introduced figs to North Africa; the Moors carried them to Spain, whose missionaries later planted the trees in California and Latin America.

Today, the fig is cultivated around the world, and there are more than six hundred different species. The most highly esteemed is the *Smyrna* fig, from Izmir, on the west coast of Turkey. (The Smyrna fig, grown in California, has become the *Calimyrna.*) The *black,* or *mission,* fig, grown in California, has a purplish skin and crimson flesh, and stems from an Iberian spe-

FEBRUARY

Yet February suns uncertain shine
For rain and frost alternately combine
To stop the plow, with sudden wintry storms—
And often fearful violence the month deforms.

EDMUND SPENSER

I F February were not the precursor of spring, it would be the most depressing month of the year. Its cold, damp weather chills us to our very marrow. The days are short; the fields are bare; and seasonal produce is at its most limited.

Originally, February had twenty-nine days, thirty in leap year, but the emperor Augustus stole a day to add to August, so that *his* month would have as many days as July, named for Julius Caesar. This makes February the year's shortest month; given its weather, few people regret its usual twenty-eight-day brevity— except, of course, those people with birthdays on February 29, which occurs only once every four years!

February is a dreary month, so it's not surprising that people have always looked for tokens of light and springtime. February 2 is Candlemas Day, which Catholics celebrate with a candlelit mass. Curiously, sunlight was the last thing English farmers wanted to see on Candlemas Day, for it was believed that clear skies on February 2 betokened six more weeks of bad weather. "Nay, tis an omen bad, the yeomen say, / If Phoebus shows his face the second day" ran an old English saying. Modern Americans are hardly less superstitious about the Pennsylvania Dutch holiday, Groundhog Day. If the groundhog sees his shadow on February 2, we are told to expect an additional six weeks of winter.

It is appropriate that this dour month be a time of expiation and repentance. February, indeed, takes its name from the Latin *februare,* "to purify." The Romas held a purification rite in February—the predecessor to Christian Lent. Lent is a forty-day period of fasting and repentance to commemorate Jesus' six-week fast in the desert. In the Middle Ages, Lent was rigorous indeed. Among the foods forbidden were butter, cheese, milk, eggs, and meat. (The eggs returned in all their hard-boiled glory on Easter Sunday.) Today's Catholics limit themselves to giving up one particularly cherished food. Spinach or rutabagas were popular choices among my less-than-devout Catholic schoolmates!

The fast officially begins on Ash Wednesday, and for centuries, Christendom has indulged itself in a wild pre-Lenten bash. This was the *carne vale,* literally the "farewell to meat"—the origin of our word *carnival.* The revels reached a crescendo on Shrove Tuesday, better known by its French name, Mardi Gras. (The former refers to the Old English verb *shriven,* "to confess"; the latter literally means "Fat Tuesday.") Forbidden foods were consumed with Gargantuan abandon. Eggs were transformed into pancakes, which are still eaten on Shrove Tuesday in England. The frenzy of meat-eating occasioned by Mardi Gras was well described by a medieval Italian: "Such boiling and broiling, such roasting and toasting, such baking, frying, mincing, cutting, carving, devouring, and gorbellied gormandizing, that a man would think that people did . . . ballast their bellies with meat for a voyage to Constantinople."

If February is a month for repentance, it is also a season for love. Its name is associated with Faunus (also called Pan), the goat-legged god of fertility. On February 15, the Romans held a festival of fertility called Lupercalia. When the Christians took over, they transformed Lupercalia into St. Valentine's Day.

The Anglo-Saxons called February *Kale-Monat,* "kale month," for this was their principal winter vegetable. The term embraced all members of the cabbage family, which to this day help sustain us through the winter months. In addition, winter squash and root vegetables are abundant. February is a summer month in the Southern Hemisphere, so we can enjoy their exotic fruits, such as cherimoyas and starfruits, during this time. Crayfish stir from their pond-bottom lairs this time of year, and shrimp are particularly succulent. In New England, February brings the first thaw, and with it a fresh batch of maple syrup. And speaking of sweets, Valentine's Day is a good occasion to show off your baking skills with chocolate.

COLLARD GREENS AND KALE

THESE leafy members of the cabbage family were a mainstay of the early English diet. The Anglo-Saxons called them *cole*, from which we derive the modern words *kale* and *collards*. The former has corrugated, crinkly, blue-green leaves, while the latter have smooth leaves, like steam-rollered cabbage. Both have a mild, cabbagey flavor that is enhanced by bacon, cheese, or soy sauce.

Kale is a venerable vegetable—a survivor from the age of dinosaurs. This hardy plant is capable of surviving frosts and even snowstorms. In fact, freezing weather is said to improve its flavor.

This crinkly leaf has endeared itself to people far and wide. In Scotland the phrase "come to cail" is an invitation to dinner. (Scottish maidens have a "he loves me/he loves me not" routine in which they strip kale leaves from their stems, instead of plucking daisy petals.) The Turks speak fondly of kale when they say: "Every green leaf you chew adds a branch to the tree of your life." Kale is indeed healthy, loaded with calcium, potassium, and a staggering 9000 units of vitamin A per cup.

As for collard greens, according to Waverly Root, they are what the ancients referred to whenever they spoke of "cabbage." Julius Caesar chewed collards after heavy banqueting to ward off indigestion. Collard greens grow well in poor soil; for this reason they were popular with the African slaves in the United States.

Collard greens with ham hocks is still a popular dish in the South.

While available most of the year, except summer, the peak season for these greens is December through March. When buying kale, look for springy, blue-green leaves on firm stalks—the smaller the leaves, the more tender. Baby kale leaves can even be eaten raw in salads. Collard greens should be jade green. When storing kale or collard greens for later use, wrap in a wet paper towel and store in an unsealed plastic bag in the refrigerator. One pound of kale or collard greens will serve three to four people.

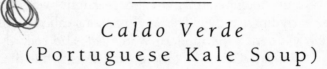

Caldo Verde (Portuguese Kale Soup)

SERVES 6

KALE soup is the national dish of Portugal. Every house has a garden, as do most apartment buildings, and in the center of every garden grows kale. The plant looks a little like a palm tree with the fronds growing up, not down. When a housewife makes kale soup (a daily occurrence), she goes to the garden, pulls off a few leaves, and adds them to the pot. There is even a special machine, which looks like a meat slicer, for cutting the leaves into ribbon-thin slivers. *Chouriço* is a spicy Portuguese sausage—any hot sausage will do.

> 4 tablespoons extra-virgin olive oil
> 1 chouriço or hot sausage
> 1 small onion or leek
> 1 clove garlic
> 2 stalks celery
> 1 large potato
> 1 pound kale
> 5 cups chicken stock (see recipe on page 472)
> Bouquet garni (see recipe on page 471)
> 1–2 tablespoons red wine vinegar
> Salt and fresh black pepper

(*1*) Heat 2 tablespoons of the olive oil in a 4-quart saucepan over a medium flame. Prick the sausage, add it to the pan, and cook it for 3 minutes per side, or until cooked. Remove the sausage from the pan, discard the fat, and set the pan aside. When the sausage is cool, cut it into ¼-inch slices and reserve. (If you are using a precooked sausage, cut it into ¼-inch slices and lightly brown these in the oil.)

(*2*) Meanwhile, finely chop the onion (or well-washed leek), garlic, and celery. Peel the potato and cut it into a fine dice. Cut the thick stems off the kale, roll the leaves into a tight cylinder, and cut them crosswise with a chef's knife into ⅛-inch strips. The idea here is to finely shred the kale. Make one or two lengthwise cuts to render the slivers a manageable length for eating.

(*3*) Add the remaining 2 tablespoons oil to the sausage pan and cook the onion, garlic, and celery over medium heat for 3 to 4 minutes, or until the vegetables are tender but not brown. Add the diced potato, stock, bouquet garni, and sausage slices, and simmer the soup for 6 to 8 minutes, or until the potatoes are almost tender. Add the kale and simmer the soup for 5 minutes, or until the kale is tender, too. Add a splash of vinegar and salt and pepper to taste. The soup is ready to serve, and it is excellent rewarmed the next day.

With kale soup serve a Portuguese wine: a crisp *vinho verde* if you like white, or a *dão* if you like red.

Fried Kale with Sesame

SERVES 4 TO 6

KALE, when fried, acquires the intriguing crispness of nori seaweed. To continue in an Eastern vein, we've concocted a tamari (dark soy sauce) and sesame dressing. Fried kale makes an attractive accompaniment for scallops, shrimp, and chicken.

1½ **pounds fresh kale**
2–3 **cups vegetable oil for frying**

For the tamari dressing:
  2 tablespoons sesame seeds
  2 tablespoons tamari
  2 teaspoons sesame oil
  1 tablespoon rice vinegar
  1 scallion
  1 ¼-inch slice of fresh ginger root

  1 wok or electric frying pan

(1) Wash and thoroughly dry the kale, the drier the better—moisture on the leaves will cause the oil to hiss and spatter. Remove the tough ribs and cut the kale into 1-inch strips.

(2) Meanwhile, prepare the dressing. Toast the sesame seeds in a dry skillet over medium heat for 1 minute or until golden brown, stirring frequently so they do not burn. (This can also be done in a hot oven but the sesame seeds must be carefully watched.) Trim and finely chop the scallion and ginger root. Combine all the ingredients for the dressing.

(3) Just before serving, heat 2 to 3 inches of oil to 380 degrees in the wok or frying pan. Fry the kale, a handful or two at a time, for 1 to 2 minutes, taking care not to burn yourself with spattering oil. Remove the fried leaves with a slotted spoon and drain on paper towels. Serve the fried kale on a platter, and pass the dressing separately; if dressed ahead of time, the kale will become soggy.

A Savory Tart of Collard Greens, Swiss Cheese, and Bacon

SERVES 8 TO 10

"THERE is no such thing as a mistake in cooking, just recipes that are waiting to be discovered." With these words I tried to console one of my students, who had dropped a Roquefort-leek tart, face down, as she was taking it out of the oven. We had used up all the Roquefort and leeks, but we still had some collard greens, Swiss cheese, and bacon. The new tart was assembled and baked in a trice. On tasting it, we toasted our good misfortune!

    1 1½-cup-batch basic pie dough (see recipe on page 476), or your own favorite recipe
    1 pound collard greens (enough to make 2 cups chopped)
      Salt
    6 strips bacon
    6 ounces Emmenthaler or Jarlsberg cheese
    3 tablespoons butter
    3 tablespoons flour
    ¾ cup milk
    ¾ cup heavy cream
    1 tablespoon Dijon-style mustard
      Fresh black pepper and freshly grated nutmeg
    3 eggs

    1 12-inch tart pan with removable bottom

(1) Prepare and chill the pie dough. Roll it out and use it to line the tart pan. Chill the shell and preheat the oven to 400 degrees.

(2) Wash the collard greens, cut the stems off, and coarsely chop the leaves. Cook them in rapidly boiling salted water for 2 minutes or until tender. Refresh the leaves under cold water and drain. Cut the bacon into ¼-inch slivers. Lightly brown the bacon in a skillet over medium heat, and drain. Cut the cheese into ½-inch cubes.

(3) Prepare the filling. Melt the butter in a saucepan and whisk in the flour to make a roux. Whisk in the milk and cream off the heat. Return the pan to the heat, and bring the sauce to a boil, whisking vigorously. Gently simmer the sauce for 3 minutes, stirring frequently. Whisk in the mustard, and salt, pepper, and nutmeg to taste. Let the sauce cool slightly, then whisk in the eggs. Gently stir in the collard greens, bacon, and cheese, and spoon the filling into the crust.

(4) Start baking the tart on the floor of the oven—the blast of heat from the bottom helps cook the bottom crust. (If you

have an electric oven and cannot place the tart on the bottom, set it on a preheated baking sheet.) After 15 minutes, raise the tart to the center rack, and continue baking for 15 minutes, or until the filling is puffed, golden, and set. Remove the tart from the oven, and cool for 5 minutes before slicing and serving. A crisp Riesling from Alsace would make an excellent accompaniment.

Collard Greens
with Spicy Relish

SERVES 4

THIS recipe features a modern twist on an old Southern favorite. Instead of being stewed with vinegar, the collard greens are blanched and served with a spicy relish. The cooking time needed varies widely for collard greens—the smaller the leaves, the more tender. As a variation, you could substitute an equal amount of kale for the collard greens.

    1 generous pound collard greens
    Salt
2–3 tablespoons butter

For the relish:
    1 small onion (½ cup chopped)
    1 small red, yellow, or green pepper (½ cup chopped)
    1 jalapeño or other hot chili
    ½ teaspoon grated fresh ginger root
    2 tablespoons butter
3–4 tablespoons red wine vinegar
    2 tablespoons brown sugar
    1 tablespoon chopped sour pickle
    1 tablespoon chopped fresh cilantro or scallion green
    Salt and fresh black pepper

(1) Wash the collard greens and remove the tough stems. Cut the leaves into 2-inch pieces and cook them in 2 quarts boiling salted water for 3 to 4 minutes, or until tender. Alternatively, the greens can be steamed, but the color won't be as nice.

(2) Meanwhile, prepare the relish. Finely chop the onion and pepper. Cut the chili in half (see Note on page 48), remove the seeds, and chop finely. (If you like fiery food, leave the seeds in.) Grate the ginger. Melt the butter in a small saucepan. Add the vegetables and ginger and cook over medium heat for 3 to 4 minutes, or until the vegetables are soft but not browned. Add the vinegar, sugar, and pickle, and gently simmer for 5 minutes. Stir in the cilantro or scallions. Season the relish to taste, adding more vinegar or sugar as necessary—the mixture should be sweet, sour, and spicy. The relish can be made up to 48 hours ahead and can be served warm or chilled.

(3) To serve, drain the cooked collard greens, toss them with butter, and mound them on a platter or on individual plates. Spoon the relish on top. Collard greens are a good accompaniment to pork.

SHRIMP

SHRIMP is America's favorite shellfish. But oh, what wretched stuff our compatriots think of as shrimp! It's caught by the ton, chemically disinfected, and flash-frozen in icy monoliths. By the time it winds up in cocktail sauce, it has about as much flavor as the boxes in which it is shipped!

There are people who take shrimp seriously. Like the French, who sell *petites grises* (tiny "gray" shrimp) and *bouquets* (pretty pink shrimp) live and wriggling at the market. Or the Norwegians, who steam tiny shrimp on their fishing boats, to be sold on the docks in paper cones, and munched, head and all, like popcorn. The sweetest shrimp I have ever tasted are the *Northern prawns* (also called Maine shrimp) fished from the icy waters off the Maine coast. The season is brief—February to April—and these sweet, baby, finger-sized shrimp are seldom seen outside the Northeast.

Shrimp is a catchall term embracing the giant *tiger prawns* of Southeast Asia (weighing up to a half-pound each) and the miniscule *hestereke* (two hundred to a pound), which Scandinavians eat on open-faced sandwiches. There are white, brown, and pink shrimp which are netted in the Gulf of Mexico, and served up by the billion in breading or cocktail sauce. Exotic varieties found at pricey restaurants include the *spot prawn,* fished on the West Coast, and the *Dublin Bay prawn,* which has claws like a miniature lobster.

The terms *shrimp, prawn,* and *scampi* have no scientific distinction, but in commercial parlance, "shrimp" refers to smaller shellfish, "prawn" to large shrimp, and "scampi" to either served in garlic butter at an Italian restaurant. In the U.S., shrimp are sold not by species but by count (number of shrimp per pound). If judged solely by price, jumbo shrimp would seem the most desirable, but I find that the smaller varieties are more succulent and tender.

Shrimp are rich in omega-3 fatty acids, a highly unsaturated fat that has been linked to lowering cholesterol and triglyceride levels, and fatty plaque deposits on the artery walls. And at least one African country is named for them. Sailing along the African coast, a Portuguese navigator discovered a bay where the waters teemed with shrimp. He called the area *Rio des Camarões,* "River of Shrimp," which we know today as the Cameroons.

COOKING SHRIMP

To shell or to leave the shrimp whole, to devein or not: these are some of the questions that arise when it comes to cooking shrimp. When boiling shrimp for munching or cocktails, I prefer to cook them in the shells: the meat remains moister.

To shell a shrimp, pinch the front legs between your thumb and forefinger, and peel off the shell as you would the rind of a tangerine. Then pinch the tail and slowly wiggle the body out of the shell.

To devein shrimp insert the tine of a fork in the rounded part of the back, just below the vein. Extract the vein by slowly pulling the fork away from the shrimp. I never bother to devein small shrimp.

Boil shrimp in a *court bouillon,* wine and water flavored with spices and root vegetables. (See the recipe on page 475 or use a good commercial spice mix.) Bring the liquid to a boil, add the shrimp, and gently simmer for 2 to 3 minutes, or just until they become firm and pink. When cooking shrimp to serve cold, cook until firm, remove from the broth, and let cool to tepid. Then return them to the broth and cool completely. This will make your shrimp exceptionally moist without overcooking them.

When eating whole shrimp, be sure to "suck" the head to extract the tasty juices. (Louisianans enjoy the whole shrimp, head and all.) To separate the head from the tail, simply twist in opposite directions.

Shrimp with Fennel

SERVES 4

THE licoricelike flavor of fennel goes well with the taste of shrimp. I make this dish with Maine shrimp (also called Northern prawns)—small pink shellfish remarkable for their sweetness. Elsewhere in the U.S., you could use brown shrimp, or spot prawns, but try to use fresh shrimp. Any anise-flavored liqueur will do for the sauce: Pernod, Ricard, anisette, ouzo, or raki.

    1½ pounds fresh shrimp
      1 large or 2 small bulbs fennel
        Salt
     ½ cup dry white vermouth
    2–3 tablespoons Pernod or other anise-flavored liqueur
      1 teaspoon fennel seeds
      1 cup heavy cream
      4 tablespoons cold unsalted butter
        Fresh white pepper and cayenne pepper

(1) Shell and devein the shrimp, as described on pages 74–75. Cut the stalks off the fennel, reserving a few of the leaves for garnish. (Save the stalks for a salad.) Cut the bulb in half lengthwise, make a V-shaped cut to remove the hard part of the core, and cut the fennel widthwise into ⅛-inch slices. Blanch the fennel in boiling, lightly salted water for 1 minute, or until tender. Refresh it under cold water and drain.

(2) Place the shrimp in a saucepan with the vermouth and 2 tablespoons Pernod. Gently poach the shrimp over medium heat for 1 minute, or until they turn pink and are slighty firm. Do not overcook. Transfer the shrimp with a slotted spoon to a bowl and cover to keep warm.

(3) Bring the poaching liquid to a boil, and reduce by half. Add the cream and any liquid in the shrimp bowl, and continue boiling until ¾ cup liquid remains. Reduce the heat to low and whisk in the butter. Add the shrimp and fennel, and correct the seasoning with salt, pepper, and cayenne, adding a few drops more Pernod, if the anise taste is too faint. Leave the sauce on the heat just long enough to heat the shrimp and fennel. Serve on a bed of fettuccine or angel hair pasta. A wine with some residual sweetness enhances this dish: try a Riesling or a Sylvaner.

Shrimp with Coconut Milk and Peppers

SERVES 4

THIS colorful dish was inspired by the cooking of northern Brazil. Brazilians and Asians use coconut milk the way we do butter or cream. You can make your own, using fresh or dried coconut (instructions are found on page 478), but good results will be had with canned coconut milk. Also called coconut cream, it is sold at Latin American or Asian markets—be sure to buy the unsweetened kind.

1½ pounds fresh shrimp
1 green bell pepper
1 red bell pepper
1 yellow bell pepper (optional)
1 hot chili pepper, like a jalapeño or serrano (optional)
1 small onion
1 clove garlic
2 ripe or 3–4 imported canned tomatoes
3 tablespoons butter
½ cup unsweetened coconut milk, plus extra if needed
   Salt, fresh black pepper, and cayenne pepper
1 teaspoon chopped fresh cilantro (see page 78) or parsley

(1) Shell and devein the shrimp, as described on pp. 74–75. Core and seed the peppers, and cut them into ½-inch pieces. Finely chop the chili (see Note on page 48), discarding the seeds, unless you like your food really spicy—the seeds are the hottest part. Finely chop the onion. Mince the garlic. Peel and seed the tomatoes (for instructions, see page 304) and coarsely chop.

(2) Heat the butter in a large, nonaluminum frying pan. Add the peppers, chili, onion, and garlic and cook over medium heat for 3 minutes, or until the vegetables are soft but not brown. Stir in the tomatoes, and cook for 1 minute. Add enough coconut milk to wet the vegetables, and bring the sauce to a boil. Reduce the heat, add the shrimp, and cook for 2 to 3 minutes, or until the shrimp are firm and pink. Season the sauce to taste with salt, black pepper, and cayenne. Spoon the shrimp into a serving dish and sprinkle with the cilantro or parsley. Serve this dish with rice or rice pilaf or with the Black-eyes and Rice on page 49.

Shrimp and Smokies

SERVES 4

THIS recipe comes from the Mucky Duck restaurant on Captiva Island, Florida. The Mucky Duck is equally remarkable for its setting (a beach on Captiva Island that offers breathtaking

sunsets over the Gulf of Mexico) and for its owner, Victor Mayeron, who likes to roam though the dining room, squirting red
strings from ketchup bottles on the laps of his panicked custom-
ers! Mayeron recommends buying twice as much beer as called
for below: half for the shrimp and half for the cook.

> **2 pounds large, unpeeled shrimp**
> **1 pound kielbasa sausage**
> **2–3 bottles imported beer for the shrimp and sausage, plus**
> **additional beer for the guests**
>
> **1 large, covered pot for steaming shrimp**

(1) Pour enough beer into the pot to cover the shrimp and
sausage (but don't put them in the pot yet) and bring it to a boil.
Meanwhile, rinse the shrimp in cold water several times. Cut the
kielbasa into ⅛-inch slices.

(2) Put the shrimp and kielbasa into the pot, cover, and
steam for 5–6 minutes, or until the shrimp turn pink. Drain the
shrimp and kielbasa and serve hot. Accompaniments could include Volcanic Horseradish Sauce (see recipe on page 439) and
a hot mustard.

Shrimp with Cilantro Sauce

SERVES 4

THIS dish is a sort of Mexican shrimp scampi. But where
an Italian would use parsley, the Mexican uses cilantro, pungent
fresh coriander leaf. Cilantro has a distinct, aromatic flavor that
leaves some people cold; its name comes from the Greek *koris,*
"bedbug," a reference to its "buggy" smell. Its pungency is mel-
lowed during cooking. There is no substitute for fresh cilantro
(the coriander seed has an entirely different flavor), but the recipe
below is also delicious when made entirely with fresh parsley.
Use the flat-leaf variety, which has more flavor.

    1½ **pounds fresh shrimp**
     2 **cloves garlic**
     4 **scallions**
     1 **bunch fresh cilantro**
    ½ **bunch flat-leaf parsley**
     1 **serrano or jalapeño chili (optional)**
     6 **tablespoons butter**
       Salt and fresh black pepper

(1) Shell and devein the shrimp according to the instructions on pages 74 and 75. Mince the garlic. Finely chop the scallions, cilantro, and parsley. You should wind up with about ½ cup of the cilantro and ¼ cup parsley. Cut the chili in half and discard the seeds. (For a note on handling chilis, see page 48.) The chili will add a slight piquancy—if you don't like spicy food, simply omit it.

(2) Heat the butter in a large skillet over medium heat. Add the garlic, scallions, chopped herbs, and chili, and cook for 1 minute. Increase the heat to high, add the shrimp, and sauté, turning the shrimp once or twice, for 1 to 2 minutes or until the shrimp become firm and pink. Do not overcook. Add salt and pepper to taste. Serve Shrimp with Cilantro Sauce over rice or fresh pasta.

EXOTIC FRUITS

FIRST it was the Chinese gooseberry, better known as the kiwi fruit. Then it was the ugli, a large, lopsided, warty-looking grapefruit. Cooks today are besieged by a veritable legion of exotic fruits: star-shaped *carambolas,* leathery-skinned passion fruits, cherimoyas that look like dinosaur eggs and are pitted like a lunar landscape. *Are they edible?* you wonder. *Are they ripe? How on earth do I eat them?* The age of innocence is gone: the savvy eater must be versed in a wide range of exotic fruits.

Most exotic fruits hail from the tropics or southern hemisphere. They come into season, mercifully, during the dreary depths of our winter. More and more of these strange flora are being cultivated in California and Florida. Here's a guide to the exotic fruits that any self-respecting gourmet should know.

Star Fruit (Carambola): The handsome, orange star fruit has taken America by storm. It's easy to see why: when cut widthwise, the slices form perfect five-sided stars. The edible skin is smooth and waxy; the juicy flesh ranges from pleasantly citric to bracingly tart (the sweeter varieties have fatter ribs). If you tasted one blindfolded, you might think you were eating a peculiar variety of orange. A native of Asia, star fruit is currently grown in Florida and Hawaii.

The season runs from November through March. When buying star fruit, look for firm, unblemished specimens with plump, juicy ribs. When ripe, the fruit will be yellow-orange and strongly perfumed. Ripen star fruits at room temperature, then store them in the refrigerator, where they will keep for up to two weeks. To enjoy the fruit by itself, wash and slice: the skin is edible.

Cherimoya (Custard Apple): If ever a fruit looked like it came from Mars, it is surely the cherimoya. Weighing anywhere from a few ounces to a few pounds, it is shaped like a lumpy pine cone; its light-green skin is pitted like a golf ball. The ivory-colored flesh has a creamy consistency that makes its nickname, custard apple, seem particularly appropriate. Mark Twain pronounced it "deliciousness itself"; the explorer Humboldt declared it worth a trip across the Atlantic. The flesh is moderately juicy and manages to be both sweet and mildly acidic. The flavor hints at papaya, pear, and vanilla. Most cherimoyas have watermelonlike seeds, although efforts are underway to develop a seedless variety.

Cherimoyas are in season from December through March. Like avocados, they are generally picked hard, to be ripened by the buyer. Look for unblemished fruit with light-green skin. Dark splotches indicate exposure to frost or poor handling. Let cherimoyas ripen at room temperature: when the fruit is soft and yielding, like a ripe avocado, it is ready to eat. To enjoy a fresh cherimoya, cut it in half or quarters, remove the seeds, sprinkle with lime juice, and eat with a spoon.

Feijoa: This small, oval, green-skinned fruit has a faint pineapple flavor, which has led it to be nicknamed pineapple guava. It is not a true guava, but a member of the myrtle family, along with cloves, allspice, and eucalyptus. The fruit is native to South America (it is named for Señor Feijo, a Spanish natural history museum director), but New Zealand is the leading exporter. Unripe feijoas are unpleasantly tart: let them ripen at room temperature till soft. To eat, cut them in half and scoop out the pulp with a spoon.

Guava: The guava is a small, round fruit with a musky flavor suggstive of bananas and strawberries. The skin ranges from yellow to green in color; the flesh is often embedded with gritty seeds. Guavas are rich in pectin and are used throughout Latin America for making jelly. The fruit should be ripened at room temperature and is ready to eat when soft. To eat, peel and seed the guava, then slice it.

Litchi: Cantonese restaurants have made most of us familiar with canned litchi nuts in syrup. I first tasted the fresh fruit at an Oriental market in Paris: it was nothing less than breathtaking. Cloaked in a leathery, rust-colored skin, fresh litchi is beguilingly sweet, refreshingly tart, and perfumed like grapes or rosewater. Peel litchis like tangerines: the opaque, grey-white flesh harbors a single shiny, dark-brown seed.

Passion Fruit: The passion fruit is known to most of us as a flavoring for exotic cocktails. It is said to be named for the passion of Christ: the spikelike styles representing the nails; the filaments, the crown of thorns; and the petals and stamens, the apostles. Native to Brazil, the passion fruit looks like a shrunken, leathery-skinned, brown and purple egg. The flesh consists of moist yellow pulp clinging to a multitude of tiny seeds. Its intense flavor suggests lemon, peach, and honey. Because of the seeds, passion fruit must be strained before eating. Look for it from November through April.

Tropical Cream Pie

SERVES 8

HERE'S a sophisticated eighties update of your childhood banana cream pie. The recipe comes from the Brown family, California's largest commercial grower of cherimoyas. Be sure to let the cherimoyas ripen till squishy soft.

For the crust:
  1 cup graham cracker crumbs
  4 tablespoons butter, melted

For the filling:
  Approximately 2 pounds fresh cherimoyas (enough to make 1½ cups purée)
  ¼ cup sugar, or to taste
  Juice of 1 lemon
  1 tablespoon Grand Marnier
  1 envelope unflavored gelatin

For the topping:
  ½ envelope unflavored gelatin
  1 8-ounce carton vanilla yogurt
  ½ cup heavy cream
  2 tablespoons sugar
  1 teaspoon vanilla

  1 9-inch pie pan

(1) Prepare the crust. Combine the butter and graham cracker crumbs, press them into the pie pan, and chill for 20 minutes.

(2) Meanwhile, peel and seed the cherimoyas, and purée in a food processor. You should have 1½ cups. Combine the sugar with 2 to 3 tablespoons water in a saucepan. Bring the mixture to a boil and remove the pan from the heat. Combine the lemon juice, Grand Marnier, and 1 tablespoon water in a bowl and sprinkle the gelatin on top. Let stand for 1 minute or until the gelatin becomes spongy. Add to the hot sugar and stir till dis-

solved. Stir in the cherimoya, let the mixture cool, and spoon it onto the crust.

(3) Prepare the topping. Sprinkle the gelatin over 3 table-spoons cold water in a small pot, and let stand for 1 minute or until spongy. Gently heat the mixture to dissolve the gelatin. In a bowl, beat the gelatin into the yogurt. In a separate, chilled bowl, whip the cream to soft peaks. Add the sugar and vanilla, and continue beating till stiff. Fold the whipped cream into the yogurt, and spread the topping on the pie. Chill the tropical cream pie for at least 2 hours before serving.

Exotic Fruit Parfait

SERVES 6

TIRED of the usual crème de menthe parfait? Here's a re-freshing dessert made with star fruit and cherimoyas.

> 1½–2 pounds ripe cherimoyas (enough to make ½ cup purée and 1 cup fruit chunks)
> 3 ripe star fruit
> Juice of 1 small orange
> Juice of 1 lemon, or to taste
> 1 cup heavy cream
> 1 cup sour cream
> ¼ cup confectioners' sugar, or to taste
> Pinch of salt
> ½ teaspoon vanilla
> 1 tablespoon Grand Marnier
> Fresh mint leaves for garnish
>
> 6 parfait glasses or saucer-style champagne glasses

(1) Peel the cherimoyas, cut into ½-inch chunks, and re-move the seeds. In a food processor or blender, purée enough cherimoya to make ½ cup, adding half the orange juice and lemon juice. Cut 1 star fruit into slices, the other 2 into ½-inch chunks. Sprinkle the slices and chunks with the remaining citrus juice to prevent discoloration.

(2) Combine the heavy cream and sour cream in a chilled mixing bowl. Beat to soft peaks, add the sugar, salt, vanilla, and Grand Marnier, and continue beating to stiff peaks. Fold in the cherimoya purée, and, if necessary, additional sugar and lemon juice to taste.

(3) Spoon a third of the exotic fruit chunks into the parfait glasses. Spoon in a layer of the cream mixture, more fruit, more cream mixture, the remaining fruit, and more cream mixture, saving a little for the garnish. Top each parfait with a slice of star fruit. Pipe a rosette of the cream mixture on each star fruit slice, and crown with a fresh mint leaf. Refrigerate until ready to serve.

Tropical Fruit Salad with Rum Sabayon

SERVES 4

THIS tropical fruit salad is nothing at all like the one Mom used to make! Sabayon, better known by its Italian name, *zabaglione,* is a mousselike sauce whipped up from egg yolks, sugar, and booze. Take care not to overcook the sabayon, or it will collapse.

For the salad:
 2 star fruit
 1 cherimoya
 2 kiwifruit
 1 mango
 1 papaya
 4 fresh mint leaves
   Juice of 1 lemon

For the Sabayon:
 4 egg yolks
 ¼ cup brown sugar
 ½ cup dark rum

(1) Cut the star fruit widthwise into ½-inch slices. Peel the cherimoya, seed, and dice. Peel the kiwi, mango, and papaya, and cut them into chunks. Combine all the fruit in a bowl. Squeeze the lemon juice over the fruit and gently mix. Shred the mint and set aside. The recipe can be prepared up to 3 hours ahead to this stage.

(2) Prepare the sabayon. Combine the egg yolks, brown sugar, and rum in a large bowl, and whisk to mix. Put the bowl over a pan of boiling water and whisk the mixture as vigorously as you can for 2 minutes, or until it is very light and frothy and thick enough to fall from a raised whisk in a silky ribbon. Do not overcook or sabayon will collapse.

(3) Spoon the fruit salad into wine glasses. Spoon the hot sabayon on top. Garnish each glass with a tuft of shredded mint and serve at once.

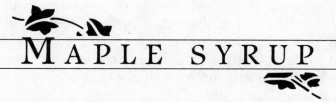

MAPLE SYRUP

NOWHERE is February gloomier than in the northern parts of New England. The sky is grey, the trees are bare, the snow is soiled and desolate. Yet with this glum month comes the first sign of springtime: the flowing of sap in the *Acer saccharum,* the sugar maple. And from this sap comes a uniquely American delicacy: maple syrup.

Some statistics: It takes a maple tree forty years to reach a ten-inch diameter—the size suitable for tapping. (The tree must be ten inches larger to accommodate a second tap.) It takes four trees six weeks to produce enough sap to make one gallon of maple syrup. Every gallon of syrup requires one four-foot log or three gallons of fuel oil to stoke the fire that evaporates the sap. And it takes forty gallons of sap boiled down in the evaporator to make a single gallon of maple syrup.

The process of maple sugaring remains much as it was in Indian times. Rising temperatures at the end of February cause the sap in the trees to expand, starting what is called a "sugar run." The Indians simply gashed the bark to release the sap; we use hollow spiles or "taps" that are hammered into the tree trunk. A four-gallon bucket hangs below the spile to collect the sap; during a good run, it must be emptied every twenty-four hours. The ideal weather for sugaring is a series of freezing storms followed by warm spells. The worse the weather, the better the sugaring, Vermonters are wont to observe.

Fresh maple sap is a watery liquid containing 2–4% sugar. It is boiled for ten to twelve hours to turn it into syrup. By the 1870s, sugarmakers were using "evaporators"—long, flat pans partitioned into a series of chambers. The pan is mounted over an "arch," or firebox, where a log or oil fire cooks the sap to the proper thickness.

Maple syrup is like wine in that the same tree in the same sugar bush will produce, depending on the year, syrups of widely varying quality. As the syrup emerges from the evaporator, it is graded by density and color in accordance with strict standards established by the state. In Vermont, the highest grade is *Vermont Fancy,* a syrup distinguished by its light amber color and fine, delicate flavor. In descending order come *Grade A Medium Amber, Grade A Dark Amber,* and last of all *Grade C.* The darker the color of the syrup, the richer and stronger its flavor. I prefer the robust caramel taste of Grade A Medium Amber to the delicate flavor of Vermont Fancy. In recent years, the traditional square cans have given way to rust-resistant plastic jugs.

Unopened, maple syrup will keep indefinitely; it should be refrigerated once the container is opened. If the syrup should crystallize, you can bring it back by placing the can in a pot of simmering water.

Other maple products include maple sugar (made by heating, stirring, and pouring the syrup into molds) and maple cream (made by cooking the syrup and whipping it when cool). The latter, not surprisingly, is delicious on biscuits and toast.

Silver Dollar Pancakes with Maple Butter

MAKES 24 TO 30 SILVER DOLLAR PANCAKES — ENOUGH TO SERVE 4

HERE'S a thoroughly American way to celebrate Shrove Tuesday. The pancakes are made with stone-ground cornmeal (the brand I use is Crutchfield's). Maple butter is delicious on pancakes, waffles, muffins, and French toast, not to mention off the end of a spoon!

For the maple butter:
½ cup maple syrup
½ cup unsalted butter, at room temperature

For the pancakes:
1 cup fine-textured stone-ground cornmeal
1 cup all-purpose flour
1 teaspoon baking soda
1 teaspoon baking powder
⅔ teaspoon salt
2 eggs
1–1½ cups buttermilk
1 tablespoon maple syrup
4 tablespoons oil
2–3 tablespoons butter

(1) Prepare the maple butter. Cream the butter in a mixer. Gradually add the maple syrup in a thin stream. Maple butter can be made ahead of time and will keep for up to 3 weeks in the refrigerator.

(2) Prepare the pancake batter. Sift the dry ingredients into a large mixing bowl and mix. (If the baking soda looks lumpy—and it often does—break it up between your fingers.) In a separate bowl, beat the eggs with ⅔ cup of the buttermilk, the maple syrup, and 2 tablespoons of the oil. Whisk the wet ingredients into the dry ones, adding additional buttermilk as necessary—the batter should be the consistency of lightly whipped cream.

(3) Heat 1 tablespoon of the remaining oil and 1½ table-

spoons of the butter in a skillet or griddle over medium heat. (For convenience, I like to use an electric frying pan set up at the breakfast table.) Use a large spoon or small measuring cup to ladle out walnut-sized blobs of batter. These will give you pancakes the size of silver dollars, which to my mind are the best. Cook the pancakes for 1 minute, or until bubbles begin to appear on the surface. Invert the cakes and cook for 1 minute on the other side. Use the remaining oil and butter to cook the remaining batter.

Serve the silver dollar cornmeal pancakes hot off the griddle, with maple butter and coffee.

Indian Pudding

SERVES 4

THIS recipe comes from Boston's venerable Locke-Ober Café. Founded in 1875, this Brahmin restaurant boasts the leather chairs, gilt wallpaper, and hand-carved Dominican mahogany of a nineteenth-century men's club. The unhurried air of the club is reflected in its traditional Indian pudding. The key to a proper Indian pudding is patience: the dish bakes in a low oven for 3 to 4 hours.

> ½ cup stone-ground cornmeal
> 3 cups milk
> 2 eggs, beaten
> ½ cup maple syrup
> ¼ cup molasses
> ¼ cup sugar
> 1 teaspoon salt
> ½ teaspoon cinnamon
> 1 teaspoon powdered ginger
> 4 tablespoons butter
> 4 tablespoons dark rum
>
> 1 5-quart soufflé dish or other ovenproof dish, thickly buttered

(1) Preheat the oven to 250 degrees. Mix the cornmeal with enough cold milk to make a liquid that pours easily (about ½

cup). Scald the remaining milk. Combine the cornmeal mixture with the scalded milk in the top of a double boiler. Cook it, stirring frequently, for 20 minutes, or until thick. Stir in the remaining ingredients and pour the mixture into the soufflé dish.

(2) Set the dish in a roasting pan with 1 inch boiling water in it (this is called a *bain marie* or water bath). Bake the Indian pudding for 3 to 4 hours in the oven, adding water to the *bain marie* as necessary. Let stand 30 minutes before serving. Indian pudding is delicious served with vanilla ice cream.

Pork Chops with Maple Barbecue Sauce

SERVES 4

In the southern United States, barbecue sauce is made with honey, mustard, and vinegar. I contrived a New England version using maple syrup instead of honey. My maple syrup barbecue sauce is delicious with pork, ham, and turkey, and it's just the thing for adding zip to lackluster baked beans.

For the maple barbecue sauce:
   4 strips bacon
   1 small onion
   1 small pickled or fresh jalapeño chili (optional)
   1 tablespoon butter
   ½ cup maple syrup
   3 tablespoons grainy mustard
2–3 tablespoons cider or raspberry vinegar
   Salt and fresh black pepper

To finish the pork chops:
   4 large fresh or smoked pork chops
   Salt and fresh black pepper
   2 tablespoons oil
   2 tablespoons butter

   1 ovenproof skillet just large enough to hold the chops

(1) Cut the bacon into ¼-inch slivers. Finely chop the onion, and seed and chop the chili (see Note on page 48). Melt the butter in a small saucepan. Add the bacon, onion, and chili, and cook over medium heat for 2 to 3 minutes, or until the onion is soft but not brown. Pour off the bacon fat. Whisk in the remaining ingredients and simmer for 2 to 3 minutes. Taste the sauce and make any necessary adjustments: it should be a little sweet, a little sour, and plenty spicy. The recipe can be prepared ahead to this stage.

(2) Preheat the oven to 400 degrees. Trim the excess fat off the pork chops and season with salt and pepper. Heat the oil and butter in a large skillet over a high flame. Add the pork chops and thoroughly brown on both sides. Pour off the fat. Spoon a little maple-barbecue sauce under the chops, then pour the rest on top. Bake the chops for 15 minutes, or until cooked to taste.

Variation: This preparation is excellent for Smithfield ham steak.

Frozen Maple Soufflé

SERVES 4

UNLIKE their baked cousins, frozen soufflés can be made ahead of time and served without worry. A frozen soufflé is nothing more than Italian meringue mixed with whipped cream. To make the meringue we cook sugar (or maple syrup) to the soft ball stage, then add it to stiffly beaten egg whites. The trick is to have the syrup reach the soft ball stage at the same moment the whites form stiff peaks. If the syrup gets too hot, add a few drops of cold water. For the best results, use a Grade A Medium or Grade A Dark syrup, which have a stronger flavor than Grade A Light.

  1 cup heavy cream
  1 cup maple syrup
  3 egg whites

Pinch each salt and cream of tartar
2 tablespoons sugar
1 teaspoon grated lemon peel
1½ cups coarsely crushed chocolate wafers or ginger cookies
Candied violets for decoration

4 ramekins or custard cups
Parchment paper or waxed paper
Oil and a pastry brush

(1) Beat the cream to stiff peaks in a chilled bowl. Set aside in a cool place and reserve. Bring the maple syrup to a boil in a heavy 3-quart saucepan (watch out—it boils over easily). Cook it to the soft ball stage (239 degrees on a sugar thermometer). To test it without a thermometer, drop a little syrup off the end of a spoon into a bowl of cold water. When rolled between the fingers, it should form a clear, pliable ball.

(2) Meanwhile, beat the egg whites to stiff peaks, adding the salt and cream of tartar after 20 seconds. Start by running the mixer at medium speed, increasing the speed to high and sprinkling in the sugar as the whites stiffen. Pour the boiling maple syrup into the stiffly beaten whites in a thin stream. Run the mixer at high speed while you are adding the syrup and until the mixture is cool.

(3) Prepare the ramekins. Cut the paper into 4- × 12-inch strips. Use them to form collars around the ramekins, tying them on with string. Lightly brush the inside of the collars with oil. Frozen soufflés don't really rise—they just look that way when you peel off the paper.

(4) Fold most of the whipped cream into the maple mixture with the lemon peel, reserving a little cream for garnish. Spoon the mixture into the prepared ramekins, alternating layers of cookie crumbs and mousse. (For a quick dessert, the mixture can be spooned or piped into wine glasses.) Freeze for at least 6 hours, preferably overnight. The recipe can be made up to 1 week ahead to this stage.

(5) Just before serving, remove the collars and pipe a rosette of whipped cream in the center of each soufflé. Crown each rosette with a candied violet and serve.

CHOCOLATE

TODAY is Valentine's Day. I will give my sweetie a box of chocolates. Millions of men all over the world will express their love the same way. Just how did chocolate and Valentine's Day come to be linked? The answer takes us back to ancient Rome and to the blood-thirsty rites of the Aztecs.

Valentine's Day occurs in February. February was sacred to the god Februus, better know as Faunus, the goat-legged god of fertility. In mid-February, the Romans celebrated a fertility festival called Lupercalia. Young men would sacrifice goats in the cave where the wolf had suckled Romulus and Remus. They then ran through the streets of Rome, clad only in loincloths, striking women with strips of goatskin to foster fertility. Roman boys chose their partners for the festival by drawing girls' names from an urn. The couples exchanged presents at the feast of Lupercalia —the origin of the modern custom of Valentine's Day gift-giving.

The early Christians knew better than to try to abolish pagan rites. So in 496 A.D., Pope Gelasius resolved to Christianize Lupercalia by transforming it into the feast of Saint Valentine. Valentine was a Roman priest who was imprisoned for aiding persecuted Christians. He restored the sight of his jailor's blind daughter, but was later clubbed to death on February 14, 270 A.D.

But how did chocolate come to be associated with the day of gallants and lovers? The cocoa tree is native to Central America, where it has been cultivated for four thousand years. It was inextricably linked with sex in most of the pre-Columbian cultures.

Columbus first tasted chocolate on his fourth expedition, in 1502; he was less than favorably impressed. Seventeen years

MARCH

I wonder if the sap is stirring yet,
If wintery birds are dreaming of a mate,
If frozen snowdrops feel as yet the sun,
And crocus fires are kindling one by one.

CHRISTINA ROSETTI

YESTERDAY it snowed. Today the warm sun drew me outdoors in my shirtsleeves. Tomorrow we will have a torrential downpour. And the wind has howled for all it's worth all week. Welcome to March, a month of wildly variable weather. One day we are still locked in the icy grip of winter. The next day we are warmed with the sunny promise of spring.

March is named, appropriately enough, for Mars, the Roman war god. There is certainly something bellicose about the intensity of the weather. Fortunately, spring officially arrives with the vernal equinox on March 20. As the sun crosses the equator, daylight increases and nighttime diminishes. Indeed, the Anglo-Saxons called March *Lenct-Monat,* "length month," because the days become longer than the nights.

This blustery month marks the commencement of the agricultural year. Seeds are sown; sheep are lambed; and mammals emerge from hibernation. March was the first month of the Greek and Roman calendar. And in England it wasn't until 1752 that New Year's Day was moved from March 25 to January 1. (In rural Europe, farm leases are still renewed in March.)

March is an important month for saints of the British Isles. March 1 is St. David's Day, honoring both the patron saint of Wales and another David, a warrior prince, who led the Welsh to victory against the Saxon king Cadwalader in the seventh century. His troops pinned leeks to their helmets so they could distinguish their comrades from the enemy. To this day, the Welsh wear leeks on their lapels and eat leek dishes on March 1 to commemorate the victory.

And, of course, St. Patrick is honored on March 17. Born in 389 A.D., Patrick was enslaved and deported by pagans when he was sixteen years old. He escaped and returned to Ireland to spread the Christian faith. When the saint lay on his deathbed, he urged his followers to celebrate, not lament his passing: the pious origin, perhaps, of the custom of drinking whisky at wakes. (Our word whisky, incidentally, comes from the Gaelic *usque-beathe,* literally "water of life.") I'm not sure what St. Patrick would think of the green beer swilled in twentieth-century taverns, but he probably wouldn't have objected to a pint or two of Guinness to wash down the traditional corned beef and cabbage.

A popular Jewish holiday called Purim also occurs in March. Purim commemorates the triumph of a Jewish maiden named Ester over an evil governor named Haman. King Ahasuerus fell in love with Ester and took her to be his queen. Unbeknownst to the king, Haman planned to execute all of Persia's Jews. (The date was to be determined by lot, hence the holiday's name, which means "Feast of Lots.") Ester barged into the king's private chambers (a crime punishable by death in those days), and exposed the plot. The evil man was strung up on the very gallows he had erected for his victims. Purim is one of the most ebullient of Jewish holidays. Worshippers sound noisemakers at the mention of Haman's name during the service and eat triangular poppyseed cakes, called *hamentaschen,* "Haman's purses."

This time of agricultural rebirth is a happy season for cooks. St. David's Day is a good occasion to enjoy leeks, which are in full season now. Sturdy leaf vegetables, such as dandelions, arugula, and rapini, are plentiful. Asparagus returns to the market, and root vegetables remain abundant. The orchards in the southern climes supply us with oranges, grapefruits, mineolas, kumquats, and ugli fruit.

March sees the return of shad to the East Coast estuaries. This silver fish is a delicacy, especially its buttery roe. What better way to celebrate St. Patrick's Day than with finnan haddie (smoked haddock), corned beef and cabbage, and Irish coffee.

March is a time of hope and renewal, of daylight and springtime, of the promise of clear skies and warm weather. But there's another reason why I am especially fond of this month, the third month of the year: March 11 is my birthday!

SPRING GREENS

HERE in the Frost Belt, March is a month of leaden skies and barren landscapes. We have come to the end of the winter squash and root season, but it is still too early for spring vegetables. All is not hopeless—our diet is brightened considerably by the appearance of three early-ripening greens: dandelions, rapini, and arugula. The first two are usually cooked, while arugula is enjoyed raw in salads.

Dandelion greens are rich in iron, calcium, and vitamin A; their virtue as a diuretic is attested to by their French name, *pissenlit,* which loosely translated means "bed-wetter." The English word comes from the French *dent de lion,* "tooth of a lion," an apt description for the jagged leaves. Their assertive, slightly bitter flavor makes them—in moderate doses—an interesting component for salads. The bitterness is attenuated by cooking.

The trick to enjoying dandelions is to get them really young. You can pick your own, but do so before the bud has flowered —the smaller and younger the leaves, the less bitter. If the stems leak a milky liquid when cut, you know the dandelions will be bitter. (Be sure the ones you gather have not been sprayed by a dog or with pesticides!) Some people eat the unfurled buds, which are said to taste vaguely like mushrooms. Cultivated dandelion leaves can be found at Italian markets. They wilt with appalling rapidity—try to eat them the same day you buy or pick them.

Rapini is another spring green popular with Italians. Its

sturdy leaves and broccolilike flowers taste like a cross between cabbage and broccoli. Actually, it's a variety of turnip, one that lacks a tuberous root. (The name comes from the Latin *rapa*, "turnip.") Rapini is a relative newcomer to the American diet: not surprisingly, it goes by many ethnic names, including *broccoli rabe, raab, brocoletto, brocoletti de rape, choy sum,* and *Chinese flowering cabbage*. Choose firm stems with relatively few buds or open flowers. Rapini is usually blanched or sautéed. Like other members of the cabbage family, it is low in sodium and calories, and an excellent source of vitamins A and C.

Once eaten only by Italian peasants, arugula has become a "designer" green, like radicchio and lamb's lettuce. A member of the radish family, arugula does indeed add a pungent, peppery tang to salads. Arugula (pronounced "a-*roo*-guh-la") has tender, dull green leaves shaped like those of the garden radish. Sometimes sold under its English name, rocket, it can be found at specialty greengrocers. Arugula loses some of its flavor when heated; cook it as briefly as possible.

Hot Dandelion Salad

SERVES 4 TO 6

THIS dandelion salad is a European version of a Midwestern favorite: hot salad with bacon. In both cases, the greens are dressed with hot bacon fat, which partially cooks the leaves and helps reduce their bitterness. Here, too, use young dandelions, as the older greens will be unpleasantly bitter. (You may wish to add other greens to further reduce the bitterness.) *Pancetta* is Italian bacon; it is dry-cured like prosciutto. In its absence, use regular bacon.

> 1 pound dandelion greens, or mixed greens such as escarole, chicory, endive, spinach, and/or romaine lettuce
> 2 eggs

2 slices country-style white bread or French bread
4–6 tablespoons extra-virgin olive oil
2 ounces Roquefort or blue cheese
4–6 ounces pancetta
1 clove garlic
2 tablespoons red wine vinegar, or to taste
Salt and fresh black pepper

(1) Preheat the oven to 400 degrees. Remove the bitter stems from the greens. Wash the greens in a bowl of cold water and spin dry in a salad spinner. Hard-cook the eggs: place then in cold water, bring to a boil, reduce the heat, and gently simmer for 11 minutes. Rinse the eggs under cold water and shell at once. Lightly brush the bread slices with a little olive oil on both sides. Cut them into 1-inch croutons, and bake in the preheated oven, turning once, for 10 minutes, or until golden brown. Cool the croutons on a cake rack. Rub them with the Roquefort or blue cheese. Grate the hard-cooked eggs and the remaining cheese on the coarse side of a grater. Cut the pancetta into ¼-inch slivers. Mince the garlic. The recipe can be prepared to this stage up to 3 hours before serving.

(2) Place the greens in a heatproof serving bowl. Just before serving, heat 1 tablespoon olive oil in a non–cast iron or aluminum skillet over medium heat. Add the pancetta and sauté until the pieces are very lightly browned. Transfer the pancetta to the serving bowl and discard all but 2 tablespoons of the hot bacon fat. Add 2 more tablespoons olive oil and the garlic. Reheat the pan until the garlic sizzles. Pour the hot fat over the greens, and toss. Add the vinegar to the hot pan and bring it to a boil. Pour the vinegar over the greens. Add salt and pepper to taste, and the grated eggs and cheese, and toss the salad thoroughly. Adjust the flavor of the dressing with additional salt, pepper, vinegar, or oil, if necessary. Garnish the salad with the croutons and serve at once.

Verdura

SERVES 4

As did a whole generation of second-generation Italian Americans, my friend Carol Spach consumed most of her childhood vegetables in the form of *verdura,* greens cooked with potatoes, garlic, and olive oil. The preparation lends itself particularly well to dandelion greens, which tend to be quite bitter by themselves. Use the youngest, tenderest dandelion greens you can find. Collard greens, turnip greens, and mustard greens can be prepared the same way.

> 1 **pound tender young dandelion greens**
> 1 **large baking potato**
>   **Salt**
> 1 **clove garlic, minced**
> 2–3 **tablespoons extra-virgin olive oil**
>   **Fresh black pepper**
>   **Juice of ½ lemon, or to taste**
> ½ **teaspoon sugar (optional)**

(1) Remove the stems from the dandelion greens. Wash the leaves. Cut the leaves widthwise into ¼-inch strips. Peel the potato and cut it into ¼-inch cubes.

(2) Place the potatoes in cold salted water, bring to a boil, reduce the heat, and gently simmer for 3 to 4 minutes, or until tender. Refresh the potatoes under cold water and drain. Meanwhile, cook the dandelion greens in rapidly boiling salted water for 1 to 2 minutes, or until tender. Refresh under cold water and drain. Mince the garlic. The recipe can be prepared to this stage up to 12 hours before serving.

(3) Just before serving, heat the olive oil in a skillet over medium heat. Add the garlic and cook for 10 seconds. Add the dandelion greens and potatoes, and salt and pepper to taste. Sauté the vegetables for 2 minutes, or until thoroughly heated. Add lemon juice to taste. If the greens are still bitter, add a little

sugar. Verdura makes a nice accompaniment to veal, chicken, or lamb.

Rapini with Italian Bacon and Garlic

RAPINI is a green in the broccoli family with a flavor that's a cross between that of kale and spinach. If pancetta is unavailable, use regular bacon or even a spicy sausage like Portuguese linguiça or chouriço.

- 2 pounds rapini
- 3 ounces pancetta or bacon
- 1–2 cloves garlic
- ½ teaspoon dried oregano
- Salt and fresh black pepper
- A few drops of fresh lemon juice (optional)

(1) Wash the rapini and remove any coarse stems (those thicker than ⅛ inch). Cut the leaves widthwise into 1-inch strips. Cut the pancetta into ¼-inch slivers. Mince or smash the garlic.

(2) Cook the pancetta in a large saucepan over medium heat for 2 to 3 minutes, or until the fat is rendered and the bacon pieces are cooked, but not brown or crisp. Push the pancetta to one side, and discard all but 3 tablespoons fat. Increase the heat to high and stir in the garlic, followed by the rapini. (The considerable bulk of the leaves will diminish as the rapini cooks.) Stir in the oregano.

(3) Cook the rapini for 5 to 10 minutes, or until the leaves are tender and have lost their bitterness, and most of the liquid has evaporated. Add salt and pepper to taste, and a few drops lemon juice, if you wish. Rapini makes a good accompaniment for veal or chicken.

Arugula and Endive Salad with Sherry Vinaigrette

SERVES 2

ARUGULA, known as "rocket" in the old herbals, is a springtime green whose leaves look like radish leaves. Its peppery flavor is reminiscent of root radish. As with other spring greens, try to buy the leaves small and tender. Sherry vinegar is available in most gourmet shops. Alternatively, you can use red wine vinegar with a splash of dry sherry.

> 1 large bunch arugula (about 1 cup)
> 1–2 heads Belgian endive
> 2 tablespoons extra-virgin olive oil, walnut oil, or hazelnut oil
> 2 teaspoons sherry vinegar
> Salt and fresh black pepper

(1) Remove the coarse stems from the arugula, wash the leaves, and dry in a salad spinner. Tear the leaves into 1½ inch pieces. Cut the endive widthwise into ¼-inch strips, discarding the last inch of the root end, which is bitter. Place the arugula and endive in a glass or white ceramic salad bowl. The recipe can be prepared to this stage up to 4 hours ahead; to keep the greens fresh, cover them with a cold, wet paper towel, and a plate or pot lid an inch smaller than the bowl. (Never tightly cover greens with plastic wrap—unable to "breathe," they will acquire a musty taste.)

(2) Just before serving, sprinkle the greens with the oil, vinegar, salt, and pepper. Toss lightly, correct the seasoning, toss again, and serve the salad at once.

NOTE: Unlike most salad dressings, the ingredients for this one are not combined ahead of time. The virtue of the recipe lies in its spontaneity and freshness.

Boneless shad is widely available in the mid-Atlantic states, and it is flown to prestige fish shops around the country. If you can't get it in your area, you must resort to other tactics. The second method is to bake the fish at a low heat for five to six hours, which softens the bones enough to make them edible. Another method is to cook shad with an acidic ingredient, like sorrel (see page 173) or vinegar, to dissolve the bones.

For many people, the fish is of small consequence—the mere packaging for another springtime delicacy, shad roe. Raw shad roe is not for the squeamish: two soft, squishy, banana-shaped egg sacs, containing thirty thousand eggs, connected by a veined, often bloody membrane. But cooked it's the sort of fare one should savor, kneeling, with one's head bared. The taste of shad roe is ineffable, but to get an idea, imagine the richness of sweetbreads, the subtle liver flavor of foie gras, and the sensuous crunch of the finest caviar. If I've failed to convince you, please pass your plate to me!

BUYING SHAD AND SHAD ROE

WHOLE shad should have bright eyes and shimmering, silvery skin. The fillets should look plump and moist. Boned shad is expensive, and the fillets will have several longitudinal slits. Beware of inexpensive "fillets": they are apt to be merely split, not boned, and literally riddled with bones. (You can feel them if you run your fingers over the surface.)

Shad roe should be plump and whole, not broken or excessively bloody. To ensure even cooking, buy roe all the same size.

Shad roe requires a master's touch at cooking, for it disintegrates when handled roughly. Overcooked, it is as dry as sawdust, but it's not the sort of fare you want to eat rare. When cooked, the roe feel firm but not springy. You can also make a small incision: the eggs in the very center should just be losing their pink.

Shad roe should be washed in cold water to remove the

blood. Take care not to remove or rupture the membrane, or the eggs will spatter. Cooks are divided on the question of a preliminary poaching in water. I like this method: it makes the roe easier to handle and reduces the risk of undercooking. To poach shad roe, place it in cold, lightly salted water to cover, bring it to the barest simmer, and cook it over low heat for 4 to 6 minutes. Drain the roe and blot it dry: you are now ready to finish it by sautéeing it in butter or bacon fat. Keep the accompaniments simple: bacon, capers, lemon juice. The richness of the roe makes saucery superfluous.

Boned Shad with Spinach and Pink Butter Sauce

SERVES 4

HERE'S a dish that's as colorful as church on Easter Sunday. The white shad cloaked with pink butter sauce reclines on a bed of green spinach. You must use completely boned shad fillets. You'll pay dearly for them, but I promise you, the ease of eating is worth every penny. Fresh sorrel can be substituted for the spinach; its acidity goes well with this moist, rich fish. The sauce derives from a classic *beurre blanc*, white butter sauce, from the Loire Valley. It owes its pink hue to the presence of rosé wine and red wine vinegar.

For the shad:
2 completely boned shad fillets (1½–2 pounds fish)
  Salt and fresh black pepper
3 tablespoons butter
2 tablespoons minced shallots
¼ cup dry white wine

For the spinach:
  Approximately 1 pound fresh spinach
3 tablespoons butter
  Salt, fresh black pepper, and freshly grated nutmeg
  Juice of ½ lemon (optional)

For the pink butter sauce:

3 tablespoons minced shallots
1 cup dry rosé wine (like a rosé d'Anjou from the Loire Valley or a California blush wine)
¼ cup red wine vinegar
3 tablespoons heavy cream
½ cup cold unsalted butter, cut into ½-inch pieces
Salt, fresh black pepper, and cayenne pepper

(1) Preheat the oven to 400 degrees. Season the fish with salt and pepper. Spread a nonaluminum baking dish with half the butter and half the shallots. Arrange the fish on top, sprinkle with the shallots and the wine, and dot with the remaining butter. Press a piece of foil or parchment paper over the fish, and bake for 20 to 30 minutes, or until the fish flakes easily when pressed.

(2) Meanwhile, get the spinach ready for cooking. Remove the stems and wash the leaves. Set aside.

(3) Prepare the butter sauce. Combine the shallots, wine, and vinegar in a heavy, nonaluminum saucepan. (You can also add the pan juices from the fish, if you like.) Boil these ingredients until only 5 tablespoons liquid remain. Add the cream, and continue boiling until only 4 tablespoons liquid remain. Whisk in the butter, piece by piece, working over high heat. The sauce may boil while the butter is being added, but must not boil once finished, or it will separate. (If it does separate, try whisking it in a thin stream into a few tablespoons of cold cream.) Season the sauce to taste with salt, pepper, and cayenne. (*Note:* These sorts of butter sauces are not served piping hot. Keep the sauce warm on the stove, but do not attempt to warm it over direct heat, or it may curdle.)

(4) Cook the spinach. Melt the butter in a large sauté pan over high heat, and cook it until it begins to brown. Add the spinach and cook, stirring frequently, for 1 minute, or until the leaves are tender and wilted. Add salt, pepper, and nutmeg to taste, and, if you wish, a squeeze of lemon juice.

To assemble the dish, spread the spinach around the edge of a platter or plates, and arrange the shad fillets in the center. Spoon the pink butter sauce over the fish. Uncork a nice Sancerre from the Loire Valley or a West Coast Sauvignon Blanc.

Six-Hour Shad

SERVES 3 TO 4

THIS recipe is for people who can't buy boned shad fillets but can find the fish whole or split. (If you pay less than $3.50 a pound for it, chances are it's not completely boned.) The five-to-six-hour baking time and the acid of the lemon juice soften the bones to the point where you can eat them right along with the fish. If you can find some fresh sorrel (see page 173), wrap the shad in it: the oxalic acid is a great tenderizer.

> 1 3–4 pound shad (ask your fishmonger to split the fish and remove the skin)
> 3 tablespoons heavy cream
> Juice of 1 lemon
> Salt
> 3 tablespoons unsalted butter
> White pepper
>
> Aluminum foil

(1) Preheat the oven to 175 degrees or the lowest setting it will register. Sprinkle the shad halves with the cream and one third of the lemon juice, and salt to taste. Spread half the butter on a large sheet of foil. Place the fish on top, fillets side by side, and dot the top with the remaining butter and sprinkle another third of the lemon juice over it. Fold the foil over to enclose the fish, and crimp the edges to make a hermetic seal.

(2) Place the wrapped shad in a baking dish, and bake it for 5 to 6 hours, or until it breaks into meaty flakes when pressed. Unwrap it just before serving, and season with pepper and the remaining lemon juice. Despite our best efforts, the fish will be somewhat dry, so serve it with a rich sauce, like the Pink Butter Sauce on page 113.

NOTE: Many recipes call for adding onion, green peppers, bay leaf, black pepper, etc. I find that by the time the shad has baked for six hours, these flavorings overpower the fish.

Shad Roe with Bacon

SERVES 2

THIS is the way shad roe is prepared in the South. It is poached in water first to firm up the eggs, then browned in bacon fat. Simple, yes, but it's the best way we know to eat shad roe.

  1 pair of shad roe
  4 strips bacon
    Salt and fresh black pepper
  1 cup flour
  1 lemon
  1 heaping tablespoon capers (optional)

(1) Gently wash the roe, removing any bloody spots or veins. (Do not remove the membrane, or the roe will crumble.) Soak the roe in salted ice water in a saucepan for 10 minutes. Place the pan on the heat, bring the water to the gentlest simmer, and cook the roe for 5 minutes. Drain.

(2) Meanwhile, sauté the bacon in a cast iron skillet over medium heat for 3 minutes, or until lightly browned. Transfer the bacon to paper towels to drain. Reserve the fat in the skillet. Season the roe with salt and pepper. Dredge the roe in the flour, shaking to remove the excess. Cook the roe in the bacon fat over low heat for 3 minutes per side, or until nicely browned.

To serve, spoon a little of the bacon fat over the roe, followed by a squeeze of fresh lemon juice. Garnish with bacon and, if you wish, capers.

Shad Roe with Black Butter

SERVES 2

BEURRE *noir,* "black butter," is a sauce often served with skate or brains. To prepare it, butter is cooked until it begins to burn (it acquires a lovely nutty flavor in the process), then deglazed with vinegar and capers. In this recipe the roe is poached in water first, then finished by sautéing.

    1 **pair of shad roe**
    4 **tablespoons unsalted butter**
      Salt and fresh black pepper
      Flour for dusting
    2 **tablespoons wine or sherry vinegar**
      Juice of ½ lemon, plus extra if necessary
    1 **heaping tablespoon drained capers**

(1) Wash the roe in cold water, and place in a saucepan with salted water to cover. Bring the water to the barest simmer over medium heat, then gently poach the roe over low heat for 4 to 6 minutes, or until firm but not springy—if anything, the roe should be slightly undercooked. Drain the roe and blot dry.

(2) Melt the butter in a sauté pan over medium heat. Meanwhile, season the roe with salt and pepper and dust with flour, shaking off the excess. Sauté the roe over medium heat for 2 to 3 minutes per side or until nicely browned and cooked. Transfer the roe to plates or a platter.

(3) Have all the remaining ingredients ready. Cook the pan juices over high heat until the butter becomes very brown and smoky. Add the vinegar, lemon juice, and capers, and stand back —otherwise the rising cloud of vinegar vapor will sting your eyes. Simmer this sauce for a few seconds, adding salt and pepper to taste, and more lemon juice if you wish. Pour the black butter over the roe and serve at once.

ASPARAGUS

PAST generations have venerated the stalks as scepters of Venus. But to eat asparagus solely for its supposed aphrodisiac properties would be to overlook one of the most sublime flavors in the vegetable kingdom. Asparagus sends up its verdant tips at the end of March and the beginning of April. French gastronome Moncelet summed up the timeliness of this delicacy, observing that "spring has sent its calling card on a plate."

There are at least fourteen species of asparagus. My favorite is the green variety grown in the United States. The Europeans go to great pains to raise white asparagus, which owes its anemic complexion to solar deprivation. (The stalks are buried with fresh dirt as they grow.) White asparagus tends to be bland and fibrous —I've never understood why the French make such a fuss about it. Nor should one overlook wild asparagus—its slim dimensions and robust taste make it good enough to eat raw.

When buying asparagus, look for unblemished, bright-green stalks with closed, compact tips. Avoid asparagus with open or moldy ends or crimped or woody stems: at least two-thirds of each stalk should be green. The Romans liked their asparagus large—Pliny raved about stalks so large that three of them weighed a pound. For me, the ideal size is ⅓-inch in diameter, but larger plants have their enthusiasts.

If you don't plan to use asparagus the same day you buy it, store it upright in a dish of cold water in the refrigerator. Wash asparagus right before you plan to cook it. If you must store it more than forty-eight hours, I find it keeps better cooked than raw. One pound will serve two as an appetizer, three to four as a vegetable.

A great deal of nonsense surrounds the cooking and eating of asparagus. The practice of peeling the stalks originated in Europe, where the white variety has a tough exterior. True, you can eat more of each stalk of the green ones if you whittle off the fibrous skin at the end (use a knife or vegetable peeler). But it's quicker and easier simply to hold the stem end firmly in one hand and bend the stalk over with the other. The asparagus will snap at the natural dividing line between toughness and tenderness.

Nor do you need a special cylindrical pot for steaming asparagus. Indeed, I prefer boiling to steaming, as it preserves the vegetable's color. Cook each pound of asparagus in 1 quart of rapidly boiling water with 2 teaspoons salt for 3 minutes, or until crispy-tender. (To test it, insert a small knife in the end: it should still be a little resistant.) Remove the asparagus from the boiling water, refresh under cold running water until cool. This prevents overcooking and fixes the color. The stalks can be reheated at the last minute in butter, oil, or vermouth. Asparagus can also be cut into bite-sized pieces and stir-fried.

Asparagus is traditionally served with melted butter and lemon, olive oil and lemon, or with hollandaise or Maltaise sauce (made with orange juice instead of lemon—see page 131). It is also delicious as a cold salad with a mayonnaise or vinaigrette dressing. In Europe it is considered perfectly polite to eat the stalks with your fingers.

Asparagus with
Lemon-Soy Glaze

SERVES 3 TO 4

HERE'S a quick, easy way to prepare asparagus. The trick is to use high heat, so the butter and soy sauce caramelize.

    1 pound asparagus
      Salt
    2 tablespoons butter
    2 tablespoons soy sauce
      Juice of ½ lemon
    1 teaspoon sugar or honey
      Fresh black pepper

(1) Wash and snap the stalks as described above. Cook in rapidly boiling salted water for 2 to 3 minutes, or until crispy-tender. Refresh under cold water and drain. The asparagus can be prepared up to 24 hours ahead.

(2) Just before serving, melt the butter in a sauté pan and add the soy sauce, lemon juice, sugar or honey, and asparagus.

Cook over high heat, shaking the pan so the stalks roll around in the sauce, for 1 minute, or until the liquids have boiled down to a glaze. Season to taste with salt and pepper. Serve at once.

Asparagus Salad with Baby Carrots and Curaçao Vinaigrette

SERVES 4

THIS colorful salad is the invention of my assistant, Marcia Walsh. When it comes to presentation, Marcia has the eye of an artist; she is also a terrific cook. Curaçao is an orange-flavored liqueur from an island in the Caribbean. If unavailable, substitute Cointreau, Grand Marnier, or triple sec.

1 pound asparagus
1 pound baby carrots
Salt

For the dressing:
12 fresh basil leaves
1 teaspoon Dijon-style mustard
Salt and fresh black pepper
1 tablespoon sherry or rice wine vinegar
1 tablespoon curaçao
4 tablespoons walnut oil or olive oil

(1) Clean and trim the asparagus as described above. Scrub or peel the carrots, leaving 1 inch of the stem intact. Tie the asparagus in bundles and cook in rapidly boiling salted water for 2 to 3 minutes, or until crispy-tender. Remove with the slotted spoon, refresh under cold water, and drain. Follow the same procedure with the carrots, cooking them for 2 to 3 minutes or until crispy-tender.

(2) Finely chop 6 of the basil leaves, leaving 6 whole for garnish. Combine the mustard, salt, pepper, vinegar, and curaçao

in a bowl. Whisk in the oil in a thin stream to make an emulsified sauce. Correct the seasoning.

(3) Arrange the vegetables on plates or a platter, like spokes around a hub, alternating asparagus and carrots. Spoon the vinaigrette sauce over the vegetables and place the basil leaves in the center.

Penne with Asparagus and Smoked Salmon

SERVES 4

THIS pasta dish makes a delightful appetizer or light entrée. *Penne* are finger-length pasta tubes, ¼ inch in diameter. The word literally means "quill"—an apt description of the diagonally cut ends.

    1 pound asparagus
      Salt
    1 cup heavy cream
    8 ounces smoked salmon, cut into slivers
    ½ cup butter, diced
    1 pound penne, or other small, tube-shaped pasta
    ½ cup freshly grated Parmesan
    2 tablespoons chopped fresh chives, scallions, or tarragon

(1) Wash and snap the asparagus stalks as described on page 117. Cut the asparagus into pieces the length of the *penne*. Cook in rapidly boiling salted water till crispy-tender, about 3 minutes, then refresh under cold water and drain. Boil the cream until reduced by half, adding the smoked salmon halfway through. Whisk in the butter, piece by piece.

(2) Cook the pasta in lightly salted water for 4 minutes, or until al dente, then drain. Return the pasta to the pan with the asparagus, salmon-cream sauce, and half the cheese. Cook over high heat, stirring gently, for 1 minute, or until the ingredients

are hot and coated with sauce. Stir in the fresh herbs. Serve the remaining cheese on the side. You'll need a crisp, dry wine with this one: a Verdicchio or Muscadet.

Roulades of Sole with
Low-fat Asparagus Mousse

SERVES 2

HERE'S a recipe for my weight-conscious friends, the ones who are always complaining that they can never use any of my cookbooks. The fish is cooked by steaming and is absolutely free of fat. The recipe can be multiplied to accommodate any number of diners.

> 1 pound asparagus
> Salt
> 4 nice sole fillets (about 1 pound fish)
> Fresh white pepper
> White part of 2 scallions
> ½ cup low-fat cottage cheese
> Juice of ½ lemon, or to taste
> A few gratings of whole nutmeg
>
> 1 wok with a fitting bamboo steamer

(1) Wash and snap the asparagus stems as described on page 117. Cook half the stems in rapidly boiling salted water for 1 minute, or until crispy-tender (more on the crisp side than the tender side). Refresh the asparagus under cold water and drain, reserving the cooking liquid. (*Note:* The asparagus can also be cooked by steaming.)

(2) Run your fingers over the fish fillets, feeling for bones. Cut away any you find with a paring knife. Season the fillets with salt and pepper. Roll each fillet around 3 or 4 asparagus spears, rolling the fish on the diagonal. Place the rolls in the steamer.

(3) Prepare the asparagus mousse. Cut the tips off the remaining asparagus; each tip should be 1 inch long. Finely chop the stalks and the scallions. Bring the asparagus water back to a boil. Add the asparagus and scallions, and cook until the small pieces are very tender, again reserving the cooking liquid. (The tips, which are larger, will still be a little crisp.) Separate the asparagus tips from the small pieces. Purée the latter in a blender or food processor with the low-fat cottage cheese and lemon juice, and salt, pepper, and nutmeg to taste. If the mousse is too thick, add a little of the asparagus water. The recipe can be prepared up to 2 hours ahead to this stage.

(4) To assemble the dish, place the steamer over a wok filled with water. Steam the sole for 10 minutes, or until it flakes easily when pressed. Meanwhile, warm the mousse. To serve, spread the asparagus mousse over the bottom of 2 warm dinnner plates. Using a spatula, set the asparagus-sole rolls on top. Decorate with the reserved asparagus tips.

If wine is allowed in your diet, try a Trefethen Chardonnay.

LEEKS

LEEKS have the honor of figuring in the world's oldest recipes, recorded by the Mesopotamians on cuneiform tablets in 1700 B.C. Leeks were an important ration of the slaves who built the pyramids. The emperor Nero ate leek soup daily to make his voice sonorous and clear for oration. More recent enthusiasts include miners in northeast England, who compete fiercely in growing leeks, nourishing their prized specimens with brown sugar, polishing them with oil and milk. (The winners have been known to attain a diameter of four inches!)

The leek looks like a giant scallion—a cylindrical, white stalk with furry roots at one end and a crown of dark green leaves at the other. Past generations have alternately revered and reviled this distinctive root; the Young Turks of the "new American cooking" have made them the aristocrats of the onion race. Leeks have a unique flavor: they are milder than onions, more mellow than garlic, similar to scallions, but more earthy and flavorful. Some people detect an asparagus flavor—whence the leek's nickname "poor man's asparagus."

Leeks are essential to soups of all sorts (such as cock-a-leekie and vichyssoise) and to such dishes as Belgian *flamiche* (cheese pie with leeks), Italian *torta pasqualina* (Easter pie), and *potée Auvergnat* (stuffed cabbage from central France).

Leeks are available much of the year but are at their best in the spring. The crown should bend easily: a rigid leek has gone to seed and will have a tough, fibrous core. Leeks come in varying diameters: the small ones are troublesome to chop but nice for salads or braising. If you need lots of chopped leeks for a soup or stew, you'd best buy a couple of giants. The leaves should be bright green and fresh-looking: avoid leeks with brown or oozy roots, or faded, anemic-looking leaves.

The best part of the leek is the white part of the stalk, which owes its mildness to its sojourn underground. (Like white asparagus, leeks are often mounded with dirt as they grow, to give them a more delicate flavor.) As a result, the stalk is full of sand and must be thoroughly cleansed before chopping.

To clean a leek, cut off the green leaves, whittling the end like the point of a pencil. (The white part continues up the stalk inside the leaves.) Cut off the furry root, leaving the base attached. Slice the outer layer of the leek lengthwise, and remove it as you would an onion skin. Next, cut the leek in half lengthwise almost to the root, rotate the stalk 90 degrees, and cut it in half again. Now holding the leek by the root end, plunge it up and down in a bowl of cold water, as you would a plumber's helper, till the layers are completely free of sand. Shake the leek to dry it out, and chop it like a carrot. (*Note:* Be sure to wipe off the cutting board first, as the grit often remains behind after the original lengthwise cuts.)

Leek Salad with Maple Vinaigrette

SERVES 6

THE unusual dressing for this dish was created for *Bon Appétit* magazine at my Taste of the Mountains cooking school, in Glen, New Hampshire. The syrup came from a sugar house across the road.

1½ **pounds leeks of the same length**

For the maple vinaigrette:
 1 **tablespoon sherry or red wine vinegar**
 1 **teaspoon Dijon-style mustard**
 ⅓ **teaspoon salt**
 ¼ **cup walnut oil**
 1 **teaspoon minced fresh herbs, such as tarragon and chives**
 2 **tablespoons maple syrup**
   Fresh black pepper

For the garnish:
 1 **hard-cooked egg**
 ¼ **cup coarsley chopped pecans**
 ¼ **cup minced fresh parsley**

(1) Cut the dark green leaves and furry roots off the leeks. Split the leeks lengthwise and wash thoroughly as described above. Tie them into 2 or 3 bundles with kitchen twine or un-waxed dental floss, then cook in 3 quarts of boiling, salted water for 8 to 10 minutes, or until tender. Refresh under cold water and drain. Blot the leeks dry and arrange them in rows or radiating spokes on a platter.

(2) Mix the vinegar, mustard, and salt in a small bowl. Whisk in the oil in a thin stream. Stir in the herbs, maple syrup, and plenty of pepper. Spoon half of the vinaigrette over the leeks, and marinate for at least 1 hour. The recipe can be prepared several hours ahead to this point.

(3) Sieve or finely chop the egg yolk and white separately.

Decoratively arrange the white and yolk, pecans, and parsley on top of the leeks. Whisk the remaining vinaigrette, spoon it over the leeks, and serve.

Flamiche

SERVES 8

A *flamiche* is a leek tart from Flanders. It is often garnished with *maroilles,* a pungent cheese that smells like athletic-wear left for too long at the bottom of a gym locker. Other cheeses that would work include Pont l'Evêque, Appenzeller, or imported Munster. To save time, the yeast dough is made in the food processor.

For the yeast dough:
- ½ cake compressed yeast, or 1 envelope dried yeast, or 2 teaspoons bulk yeast
- 1 tablespoon sugar
- 2 cups white flour
- 2 eggs
- 1 tablespoon vegetable oil
- 1 scant teaspoon salt

For the filling:
- 6 leeks, furry roots and dark green leaves discarded
- 4 tablespoons butter
- 2 tablespoons chopped fresh parsley and other herbs
- ⅓ cup heavy cream
  Salt, fresh black pepper, cayenne pepper, and freshly grated nutmeg
- ½ pound maroilles or other pungent cheese

- 1 12-inch tart pan with removable bottom

(1) Prepare the dough. Place 3 tablespoons warm water in a small bowl and sprinkle the yeast and sugar on top. After 4 to 5 minutes, the mixture should begin to foam like the head of a beer. Place the yeast mixture and the remaining ingredients for

the dough in a food processor bowl, and process in short bursts for 2 to 3 minutes, or until the dough comes together into a smooth ball. (*Note:* It may be necessary to add a few tablespoons water or flour to obtain the proper consistency. The dough should be soft but not sticky.) Knead it for a few minutes by hand.

(2) Place the dough in an oiled bowl, cover with plastic wrap, and set the bowl in a warm spot for 1 to 2 hours, or until the dough has doubled in bulk. Punch the dough down, roll it out, and use it to line the tart pan. The recipe can be prepared to this stage up to 24 hours ahead, but refrigerate the dough, and punch it down again before rolling it out.

(3) Meanwhile, wash the leeks as described on page 123, and finely chop. Melt the butter in a large frying pan over medium heat, and cook the leeks for 5 minutes, or until soft but not brown. Add the herbs and cream and gently simmer for 5 minutes: the cream should be mostly absorbed by the leeks. Add salt, black pepper, cayenne pepper, and nutmeg to taste: the mixture should be highly seasoned. Cut the cheese into slices ¼-inch thick and just slightly smaller than playing cards.

(4) Spoon the leek mixture into the crust. Arrange the cheese slices on top around the edge of the tart, leaving the center open. Preheat the oven to 375 degrees, and let the tart stand in a warm place for 30 to 40 minutes. Bake the *flamiche* for 30 to 40 minutes or until the crust is browned and sounds hollow when tapped. (If the edge of the crust browns too fast, protect it with a piece of foil.) Cool slightly before serving. A fruity wine from Alsace, like a Riesling or Gewürztraminer, would make the perfect beverage.

Gratin of Leeks with Smoked Cheese

SERVES 4

A gratin is a vegetable casserole baked crusty and brown in the oven. The word comes from the French *gratter,* "to scratch" or "scrape," for this is what you must do to get at the best part —the cheese that bakes into the corners of the pan. For an unusual touch we use smoked cheese, but the unadventurous could substitute freshly grated Parmesan.

> 2 pounds fresh leeks
> Salt
> Fresh black pepper and freshly grated nutmeg
> 3 tablespoons butter
> 1 cup grated smoked mozzarella or other mild smoked cheese
> ½ cup lightly toasted bread crumbs
> Approximately 1 cup heavy cream

(1) Preheat the oven to 375 degrees. Cut the dark green leaves and the furry roots off the leeks. Cut each leek in half, lengthwise, almost to the root. Wash the leeks thoroughly and tie them into small bundles with string, to prevent them from falling apart while cooking. Cook them in rapidly boiling, lightly salted water for 8 to 10 minutes, or until tender. Refresh under cold water and drain.

(2) Lightly butter a baking dish just large enough to hold the leeks. Arrange a layer of leeks in the bottom. Sprinkle with a little salt, pepper, and nutmeg, and dot with half the butter. Then sprinkle on half the grated cheese and bread crumbs. Add another layer of leeks and sprinkle with seasonings. Add enough cream to almost cover the leeks, and sprinkle the remaining butter, cheese, and crumbs on top. The recipe can be prepared to this stage up to 8 hours ahead.

(3) Bake the gratin in the preheated oven for 30 minutes, or until the cream is mostly absorbed by the leeks and the top is browned and crusty.

Braised Leeks

SERVES 4 TO 6

BRAISING is a moist cooking method well suited to cooking fibrous foods; it is ideal for such stringy vegetables as celery, Belgian endive, and leeks.

>   8 medium-sized leeks (2–2½ pounds)
>   Salt
>   1 small onion
>   1 clove garlic
>   1 carrot
>   1 stalk celery
>   2 ounces cooked ham or prosciutto
>   3 tablespoons butter
>   Fresh black pepper
>   ¾ cup brown stock, plus extra if necessary (see recipe on page 473)
>   Bouquet garni (see recipe on page 471)
>   3 tablespoons chopped fresh parsley for garnish (optional)

(1) Cut off the dark green tops and furry roots of the leeks, and clean them as described on page 123. To keep them together, tie the leeks with twine or unwaxed dental floss, and blanch them in rapidly boiling, heavily salted water for 5 minutes, or until they begin to soften. Refresh under cold water, and drain.

(2) Preheat the oven to 400 degrees. Peel and finely chop the onion, garlic, and carrot. Clean and finely chop the celery. Coarsely chop the ham.

(3) Melt the butter in a small frying pan over medium heat. Add the chopped vegetables and ham and sauté for 3 to 5 minutes, or until the vegetables are soft and just beginning to brown. Spread the vegetables in a baking dish just large enough to hold the leeks. Arrange the leeks on top. Add the pepper, stock, and bouquet garni—the stock should come halfway up the sides of the leeks. Press a piece of buttered foil on top of the vegetables and tightly cover the pan. The recipe can be prepared to this stage up to 12 hours before baking.

(4) Bake the leeks in the preheated oven for 30 to 40 minutes, or until tender. If too much stock evaporates, add more. To serve, transfer the leeks to a warm platter. Boil the braising liquid in a small saucepan until 5 to 6 tablespoons liquid remain. Adjust the seasoning and spoon this liquid over the leeks. Garnish with chopped parsley, and serve.

WINTER CITRUS

THERE once was a time when youngsters would find oranges in their Christmas stockings. While few parents would give their kids fruit today (they would face a mutiny Christmas morning), the custom does serve to remind us that citrus fruits were once relatively rare and that winter is the best time to eat them.

The orange is one of the few trees that simultaneously bears leaves, flowers, and fruit. In many cultures orange blossoms are a symbol of innocence and fertility, worn by brides to ensure a fruitful marriage.

The Chinese are credited with domesticating the orange; commercial groves were recorded as early as 2400 B.C. The fruit remained a status symbol in Europe up through the eighteenth century. No self-respecting palace was without its *orangerie,* or citrus greenhouse: that of Versailles contained twelve hundred silver tubs planted with orange trees (the fruit was used for show rather than for eating). The Louvre's orangerie currently houses the water lily murals painted by impressionist Claude Monet.

The longer oranges stay on the tree, the sweeter they become. But the fruit is very vulnerable to cold: at 28 degrees it becomes frozen in only four hours. The best oranges and grapefruits come from Indian River, in central Florida, where special soil conditions and a particularly mild climate enable them to ripen to their peak.

Most of our foods have existed since recorded history, but not that giant of the citrus kingdom, the grapefruit. Derived from a bitter Malaysian fruit called *pummelo,* the grapefruit was "invented" in Jamaica in the early nineteenth century. It hardly tastes like a grape, but the tree is so prolific (yielding thirteen hundred to fifteen hundred pounds of fruit a year) that the fruits appear to grow in grapelike clusters.

Grapefruits come in two main types: white and pink. The latter are marginally sweeter but less flavorful than the former. There are numerous varieties, including the Florida Duncan (excellent for squeezing) and Texas Ruby Red (one of the few with pink juice as well as pink flesh).

Also from Jamaica and related to the grapefruit is the ugli, a pear-shaped fruit that's a hybrid between the grapefruit and the tangerine. With its thick, bumpy skin and mottled greenish-yellow color, the fruit is indeed worthy of its name. The flesh is succulent, however, and tastes like a cross between its above-mentioned ancestors.

Sicilian Orange Salad

SERVES 4

THIS unusual recipe comes from a former student, Joe Burgio, who learned to make it from his Sicilian grandfather. (Grandfather used considerably more red pepper and wine than the amounts listed below.) The oranges should be fragrant and juicy: Joe recommends Temples or blood oranges.

> 4 plump, juicy oranges
> 1 clove garlic (optional)
> 2 tablespoons extra-virgin olive oil
> 3–4 tablespoons dry red wine
> 2 tablespoons toasted pine nuts (see Note below)
> ½ teaspoon balsamic or red wine vinegar
> ¼ teaspoon crushed dried red pepper flakes, or to taste
> Salt and fresh black pepper to taste

Peel and skin the oranges: cut the segments away from the membranes, working over a bowl to catch the juice. Cut the garlic in half and use one half to rub the inside of a glass or ceramic mixing bowl. Place the orange segments and juice in the bowl with the remaining ingredients, adding additional oil, wine, or vinegar to taste. Let the mixture marinate for 5 to 10 minutes before serving. The recipe can be prepared up to 1 hour ahead. I like to serve Sicilian orange salad as a midmeal palate refresher or an accompaniment to fish.

NOTE: To toast pine nuts, place them on a baking sheet in a preheated 400-degree oven or toaster oven for 5 minutes, or until lightly browned, shaking the pan once or twice to turn the nuts.

Blood Orange Maltaise Sauce

MAKES 1½ CUPS SAUCE

MALTAISE sauce is traditionally made with sour oranges from Malta. In this recipe we use blood oranges—the color is much more striking. Maltaise sauce is delicious on asparagus, grilled fish, and sautéed sweetbreads.

¾ **cup butter**
4 **egg yolks**
   Juice of 1 blood orange, or to taste
   Salt, fresh white pepper, and cayenne pepper
   A few drops lemon juice (optional)

(1) Melt the butter in a small saucepan over a low flame, then set aside in a warm place. Have a large bowl of cold water nearby. Place the egg yolks and 1 tablespoon of the orange juice in a large stainless steel bowl, whisk together, and place over a pan of simmering water, set over a medium flame. (Often double boilers do not provide enough whisking space.) Whisk the yolks as vigorously as you can. After 60 seconds or so, the mixture will

become light and moussy; continue whisking until it thickens to the consistency of mayonnaise and you can see traces of the bottom of the bowl with each stroke of the whisk.

(2) Remove the bowl from the simmering water as soon as the sauce begins to thicken, as the residual heat from the metal bowl will continue to cook the yolks. If the yolks start to over-cook (turn into scrambled eggs), set the bowl in the bowl of cold water. A trace of scrambling is normal and will not harm the final sauce.

(3) Add the warm butter in a very thin stream, whisking constantly. The sauce should thicken. It is better to add the butter too slowly rather than too quickly. Add the remaining orange juice a few drops at a time, then whisk in salt, pepper, and cayenne to taste. Add lemon juice if the sauce is too sweet, more orange juice if that flavor does not come through. The sauce should be a highly seasoned balance between sweet and tart.

Grapefruit Mousse

SERVES 4

THIS recipe works equally well with white or pink grape-fruit, but you may need to increase or decrease the sugar, de-pending on the sweetness of the fruit. To enhance the flavor and appearance, the mousse is served in hollowed grapefruit shells.

    2 large grapefruit
    1 envelope gelatin
    ¼ cup Cointreau or triple sec
    3 egg yolks
      Approximately ¾ cup sugar
    ⅔ cup light cream
    1 cup heavy cream
      Fresh mint leaves or candied violets for garnish

(1) "Wolf" the grapefruit. Cut a small slice off the top and bottom of the fruit, without exposing the flesh, so that the halves stand straight without wobblng. Place the fruit on its side on the cutting board. Using a large knife, and holding it vertically, make a series of zigzag cuts around the middle of the fruit—the equator, so to speak—to cut the grapefruit in half. Each cut should go slightly deeper than halfway. Pull the two halves apart: their jagged edges will resemble the teeth of a wolf.

(2) Carefully hollow out each grapefruit half, working over a bowl to catch the juice. Press the pulp through a strainer; you should have a little more than 1 cup grapefruit juice. Discard the pulp, but reserve the grapefruit shells. Sprinkle the gelatin over the Cointreau in a small, heatproof bowl and let stand until spongy. Place the bowl in a pan of simmering water to completely melt the gelatin.

(3) Whisk the egg yolks with ½ cup sugar in a large bowl. Heat the light cream with ⅓ cup grapefruit juice in a heavy saucepan. Gradually whisk the hot cream into the yolk mixture. Return it to the pan and cook over medium heat, stirring with a wooden spoon, for 2 minutes, or until the mixture loses its raw-yolk smell and thickens to the consistency of heavy cream. (It should thickly coat the back of the wooden spoon.) Do not allow the mixture to boil, however, or it will curdle. Strain the cream mixture back into the mixing bowl and whisk in the melted gelatin, the remaining grapefruit juice, and additional sugar, as necessary. Set the bowl over a pan of ice, stirring occasionally with a rubber spatula as the mixture chills.

(4) Beat the heavy cream to stiff peaks and keep cool. When the grapefruit mixture is on the verge of setting, fold in most of the whipped cream, reserving ¼ cup for decoration. Spoon the mousse mixture into the hollowed grapefruit shells and refrigerate for at least 4 hours or overnight. The recipe can be made to this stage up to 48 hours before serving.

(5) Just before serving, decorate each mousse with a rosette of whipped cream and garnish it with mint leaves or candied violets.

Ugli Fruit Sorbet

MAKES 1 PINT

THE term *sorbet* comes for the Arabic *sharbah*, "cold drink." The original sherbets were chilled with mountain snow—no mean feat in the Near East and ancient Rome. If ugli fruit are unavailable, substitute grapefruit.

> 3–4 ugli fruits (enough to make 2 cups juice)
> Juice of 1 lemon, plus extra if necessary
> ¾ cup sugar, plus extra if necessary
> 2 tablespoons fresh tarragon or mint leaves, plus a few whole sprigs for garnish (optional)
> 1 egg white
>
> 1 ice cream machine, ice, rock salt

(1) Squeeze the ugli fruit to obtain 2 cups juice. Squeeze the lemon. Combine the sugar with ½ cup water in a large saucepan and bring it to a boil. Coarsely chop the tarragon or mint: you should have 2 tablespoons. Let the sugar syrup cool to room temperature. Stir in the ugli and lemon juices, chopped herbs, and egg white, adding additional sugar or lemon juice to taste.

(2) Place the sorbet in the ice cream machine and freeze according to the manufacturer's instructions. Serve small balls of sorbet in wine glasses or ramekins. Garnish each with a sprig of tarragon or mint. Ugli fruit sorbet makes an excellent midmeal palate refresher or light dessert.

APRIL

When proud-pied April, dress'd in all his trim,
Hath put a spirit of youth in everything.

SHAKESPEARE

''A P R I L is the cruelest month," observed T. S. Eliot. True, this is a time of gray skies and unpredictable weather. But April is also a month of rebirth and renewal, a time when leaves bud, fields are sown, and birds return from migration. Our word April comes from the Latin *aprilis,* "to open," an apt allusion to the sprouting seeds and burgeoning tree buds.

April opens on a whimsical note—Fools' Day—thought to stem from a French calendar reform in 1564, which moved New Year's Day from April 1 to January 1. A person who persisted in celebrating the old New Year's Day was called a *poisson d'avril,* "April fish"—an April fool. For Catholics, April brings an end to the dietary rigors of Lent. It is also a time of movement and restlessness, the month when Chaucer's pilgrims set forth on their journey to Canterbury.

Two major holidays take place in April: Easter and Passover. Easter was originally a Pagan holiday, named for Eastre, the Celtic goddess of spring. Easter celebrates Christ's death and resurrection—a spiritual rebirth paralleled in nature by the return of life to the fields. Passover is a holiday of spiritual redemption, commemorating the escape of the Hebrews from Egyptian bondage. It is a time of purification, when Jews use a special set of dishes and do a ritual spring cleaning.

Eggs are associated with both holidays—an apt symbol of new beginnings. The medieval church proscribed eggs during Lent—they returned in all their hard-boiled splendor on Easter Sunday. Roasted eggs appear on the Passover table, an emblem of the return of spring. Lamb is another food traditionally associated with Easter and Passover—Christ is traditionally symbolized by a lamb, and the Hebrews marked their doorsills with the blood of a lamb to ward off the Angel of Death as it passed over Egypt. No doubt the religious use of lamb served a practical purpose: lambs born in the winter reach eating size in April. Another ritual food of Passover is parsley, representing the budding of a new season's crop.

April is a happy month for epicures. Rhubarb raises its crimson stalks; artichokes bloom in abundance. Trout surface from their winter lairs; shad and shad roe are in season. Carnivores take special pleasure in lamb, not to mention ham for Easter Sunday. And April is the best month of the year for enjoying pineapple.

Children delight in painting and hunting Easter eggs during April, while Christians of all ages enjoy a variety of freshly baked Easter breads. Jews console themselves for the loss of bread (forbidden during the ten days of Passover) with such holiday delights as gefilte fish, matzoh ball soup, and fried matzoh.

For poets, April may be a month of lovelorn tears and uncertainty. For cooks, it's a cornucopia of culinary delights.

ARTICHOKES

HAVE you ever wondered how our forebears learned to eat inaccessible or seemingly inedible foods? Honey gatherers had to contend with bee stings, for example, and in its raw state rhubarb is toxic. But the greatest mystery to me is how early man contrived to eat artichokes. The man-high plant has prickly leaves; the fruit wears its spiny petals like a botanical suit of armor. Even without the spines, you wouldn't want to eat a raw choke: the flesh is astringently bitter. Pliny called artichokes "the most monstrous productions of earth," but that did not prevent the Greeks and Romans from devouring them with gusto.

Artichokes are still immensely popular with Italians and the French. The plant was probably introduced to the Americas by French settlers in Louisiana or Spanish missionaries in California. The latter is the state that grows the most today. Castroville, California, is America's self-proclaimed artichoke capital: some fifty billion pounds are harvested here each year. Most are destined for eating, but artichoke juice is also used for curdling milk to make rennetless cheese. There is even an artichoke-based aperitif called Cynar.

The most common way to enjoy artichokes is boiled or steamed, eaten petal by petal. The petals are traditionally dipped in melted butter. Large artichokes are ideal for stuffing, and the smaller ones are excellent preserved in oil or fried. The French have perfected a technique for carving out the meaty heart, which they poach in acidulated water and often crown with cheese sauce or a poached egg. Boiled baby artichokes are sold on street corners in Sicily, where they are munched, like popcorn, for a snack.

Artichokes are available most of the year but are at their prime in March and April. Choose plump, compact specimens, a consistent green in color, that feel heavy for their size. Avoid artichokes that are moldy or shriveled; they have been sitting around too long. Hard or spreading "scales" (the pointy leaf tips) indicate a choke that is overripe.

Artichokes have a "second" season in late fall and early winter. At that time of the year, look for chokes with bronze-colored scales or whitish skin—the result of frost, which is supposed to increase the vegetable's sweetness.

Artichokes Stuffed with Pancetta and Shrimp

SERVES 4

A delicious appetizer or light entrée, this dish dates from my student days at the Cordon Bleu in Paris. Pancetta is Italian bacon —if unavailable, use good smoked bacon or prosciutto or Westphalian ham. The dish is also delicious made with crab. The artichokes can be boiled, steamed, or cooked in the microwave.

> 4 large artichokes
> ½ lemon (save rind for the stuffing)
> Salt
> Pinch of baking soda

For the stuffing:
> ½ pound shrimp (fresh if possible)
> 4–5 thin slices pancetta
> 2–3 scallions, green part only
> ¼ cup pine nuts
> Rind of ½ lemon
> ¼ cup freshly grated Parmesan
> 2 tablespoons chopped fresh parsley, basil, tarragon, or other fresh herbs
> 1 teaspoon vegetable oil
> 1 tablespoon butter or extra-virgin olive oil
> Salt, fresh black pepper, and cayenne pepper

(1) Cut off the stems of the artichokes flush with the bottom. Using a sharp knife, cut off the top quarter of the crown. Using kitchen scissors, snip off the tips of the leaves. Rub the artichokes with lemon to prevent them from discoloring. Cook the artichokes in 3 quarts rapidly boiling, salted water with a pinch of baking soda for 30 minutes, or until the hearts are easily pierced with a skewer. Refresh the chokes under cold water, invert, and drain. Alternatively, the artichokes can be steamed for 20 minutes or cooked al dente in a microwave oven, following the directions of the manufacturer.

(2) Meanwhile, prepare the stuffing. Shell the shrimp and

chop into ¼-inch dice. Cut the pancetta into ¼-inch slivers. Finely chop the scallions. Lightly toast the pine nuts in a toaster oven or under the broiler. Grate the lemon rind and cheese. Finely chop the herbs. Heat the vegetable oil in a small pan, and sauté the pancetta over medium heat for 2 minutes or until lightly browned. Pour off the excess fat. Add the shrimp, and cook for 1 minute. Remove the pan from the heat and stir in the remaining ingredients, adding salt, black pepper, cayenne, and grated lemon rind to taste.

(3) Preheat the oven to 400 degrees. Pull out the inside leaves of the artichokes to make a 1½-inch cavity. Use a melon baller or grapefruit spoon to scrape out the fibrous "choke" at the bottom, taking care not to pierce the heart. Spoon the filling into the artichokes, and top with a piece of butter or a few drops of olive oil. The recipe can be prepared to this stage up to 8 hours before baking.

(4) Cook the stuffed artichokes in the preheated oven for 10 to 15 minutes, or until thoroughly heated, and serve. The perfect wine for this dish is a Pouilly-Fumé from the Loire Valley.

Carciofi alla Giudia
(Fried Baby Artichokes)

SERVES 4

THIS dish has its roots in the Jewish ghettos of Renaissance Rome. (The name means "artichokes in the style of the Jews.") The recipe was inspired by one in the *Lexicon of Jewish Cooking* by Patti Shosteck. Baby artichokes are best for this recipe—their "chokes" are either undeveloped or small enough to be eaten. If baby artichokes are unavailable, you can use the adult size: trim off the outside leaves, cut the artichokes in quarters, and remove the choke. Do not despair about the quantity of olive oil used in the recipe—it can be filtered and saved for later use in salad dressings and other recipes that will benefit from its mild garlic flavor.

16 baby artichokes
4 cups extra-virgin olive oil
3 cloves garlic
1 sprig rosemary
Salt and fresh black pepper
1 lemon, cut into 8 wedges

(1) Remove any blemished or stiff outer leaves from the artichokes, and trim ½ inch off the points and top. Cut off the bottom portion of the stem and discard. Wash the artichokes, drain, and blot dry.

(2) In a deep saucepan or wok over a medium flame, heat the olive oil to 350 degrees. While the oil is heating, peel the garlic and add to the oil with the rosemary. When the oil is hot, add the artichokes in one or two batches and fry for 10 to 15 minutes, or until golden brown. Drain the artichokes on paper towels and keep them warm in a low oven until you are ready to serve them.

(3) Gently flatten the leaves of each artichoke to make it look like an open flower. Season with salt and pepper, and serve warm, with lemon wedges.

Poached Eggs Massena

SERVES 4 AS AN APPETIZER, 2 FOR BRUNCH

HERE'S an interesting variation on eggs Benedict. The eggs are served on fresh artichoke hearts and crowned with béarnaise sauce instead of hollandaise. The dish was named after André Massena, a general under Napoleon. He won the battle of Rivoli, for which the stately Rue de Rivoli in Paris is named. (*Note:* You must use fresh tarragon for the sauce. If unavailable, top the eggs with hollandaise sauce or the blood orange Maltaise on page 131.)

4 large artichokes
½ lemon
Salt

For the béarnaise sauce:
⅔ cup dry white wine
⅓ cup tarragon vinegar
 3 tablespoons minced shallots
 2 tablespoons chopped fresh tarragon
   Fresh white pepper
½ cup unsalted butter
 3 egg yolks
   Salt and cayenne pepper

 4 very fresh eggs
 1 tablespoon wine vinegar

(1) Cut the stems and the top two thirds of the leaves off the artichoke. Using a paring knife, whittle off the leaves at the base of the artichoke to expose the heart. Using a melon baller, scrape out the fibrous "choke"—the idea here is to cut away everything but the disk-shaped heart. Rub the artichoke hearts with the lemon to prevent them from discoloring. Cook them in rapidly boiling salted water for 6 to 8 minutes, or until tender. Refresh under cold water and reserve.

(2) Prepare the béarnaise sauce. Combine the wine, tarragon vinegar, shallots, 1 tablespoon of the chopped tarragon, and 10 grinds of white pepper in a heavy nonaluminum saucepan. Boil this mixture until only 3 tablespoons liquid remain. Let the mixture cool. Meanwhile, melt the butter and let cool slightly. Have ready a large bowl of cold water. Add the egg yolks to the vinegar mixture, and cook over a very low heat, whisking constantly, for 1 minute or until the mixture thickens to the consistency of mayonnaise and you can see traces of whisk on the bottom of the pan. Do not overcook, or the mixture will curdle. (If the yolks start to scramble, set the pan down in the cold water. A trace of scrambling is normal and will not harm the final sauce.) Whisk the warm melted butter in a very thin steam into the wine mixture—the sauce will thicken. Whisk in the remaining tablespoon of chopped tarragon, and salt, cayenne, and white pepper to taste. The sauce should be highly seasoned. Keep it warm. (*Note:* Keep béarnaise sauce warm on a warm corner of the stove, or in a pan of hot [faucet hot] water. Do not attempt to warm the sauce over direct heat or in a double boiler, or it will curdle.)

(3) Poach the eggs. In a deep saucepan, bring 2 quarts water and 1 tablespoon vinegar to a boil. Crack the eggs into the bubbling spots—the swirling of the water will help wrap the whites around the yolks. Poach the eggs for 3 minutes, or until cooked to taste. Remove them with a slotted spoon, trim off any ragged edges, and keep warm in a bowl of hot water. The recipe can be prepared up to 2 hours ahead to this stage.

(4) To assemble the dish, heat the artichoke hearts and poached eggs in hot water or a low oven. Blot the hearts dry. Spoon a little béarnaise sauce into each artichoke heart. Place a poached egg on top and spoon the remaining béarnaise sauce over the eggs. Serve at once.

Variations: Try sandwiching the eggs and artichoke hearts with slices of steak, Canadian bacon, or smoked salmon.

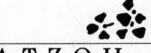

MATZOH

"THIS is the bread of affliction our forefathers ate." With these words opens the seder, the Passover feast celebrated by Jews all over the world. The affliction was the slavery of the Jewish people in Egypt. The term *Passover* refers to the Angel of Death, who visited the tenth plague on the Egyptians, that of slaying their first-born sons, but "passed over" the Jewish homes without harming them. The holiday commemorates the escape from Egypt, but in a broader sense honors the ideal of freedom for all peoples in the world.

The Jews' departure from Egypt was hasty—so hasty that there was no time for the bread made daily to rise. So they baked it as flatcakes, unleavened loaves and ever since, Jews have eaten matzoh during Passover. Bread is proscribed during the holiday,

(2) Bring 2 to 3 gallons lightly salted water to a rolling boil. Drop the matzoh balls in, one by one, and boil them for 45 minutes, or until firm. Using a slotted spoon, transfer the balls to a colander.

To serve, heat the broth and add salt and pepper to taste. Place one or two matzoh balls in each bowl and ladle the broth on top. The apropriate wine? Why, Manischewitz, of course!

LAMB

MARY had a little lamb. Mary should count herself lucky. It's almost impossible to find little lamb at the supermarket. By "little lamb," I mean milk-fed lamb (also called *baby lamb* or *hothouse lamb*), a diminutive creature taken a month or two after birth, before it has had a chance to graduate to a flesh-toughening diet of grasses. Raised solely on milk, baby lamb has pale pink, incredibly mild-flavored flesh. Alfred Hitchcock was so enamored of it he would send his private jet to the East Coast to fetch this Lilliputian delicacy to Hollywood.

Lamb has experienced a remarkable comeback in recent years. For decades, our otherwise staunchly carnivorous Midwest spurned it, and even East Coasters generally overcooked it to the toughness of shoe leather. The French taught us to enjoy lamb medium-rare, and today, at fine restaurants, it is every bit as popular as beef. And the grassroots movement that is sweeping the food industry has increased the availablity of free-ranging, chemical-free meat.

Lamb was probably man's first barnyard animal: domesticated sheep bones dating from 9000 B.C. have been found in Iraq. It is still the principal meat in the Middle East, North Africa, and Greece. Australia ranks first among the world's lamb-raising countries: there are 60 million sheep to a population of 3 million people. The Italians are famed for their *abbacchio,* month-old milk-fed lamb, which is roasted with rosemary, garlic, and anchovies in Rome. The French favor *pré-salé,* "salt meadow" lamb, pastured on the salty marshes of Brittany.

When buying lamb, the younger the animal, the paler and more delicate the meat. The French have six grades, starting with *agneau de lait,* "suckling lamb," which is sold at poultry shops, not the butchers'.

In America we have only three grades: **genuine spring lamb**: slaughtered between March and October, when less than six months old; **spring lamb**: an animal of inferior quality, slaughtered between November and February; and **lamb**: any animal that is less than one year old.

Baby lamb is raised in limited quantities in New Jersey and Pennsylvania. Although there is no legal appellation, it is generally dispatched when three to nine weeks old. In the U.S., lamb doesn't become mutton until it is one year old. Lamb is one meat you are better off buying at a butcher shop. Supermarket lamb is usually Choice, not Prime, and is geared more toward stewing and roasting.

Greek Lamb Stew with Romaine Lettuce and Dill

SERVES 6

MY aunt, Rosa Miller, is an extraordinary cook. But because I was a finicky eater when I was growing up, I used to dread going to her house for dinner. Rosa was forever serving "weird" foods, like feta cheese or chick-peas. (She is Greek.) Now I relish her and her mother Lily's cooking. Here's their recipe for lamb stew with romaine lettuce and dill.

Lamb *Berbère*

SERVES 6

LAMB *Berbère* is lamb prepared in the style of the Berbers, a nomadic tribe in North Africa. I was first introduced to the fiery spice paste that they use by a fine cook named Stephanie Elkind. Fenugreek is a rectangle-shaped seed with an agreeably bitter flavor. I also use this spice mixture on tuna, pork tenderloin, and steak.

> 2 pounds leg of lamb
> 1 very small onion
> 2 cloves garlic
> 1 1-inch piece fresh ginger root
> 2 teaspoons cracked black peppercorns
> 1 teaspoon coriander seeds
> 1 teaspoon cardamom seeds
> 1 teaspoon fenugreek seeds
> Generous pinch each of ground cloves, cinnamon, and allspice
> 2 teaspoons red pepper flakes, or to taste
> 1 tablespoon salt, or to taste
> ⅓ cup imported paprika
> ½ cup extra-virgin olive oil
> Juice of 1 lemon

(1) Trim the lamb and cut it into 1- to 1½-inch cubes. Finely chop the onion; you should have 3 to 4 tablespoons. Mince the garlic and grate the ginger root. Place the onions, garlic, ginger, and all the spices in a dry skillet and cook over medium heat for 1 to 2 minutes, or until the spices are lightly roasted.

(2) Combine the roasted spices with the olive oil and lemon juice in a blender, and purée to a smooth paste. Smear this paste on the lamb and marinate for 3 to 4 hours or overnight. Thread the meat cubes on bamboo skewers, and broil or grill for 4 to 5 minutes per side. Serve the lamb Berbère with rice pilaf and a tall, frosty mug of beer.

RHUBARB

I was the first kid on the block to eat rhubarb. For that matter, I was the *only* kid on the block to eat rhubarb. My playmates (not to mention their parents) disparaged this strange, sour plant, its stalks resembling red celery. They were no better than the ancient Greeks, who believed that rhubarb was fit only for the barbarians who lived in the savage lands beyond the Volga River. Indeed, in Greek *rheum-barbarum* means "barbarians from the river Rha" (the Greek name for the Volga), which is how rhubarb got its name.

Both the ancient Greeks and my childhood friends didn't know what they were missing. When sweetened, rhubarb has a fine flavor—tangy and tart, with an intriguing hint of spice. Rhubarb's bum rap may come from the fact that its leaves contain toxic quantities of oxalic acid. The stalks are incredibly tart in their natural state, but that does not prevent Eskimos and Afghani tribesmen from eating them raw.

When buying rhubarb, look for plump, firm, moist stalks. The color can be green or red, or any hue in between. Avoid shriveled stalks, or those with brown or slimy ends. Thick stalks are just as tender as thin ones, and are quicker to wash and chop.

In this country, rhubarb is used for preserves and desserts, but in Europe its tartness is often matched with fowl, game, and even fish. Rhubarb contains a great deal of water, so you needn't use much liquid to cook it. To ready rhubarb for cooking, cut off the ends and wash the stalks.

Rhubarb Compote with Ginger

SERVES 4

DURING the rhubarb season, this compote graces my table nightly. It is easy to make, can be served as a vegetable or dessert, and keeps almost indefinitely. The most popular brand of ginger wine is Stone's—if unavailable, substitute ginger beer (sold at Jamaican markets) or water.

      1 **pound fresh rhubarb**
      1 **1-inch piece fresh ginger root**
  ⅓–½ **cup sugar, or to taste**
      ½ **cup ginger wine, ginger beer, or water**
      2 **strips lemon peel**

(1) Wash the rhubarb and cut off any leafy tops. Cut the rhubarb stalks into 1-inch slices. Cut the ginger into ¼-inch slices. Combine all the ingredients in a large saucepan, cover the pan, and cook the compote over a medium heat for 8 to 10 minutes, or until the rhubarb is just tender. The trick to rhubarb is cooking it enough to remove its bitterness, but not so much that it falls apart. Take care to stir the compote occasionally or it may boil over.

(2) Serve rhurbarb compote chilled. It is delicious by itself, or is well accompanied by lightly sweetened whipped cream, ricotta cheese, or softened Mascarpone (a rich Italian cream cheese).

Rhubarb Muffins

MAKES 8 GIANT MUFFINS OR 12 REGULAR ONES

ALMA Hecht is the founder of a wildly successful chain of muffin shops. Her muffins come in over a hundred different flavors, including the buttery rhubarb muffins below. An ice cream scoop makes a handy tool for spooning the batter into the tin. The pan of water is the oven ensures moistness. When the muffins are cooked, a skewer or toothpick inserted in the center will come out clean.

    2 cups unbleached white flour
    ½ cup sugar
    ½ teaspoon salt
    ½ teaspoon baking soda
    1 tablespoon baking powder
    1 teaspoon cinnamon
  5½ tablespoons unsalted butter
    1 cup buttermilk
    1 egg
    1 teaspoon vanilla extract
    1 cup finely chopped fresh rhubarb
    3 tablespoons cinnamon sugar for sprinkling

    1 muffin tin, thoroughly buttered and floured

(1) Preheat the oven to 375 degrees. Combine the dry ingredients in a large mixing bowl. Cut the butter into ¼-inch pieces, and using a food processor or by hand, cut it into the flour mixture. Add the wet ingredients and rhubarb and process, or stir, just to mix. Do not overmix; lumps are fine—they disappear when cooked. Bring 2 to 3 cups water to a boil in a shallow ovenproof pan.

(2) Spoon the batter into the prepared tin and sprinkle the top of each muffin with cinnamon sugar. Place the muffin pan in the oven next to the shallow pan of boiling water. Bake the muffins for 18 minutes, or until an inserted toothpick comes out clean. Turn the muffins onto a cake rack to cool, and serve with plenty of sweet butter.

Jean True's Rhubarb Meringue Pie

SERVES 8 TO 10

JEAN True is a caterer and fine cook from Glen Ellyn, Illinois, near Chicago. Her rhubarb pie is so good, it will make you want to throw stones at the usual lemon meringue!

1 batch basic pie dough made with 1½ cups flour (see recipe on page 476), or use your favorite recipe

For the filling:
1½ pounds fresh rhubarb
1¾ cups sugar (or a little less, according to taste)
3 eggs
3 tablespoons milk
4 tablespoons flour
¼ teaspoon cinnamon
1 teaspoon vanilla

For the meringue:
3 egg whites
¼ teaspoon salt
¼ teaspoon cream of tartar
⅓ cup sugar

1 9- or 10-inch tart pan with removable bottom
Piping bag with large star tip

(1) Prepare the pie dough and chill for 20 minutes. Roll it out to a ³⁄₁₆-inch thickness and use it to line the tart pan. Chill the crust for 5 minutes. Preheat the oven to 375 degrees.

(2) Prepare the filling. Cut the rhubarb into ¼-inch slices: you should wind up with about 4 cups. Mix it with the sugar in a bowl and let stand for 15 minutes. Lightly beat the eggs in a large bowl. Beat in the milk, flour, and flavorings. Stir in the rhubarb and sugar. Pour this mixture into the pie shell and bake for 40 to 50 minutes, or until the filling is set. Remove the pie from the oven, but keep the oven set at 375 degrees.

(3) Prepare the meringue. Beat the whites in a mixer at medium speed for 20 seconds. Add the salt and cream of tartar, and continue beating for 1 minute, or until the whites are light and frothy. Gradually add the sugar, increasing the mixer speed to high, and continue beating the whites until stiff. Do not overbeat. Using a piping bag fitted with a star tip, pipe rosettes of meringue on top of the pie. Alternatively, you can spread the meringue on top of the pie with a spatula. (*Note:* it is important that the meringue, whether piped or spread, cover the entire surface of the pie.)

(4) Return the pie to the oven and bake for 5 to 10 minutes, or until the meringue is nicely browned. Meringue burns like kindling—watch it closely! Serve rhubarb meringue pie at room temperature, ideally within 4 hours of baking. A chilled muscat, like a Quaddy Vineyards Essencia, would make a lovely dessert wine.

PINEAPPLE

IN 1493, Europeans got their first taste of pineapple. To put it mildly, they were impressed. Early accounts from the New World describe it as "the king of fruits" . . . "an excellent arouser of the appetite" . . . "of such excellence that it should be picked only by the hands of Venus." (Given the sharpness of its leaves, I hope that Venus would wear gloves!)

This was no news to the Caribbean natives, who had enjoyed the pineapple for centuries. The explorers took it around the world: its abundant vitamin C helped prevent scurvy. Whaling ships would return to New England with pineapples from the tropics. It quickly became a symbol of hospitality and a popular architectural motif.

The pineapple is a member of the Bromeliaceae family, which also includes Spanish moss. It grows from the crown of another pineapple and it requires eighteen months to bear fruit. Pineapples grow in warm climates around the world; Hawaii alone has forty thousand acres under cultivation. Pineapples are generally available year-round but are best in March, April, and May.

When buying pineapples look for bright-green leaves and a firm skin. Soft pineapples or brown spots indicate internal fermentation. Smell the base of the fruit: if it has a nice pineapple smell, chances are it will have a good flavor. Pineapple should be refrigerated until used. To remove the fruit's leafy crown, simply twist the pineapple in one direction and the leaves in the other. To remove the fibrous core, cut the pineapple in half lengthwise, and make a V-shaped cut down the center. To hollow the shell for serving, leave the leaves on and use a serrated, curved-blade grapefruit knife to cut the flesh away from the skin. Pineapples can also be hollowed vertically to make a nifty cup for piña coladas.

Pineapple Salsa

MAKES 2 TO 3 CUPS

NINETEEN eighty-six will be remembered as the year that Americans discovered salsas. Traditional Tex-Mex tomato salsa has given way to a host of exotic condiments, like the pineapple salsa below.

    1 small ripe pineapple
2–3 fresh jalapeño chilies
    1 bunch scallions, green part only
    1 ½-inch piece fresh ginger root
    1 bunch cilantro
2–3 tablespoons brown sugar, or to taste
    Juice of 2 limes, or to taste
    Salt and fresh black pepper (optional)

(1) Skin and core the pineapple, and cut it into ½-inch pieces. Split and seed the chilies (see Note on page 48) and discard the seeds (unless you like your food really hot, in which case add them). Finely chop the ginger. Finely chop the green part of the scallions. Remove the stems from the cilantro and finely chop the leaves.

(2) Combine the ingredients in a bowl, adding lime juice and sugar to taste. Add salt and pepper to taste, if you wish. Let the salsa "ripen" for at least 2 hours before serving. I find pineapple salsa delicious with fish and grilled poultry; then again, I have been known to eat it right off a spoon.

Pineapple Salad with Chayote and Chili

SERVES 8

HERE'S an unusual salad for a warm spring day. *Chayote* (pronounced "shy-*oat*") is a kind of gourd popular in Asia and Latin America. It looks like a flat, pale-green avocado and tastes like a cross between squash and cucumber. Chayotes can be found at a gourmet greengrocer or Latin American market. If unavailable, substitute cucumbers. Fish sauce is used in Southeast Asia the way soy sauce is in China. The latter can be used in place of the former.

> 2 chayotes or cucumbers
> 1 small ripe pineapple
> 2–3 scallions, green part only

For the dressing:
> 3 tablespoons fish sauce or soy sauce
> 2 tablespoons rice wine vinegar
> 1 tablespoon sugar
> 1 clove garlic, minced
> 1 teaspoon grated or minced ginger root
> 1 teaspoon hot pepper flakes or chili sauce, or to taste
> 4 tablespoons chopped fresh parsley or cilantro

MAY

M A Y is the month of passion. In centuries past, villagers erected May Poles and danced round them in exuberant revels. In our own day, socialists raise phallic symbols of a different sort —missiles—which are paraded through Red Square to bear tribute to the International Workers Movement. After winter's chill and April's intransigence, spring bursts forth in all its glory. Green returns to field and forest; flowers bloom; and sap of an amorous sort flows in the hearts—and loins—of men.

May was the second month of the Alban calendar, the third month of the Roman one, and is the fifth month of today's. It is probably named for Maia, daughter of Atlas and mother of Hermes, whom Romans worshipped as the goddess of growth and increase. (Her star is in the constellation Pleiades.) Some scholars maintain that the month was named for the *Maiores,* the "Elders" of the original Roman senate and the origin of our word mayor.

The May Day celebration has its roots in Celtic ritual. In the Celtic calendar, summer officially commenced on May first. The day was sacred to Baal, god of agriculture and livestock. Huge bonfires were kindled, and grain and cattle were sacrificed to petition for agricultural plenty. On a darker note, a large round oat cake was roasted over the fire and broken into pieces, and placed in an urn or bonnet. Blindfolded, the celebrants drew the cakes: the person who got the darkest piece was ceremoniously placed on the pyre!

The maypole originated with the tree worship of the Druids. In medieval England, maypoles were cut from tall fir trees and erected in the town square. The frolicking often took a licentious turn: the pious complained that for every ten maidens who set forth a-maying, "nine came home with childe." When the Puritans took over in 1644, Parliament outlawed maypoles and May Day celebrations. May celebrations resumed when the monarchy returned to power. In Tudor England, women bathed their faces with May morning dew, believing it would enhance their beauty.

Other May holidays include Chimney Sweep Day, celebrated in London on May 1, and Dismal Day (May 3), which Scottish Highlanders believe was the day Lucifer and his rebellious angels fell from heaven. And speaking of evil, the evening before May Day is Walpurgis Night, when witches dance around bonfires and are at the height of their malevolent powers. Jews celebrate the holiday of Shavuot in May, commemorating the arrival of the Israelites at Mount Sinai and the giving of the Ten Commandments. And daylight saving time returns in May, giving us extra hours to enjoy the sunshine.

The Kentucky Derby takes place on the first Saturday in May at Churchill Downs in Louisville. Dust off your silver cup and prepare a batch of mint juleps. On the second Sunday in May we honor America's moms, as we've done since 1914, when Congress recognized Mother's Day. May 8 is Stork Day in Denmark, marking the return of these winged obstetricians. May 25 is sacred to St. Urban, the patron saint of vintners. Stravinsky's *Rite of Spring* was first performed on May 29, 1913; the music was so controversial, the audience came to fisticuffs.

This merry month brings glad tidings to the cook, in the form of spring greens, like spinach and sorrel. The backwoods of Maine and New Hampshire provide a fleeting treat: the edible fronds of the fiddlehead fern. Fungi fanciers hit the trail in search of morels and other wild mushrooms. May is a good month to eat mussels, not to mention mackerel and haddock. ("The haddocks are good, when dipped in May flood," goes an old English saying.) Salmon have begun to come into season (particularly sockeye and chinook) and fresh squid, too, is abundant. Fruits to look for are mangos and papayas.

The month of May has long been associated with dairying and cheese-making. The cattle return to the pastures to graze;

their milk is especially plentiful. The Anglo-Saxons called May *Tri-Milchi,* "three-milking" month, for during this fertile month cows were said to give milk three times a day.

A merry month indeed is May, not just for lovers, but for cooks!

FIDDLEHEAD FERNS

FIDDLEHEAD ferns are a vernal delicacy found all over New England, especially in Maine, New Hampshire, and Vermont. (They also turn up in Michigan and Minnesota, and even as far south as Virginia.) Fiddleheads are the unfurled frond of the ostrich fern, newly risen above the earth. They resemble a bishop's crosier, or the head of a violin, which is how they got their name. A young fiddlehead is about the size of a curled index finger. The flavor is reminiscent of asparagus, spinach, and okra and is positively unique.

Fiddlehead season starts the first or second week of May and lasts only three weeks. Once the frond has unfurled, the fern is no longer good to eat. If you live in one of the northern states, you can pick your own. There are only two edible varieties. The best is the ostrich fern, also known as *Matteuccia struthiotteris.* Be sure you can differentiate between the ostrich fern and the bracken fern, its cousin; brackens are thought to be carcinogenic. The ostrich fern is distinguished by its vivid green color and a deep groove on the inside of its stem. The other edible fern, the cinnamon fern (*Osmunda cinnamonea*), is similar in appearance to the ostrich fern, except that it is covered with a brownish down. All ferns with rounded stems are considered inedible.

Fiddlehead ferns are available in specialty markets in most

major American cities. When buying fiddleheads, look for jade green, crisp-looking, tightly furled fronds. The stem darkens where it is cut, but the rest of the fern should be free of blemishes. One pound of fiddleheads will feed four.

Cook fiddleheads the way you would any green vegetable: by steaming or in rapidly boiling salted water for 2 to 3 minutes or until crispy-tender. (If you don't plan to serve the ferns right away, refresh them in cold water to prevent overcooking). They are also good stir-fried with sesame oil or butter and lemon. If you're eating fiddlehead ferns for the first time, keep the accompaniments simple: a little melted butter, olive oil and lemon juice, or hollandaise sauce. They are also excellent in soups, salads, and Oriental preparations.

Fiddlehead Gumbo

SERVES 8 TO 10

THIS recipe was created by chef Rick Spencer of the Bernerhof Inn, in New Hampshire. Gumbo, of course, is a thick Cajun soup often garnished with sausage and seafood; it takes its name from the African word for okra. Gumbos are thickened with roux, a dark-brown paste made of flour and oil. If you have never made a Cajun roux before, read Step 2 especially carefully. Filé powder is made from ground sassafras leaves; it is used for additional thickening and flavor. By the way, the gumbo is perfectly delicious when made with other green vegetables, like asparagus or okra.

> 4 cups fiddlehead ferns
> 2 green bell peppers
> 1 red bell pepper
> 2 hot chili peppers, or to taste
> 1 large or 2 small onions
> 2–3 stalks celery

  2 cloves garlic
  ½ cup vegetable oil
  ½ cup flour
  6 cups chicken stock (see recipe on page 472)
  2 tablespoons gumbo filé powder
  ½ pound crabmeat or small, shelled, deveined shrimp
  ½ pound smoked cooked ham, cut into ¼-inch pieces
  ½ teaspoon dried thyme
    Salt, fresh black pepper, and cayenne pepper
  2 cups cooked rice (optional)

(1) Wash the fiddlehead ferns in a bowl of cold water, pulling off any bits of papery brown membrane. Discard any brown ends and cut off any long stems, leaving the curled fronds intact. Cut these stems into ¼-inch dice. Core and seed the peppers and chilies (see page 48 for a note on handling chilies). Cut the peppers into ¼-inch dice: you should have a little more than 1 cup. Cut the onion and celery into ¼-inch dice: you should have about a cup of each. Mince the garlic and the cored, seeded chilies.

(2) Prepare the roux. Place the oil and flour in a large (12-inch) cast iron frying pan. Have the chopped vegetables handy, and place the pan over medium heat. Cook the roux for 4 to 5 minutes, stirring constantly with a whisk until it is dark and reddish-brown in hue—almost the color of coffee. You must whisk constantly, for if any black spots appear, the roux will taste burnt and bitter. Work over a medium heat the first time you make roux—you can graduate to higher heat with practice. As soon as the roux turns dark brown, lower the heat and stir in the chopped vegetables. (This prevents the roux from overcooking, and gives the vegetables a fine, toasty flavor.) Continue to cook the vegetables for 2 to 3 minutes or until slightly tender, then remove the pan from the heat. (*Note:* Take care not to let the roux splash on your hands while you are stirring it—it's not without reason that chefs call this mixture "Cajun napalm"!)

(3) Heat the chicken stock in a large saucepan. Gradually add the vegetable mixture, stirring constantly, and bring the gumbo to a boil. Stir in the fiddlehead ferns, filé gumbo, crabmeat or shrimp, ham, thyme, and seasonings to taste, and sim-

mer the gumbo for 4 to 5 minutes, or until the fiddleheads are tender. Stir in the rice, if using, bring the soup back to a simmer, and correct the seasoning.

This gumbo can be served as a rich soup course, but it also makes a great meal in itself, accompanied by crusty bread and a salad.

Tempura of Fiddlehead Ferns

SERVES 4

THE Japanese are the world's undisputed masters when it comes to the art of frying. Consider tempura. No other batter is as crispy and light. It is the perfect accompaniment for tender young ferns. My thanks to Alice Kovler for the idea.

> 1 pound fiddlehead ferns
> 1 quart peanut oil for frying

For the batter:
> 1 cup ice water
> 1 egg yolk
> ¾–1 scant cup unsifted flour

(1) Wash the fiddlehead ferns in a bowl of cold water, pulling off any bits of papery brown membrane. Trim off the ends. Heat the oil in a saucepan or wok to 375 degrees.

(2) Prepare the batter. Combine the ice water and yolk in a bowl and lightly beat with chopsticks. Add the flour and beat for 10 or 12 strokes with the chopsticks: the ingredients should be *barely* mixed. The batter should be quite thin, a little thinner than cream, but if it is too watery, add a little more flour.

(3) Just before serving, dip the fiddleheads into the batter and drop them with chopsticks into the hot oil. Fry the tempura

for 1 minute, or until the pieces are golden brown. Transfer the pieces to paper towels to drain, then serve at once with the dipping sauce below.

Tempura Dipping Sauce

MAKES ABOUT 1½ CUPS

TEMPURA dipping sauce is traditionally made with *dashi*, a stock made with dried bonito flakes and sea kelp (see Note below). Both ingredients can be found at any Japanese market. If these are unavailable in your area, use chicken stock. *Mirin* is sweet rice wine. *Daikon* is a white radish used in Oriental cooking.

  1 cup dashi or chicken stock
  ⅓ cup mirin or dry sherry
  ⅓ cup Japanese or light soy sauce
  4 tablespoons grated daikon (optional)
  1 teaspoon grated fresh ginger

Combine the above ingredients in a small saucepan and heat over a low flame. Serve warm with additional daikon or ginger as desired.

NOTE: Most Asian markets sell instant dashi, packaged granules that dissolve in hot water. To make dashi from scratch, combine 1 ounce *kombu* (giant kelp) with 1 quart water, bring almost to a boil, and discard the kelp. Add 1 ounce *Hana-katsuo* (dried bonito flakes), and bring the water just to a boil. Add 2 or 3 ice cubes, and bring the water just to a boil again. Let the broth stand for 2 minutes without heat, then strain.

Fiddlehead Ferns with Escargot Butter

SERVES 4

ESCARGOT butter—flavored with garlic and parsley—customarily accompanies snails and mussels. But it is also delicious for sautéing green vegetables, like fiddlehead ferns. The garlic, shallot, and parsley should be so finely chopped that a sneeze would blow them away!

> 1 pound fresh fiddlehead ferns
> Salt

> *For the escargot butter:*
> 4 tablespoons unsalted butter, at room temperature
> 1 clove garlic, minced
> 1 tablespoon very finely chopped shallot
> 3 tablespoons very finely chopped parsley
> Salt, fresh black pepper, and cayenne pepper
> A few drops fresh lemon juice

(1) Wash the fiddlehead ferns in a bowl of cold water, pulling away any bits of papery brown membrane. Trim off the ends. Cook the fiddlehead ferns in at least 2 quarts rapidly boiling, salted water for 20 seconds. Refresh under cold water and drain.

(2) Prepare the escargot butter. Cream the butter with a whisk or wooden spoon, and gradually whisk in the flavorings, adding the salt, black pepper, cayenne and lemon juice to taste. The recipe can be prepared ahead to this stage.

(3) Just before serving, melt the escargot butter in a large frying pan over medium heat. Add the ferns, and sauté for 1 to 2 minutes, or until the ferns are hot. Serve immediately.

SORREL

IN French it is called *oseille,* and cooks use it as an accompaniment to fish. In Yiddish it is called *schav,* and cooks use it to make a tart, chilled soup. In English it's called sorrel (and occasionally "sour grass"), but few people have ever heard of it—which is a shame, because few greens are as zestily tart as this arrow-shaped herb.

Sorrel is a member of the buckwheat family. It looks like young spinach: broad, bright-green leaves on single stems, tapering to a rounded point at the end. The similarities stop here, for the flavor is assertively acidic, like lemon. (For this reason, sorrel is often served with fish.) The herb owes its tartness to an abundance of oxalic acid, the chemical that gives rhubarb its sourish tang. Our name for it comes from the Old German *sur,* "sour."

Sorrel (pronounced "*sor*-el") is no newcomer to the kitchen. Gaius Lailius praised it for its "philosophic superiority" (for reasons unclear today). A seventeenth century physician recommended it for the treatment of scurvy. Laplanders make a vitamin-rich beverage with reindeer milk and boiled sorrel. The French are its biggest consumers: at the turn of the century, reports Waverly Root, Parisians alone ate 44 million pounds.

Look for fresh sorrel in late spring or summer. (Greenhouse sorrel is available year-round—at prices that would break Fort Knox.) It's mainly found at specialty shops, so you may wish to buy some seeds and grow your own. When buying sorrel, look for springy, emerald-green leaves. Sorrel is highly perishable, so store it in an unsealed plastic bag with a wet paper towel in the refrigerator, and try to use it the day you buy it or pick it.

Fresh sorrel leaves can be used to spice up a salad—a little of this lemony herb goes a long way. More often, it's consumed cooked, in the form of soups and sauces. Sorrel diminishes in bulk when cooked: a pound of fresh leaves will give you less than a cup of purée. Due to its high acidity, sorrel should never be cooked in unlined aluminum or cast iron. The herb is often added to sauces in the form of a *chiffonade,* ribbonlike strips. To cut a chiffonade, lay the leaves one on top of another, roll them into a tube, and cut widthwise into ¼-inch slices.

Shirred Eggs with Sorrel and Smithfield Ham

SERVES 4 AS AN APPETIZER OR 2 AS A LIGHT MAIN COURSE

HERE'S an unusual variation on that brunch standby, eggs Florentine. Shirred eggs are similar to poached or fried eggs, but they are baked in the oven. This dish was inspired by food columnist Sheryl Julian.

> 4 cups fresh sorrel leaves
> 3 scallions
> 3 tablespoons butter
> ½ cup heavy cream
>   Salt, fresh black pepper, and cayenne pepper
> 3 ounces Smithfield ham or bacon
> 4 large eggs

For the toast fingers:
> 4 slices country-style white bread
> 3–4 tablespoons butter, melted

> 4 ½-cup ramekins, thoroughly buttered

(1) Preheat the oven to 400 degrees. Stem and wash the sorrel leaves, and cut them into ¼-inch ribbons. Finely chop the scallions. Melt 1½ tablespoons of the butter in a large sauté pan over high heat. Add the scallions and cook for 1 minute. Add

the sorrel and cook, stirring, for 2 to 3 minutes, or until it has reduced to purée. Stir in the cream, and salt, black pepper, and cayenne to taste. Let the sorrel mixture cool and divide it among the 4 ramekins.

(2) Cut the ham or bacon into ¼-inch dice or fine slivers. Melt the remaining 1½ tablespoons butter (only necessary for ham) in a small pan and lightly sauté the ham or bacon. Add half of it to the ramekins. Crack an egg into each ramekin, taking care not to break the yolk. Sprinkle the remaining meat and a few twists of black pepper on top.

(3) Prepare the toast fingers. Cut the crusts off the bread and lightly brush each slice with melted butter. Cut each slice into ½-inch strips. Bake the toast fingers on a baking sheet in the preheated oven (turning them once) for 6 to 8 minutes, or until golden brown. Cool the toast fingers on a cake rack. (The recipe can be prepared to this stage up to 3 hours before baking. Keep the egg-filled ramekins in the refrigerator.)

(4) Preheat the oven to 350 degrees. Just before serving, set the ramekins in a roasting pan with ½-inch boiling water. Bake for 10 to 12 minutes, or until the eggs are cooked to taste. Warm the toast fingers in an oven or toaster oven. Serve the shirred eggs with the toast fingers, using the latter to scoop up the yolks.

Schav
(Chilled Sorrel Soup)

SERVES 4 TO 6

SCHAV is a sort of cold borscht made with sorrel instead of beets. It was invented by the Jews of Eastern Europe and is beloved by Jews around the world. I grew up on bottled schav, because fresh sorrel was not available. Here's how you make this unusual soup from scratch—Manischewitz never tasted so good!

1 pound fresh sorrel
2 medium white potatoes
1 leek
3 tablespoons butter
 Salt and fresh black pepper
2 cups chicken stock (optional—see recipe on page 472)
1 tablespoon sugar, plus extra if necessary
1 cup heavy cream
 Juice of 1 lemon, or to taste
1 cup sour cream for serving
6–8 tablespoons chopped scallions

(1) Stem and wash the sorrel, and cut the leaves into ribbons. Peel the potatoes, and cut them into ½-inch dice. Discard the furry root end and dark green leaves of the leek, cut it in half, wash thoroughly, and finely chop.

(2) Melt the butter in a large saucepan, and cook the leek for 2 minutes over medium heat. Add the sorrel and potatoes, and cook for 5 minutes. Add the stock, 2 cups water, salt and pepper to taste, and the sugar, and simmer for 15 to 20 minutes, or until the potatoes are very tender.

(3) Purée the soup in a blender or food processor. (The former works better than the latter; if you use the latter, purée the solids first and gradually add the liquids.) Stir in the cream and let the soup chill for at least 1 hour. Just before serving, add the lemon juice and additional sugar and salt, if necessary—the soup should be refreshingly tart but a little sweet. Serve schav in bowls with dollops of sour cream. Garnish each bowl with chopped scallions.

Sorrel Sauce

MAKES 1 CUP

THIS tart green sauce makes a perfect accompaniment to poached salmon, shad, or halibut.

¾ pound fresh sorrel (about 3 cups when cut into ribbons)
3 tablespoons butter

½ cup heavy cream
  Salt, fresh black pepper, cayenne pepper, and freshly grated
  nutmeg

Remove the stems and wash the sorrel. Cut the leaves into
½-inch ribbons. Melt the butter in a large saucepan. Add the
sorrel and cook, stirring, over medium heat for 2 to 3 minutes,
or until the sorrel dissolves into a purée. Whisk in the cream.
Simmer the sauce for 2 to 3 minutes, adding salt, pepper, cayenne, and nutmeg to taste.

MACKEREL

Mackerel scales and mare's tails
Make lofty ships carry low sails.

OLD SAILORS' SAYING

THE mackerel is a handsome fish with a tarnished reputation. The sailor fears a "mackerel sky," grey and white clouds
that betoken a storm. In French the word *maquereau* is a slang
expression for a pimp—an allusion, no doubt, to the fish's gaudy
colors. And when Americans cry, "Holy mackerel!" they don't
mean their favorite fish on Friday.

It's high time to rehabilitate mackerel, a tasty fish with a rich
flavor not dissimilar to that of tuna. Moreover, it is excellent for
your health: medical research has linked a diet of fatty fish, like
mackerel, to reduced cholesterol levels and fewer heart attacks.
Mackerel is a bargain, costing a fraction of the price of other oily
fish, like tuna or swordfish. It only tastes "fishy" when it isn't
impeccably fresh.

The mackerel's bum rap comes in part from the fact that it's
an oily fish, with a high proportion (6–12 percent) of fat. This

oil makes it highly perishable: indeed, in 1698, the London legislature enacted a special ordinance allowing fishmongers to cry mackerel through the streets on Sunday.

Mackerel are plentiful throughout the Atlantic; varieties are found as far north as Nova Scotia and as far south as Brazil. The fish fast during the winter months and spawn in the summer, so they are best to eat in spring or fall.

"Mackerel cannot be eaten in perfection except at the seaside," opined a nineteenth-century cookbook. Refrigeration made the fish more transportable, but you should still try to buy mackerel the day that you plan to eat it. The fish is usually sold whole. Look for bright, clear eyes and a firm, iridescent body.

Three-Mustard Mackerel

SERVES 4

MACKEREL is a rich fish, and the sharp flavor of mustard helps cut its inherent oiliness. In this preparation, the fish can be either baked or broiled. If you have an electric oven, set it on "Preheat," so both the top and bottom coils glow.

1½ **pounds mackerel fillets**

For the mustard sauce:
   2 **tablespoons minced shallots**
   1 **teaspoon each yellow and black mustard seeds**
   ½ **cup dry white wine**
   ½ **cup heavy cream**
   ½ **cup sour cream**
3–4 **tablespoons Meaux-style grainy mustard**
   Salt and fresh black pepper

(1) Remove the skins from the mackerel fillets, and make a V-shaped cut the length of the fish to remove the vein of dark-red meat. (This tends to have a strong fish flavor.) Lightly oil a baking dish just large enough to hold the fillets, and arrange the fish on the bottom.

(2) Combine the shallots, mustard seeds, and wine in a heavy saucepan and boil until only 2 tablespoons liquid remain. Add the cream, and boil until only 3 tablespoons liquid remain. Let the mixture cool, and whisk in the sour cream, grainy mustard, and salt and pepper to taste. Spoon this sauce over the fish. The recipe can be prepared to this stage up to 4 hours ahead.

(3) Preheat the broiler (or oven, if using, to 450 degrees). Cook the mackerel for 10 to 15 minutes, or until the topping is browned and bubbling and the fish breaks into firm flakes when pressed. Serve with boiled new potatoes. A Chablis or California Chardonnay would be a good wine.

Mackerel *alla Puttanesca* (with Capers and Anchovies)

SERVES 4

SPAGHETTI *alla puttanesca* is a traditional Roman dish, originating in the Trastevere, a poor neighborhood frequented by prostitutes. It owes its name (a *puttana* is a prostitute) to the fact that it is hot and saucy and very quickly made! The pungent garnish of olives, anchovies, capers, and garlic goes well with a strong-flavored fish like mackerel. Kingfish and bluefish would make good substitutes.

1½ pounds mackerel fillets
   Salt and fresh black pepper
 6 tablespoons very good extra-virgin olive oil
 2 cloves garlic, minced
 8 anchovy fillets, cut into ¼-inch pieces
½ cup chopped pitted Greek or calamata olives
 1 pound fresh tomatoes, or 1 15-ounce can imported plum tomatoes
½ teaspoon dried red pepper flakes, or to taste
 4 tablespoons capers
 4 tablespoons chopped fresh parsley

(1) Preheat the oven to 400 degrees. Run your fingers along the mackerel fillets and remove any bones you feel, using pliers

or tweezers. Sprinkle the fillets with salt and pepper. With a little of the olive oil, grease a baking dish just large enough to hold the fish, then arrange the fish fillets in the dish. Mince the garlic, chop the anchovies, pit and chop the olives. Peel and seed the tomatoes, as described on page 304, and coarsely chop.

(2) Heat the remaining olive oil in a saucepan and add the garlic, anchovy fillets, and pepper flakes. Sauté over medium heat for 20 seconds. Add the tomatoes and capers, increase the heat to high, and cook the mixture for 3 minutes, or until most of the liquid evaporates. Add the parsley, and salt, black pepper, and additional pepper flakes to taste. The recipe can be prepared to this stage up to 2 hours before baking.

(3) When ready to bake, spoon the tomato mixture over the mackerel, set it in the preheated oven, and bake for 6 to 8 minutes, or until the fish flakes easily when pressed. Serve mackerel alla puttanesca with pasta, a green salad, and a sturdy wine, like Verdicchio or Corvo from Sicily.

Mackerel Gravlax

SERVES 4

GRAVLAX is a Scandinavian dish, made by curing fresh salmon with salt, dill, and sugar. The salt will draw liquid from the fish; this should be drained off. Once cured, the fish will keep for up to a week.

> 2 whole mackerel, heads removed, split and boned
> 3 tablespoons granulated sugar
> 3 tablespoons brown sugar
> 3 tablespoons salt
> 1 teaspoon coarsely crushed white pepper
> 1 bunch fresh dill, chopped
>
> Glass dish just large enough to hold the fish

(1) Run your fingers over the mackerel fillets, feeling for bones, and remove any you find with a tweezers or needle-nose pliers. Mix the sugars, salt, and pepper. Coarsely chop the dill.

(2) Line the bottom of the dish with dill and sprinkle with a little of the salt mixture. Place two fillets, skin side down, on top. Sprinkle the fish with more of the salt mixture, add another layer of dill, and sprinkle on more of the salt mixture. Place the remaining fillets on top, skin side up, and cover with the remaining salt mixture and dill. Place a plate or other weighted object on top.

(3) Let the mackerel cure for 24 hours in the refrigerator, and turn the fillets once. Pour off the liquid that is drawn off. To serve, scrape the dill and salt mixture off the fillets, and cut the fish on the diagonal into thin slices. Serve with the mustard sauce below.

———

Mustard Sauce
for Mackerel Gravlax

  3 tablespoons Dijon-style mustard
  2 teaspoons dry mustard
  1 tablespoon sugar
  2 tablespoons wine vinegar
  ⅓ cup vegetable oil
3–4 tablespoons chopped fresh dill
  Salt and fresh black pepper

Whisk the first 4 ingredients together in a bowl. Gradually whisk in the oil in a thin stream—the sauce should thicken like a mayonnaise. Whisk in the dill, and salt and pepper to taste. The sauce can be prepared ahead to this stage, but you may need to whisk the ingredients into a smooth paste just before serving.

MUSSELS

MUSSELS are the Horatio Algers of shellfish. Twenty-five years ago most Americans ignored their very existence. Today they turn up at the most fashionable restaurants. The French like the black bivalve enough to eat eighty thousand tons a year. In Belgium mussels and french fries are as popular as hamburgers are in the United States.

Mussels were among the first seafood to be "farmed"—as early as 500 B.C., the bivalves were grown on branches submerged beneath piers. Today they are raised on ropes hung from rafts. Cultivated mussels account for a substantial portion of the shellfish we eat. They have the advantage of being protected from predators, and because they are suspended in water, they are relatively free of grit. Occasionally, mussels will contain tiny pearls, which are perfectly harmless but annoying to eat.

Mussels are by far the most affordable shellfish, costing as little as fifty cents a pound. There are fifteen to twenty mussels to a pound, which will feed one person. Look for bivalves with tightly closed shells and a fresh, ocean smell. It's normal for a few shells to be gapped, but these should close when the bivalve is tapped.

Cultivated mussels have the advantage of being relatively sand-free. But the best mussels I have ever tasted were those I gathered at low tide on the rocky coast of Islesboro, Maine. (If you plan to gather mussels yourself, pick only the smooth-black-shell variety, not the ridged-shell kind. Also consult the local shellfish warden about the presence of "red tide" before eating them.) The color of mussel flesh ranges from bright orange to tan—a function of the mussel's diet, not quality, although I have found that the orange ones taste saltier and more succulent.

To prepare mussels for cooking, scrub the shells with a brush, scraping off any barnacles with the back of a knife. Find the tuft of threads at the "hinge" where the shells meet, and pinching them between your thumb and the back of a knife, pull them out. Discard any mussels with cracked shells, or gapped or open shells that fail to close within thirty seconds when the bivalve is tapped.

The first step to cooking mussels is to steam them open in dry white wine, with onion, garlic, and herbs. Mussels steamed this way are called *moules à la marinière* ("mussels seaman-style") and are a delicacy in their own right. Enjoy them with dry white wine and crusty French bread. When steaming more than two or three pounds of mussels, shake the pot or stir the mussels a few times to release the ones pinned on the bottom. Be sure to save the broth for soups or sauces; strain it through a cheesecloth, leaving the silty dregs in the pot. When serving mussels whole, be sure to provide a bowl for the empty shells.

Mouclade Vendéenne

SERVES 4 AS AN APPETIZER

THE Vendée is a region in Brittany famed for its shellfish, especially its mussels. A *mouclade* is a stew made with mussels and wine. There are numerous versions of mouclade—this one features curry, onions, and cream.

2 pounds mussels
½ cup dry white wine for steaming
3 tablespoons butter
1 small onion, finely chopped
1 clove garlic, minced
1 teaspoon curry powder
1 tablespoon flour
¼ cup heavy cream
Fresh black pepper and perhaps a little salt

(1) Clean and steam the mussels in wine as described on page 183. When cooked, let the mussels cool in the shells, and strain off ¾ cup of the broth.

(2) Meanwhile, prepare the sauce. Melt the butter in a saucepan and sauté the onion, garlic, and curry powder over medium heat for 2 minutes, or until the former are soft but not brown. Stir in the flour and cook for 1 minute. Off the heat whisk in the ¾ cup mussel broth and cream, then return pan to medium heat and simmer for 2 to 3 minutes, adding pepper and salt to taste. (*Note*: Salt may not be necessary as the mussels are already quite salty.)

(3) Remove the mussels from the shells, reserving the prettiest shells. Arrange the shells in concentric circles on a round platter. Place one or two mussels in each shell, and pour the hot sauce over them. You couldn't choose a better beverage than a cold, semidry Vouvray from the nearby Loire Valley.

Chicken with Mussels

SERVES 4

CHICKEN lends itself well to sauces flavored with seafood. Chicken with crayfish, for example, is a traditional dish from Lyon. Feel free to substitute clams, oysters, or even lobster in the recipe below.

    1 3-pound chicken
      Salt and fresh black pepper
    2 tablespoons vegetable oil
    2 tablespoons butter
    2 tablespoons flour
    ¾ cup dry white wine
    ½ cup chicken stock
    ½ cup heavy cream
    ⅛ teaspoon saffron
    2 pounds mussels

(1) Cut the chicken into eight pieces and season with salt and pepper. (Go lightly on the salt initially, because the mussel juice added later will be quite salty.) Heat the oil in a sauté pan over a high flame and lightly brown the chicken pieces on all sides. Transfer the chicken to a platter and pour off all the fat. Melt the butter in the pan and whisk in the flour. Add ½ cup of the wine, scraping the bottom of the pan to dissolve the pan juices. Add the chicken, stock, cream, and saffron—the liquid in the pan should almost cover the chicken. Bring the sauce to a boil, reduce the heat, and simmer for 20 to 30 minutes, or until the chicken pieces are cooked and tender.

(2) Meanwhile, clean and prepare the mussels as described on page 183. Bring the remaining ¼ cup wine to a boil in a large saucepan. Add the mussels and tightly cover the pan. Cook the mussels over high heat for 4 minutes, or until all the shells open, shaking the pan once or twice to free the mussels that are at the bottom. Do not overcook. Extract most of the mussels from the shells, discarding the latter, leaving 12 mussels in the shell for garnish. Strain the mussel broth through cheesecloth onto the chicken, leaving the silty liquid at the bottom of the mussel pan.

(3) To finish the dish, transfer the chicken to a warm serving dish and boil the sauce until it is richly flavored and reduced to about 1 cup. Add the shelled mussels to the sauce and correct the seasoning. Spoon the sauce over the chicken, and garnish with the mussels in the shells. To accompany chicken with mussels, serve a nice Montrachet or Mersault.

Variation: This dish is delicious when prepared with cherry-stones; substitute dry white vermouth for the wine and browned bacon or pancetta for the saffron.

Mussels with Cilantro and Chili

SERVES 8 AS AN APPETIZER

HERE'S a Mexican version of the classic French *escargots à la bourguignonne*.

> 3 pounds mussels
> 1 cup dry white wine
> 1 small onion, finely chopped
> Bouquet garni (optional)

For the cilantro butter:
> ¾ cup unsalted butter, at room temperature
> 1 bunch cilantro (fresh coriander leaf)
> 2–3 scallions
> 1 small jalapeño or serrano chili
> 1–2 cloves garlic
> Salt and fresh black pepper
> A few drops fresh lemon or lime juice

1–2 cups kosher salt to line the baking dish (optional)

(1) Preheat the broiler or oven to 450 degrees. Prepare the mussels. Scrub the shellfish and remove the threads. Place the wine and flavorings in a large pot and bring to a boil. Add the mussels, cover the pot, and cook over high heat for 5 minutes, or until the shells just open. Let cool.

(2) Meanwhile, prepare the cilantro butter. Cream the butter with a mixer or a wooden spoon. Finely chop the cilantro and scallions. Seed and mince the chili (see page 48 for a note on handling chilies). Peel and mince the garlic. Beat the cilantro, scallions, chili, and garlic into the butter, with salt, pepper, and citrus juice to taste.

(3) Remove the mussels from the shells, reserving half the shells (the prettiest ones). Arrange these shells on an ovenproof baking dish spread with ¼-inch kosher salt. (The salt keeps the shells from tipping.) Place one or two mussels in each shell, and

top each with a spoonful of cilantro butter. The mussels can be prepared to this stage up to 24 hours ahead.

(4) Just before serving, cook the mussels in the preheated oven for 5 minutes, or until the shellfish are hot and the butter bubbling. Serve at once with plenty of Superior or Dos Equis beer.

Variations: This recipe can also be prepared with littlenecks or cherrystones. Or use the cilantro butter for sautéing fresh shrimp, to make a Mexican version of scampi.

JUNE

J U N E is named for Juno, wife and sister of Jupiter, king of the gods on Mount Olympus. Juno was, appropriately, the Goddess of Marriage and the protectress of wedded women. The Romans considered June the best month to get married in, especially on the day of the full moon. The anonymous author of *Poor Robin's Almanac* (published in 1683) summed up the month's amorous appeal:

> *This is the best month to enter marriage state*
> *To try the love each bears unto his mate*
> *For if that they do now lay close together*
> *No doubt they'll do the same in colder weather!*

June is one of the most temperate months of the year. The weather is warm; the sun is bright; the fields and forests are verdant. The Anglo-Saxons called the month *Weyd-Monath,* "meadow month," mindful of the excellent pasturage for cattle. A profusion of flowers bloom in June, their blossoms abuzz with bees gathering nectar to make into honey. On a less idyllic note, allergy sufferers—the author among them—break out their nasal sprays and tissues!

On the ninth of June, the Romans celebrated the festival of Fornax, the Goddess of the Oven. Oven doors were decorated with flowers; garlands were hung on the necks of the mules that turned the grindstones. Incidentally, it is from the Latin word *fornus,* "oven," that our term *fornication* derives. The proverbial bun-in-the-oven is an apt metaphor for the fruits of vernal passion!

June is a felicitous month for fish lovers. Both Atlantic and Pacific salmon are at their prime. Schools of fresh herring ply the waters of the East Coast—try pickling them yourself or enjoying them fresh, grilled with lemon. June has long been associated with crab, as observed by the poet Spenser:

Upon a crab he [June] rode, that did him bear,
With crooked crawling steps, an uncouth pace,
And backward rode . . .

The blue crab molts (sheds its shell) in June, providing us with an ephemeral delicacy: soft-shell crab. This is also the month for fresh sardines and tiny whitebait—the former are excellent grilled; the latter delicious fried in cornmeal.

Other June delicacies include sugar-sweet onions from Vidalia, Georgia; Maui, Hawaii; and Walla Walla in Washington State. Fresh peas are plentiful; so are sugar snap peas, which are so sweet you eat them pods and all. After a winter of cottony hothouse fruit, we can finally enjoy vine-ripened strawberries. Blueberries and blackberries make their first appearance, their price dropping in the weeks to come. From now till September, I do most of my cooking on the barbecue grill. And the warm weather is reason enough to enjoy many meals al fresco.

June is truly a fair-weather month for cooks!

SWEET ONIONS

WHAT'S wrong with this picture? A child is taking a bite of an object that looks like an apple, only the apple isn't an apple —it's an onion! But the child is smiling, not weeping. It's a Vidalia onion from Georgia, and it's mild enough to chomp raw.

Vidalia is to onions what Pauillac is to wine, a microclimate where a unique combination of loamy soil, mild weather, and a fifty-year tradition have conspired to raise the lowly onion to the level of art. Vidalia onions are protected by the closest thing America has to an *appellation controllée:* "bootleggers" caught using the Vidalia name for onions grown outside the region can be fined up to twenty thousand dollars.

Vidalia covers thirteen counties in southeast Georgia. Onions have been raised commercially here since the early 1940s. The secret is not the onion variety: the yellow Granix is planted all over the United States. What's unique are the growing conditions that enable farmers to harvest early, before the onions have had time to develop a strong taste. Vidalia onions contain a large proportion of water and a whopping 12.5 percent sugar. Yes, Virginia, that's more natural sugar than is in an apple, even more than is in Coke.

Vidalia isn't the only region to lay claim to the nation's best onions. The island of Maui similarly boasts the growing conditions necessary to produce mild, sweet onions. Like Vidalias, Maui onions are slightly flattened, and range in color from yellow to pearl.

Not to be outdone, the farmers of Walla Walla, Washington, have bred an Italian onion variety into a strain remarkable for its delicate flavor and perfectly spherical shape. Walla Walla "sweets" can grow quite large, weighing as much as one and a half pounds apiece. The thick, crunchy layers make Walla Wallas excellent for onion rings. They are also delicious in salads.

Sweet onions are among the most fleeting of vegetables, their season lasting only six to eight weeks. Fortunately, the seasons are staggered, so the onion addict can find a fix from April to the end of August. Vidalia onions are in season from May to mid-June; Mauis, from April to June; and Walla Wallas, through July and August. Occasionally, you'll find them at specialty shops, but most often they are ordered by mail.

Because of their high water content, sweet onions are highly perishable. Successful storage depends on three factors: a cool, dry environment; good air-circulation; and luck. The first condition can be met by storing the onions in a dry corner of the basement. In Vidalia, to ensure good air-circulation, the onions are tied in old stockings, with a knot tied between each one. Alternatively, they can be stored on a window screen—the important thing is that they not touch a flat surface. If you don't have a basement, store them in the refrigerator, individually wrapped in foil. Gourmet onions will keep for extended periods, but they rapidly loose their sweetnesss. If I can't eat them in season, I don't bother to eat them at all.

For further information, contact the Vidalia Chamber of Commerce, P.O. Box 306, Vidalia, Georgia, 30474 (Tel.: 912/537-4466). Many farms sell the onions mail-order: I've had good luck with Bland Farms, P.O. Box 506, Glennville, Georgia, 30427 (Tel.: 1-800-VIDALIA).

COOKING WITH SWEET ONIONS

THE chief advantage of sweet onions is that they are mild enough to eat raw. Thinly sliced, use them in salads or on sandwiches—anywhere a regular onion would be too strong. When cooking sweet onions, keep the preparation simple: grill them; wrap them in foil and roast them (30 minutes at 400 degrees);

slice them up for soups, pies, or tempuras. *Note:* To keep from crying when chopping any onion, stick a slice of bread in your mouth.

Vidalia Onion Cream Sauce

MAKES 2 CUPS

THIS unusual onion sauce comes from an early nineteenth-century cookbook (*The Complete Woman,* published in 1800). It is particularly tasty made with sweet Vidalia onions. Onion sauce makes a fine accompaniment to roast beef, pork, or veal, and to poached or grilled chicken or fish.

> 1 pound Vidalia onions
> 3–4 tablespoons butter
> ½–¾ cup heavy cream
> Salt, fresh black pepper, cayenne pepper, and freshly grated nutmeg

(1) Peel the onions, quarter them, and place them in a saucepan with cold water to cover. Bring to a boil, reduce heat, and gently simmer the onions for 10 to 15 minutes or until tender. Drain.

(2) Purée the onions in a food processor or through a food mill. Return the purée to the saucepan with the butter, cream, and seasonings to taste. Simmer the sauce for 5 minutes, or until nicely thickened, adding more seasonings as necessary.

Grilled Onion and Goat Cheese Tart

SERVES 6

GRILLING imparts a wonderful smoky flavor to the onions. As I do most of my cooking out-of-doors this time of year, I usually throw the onions on the grill after I've made dinner, allow them to cook while I'm eating, and make the tart the following day. Another recipe from my assistant, Marcia Walsh.

> 1½ pounds Vidalia or Walla Walla onions
>   Extra-virgin olive oil
> 1 2-cup batch basic pie dough (see recipe on page 476), or your favorite recipe
> ¾ pound soft, mild goat cheese, like montrachet
> 2 eggs
> 2 egg yolks
> 1½ cups milk or light cream
>   Salt and fresh black pepper
> ½ pound walnut halves
>
> 1 12-inch French tart pan with removable bottom

(1) Cut the onions in half, leaving the skins on. Peel back and remove the skins, leaving the shoot and roots intact (These help hold the onion together during grilling). Brush the onions with olive oil and grill over a low heat for 20 to 30 minutes, or until tender.

(2) Preheat the oven to 400 degrees. Line the tart pan with the pie pastry. Once the onions have cooled, slip off the outermost layer and trim off the roots and shoots. Lay the onions flat side down on the cutting board and cut each half into quarters. Arrange the onion wedges in the tart pan, points toward the center.

(3) Cream the goat cheese in a large mixing bowl, then beat together with the eggs, egg yolks, and milk or cream until there are no large lumps of cheese remaining. Season the mixture with salt and pepper and pour it over the onions. Bake the tart in the preheated oven for 30 minutes, or until partially set, and remove to a wire rack. Arrange the walnut halves on the tart in concentric circles, and return it to the oven for an additional 20 minutes, or until the custard is set and an inserted skewer comes out clean. Serve at room temperature. A Sancerre or Pouilly-Fumé would make an appropriate wine.

Baked Vidalia Onions

SERVES 4

THIS recipe comes from a friend's father, Big Jim Walsh, who insists that the key to enjoying Vidalia onions is simplicity of preparation.

    4 large Vidalia onions
    2 tablespoons butter
    4 strips country-style bacon
    4 tablespoons cream cheese, at room temperature
    1 teaspoon Worcestershire sauce
      Salt and fresh black pepper

(1) Preheat the oven to 350 degrees. Beginning at the pointy end, core the onions almost through to the other side, leaving the root end intact to hold the onion together. Remove the skin. Place a pat of butter in each onion, wrap tightly in foil, and bake for 20 to 25 minutes, or until the onions are just beginning to get soft.

(2) Meanwhile, butter a baking dish just large enough to hold the onions. Cut the bacon into ¼-inch slivers and fry over medium heat until golden. Drain the bacon on paper towels and reserve. With a fork or wooden spoon, beat together the cream cheese, Worcestershire sauce, and bacon. When the onions are ready, remove them from the foil and stuff them with the mixture. Arrange the onions in the baking dish, and season to taste with salt and pepper. (The recipe can be prepared to this stage up to 4 hours before serving.) Just before serving, return the onions to the 350-degree oven for 15 to 20 minutes, or until the onions are very tender and the cheese mixture is heated through.

HARD- AND
SOFT-SHELL CRABS

IF you could choose your last meal on earth, what would you pick? Truffles? Foie gras? Caviar? Something hideously rich and French? I know what I would pick, and it wouldn't take much soul-searching. For my last supper I would have a meal of Maryland crab.

I would start with crab soup, brimming with vegetables and fiery with pepper. Next, I'd wolf down some soft-shell crabs—extra capers, please! The third course would be Maryland crab cakes, loaded with snowy backfin meat. The *pièce de résistance* would be Maryland-style steamed crabs, steamed in beer, smeared with lip-stinging spice paste. No damask tablecloth or bone china would be necessary for my last meal, no venerable vintages: the table would be spread with old newspapers, my cup would runneth over with beer. And I wouldn't trade a single bite of my crab feast for all the lobster in Maine. I would cheerfully depart for the hereafter, knowing I'd already found heaven on earth!

America's waters are blessed with an abundance of crab: blue crabs from the Chesapeake Bay, stone crabs from Florida, Dungeness crabs from the West Coast, giant king crabs from Alaska. There are over four thousand varieties of crab in the world, ranging from pea crabs—tiny enough to live in mussel shells—to the Japanese giant crab, which may attain a leg-span of twelve and a half feet. Crabmeat is incredibly versatile, suitable for preparations as diverse as soups, gratins, soufflés, stir-fries, and sushi. Maryland crabmeat comes in three forms: lump meat (large, white, meaty chunks from the body—use for crab cakes and salads); flake meat (small, white pieces from the body—use for soups and sautées); and claw meat (very sweet but brownish in color—use for dipping).

Like all crustaceans, crabs periodically molt to make way for a larger carapace. Newly molted blue crabs (called "peelers" by the fishermen) are eaten carapace and all, a delicacy known as soft-shells. Soft-shell crabs come into season in June, and are irregularly available through September. Pan-fried in butter, they are truly a treat.

When buying whole crabs for steaming, one rule holds: they should be feisty and kicking. The same holds true for soft-shell crabs, which are even more perishable than hard-shells. Many people prefer female crabs: they are recognizable by the wide, V-shaped, tablike "apron" on the belly.

Live crabs are generally cooked by steaming. In Maryland, they are steamed in a pungent mixture of vinegar, beer, and spices (see below). Soft-shell crabs taste best sautéed or deep-fried. To prepare a live soft-shell for sautéing:

(1) Make a V-shaped cut with a knife or scissors to remove the mouth and eyes. (This kills the crab instantly, although it may continue to wriggle.)

(2) Remove the "apron," the V-shaped tab on the belly.

(3) Lift the pointed flaps of the carapace (top shell), and remove the spongy, featherlike gills just underneath.

This procedure is not for the squeamish—you may wish to have your fishmonger do it instead. In that case, be sure to eat the crabs the same day you buy them.

Maryland Crab Soup

SERVES 6 TO 8

THIS spicy soup begins a triumvirate of Maryland crab delicacies. Imagine a rich vegetable soup lavished with snowy crab meat and ignited with hot sauce. I know of no better remedy for a cold! The soup can be an intimidating dish to eat at a Maryland restaurant: it is usually served with half a crab, claws raised, in each bowl! If you have any steamed crabs left over from the Maryland steamed crab recipe on page 202, add them, pepper sauce and all. The soup can be made with shelled crabmeat, but it will be richer if you can find a couple of whole crabs to add to the broth.

3–4 live blue crabs (about 2 pounds), or 1 pound crab meat
 1 onion
 1 leek, trimmed and washed
 2 large carrots
 2 ribs celery
 2 cloves garlic
 1 28-ounce can imported peeled plum tomatoes, or 2 pounds
 fresh tomatoes if in season
 4 tablespoons butter
 6 cups bottled clam broth, fish or chicken stock, or water
 Bouquet garni (see recipe on page 471)
2–3 teaspoons Old Bay Seasoning (see Note on next page)
 1 teaspoon Tabasco or Pickapepper sauce
 2 potatoes
2–3 ears of corn (if available)
 ¼ pound fresh green beans
 ½ pound fresh peas
 Salt and fresh black pepper

(1) Have the crabs ready—they should be live and kicking. If using crabmeat, pick through it to remove any shells. Finely chop the onion, leek, carrots, celery, and garlic. Coarsely chop the tomatoes, and reserve the juices. (*Note:* If you are using fresh tomatoes, you may need to add an extra cup of clam broth or water.)

(2) Melt the butter in a large (8-quart) pan. Add the vegetables and cook over medium heat for 3 minutes, or until tender. Add the tomatoes, reserved juices, and clam broth, stock, or water, and bring the soup to a boil. Add the crabs and bouquet garni, half the Old Bay Seasoning, and half the hot sauce. Reduce the heat and simmer the soup while you prepare the other ingredients—20 to 30 minutes in all.

(3) Peel the potatoes and cut them into ½-inch cubes. Cut

the kernels off the corn. Snap the ends off the green beans, and cut the beans into ¼-inch pieces. Shuck the peas. Add the potatoes to the soup, and simmer for 10 minutes. Add the beans and peas, and simmer for 5 minutes, or until tender.

(4) Just before serving, remove the crabs with a slotted spoon. Lift the carapace, and scrape out the featherlike gills and spaghettilike entrails. Cut the crabs into quarters and return to the soup. Add the remaining Old Bay Seasoning and hot sauce —the soup should be very spicy—and salt and pepper to taste. The soup is great now and is guaranteed to improve with age.

NOTE: Old Bay Seasoning is made in Baltimore and distributed on a limited basis throughout the U.S. The predominant flavorings are salt, celery seed, mustard seed, pepper, bay leaves, cloves, ginger, mace, cardamom, and paprika. It can be ordered from the Baltimore Spice Company, Baltimore, Maryland, 21208. Or try adding a pinch of each of these ingredients, if Old Bay Seasoning is unavailable in your area.

Maryland Crab Cakes

MAKES 4 CAKES—SERVES 4 AS AN APPETIZER OR
2 AS A MAIN COURSE.

SOME time ago, I was talking about crab cakes on a Baltimore radio talk show. The host asked listeners to call in with their favorite recipe for crab cakes—the variations were endless. Here's the recipe I favor.

    1 pound jumbo lump crabmeat
    2 slices fresh white bread, crust removed
    1 egg
    1 generous tablespoon mayonnaise (see recipe on page 477 or use
      a good commercial brand)
    ⅛ teaspoon dry mustard
    1 teaspoon Dijon-style mustard
      Salt and fresh black pepper
    3 tablespooons butter, if frying

(1) Pick through the crab, removing any shell but leaving the lumps as large as possible. Cut the bread into ¼-inch cubes. Beat the egg in a bowl with the mayonnaise, seasonings, and bread cubes. Add the crab and mix the ingredients as gently as possible with your hands. Form the crab mixture into four thick, round patties, and refrigerate these for 2 to 3 hours.

(2) Just before serving, preheat the broiler. Broil the crab cakes on a buttered rack for 5 minutes per side. If you prefer, melt the butter in a skillet and pan-fry the crab cakes over medium heat, 3 to 4 minutes per side. Serve with the homemade tartar sauce below.

Tartar Sauce

MAKES ABOUT 1¼ CUPS

CLASSIC tartar sauce is an emulsified sauce, like mayonnaise, but is made with hard-cooked, not raw, egg yolks. Here's a quick version, made with commercial mayonnaise but enriched with freshly chopped flavorings. Purists can make their own mayonnaise (see recipe on page 477).

1 cup good-quality mayonnaise
2 teaspoons of each of the following: Dijon-style mustard, chopped capers, chopped cornichon pickles, chopped fresh chives, and chopped fresh tarragon
Plenty of fresh black pepper

Whisk the flavorings into the mayonnaise, seasoning to taste.

Maryland Steamed Crabs

SERVES 3 TO 4 NORMAL PEOPLE,
ALTHOUGH I CAN EAT A DOZEN ALL BY MYSELF

BALTIMORE crab-buffs argue the merits of the various fish houses the way Michelin judges debate which twenty restaurants in all of France deserve their coveted three stars. (The latter are the unfortunate ones, for the French don't serve steamed crabs.) One of Baltimore's most famous crab houses is a sprawling, blue-collar tavern called Bo Brooks. The owners, Stevie and Billy Martin, were kind enough to provide their recipe for steamed crabs below. The proper crab for steaming is the blue crab, native to the Chesapeake Bay and the Gulf of Mexico.

> **12 large live blue crabs—the feistier, the better**
> **1½ cups beer, at room temperature**
> **¾ cup distilled white vinegar**
> **4 tablespoons Old Bay Seasoning (see Note on page 201)**
> **1 tablespoon dry mustard**
> **1 handful kosher salt**
> **1 generous shake of cayenne pepper**
>
> **1 large (at least 4-gallon) nonaluminum steaming pot with a tightly fitting lid and a rack to keep the crabs above the boiling liquid**

(1) Keep the crabs on ice until you are ready to steam them. (This quiets them down.) Add 1½ cups warm water, the beer, and the vinegar to the pot. In a small bowl, combine the spices and seasonings. Place the crabs in the pot in three layers, sprinkling a third of the spice mixture on each layer. Cover the top and weight the cover with a brick or can. (My grandfather once neglected to do this and had crabs crawling all over the kitchen!)

(2) Place the pot over high heat and steam the crabs for 15 to 20 minutes, or just until the top crab turns bright red.

To serve Maryland steamed crabs, spread your table with newspaper. Provide each guest with a wooden mallet, a small paring knife, and a stein (better yet a pitcher) of beer. Eat the crabs with your hands, claws first, then the backfin meat. (To get to the latter, pry up the tablike apron, pull the carapace away from the body, and break the body in two.) The "mustard," creamy yellow fat in the pointy ends of the shell, is considered a delicacy. Don't forget to suck the meat out of the small legs!

Soft-shell Crabs with Sesame Sauce

SERVES 4

THIS dish ranges freely across national borders, using crabs from Maryland, tahini (sesame seed paste) from the Middle East, and soy sauce and rice wine vinegar form the Orient. The recipe comes from one of Boston's most talented chefs, Jasper White of the restaurant Jasper. Jasper serves the crabs on a bed of rice noodles, but there's no reason you couldn't use Japanese *soba* (buckwheat noodles), fettuccine, or even shredded lettuce.

For the sesame sauce:
- ¼ cup tahini (available in any Middle Eastern market)
- 3 tablespoons soy sauce
- 3 tablespoons rice wine vinegar
- 1 tablespoon Oriental sesame oil
- ¼–½ teaspoon hot chili oil
- 2 teaspoons sugar
- 1 small clove garlic, minced
- Fresh black pepper

For the crabs:
- 12 small or 8 large soft-shell crabs
- Salt and fresh black pepper
- Approximately 1 cup milk
- Approximately 1 cup flour
- 6–8 tablespoons peanut oil

(1) Prepare the sesame sauce. Place the tahini in a bowl and gradually whisk in the remaining ingredients. The sauce should emulsify. This sauce can be prepared well ahead and is delicious on just about anything.

(2) Prepare the crabs as described on page 199, or have your fishmonger do it. Season each crab with salt and pepper, and dip it in milk, then in flour, patting it to shake off any excess flour. Heat the oil in one large or two small frying pans. Sauté the crabs over medium heat for 3 minutes per side, or until golden brown.

Place the crabs on paper towels to drain. Spoon the sesame sauce over the crabs just before serving.

NOTE: To make a noodle salad, soak 8 ounces rice noodles in cold water and drain (or cook other noodles according to your favorite method). Toss the noodles with a dressing made from 2 teaspoons each rice wine vinegar, sesame oil, soy sauce, finely chopped scallion, and a little grated ginger. Shredded lettuce (this is one case where the crispness of iceburg is welcomed) could be dressed in a similar way.

Soft-shell Crab Sandwich

SERVES 4

THERE is a fishmonger called Fadley's in Baltimore's Lexington Market, and for almost a century it has provided Maryland seafood buffs with some of the best oysters, clams, and blue crabs found anywhere on the East Coast. On a recent visit I ordered a soft-shell crab sandwich: the cook fished a wriggling crab from a basket, cleaned it, dropped it into a vat of hot oil, and slapped it between two slices of Wonderbread. The sandwich took 60 seconds to make, and remains one of the most memorable meals I have eaten. Here's a soft-shell crab sandwich, however, with a little more finesse. Of course, you can omit the bread and just sit down to a plate of sautéed soft-shells.

    4 large or 8 small soft-shell crabs
      Salt and fresh black pepper
      Approximately 1 cup milk
      Approximately 1 cup flour
  4–5 tablespoons clarified butter (see page 471)
    4 slices country-style white bread, bulky rolls, or challah (the
      last is delicious, if sacrilegious)
    1 batch homemade tartar sauce (see recipe on page 202)
    1 fresh lemon, cut in half

(1) Prepare the crabs as described on page 199, or have your fishmonger do it. Season each crab with salt and pepper, and dip it in milk, then in flour, patting it to shake off any excess flour. Heat the butter in one large or two small frying pans.

(2) Sauté the crabs over medium heat for 3 minutes per side, or until golden brown. Meanwhile, lightly toast the bread, and spread each slice with tartar sauce. When the crabs are cooked, place them on towels to drain, reserving the pan juices. Arrange the crabs on the bread slices to make open-faced sandwiches. Spoon some of the pan juices over each sandwich and squeeze a little lemon on top.

Variation: For sautéed soft-shells, flour and sauté the crabs as described above. Sprinkle the crabs with a heaping tablespoon of capers, some chopped anchovy (if you like anchovy), some chopped parsley, and a little butter from the frying pan. Let restaurant chefs concoct lavish sauces: there is no better way to enjoy soft-shells than this.

SALMON

"SALMON and poverty go together," wrote Dickens. Imagine his surprise if he were to venture into a fish market today! This red-fleshed fish has become an ocean aristocrat, costing as much per pound as prime beef. You would never guess that it was so common in Colonial America that indentured servants had clauses in their contracts limiting the number of times per week they could be served salmon!

Salmon have a migratory instinct as keen as that of any bird: they've been known to swim 2500 miles to return to their native river for spawning. Our word *salmon* comes from the Latin *salire*, "to leap" or "to jump"—a reference to the salmon's ability to leap rapids and waterfalls on its way upstream. From a cook's point of view, salmon are at their best when they set out on their homeward journey, usually in late spring, for spawning. Their flesh is packed with fats and nutrients to give them strength for their journey. They are also good fished from the ocean, where they feed on crustaceanlike plankton, whence their bright red flesh. Much of the salmon we buy comes from "farms" in Norway —pond-raised fish that are softer and less flavorful than their brethren from the deep.

This handsome fish once plied the Seine, the Thames, and the Rhine, not to mention our own Hudson and Connecticut rivers. Today, salmon comes from two major regions: the Atlantic (particularly off the coast of Canada, the British Isles, and Scandinavia), and the Pacific Northwest.

When buying whole salmon, look for fish with bright eyes and scales and a plump belly. The flesh should be orange-red to rose pink. (As a rule, the brighter the color, the more flavorful the fish.) The flesh should feel firm, not squishy. If you find salmon with deep, white marbling, you are in for a special treat.

Salmon lends itself to a myriad of preparations. Its natural fats keep it moist during broiling and grilling. It holds together when poached or baked. Salmon is equally delectable served hot, chilled, or raw. If you plan to serve it chilled, let it cool in its poaching liquid—this keeps the flesh nice and moist. Salmon fillets are better for broiling and grilling. Salmon steaks are well suited to poaching and baking.

Hot salmon goes well with the following: Blood Orange Maltaise Sauce (page 131) and Saffron Butter Sauce (page 355). Cold salmon goes well with Spicy Tartar Sauce (page 271) and Volcanic Horseradish Sauce (page 439).

Salmon Tartare

SERVES 8 AS AN APPETIZER

THE Tartars were a nomadic tribe in what is now eastern Turkey. They were so busy marauding and pillaging they didn't have time for cooking and ate their meat raw. Like its beef cousin, salmon tartare is flavored with mustard, capers, and olive oil. In place of the anchovy used with beef, we substitute smoked salmon. Excellent tartare can be made with tuna or swordfish (use 6 anchovy fillets in place of the smoked salmon).

> 1 **pound fresh salmon fillets**
> ¼ **pound smoked salmon**

For the sauce:
> 1 **egg yolk**
> 1 **tablespoon Dijon-style mustard**
> 2–3 **tablespoons extra-virgin olive oil**
> **Juice of ½ lemon, or to taste**
> 1 **teaspoon Worcestershire sauce**
> 3 **tablespoons finely chopped parsley**
> 3 **tablespoons finely chopped scallion (green part)**
> 3 **tablespoons capers, drained**
> **Pinch of cayenne pepper**
> **Salt and fresh black pepper**

For the garnish:
> **Sprigs of parsley or chervil**
> 1 **egg yolk (optional)**
> 16–20 **slices pumpernickel or black bread, cut into triangles**

(1) Remove the skin from the salmon fillets. Run your fingers over each fillet, feeling for bones; use tweezers or pliers to pull them out. Finely chop the fish with a chef's knife (the food processor does not work well for chopping the fish, as the whirling blade tends to mash, not chop, it.

(2) Place the egg yolk and mustard in a large bowl. Gradually whisk in the oil, followed by the liquid flavorings. Whisk in the parsley, scallions, capers, cayenne pepper, and black pepper to

taste. Not more than 30 minutes before serving, add the chopped salmon, tossing with wooden spoons to thoroughly mix. Add salt and additional lemon juice to taste, but remember, the smoked salmon is already quite salty.

(3) To serve, mound the salmon tartar in the center of a platter and decorate it with sprigs of fresh herbs. (Some people like to make a depression in the center and garnish it with a raw egg yolk.) Arrange the pumpernickel triangles around the salmon. For a beverage, I would suggest a tart wine, like a Muscadet or Sauvignon Blanc, or a bitter beer, like stout.

_____

Rillettes of Salmon

SERVES 8 TO 10

RILLETTES is a sort of rich potted pork popular on sandwiches served at French cafés. My teacher and mentor, chef Fernand Chambrette, had the brilliant idea one day to remake this charcuterie classic using fresh and smoked salmon instead of pork. Spread it on toasted French or whole wheat bread.

>   1 pound fresh salmon, with bones if possible
>   1 cup dry white wine
>   ¾ cup butter, at room temperature
>   ¾ pound smoked salmon (do not use lox—it is too salty)
>   Salt, fresh black pepper, and freshly grated nutmeg

(1) Trim the skin from the fresh salmon, and remove the bones (using tweezers or pliers) and place them in a shallow pan with the wine and 1 cup water. Bring the liquid to a boil, reduce the heat to a gentle simmer, then add the salmon and poach it for 6 minutes, or until the fish is just cooked. Leave the salmon to cool in the poaching liquid, then remove the fish and discard the skin and bones. Pour off all but 3 tablespoons of the poaching liquid. (Freeze the poured-off poaching liquid for later use as a soup or stew base.)

(2) Melt 2 tablespoons of the butter with the reserved poaching liquid and gently cook the smoked salmon for 2 minutes, or until it turns opaque. Leave it to cool. Combine the fresh and smoked salmon in a large bowl, breaking the fish into shreds.

(3) Cream the remaining butter in a separate bowl, and into it, using a wooden spoon, beat the cooled, shredded salmon little by little. Season the mixture with pepper and nutmeg to taste, but go easy on the salt. Traditionally, *rillettes* is served in earthenware crocks, so that the guests may dole out their own helpings onto squares of toast or crackers. To avoid a crush around the buffet table, you may wish to spread slices of bread with the mixture beforehand and pass them from platters. Salmon rillettes may be prepared a day or two ahead of time and refrigerated, but warm it to room temperature 2 to 3 hours before serving.

Salmon with Soy Sauce, Cider Vinegar, and Spinach-Flavored Ricotta

SERVES 6

THIS intensely flavorful and exotic recipe comes from a caterer—Susan Layton of Fairfield, Connecticut. Susan serves the dish chilled for a summer buffet, but it would also be good hot.

2½–3 pounds fresh skinless salmon fillets

For the marinade:
  1 cup soy sauce
  ½ cup cider vinegar
  2 cloves garlic, peeled and thinly sliced

For the spinach-flavored ricotta:
  ¾ pound fresh spinach
  1 medium onion
  3 tablespoons butter
  1 pound ricotta cheese
  Salt, fresh black pepper, and freshly grated nutmeg

½ cup unsalted butter, melted

Barbecue grill

(1) Run your fingers over the salmon fillets, feeling for bones. Remove any bones with tweezers or pliers. Cut the fillets into 6 even portions. Combine the ingredients for the marinade in a large stainless steel or glass pan. Marinate the salmon fillets for 1 to 1½ hours.

(2) Meanwhile, prepare the spinach-flavored ricotta. Stem and wash the spinach. Cook the spinach with ¼ cup water in a large pan over high heat for 1 minute, or until the leaves are tender. Refresh under cold water and drain. Tightly wring the spinach with your hands to extract all the liquid. Finely chop the onion. Melt the 3 tablespoons butter in a skillet and cook the onion over medium heat for 3 to 4 minutes, or until soft and sweet but not browned. Let cool. Purée the spinach, onions, and ricotta in the food processor or blender, adding salt, pepper, and nutmeg. The mixture should be highly seasoned.

(3) Preheat the grill. Dip each piece of salmon in melted butter and cook it over medium heat with the grill set as high over the coals as possible. The aim is to smoke the salmon, as well as cook it. The fish will continue cooking after you remove it from the grill, so leave it a little pink in the center. Let the fish cool.

(4) To serve the salmon, spoon a low mound of ricotta mixture on each plate. Place a piece of fish on top. An oaky Chardonnay, like Château St. Jean or Acacia Vineyards, would be an excellent wine.

Salmon *Saltimbocca*

SERVES 4

SALTIMBOCCA is a dish of Roman origins, traditionally made by rolling veal around sage leaves and prosciutto, then pan-frying it. The result is so tasty, it "jumps in your mouth," which is what *saltimbocca* literally means in Italian. This recipe substitutes salmon for the veal, and smoked fish for the prosciutto. Fontina is a creamy, full-flavored cheese from northern Italy. You could also use Bel Paese or Gouda.

> 1½ pounds fresh salmon fillets
> 6 ounces thinly sliced smoked salmon
> ⅓ pound imported fontina
> Fresh sage leaves
> 4 tablespoons butter
> Salt and fresh black pepper
> ½ cup flour for dusting
> 4 tablespoons Marsala wine
> 4 tablespoons heavy cream
> A few drops lemon juice (optional)

(1) Remove the skin from the salmon fillet(s) and run your fingers over it, feeling for bones. Use tweezers or needle nose pliers to pull out any bones. Slice the salmon fillet on the diagonal into *escalopes* that are ¼-inch thick and 3 to 4 inches square. Lightly pound each of these between two sheets of moistened parchment paper or wax paper, with the side of a cleaver or a wooden mallet.

(2) Cut the smoked salmon into squares somewhat smaller than those of the fresh salmon. Cut the cheese into thin slices the size of the smoked salmon squares. To assemble each saltimbocca, place a piece of smoked salmon on top of a square of fresh salmon. Top it with a single sage leaf, a slice of cheese, and a second square of fresh salmon. Lightly pound the saltimbocca with the side of a cleaver to seal the sides. Prepare the other saltimboccas the same way, using the remaining ingredients: you should wind up with two or three pieces per person. The recipe can be prepared to this stage up to 5 hours before cooking.

(3) Melt the butter in a large frying pan over medium heat. Season the saltimbocci with salt and pepper, and lightly dust them with flour, shaking off the excess. Add the saltimbocci to the pan and sauté them for 1 minute per side, or until cooked (the fish will flake easily when pressed). Transfer the fish to a warm platter. Add the Marsala to the frying pan and bring it to a

boil. Add the cream and continue boiling the sauce until it is reduced by one-third and slightly thickened. Add salt and pepper to taste, perhaps a few more drops Marsala, and even a few drops of lemon juice, if you wish.

(4) Serve the salmon saltimbocca at once, with rice pilaf or buttered pasta on the side. Spoon the sauce on top. For wine, try a full-bodied white from the south of Italy, like Grecco de Tufo.

PEAS

DID you eat your peas when you were young? If not, chances are your mother bought the wrong kind. If she was like my mother, she probably served big, bright green, perfectly round peas that were about as appetizing as a plateful of vitamin pills. (Never mind the trouble you had getting them on your fork!) And if you were like me, they probably wound up wadded in your napkin or fed to an obliging canine.

If only Mom had known about good peas: snow peas as crisp as apples, snap peas dulcet as honey. Peas are the first of the springtime vegetables to ripen. Gardeners impatiently await their arrival in the early weeks of June. Nothing is so sweet, so eminently satisfying as freshly harvested peas. The secret to selecting sweet shell peas is to choose the smaller, more wrinkly specimens.

The Norse believed that the pea was sent to man as punishment from the gods. Thunder-god Thor dispatched flying dragons to drop peas in wells, so they would rot and foul the water. But some of the peas fell in fields and grew, and the humans were so grateful they dedicated the new vegetable to Thor, and ate peas only on his day, Thursday.

Catherine de Medici is credited with popularizing the *petit pois*. By the seventeenth century, fresh peas had become a cult food. "The subject of peas continues to absorb all others," wrote Madame de Maintenon in 1696. "The anxiety to eat them, the pleasure of having eaten them, and the desire to eat them again are the three great matters which have been discussed by our princes for four days past." Her compatriots were enjoying a highly nutritious vegetable: 1 cup of peas provides 458 milligrams potassium, 168 milligrams phosphorus, and 903 units of vitamin A, not to mention the exercise required to shuck them!

The pea family is a single species, but there are hundreds of varieties. The major types to look for are:

Shell Peas: mature peas that are eaten after the pod has been discarded.

Snap Peas: a recent addition to the American larder, and a welcome one at that. Snap peas look like miniature shell peas. They are tender and sweet, and are enjoyed pod and all.

Snow Peas: immature peas that are eaten along with the flat pod. Snow peas were popularized by the Chinese, and are now widely grown in the United States. The smaller the pod, the better.

When buying shell peas, look for plump pods, with well formed "berries" (as canners call individual peas). The color should be bright green, and the pod should feel velvety to the touch. The more wrinkled the skin of each pea, the greater the proportion of sugar and the smaller of starch.

When buying snap peas, look for plump, tender pods. With snow peas, look for pods with immature berries. The best time for picking peas is in the morning, when the weather is still cool. Store fresh peas in a moisture-proof container.

Sweet Pea Vichyssoise

SERVES 6

VICHYSSOISE is a chilled soup of potatoes and leeks, invented by chef Louis Diat to fete the opening of the Ritz Carlton

Hotel in New York. (Diat grew up in a village near Vichy in Central France—thus the soup's name.) The twist here comes in flavoring the soup with sweet green peas. If the Prince and Princess of Wales are coming to dinner, force the peas through a sieve to remove the skins; for the rest of us, puréeing in a blender is sufficient.

> 1 pound peas (approximately 2½ cups shelled)
> 2–3 leeks (enough to make ¾ cup chopped)
> 3 tablespoons butter
> 1 medium potato, peeled and diced
> 4 cups chicken stock (see recipe on page 472)
> Bouquet garni (see recipe on page 471)
> 1 cup light cream
> Salt and fresh black pepper
> 1 cup heavy cream
> Fresh mint leaves for garnish

(1) Shell the peas and cook ½ cup of them in rapidly boiling, salted water for 4 to 5 minutes, or until crispy-tender. Refresh the peas in cold water and reserve. Clean and finely chop the leeks.

(2) Melt the butter in a large saucepan. Add the leeks and cook them over medium heat for 3 minutes, or until soft. Add the potato, stock, bouquet garni, light cream, and a little salt and pepper. Simmer the soup for 20 minutes, or until the potatoes are almost tender. Add the raw peas and simmer the soup for 5 to 6 more minutes, or until all the vegetables are very tender.

(3) Remove the bouquet garni and purée the soup in a blender. (The blender works better than the food processor.) Add salt and pepper to taste. (*Note:* Because this soup is served cold, you will need to overseason it slightly.) Chill the soup over ice, or let it come to room temperature, then chill it in the refrigerator. The recipe can be prepared to this stage up to 48 hours before serving.

(4) Just before serving, stir the heavy cream into the soup, and ladle it into chilled mugs or bowls. Sprinkle the top of each serving with chopped mint leaves and decorate with the blanched peas.

Sugar Snap Peas with Roquefort Cream

SERVES 4 TO 6

THE salty tang of Roquefort makes an unexpected flavoring for peas. In the absence of sugar snap peas—their season is lamentably short—you can substitute snow peas.

> 1 **pound sugar snap peas**
> **Salt**
> ½ **cup heavy cream**
> 1–2 **tablespoons Roquefort cheese, or to taste**
> 2 **tablespoons butter**
> **Fresh black pepper**

(1) Snap the ends off the peas and carefully draw out any strings. In a heavy saucepan, bring 1 quart water to a boil with 2 teaspoons salt. Add the peas and cook for 20 seconds. Refresh them under cold water and drain.

(2) Place the cream in the saucepan and bring it to a boil. Meanwhile, mash the Roquefort with a fork and add it to the cream, whisking until the sauce is smooth. Remove the pan from the heat and whisk in the butter and pepper to taste. Taste the sauce: add more Roquefort or salt as necessary. (You probably won't need the latter, as the Roquefort is already quite salty.) Stir in the peas and warm if necessary over a low heat.

Snow Pea Salad with Jicama and Mirin

SERVES 4

THIS pretty dish can be made with any crunchy white vegetable: jicama, Jerusalem artichokes, or fresh water chestnuts. Jicama is a brown-skinned, light-fleshed root grown in the Southwest—its flavor is a cross between that of an apple and a potato. Mirin is a sweet rice wine from Japan. It is available at most health food stores or Oriental markets, or you can use cream sherry.

½ pound snow peas
1 small jicama root
  Salt
2 teaspoons mirin
2 teaspoons sesame oil
  Fresh black pepper

(1) Snap the ends off the snow peas and remove the strings. Peel the jicama and cut it into ⅛-inch thick slices. Cut these slices into ½-inch strips, so that they are the same width as the snow peas.

(2) In a large saucepan, bring 1 quart water to a boil with a pinch of salt. Blanch the snow peas for 10 seconds, refresh under cold water, and drain. Just before serving, toss the snow peas and jicama with the mirin and sesame oil, adding salt and pepper to taste.

BERRIES

Curly-locks, Curly-locks,
Wilt thou be mine?
Thou shalt not wash dishes
Nor yet feed the swine.
But sit on a cushion
And sew a fine seam,
And feed upon strawberries,
Sugar and cream.

NURSERY RHYME

FOR nine months a year, the strawberry is a pitiful fruit, bred for shelf-life, not flavor; plucked before fully ripe; entombed in cellophane shrouds; and shipped across continents. Then come June and the first local vine-ripened berries, and Amphitryons have reason to celebrate.

Strawberries are our most common berry, existing in both cultivated and wild form. This cone-shaped, ruby-red fruit was sacred to the Norse goddess Freya (who gave her name to Friday). When the Vikings converted to Christianity, they dedicated the berry to the Virgin Mary. It was considered a sin to eat strawberries prior to St. John's Day (which falls in June)—a sensible practice which spared Norsemen from eating underripe berries. Even today, the start of strawberry season signals that summer has finally begun.

One of the most curious uses for the strawberry was dreamed up by Madame Tallien, a ninteenth-century beauty who added the juice to her bathwater to keep her skin smooth and soft—twenty-two pounds of berries were required for each bath! We can think of more sensible uses, like serving strawberries with sweet cream, shortcake, or sherbet. The French dote on *fraises des bois*, tiny wild strawberries whose haunting flavor justifies their exorbitant price. These strawberries also grow wild in North America and are starting to turn up at the better restaurants.

Blueberries are my personal favorite—I await their arrival as eagerly as a broker awaits an inside stock tip. The first blueberries to reach the market are the large, high-bush berries from the Carolinas; look for them in June. As the harvest moves up the coast from New Jersey to Maine, the price drops until it is almost reasonable. Low-bush blueberries, treasured for their intense, sweet-tart flavor, come into season in August. Their cultivation is centered in Washington and Hancock counties in Maine.

High-bush blueberries have the advantage of being easy to clean, and are best eaten by themselves or with cream. They seem to get bigger every year—some are the size of grapes! Low-bush blueberries are tiny and stemmy, but intensely flavorful. It takes fifteen hundred of them to make a pound (as opposed to high-bush berries, which come five hundred to a pound). Difficult to clean for straight eating, they are relegated to muffins, pies, and preserves.

Raspberries can be found as early as June, but they won't be plentiful till August. The brilliant hue of their flesh makes them a popular fruit for sauce. The classic way to purée raspberries is by forcing them through a hoop sieve—a messy and time-consuming process. The berries can be puréed in the food processor, but run the machine in spurts and as little as possible. (You want to avoid crushing the seeds, which will make the sauce bitter.) To my thinking, the best way to enjoy raspberries is with sugar and a dollop of *crème fraiche*.

Blackberries are another early ripener. The berry is large, fleshy, and sturdy—well suited to pies and gratins. The blackberry, by the way, was the burning bush of the Bible.

I believe in eating berries in season or not eating them at all. When buying berries, look for plump, brightly colored fruits: blueberries should be a dark blue, strawberries and raspberries bright red. A tinge of green at the base is an indication of underripeness. Avoid any berries that are wilted-looking or moldy.

Berries are extremely perishable, so buy them from a shop that has rapid turnover. Better still, visit a farm where you can pick your own.

Candy-coated Strawberries

MAKES 12 TO 16 BERRIES

CANDY-COATED strawberries make an unusual petit four. At the restaurant where I worked in Brittany, we would dip the berries in molten sugar and serve them with the check (in an effort to sweeten the moment of reckoning). The process is simple: sugar is cooked to the hard-crack or light-caramel stage. Ripe, unblemished berries are dipped into the sugar, which forms a brittle candy shell when cool. Macho chefs test the temperature of the sugar by hand (you dip your fingers in ice water first to prevent them from burning), but a candy thermometer works just as well. *Warning:* Molten sugar causes a painful burn, so take care not to drip any on your skin.

1 pint ripe, unblemished strawberries
1½ cups granulated sugar

Needlenose pliers or tweezers
1 very lightly oiled marble slab or baking sheet

(1) Wash the strawberries, leaving the hulls on. Blot dry with paper towels.

(2) Place the sugar with ⅓ cup cold water in a clean, heavy, non-tin-lined saucepan. Cover the pan, and place it over high heat for 1 minute. Remove the cover, and continue cooking the sugar, without stirring, for 3 to 4 minutes, or until it reaches the hard-crack or light-caramel stage (295 to 330 degrees on a candy thermometer). Remove the pan from the heat.

(3) Dip the strawberries in the molten sugar, holding each berry by the stem with pliers or tweezers. Hold the berries over the pan to allow the excess sugar to drip off, then lay them on the oiled slab or baking sheet. When the sugar has cooled to a

glasslike shell, gently pry the berries off the oiled surface and arrange them on a platter.

Candy-coated strawberries are very perishable—the fruit juices dissolve the sugar. Try to serve them within two hours of dipping.

Italian Peppered Strawberries

SERVES 6

THIS recipe comes from Lotte Mendelsohn, host of a popular New England talk show and author of *Italian Provincial Cooking* (Yankee Press). Mendelsohn got the recipe from a listener, who says that Italians are devouring peppered strawberries with an enthusiasm bordering on frenzy.

    1 quart fresh strawberries (about 3 cups sliced)
    ½ cup granulated sugar, or to taste
    ¼ cup sambuca or other Italian anise-flavored liqueur
    ¼ cup Grand Marnier or other orange-flavored liqueur
        Fresh black peppercorns in a grinder (set on coarse grind)

    3 cups vanilla ice cream (optional)

(1) Wash, drain, and hull the strawberries, and cut them lengthwise into ¼-inch slices. Place in a large glass bowl.

(2) Ten minutes before serving, mix in the sugar, liqueurs, and 10 grinds of black pepper. Spoon the ice cream into chilled bowls. Spoon the strawberry mixture over the ice cream. Grind a little more fresh pepper on top and serve at once.

The World's Best Blueberry Pie

NORMALLY SERVES 8,
BUT CAN BE DISPATCHED BY 1 OR 2 PEOPLE

I am leery about using the word "best" to describe a recipe. But not only was the following blueberry pie the best I ever tasted, it was so delectable I single-handedly devoured the whole thing at one sitting. The recipe comes from my longtime friend and cooking associate, Chris Kauth. The technique is a bit involved, but worth it once you understand the rationale. There are two methods of making fruit pies, Chris reasoned. In the first, you add the raw fruit to the crust, and wind up with a great fruit flavor but a filling that is as watery as soup. In the second method, you cook the fruit first to remove the excess liquid, but the resulting pie tastes suspiciously like it was made with canned fruit. Chris's innovation, and I have no doubt that it will revolutionize the art of baking, lies in cooking half the fruit to bind the liquid, and adding the other half of the fruit raw.

> 1 batch basic pie dough made with 2 cups flour (see recipe on page 476), or use a family favorite

> *For the filling:*
> 2 pints fresh blueberries
> 6 tablespoons butter
> ¾ cup brown sugar
> ⅓ teaspoon cinnamon
> Grated zest of 1 lemon
> Juice and grated zest of 1 orange
> ¼ cup white sugar, or more to taste if the berries are tart
> ⅓ cup cornstarch
> ½ teaspoon vanilla extract
> Juice of 1 fresh lime, or to taste

> *For the glaze:*
> 3 tablespoons milk
> 1 egg yolk

(1) Roll out two-thirds of the pie dough and use it to line a 10-inch glass pie pan. Save the remaining dough for the top.

(2) Wash and pick through the blueberries, removing any stems or withered berries. Place half the blueberries in a heavy saucepan with the butter, brown sugar, cinnamon, and citrus zest. Bring this mixture to a boil, and cook the berries for 3 to 5 minutes, or until tender.

(3) Whisk the orange juice, white sugar, and cornstarch to a smooth paste in a small bowl. Stir this mixture into the blueberries, and bring the mixture to a boil—it should thicken. Remove the pan from the heat and cool. When the mixture is completely cool, whisk in the remaining blueberries, plus the vanilla and lime juice to taste. Add additional sugar if necessary: the mixture should be pleasantly sweet and refreshingly citric.

(4) Preheat the oven to 425 degrees. Spoon the filling into the pie crust. Roll out the remaining dough and make a crust or lattice for the top. Beat the milk and egg yolk together to make the glaze. Brush the edges of the crust with glaze to seal the top to the bottom crust. Brush the top crust with glaze. Bake the pie at 425 degrees for 15 minutes, then reduce the heat to 325 degrees and continue baking for 30 to 45 minutes, or until the crust is nicely browned. Blueberry pie is delicious warm (try it with vanilla ice cream); it isn't bad cold, either!

Blackberry Gratin with Mascarpone Custard

SERVES 6 TO 8

JOHANNA Killeen and her husband, George Germon, run a remarkable restaurant called Al Forno. Its location is Providence, Rhode Island, but it might well be a village in Tuscany: the grilled pizza will make you feel like you've rediscovered the art of eating. That's not to pooh-pooh the desserts: this berry gratin left us speechless. The custard owes its incredible richness to Mascarpone, an Italian cheese that is a cross between a French triple crème and Devonshire clotted cream. Mascarpone is sold at most gourmet shops, but acceptable results can be obtained with softened cream cheese.

2 pints fresh blackberries or raspberries

For the custard:
 1 cup milk
 ½ cup granulated sugar
 2 egg yolks
 ¼ cup flour
 1 tablespoon butter

To finish the gratin:
 ½ cup Mascarpone cheese
 ⅔ cup heavy cream
  Approximately ¼ cup confectioners' sugar

1 large or 6 to 8 small gratin dishes

(1) Pick through the berries but do not wash. Prepare the custard. Place the milk with ¼ cup of the sugar in a heavy saucepan and scald it over medium heat. Meanwhile, combine the egg yolks and remaining ¼ cup sugar in a large bowl and whisk until smooth. Whisk in the flour. Whisk in the scalded milk in a thin stream. Return this mixture to the saucepan and simmer for 2 to 3 minutes, whisking vigorously—the sauce will thicken. Transfer the custard back to the bowl, dot the top with butter to prevent a skin from forming, and let cool.

(2) Using a whisk or wooden spoon, cream the Mascarpone with 2 tablespoons of the heavy cream: the cheese should be light and fluffy. Fold it into the cooled custard. Beat the remaining cream to soft peaks and fold it into the custard mixture.

(3) Assemble the gratin. Lightly butter the gratin dish or dishes and fill with half the custard mixture. Arrange the berries on top and sprinkle them with a light dusting of confectioners' sugar. Spread the remaining custard on top. The recipe can be prepared to this stage up to 4 hours before baking.

(4) Just before serving, preheat the oven to 500 degrees. Bake the gratin for 4 to 5 minutes or until the top is lightly browned and the fruit begins to juice. Lightly sprinkle the gratin with more confectioners' sugar, and serve at once.

JULY

Then came hot July, boiling like to fire
That all his garments he had cast away;
Upon a lion raging yet with ire
He boldly rose, and made him to obey.

EDMUND SPENSER

M O S T months are named for goddesses or gods, but July honors a mortal. His name is well-known to students of Latin: Gaius Julius Caesar. August is the vacation month, but the weather is actually hotter in July. Sirius, the Dog Star, rises with the sun this month, and the Romans believed that their combined rays were responsible for heat waves. The hottest days of the year, July 3 to 11, became known as the *caniculares dies*, the "dog days," an expression we still use today. The Anglo-Saxons called July *Hen-Monath*, "hay month," and the profusion of flowers and summer grasses is well-known to sufferers of hay fever. Despite the heat—or perhaps because of it—July has traditionally been a time of revolution.

July 25 is St. James' Day, sacred to the patron saint of Spain, whose emblem is the sea scallop. According to folklore, chicory gathered at noon on St. James' Day has the power to make you invisible—but only if you cut it with a golden knife. (We prefer the Louisianan use for this bitter root as a flavoring for coffee.) Eat oysters on St. James' Day, the English believed, and you'll never want for money.

July also brings a profusion of stone fruits: peaches, plums, apricots, and nectarines. It was in July of 1904 that St. Louis confectioner Charles F. Menches wrapped some ice cream in a waffle for a lady who was carrying flowers (she couldn't hold both), thereby inventing the ice cream cone. Ice cream is, indeed, an excellent remedy for assuaging the dog day torpors. July is a prime month for seafood buffs. Swordfish and tuna are plentiful, and if you vacation at the shore, you can dig for quahaugs and steamers. Be on the lookout for fresh herbs in July, and remember that flowers aren't just for smelling. I look forward to pickling nasturtium buds in July and adding the peppery orange flowers to salads.

FLOWERS

F is for flower. The occupant of a well-dressed button hole. The centerpiece of a properly set table. Most of us use these blossoms strictly for decoration. However, many flowers are also edible, and can add substance, not mere style, to a meal. Not that eating flowers is anything new. Artichokes are a sort of budding sunflower, and saffron is the stamen of a crocus. Gardens burst into bloom in July. Here's a selection of edible flowers to lend a summer touch to your food.

Squash Blossoms: For centuries, Italians have gathered fresh squash blossoms for stuffing, breading, and frying. The squash blossom is a papery orange cone—just large enough to accommodate a snippet of cheese or a strip of prosciutto. In the south of France, squash blossoms are deep-fried and dusted with confectioners' sugar. To harvest squash blossoms, cut just below the point where the fruit meets the flower.

Nasturtiums: Here's another flower that is excellent for eating. The plant is closely related to mustard and watercress. (The name comes from the Latin words *nasus*, "nose," and *torquere*, "to twist" or "turn.") The bright orange-yellow flowers do indeed "twist your nose," adding a peppery, watercresslike flavor to salads. The rounded leaves are a tasty green in their own right. The seeds and buds can be pickled as a substitute for capers. Nasturtiums are a perfect flower for city dwellers; they prosper in poor, dry soil, uncomplainingly delivering their bouquets.

Roses: "A rose is a rose," observed Gertrude Stein. This fragrant flower has been associated with fine dining for over two thousand years. The Roman Emperor Heliogabalus doted on rose wine—for bathing as well as drinking! Nero spent the equivalent of $150,000 on roses to embellish a single feast. Rose-flower water is an important flavoring in the desserts of the Near East. Rose hips are made into preserves (see recipe on page 467), and in France the petals are candied to make an edible decoration for cakes.

Violets: These tiny purple flowers are hardly a staple these days, but at one time they were highly regarded as a flavoring. They were added whole to salads, and preserved in syrups, powders, and conserves. Violets lent their perfumy fragrance to numerous liqueurs, one of which is still made: Parfait Amour. (Parfait Amour is bottled by the Dutch distilling concern Bols, and is an ingredient in the multicolored after-dinner drink *pousse café*). Candied violets are used by the French for decorating desserts.

Borage: The star-shaped flowers of this medicinal herb are purple, with a white base and black stamens. Borage flowers taste like spicy cucumbers: use them in salads or to garnish a Pimm's Cup cocktail.

Chive Flowers: The chive flower looks like a purple cotton-ball. When picked in the unfurled-bud stage, it is excellent in soups and salads.

Hyssop: Hyssop was a popular cooking herb during the Middle Ages. The tiny purple flowers lend a colorful note to salads.

Lavender: This perfumy flower is one of the flavorings in classical herbes de Provence. The French use it to flavor vinegar, and one chef I know adds it to the spice powder used in pan-blackening.

Lily Buds: If you've ever eaten Chinese hot and sour soup, you've probably tasted this flower. The slender, elongated, unfurled bud of the tiger lily is popular in China, where it is dried for later use as a texture food in soups and stir-fries. To use, soak the buds in warm water for 30 minutes or until supple.

Marigold: The yellow petals of this summery plant add a nutty flavor to stews and custards. According to herb expert Annie Carter, the best variety for eating is the single-flowered pot marigold.

The only edible flowers commercially sold are squash blossoms (and on rare occasion, nasturtiums). You may be able to find some of the others at an herb grower or nursery. When using flowers from a garden, make sure they haven't been sprayed with pesticides or treated with systemics. I have kept squash blossoms for up to three days by storing them, loosely wrapped in a wet paper towel, in an unsealed plastic bag in the refrigerator. But most flowers are highly perishable: try to use them the same day you pick them.

Stuffed Squash Blossoms

SERVES 6 TO 8 AS AN HORS D'OEUVRE

IF you have a garden, this dish is a delectable method of squash population control! The following recipe features four different stuffings: prosciutto, anchovies, sun-dried tomatoes, and sage leaves. Fontina is a rich, pungent, meltingly soft cheese —be sure to use authentic Italian fontina.

1 pound (30–35) squash blossoms

For the fillings:
½ pound Italian fontina
1–2 very thin slices of prosciutto
6–8 anchovy fillets, drained
6–8 sun-dried tomato halves
6–8 sage leaves

For the batter:
1 cup ice water
1 egg yolk
1 cup flour

1 cup olive oil
1 cup vegetable oil
Salt and fresh white pepper

(1) Gently open the squash blossoms and pinch out the stamens (the upright filaments in each flower). Wash the blossoms and gently pat dry with a paper towel. Cut the cheese into matchstick-sized pieces 2 inches long and ¼ inch square. Cut the prosciutto and sun-dried tomatoes into thin slivers, the anchovies in half lengthwise.

(2) Divide the blossoms into four batches. Stuff one batch with slivers of cheese and prosciutto, one of each to a flower. Stuff the second batch with cheese and anchovy fillets. Stuff the third with cheese and sun-dried tomatoes. Stuff the fourth with cheese and sage leaves.

(3) Just before serving, heat the oils to 375 degrees in a shallow frying pan. (There should be ¾ inch of oil in the pan.) Combine the ice water and egg yolk in a bowl. Add the flour, and using a fork or chopstick, beat the ingredients just to mix. Do not overbeat or the batter will be tough. Dip each squash blossom in batter and fry it in oil for 30 seconds per side or until golden. Drain on paper towels. Season with salt and pepper and serve at once.

Squash Blossoms *Rellenos*

MAKES 16 PIECES—
SERVES 4 AS AN APPETIZER OR LIGHT ENTRÉE

THIS recipe gives an Italian twist to that Mexican favorite, *chiles rellenos*. The best blossoms for stuffing are zucchini flowers. Use a mild cheese, like Monterey Jack or Munster. Serve Squash Blossoms Rellenos with Tomato Vinaigrette with Dill (see recipe on page 305).

16 large unblemished squash blossoms

2 fresh or pickled jalapeño chilies
6 ounces mild white cheese, coarsely grated
2–3 tablespoons pine nuts
16 small sprigs cilantro (optional)

For the batter:
3 eggs, separated
Pinch each of salt, cream of tartar, and white pepper
Approximately 1 cup flour

Approximately 2 cups oil for frying

(1) Gently open the squash blossoms and pinch out the stamens (the upright filaments in each flower). Wash the blossoms and gently pat dry with a paper towel. Roast and peel the chili or chilies, as described on page 318, and cut into 16 slivers (see Note on page 48). Stuff each squash blossom with grated cheese, a few pine nuts, a sliver of chili, and a sprig of cilantro, if using. The recipe can be prepared to this stage up to 24 hours before frying.

(2) Just before serving, prepare the batter. Beat the egg whites to firm peaks, adding salt and cream of tartar after 10 seconds. The whites should be stiff but not dry. Beat the yolks in a small bowl. Whisk a quarter of the whites into the yolk mixture and gently fold back into the remaining whites. Meanwhile, heat the oil in a heavy shallow pan to 375 degrees. Dip each stuffed squash blossom in flour, shake off the excess, and dip it into the egg mixture. Fry the blossoms in hot oil for 30 seconds per side, or until golden brown. Drain on paper towels.

To serve, spread a platter or plates with tomato vinaigrette or salsa and arrange the blossoms on top.

Pickled Nasturtium Buds

MAKES 6 CUPS

PICKLED nasturtium buds are a good substitute for capers. I like to use them for antipasti—people have no idea what they are. Like all preserves, these make great gifts for the holidays.

4–5 cups nasturtium buds

For the brine:
  ½ cup salt

For the pickle mixture:
  3 cups white wine vinegar
  6 cloves garlic
  3 bay leaves, broken in half
  6 sprigs fresh thyme
  2 teaspoons mustard seeds
  2 teaspoons black peppercorns

  6 1-cup canning jars

(1) Prepare the brine in a large nonaluminum mixing bowl by dissolving the salt in 2 quarts water. Wash the nasturtium buds and soak in the brine for 24 to 36 hours. Place a plate on top to keep them submerged.

(2) Combine the ingredients for the pickling mixture and 1 cup water in a medium saucepan, and simmer over a low flame for 5 minutes. Meanwhile, sterilize the canning jars. Drain the nasturtium buds and divide evenly among the jars. Ladle the pickling mixture over the buds, trying to place a garlic clove, bay leaf, thyme sprig, some mustard seeds, and some peppercorns in each jar. Seal the jars and store at least 2 weeks before using. Continue to refrigerate the nasturtium buds once the jars are open.

Rose Petal Preserves

MAKES 2 TO 3 PINTS

ROSE petal preserves make a wonderful gift and you can be reasonably certain that the recipient does not own a jar already! The preserves make elegant jam tarts. Prepare a batch of *meurbeteig* (see recipe on page 263) and roll it out to a ¼-inch thickness. Cut out 2-inch circles, make a depression in the center of each, and fill with a half teaspoon of preserves. Bake the cookies in a preheated 375-degree oven for 5 to 10 minutes, or until golden. A perfect treat for your next afternoon tea! Another recipe from my assistant, Marcia Walsh.

> 1½–2 quarts gently packed, clean, unsprayed rose petals
> 1 cup unsweetened apple juice
> 4 cups sugar
> ¼ cup fresh lemon juice
> 2 strips lemon peel (removed with a vegetable peeler)
>
> 6 1–cup jars

(1) Remove the white heel from the petals (it tends to be bitter), place the petals in a large nonaluminum saucepan or stockpot, and pour 3 cups boiling water over them. Using a wooden spoon, gently push the rose petals down into the water, bruising them to release their flavor. Cover the pan and allow the petals to steep for 20 to 30 minutes. With a slotted spoon, transfer the petals to a piece of cheesecloth and squeeze the juice out of them into the pan. Reserve the petals.

(2) Add the apple juice, sugar, lemon juice, and lemon peel to the rose water and bring to a full rolling boil. Reduce the heat and simmer until the liquid reaches 220 degrees on a jelly thermometer, or until it sheets when dropped from a metal spoon. Skim off the froth and remove the lemon peel.

(3) Return the petals to the preserves, and stir to separate the petals and distribute them evenly. When the mixture returns to the jelly stage, remove from the heat and ladle into hot, sterilized

jars. Wipe any drips from the edge of the jar with a damp paper towel, and seal with preserving lids or paraffin. If using the former, turn the jars upside down and right them again before allowing them to cool. This kills any bacteria that may be present on the lids of the jars. Store in a cool, dry place.

CLAMS

CONSIDER the clam—a most remarkable creature. It has lived on earth unchanged since eons before dinosaurs existed. It ranges in size from a few microns to six feet across, and changes its sex according to season. Clams are delectable raw, steamed, baked, and fried; they turn up in preparations as varied as pasta, pie, and pancakes. Americans like hard-shell clams enough to eat 16 million pounds a year.

Long before the beatniks spoke of "bread" and "clams," this bivalve was associated with money. The Indians made wampum —beads used for currency—from the purple lining of the quahaug shell. The Latin name for the common clam is *venus mercenaria,* "money-loving beauty." Our term *clam* comes from the Anglo-Saxon *clam,* a "bond" or "fetter," and is related etymologically to the word *clamp.*

Quahaugs: What most people mean by "clams" are really quahaugs (pronounced "*ko*-hogs"), also known as hard-shell clams. Quahaugs are sold by size, the smallest fetching the highest price.

Named for Little Neck Bay on Long Island, *littlenecks* are the smallest quahaugs, and the best clams for enjoying on the half shell. A true littleneck measures less than two inches across— the meat is incredibly sweet and tender. *Cherrystones,* named for Cherrystone Creek, in Virginia, are medium-sized quahaugs, measuring from two to two-and-a-half inches across. These too are good raw on the half shell, and are also nice for steaming. What are called *chowder clams* measure over three inches across —these are full-grown quahaugs. They are too tough to eat raw, but add lots of flavor to chowders and pies, and are excellent, minced, in stuffings.

Soft-shell Clams (*Steamers*): The soft-shell clam is an East Coast delicacy, although fifty years ago it was considered fit only for bait. It takes its name from its thin, fragile shell, which never closes completely. Soft-shells are elongated, ranging from one to three inches in length. Another distinguishing feature is the "neck," a long, protractable syphon capable of squirting a sharp stream of water when the clam is in danger—a Cape Cod nickname for the soft-shell is "piss clam"! The best way to enjoy soft-shells is steamed with melted butter for dipping, or battered and fried to a golden brown.

Razor Clams: The razor clam is spurned on the East Coast but relished in the Pacific Northwest. It is shaped like an old-fashioned straight razor, and the thin shell is as sharp as a blade. Razor clams are fast diggers, so gathering them is a challenge. (The most efficient method is to pour salt on the hole—the clams will pop out of the sand like asparagus. This practice is forbidden in many states, so consult the local shellfish warden before trying it.) The razor clam is exceptionally meaty (the digging foot accounts for over half the body). The flavor lies somewhere between that of a quahaug and a scallop.

Goeduck (pronounced "*goo*ey duck"): This is another giant clam, and the only one "hunted" with a "gun," actually a slender tube, which is placed over the hole and covered—the suction enables the hunter to pull the clam out of the sand. This long, phallus-shaped bivalve is a popular item at sushi bars.

Pacific Butter Clams: This small, thin-shelled clam is a treat seldom seen outside the Pacific Northwest. It is usually eaten in chowder.

When buying clams look for bivalves with tightly closed shells. Limp, drooping necks on steamers and razor clams are a sign that the clam has been out of the water too long. Store clams on ice or at the bottom of the refrigerator; if they are fresh, they will keep one to two days. Scrub the shells with a brush to remove surface sand and grit. Discard any bivalves with broken shells or shells that fail to close when tapped.

Clams are most tender when raw, so keep cooking times brief. The larger, tougher quahaugs should be ground or very finely chopped.

Soft-shells (steamers) taste best steamed. Clean them as described above and place in a large pot with ½ inch water, white wine, or sea water. Cover the pot and steam the clams for 5 minutes, or until the shells just open. Serve the steamers in one bowl, the broth in another, and melted butter in a third, and provide a fourth bowl for the empty shells. Remember to pull the black membrane off the "neck" (the siphon), then dip the clam in broth, then butter, and pop it in your mouth.

Both hard-shells and steamers can be barbecued. Place the bivalves on a grill or on glowing coals till the shells gap, then remove them with tongs. Delicious!

Rhode Island Stuffies

SERVES 4

A "stuffie" is what Rhode Islanders call a stuffed quahaug. (This diminutive state harvests more quahaugs than any other.) This recipe won a blue ribbon at the Annual International Quahaug Festival in North Kingston, Rhode Island.

```
12 3-inch quahaugs
 4 strips bacon
 1 small onion
 1 clove garlic
4–6 tablespoons butter
 ½ teaspoon each dried marjoram, thyme, and oregano
 4 tablespoons chopped fresh parsley
1½ cups fresh bread crumbs, plus extra if necessary
    salt and fresh black pepper
    Pinch of cayenne pepper, or to taste
```

(1) Scrub the quahaugs and place in a large pot with 2 cups water. Cover tightly and boil for 5 to 10 minutes, or until the shells just begin to open. Let the quahaugs cool, then take them from their shells, reserving the shells and 1 cup of the cooking liquid. Chop the quahaugs—but not too finely—by hand, or in a food processor or meat grinder. This can be very messy, so work over a large pan to catch any juices.

(2) Meanwhile, cut each strip of bacon into three, and cook in a sauté pan over medium heat for 4 to 5 minutes, or until the bacon is crisp. Transfer the bacon to paper towels to drain, reserving 1 tablespoon of the fat. Peel and finely chop the onion and garlic. Add 2 tablespoons of the butter to the pan, followed by the onion, garlic, and herbs. Cook over medium heat for 2 minutes, or until the onion is soft. Add the chopped quahaugs and sauté for an additional 2 minutes, or until the clams are heated through.

(3) Preheat the oven to 350 degrees. Spread the bread crumbs on a baking sheet and lightly toast them in the oven. Moisten them with 1 cup of the reserved quahaug broth strained through a cheesecloth. Combine the crumbs with the mixture in the frying pan. Add salt, black pepper, and cayenne to taste. If the mixture is too wet, add a handful of bread crumbs.

(4) Select the 12 best-looking shells and fill each one with the quahaug mixture, mounding it high in the center. Top each stuffie with a curl of bacon and a pat of butter. The stuffies can be prepared ahead to this stage; they can even be frozen.

Bake the stuffies in the preheated oven for 15 minutes, or until piping hot. Provide a little Tabasco sauce on the side for those who require more spice.

Taiwanese Marinated Clams

SERVES 4

THIS cold marinated-clam appetizer is popular in Taiwan. The recipe comes from Nina Simonds, a cooking teacher, author, and friend, who spent several years in Taiwan. Black vinegar is sold at Chinese grocery stores; if unavailable, use equal parts Worcestershire sauce and wine vinegar.

> 24 **cherrystone clams**
> 2 **cloves garlic**
> 1 **slice (¼-inch) fresh ginger root**
> 2 **scallions**
> 1 **chili**
>
> *For the marinade:*
> ¼ **cup soy sauce**
> 2 **tablespoons rice wine or sherry**
> 1 **tablespoon black vinegar**
> 2 **teaspoons sugar**

(1) Scrub the cherrystones. Mince the garlic, ginger, and scallions. Discard the seeds of the chili and mince as well (see page 48 for a note on handling chilies). Add these flavorings to the clams with ½ cup water. Cover the pan and steam the clams for 6 to 8 minutes, or until the shells just barely open.

(2) Combine the ingredients for the marinade in a large bowl. Transfer the clams to the bowl with a slotted spoon. Add most of the steaming liquid and spices, leaving the sandy dregs in the pot. Marinate the clams in this mixture for 12 to 24 hours stirring form time to time.

To serve, transfer the clams to individual bowls, spooning a little of the marinade on top.

Chappaquiddick Clam Chowder

SERVES 4

NEW England clam chowder is a gastronomic glory that has fallen on hard times. These days, it's apt to be made with canned clams from God-knows-where and thickened to the consistency of mud. The best chowder I ever tasted, all modesty aside, was one I made while staying on Chappaquiddick. Every morning I would sail my windsurfer to the shallows of Katama Bay and dig up a few dozen littlenecks for dinner. Now that was chowder!

    18–20 littlenecks, or 12 3-inch chowder clams
        6 strips bacon
        1 leek, green leaves and furry root discarded
        2 tablespoons flour
          Approximately 2 cups bottled clam broth or liquid reserved
          from cooking mussels or steamers
        2 large potatoes
        1 cup heavy cream
          Salt and fresh black pepper

(1) Shuck the clams, working over a bowl to catch the clam juice or liquor, as it is called. (If you live in a seaside town, you may be able to purchase your clams already shucked.) Coarsely chop the clams by hand or in a food processor. Measure the reserved liquor and add to it enough bottled clam broth to obtain 4 cups liquid.

(2) Cut the bacon into ¼-inch slivers. Wash and finely chop the leek. Place the bacon in a large saucepan over medium heat, and cook it for 1 minute, or until the fat begins to render. Add the leek, and continue cooking until the bacon is lightly browned and the leek pieces are tender. Stir in the flour. Stir in the clam broth and reserved clam liquor and bring to a boil. Peel the potatoes and cut them into ½-inch cubes. Add the potatoes to the chowder and gently simmer till almost tender. The recipe can be prepared to this stage up to 24 hours before serving.

(3) Just before serving, add the heavy cream and chopped clams. Gently simmer the chowder for 2 to 3 minutes, or until the clams are cooked, adding salt and plenty of fresh black pepper to taste. (*Note:* Chowder is even better the second day, but reheat it as gently as possible.)

Quahaug Pie

NO Cape Cod recipe generates as much controversy as the one for quahaug pie. Should it be made with salt pork or butter? One crust or two? Should the clams be coarsely chopped or ground as fine as hamburger? Traditionally, a small cup is placed in the center of the pie to keep the top crust from becoming soggy. This looks silly, so feel free to omit it when serving the pie to guests.

For the pie:
　　1 2-cup batch basic pie dough (see recipe on page 476)

　　2–3 dozen quahaugs (enough to make 2½ cups meat)
　　½ cup cracker crumbs
　　1 small onion
　　2 stalks celery
　　3 tablespoons butter
　　1 cup milk
　　¼ cup clam liquor
　　1 egg
　　2 egg yolks
　　　Fresh black pepper, cayenne pepper, and perhaps a little salt
　　1 egg beaten with a pinch of salt for glaze

For the sauce:
　　3 tablespoons butter
　　3 tablespoons flour
　　1 cup reserved clam liquor or clam broth
　　1 cup light cream

　　1 9- or 10-inch pie pan
　　1 small teacup or shot glass

(1) Prepare the pie dough and chill for 30 minutes.

(2) Shuck the clams, working over a bowl to collect the liquor. Set the liquor aside. You should have between 2 and 2½ cups meat. Chop it as finely as possible or grind it in the food processor. Stir in the cracker crumbs.

(3) Finely chop the onion and celery. Melt the butter in a small sauté pan and cook the vegetables over medium heat for 3

to 4 minutes, or until soft but not brown. Stir them into the clam mixture. Add the milk, egg, egg yolks, seasonings, and ¼ cup of the reserved clam liquor, and beat until smooth.

(4) Preheat the oven to 350 degrees. Divide the dough in two. Roll out the larger half and use it to line the pie pan. Spoon in the filling. Brush the edge of the lower crust with egg glaze and set a small teacup or shot glass in the center. Roll out the remaining dough and drape it over the pie to form a top crust. Cut off the excess dough, crimp the edges with a fork, and brush the top crust with egg glaze. Bake the quahaug pie for 1 hour, or until the crust is nicely browned.

(5) Meanwhile, prepare the sauce. Melt the butter in a small saucepan and stir in the flour to make a roux. Cook the roux for 1 minute. Strain in the clam liquor or broth off the heat, add the cream, then simmer the sauce for 3 to 4 minutes, adding pepper, cayenne, and salt (if necessary) to taste. Serve clam pie in wedges, with the sauce spooned over it. Drink a Muscadet or Samuel Adams beer.

SWORDFISH

Nature her bounty to his mouth confined
Gave him a sword, but left unarmed his mind.

Thus wrote Oppian about *xiphas gladius,* the swordfish. (The *gladius* was the sharp sword carried by Roman legions, which gave us the word *gladiator*.) Nautical books abound with accounts of attacks on wooden boats by this rapier-billed creature. Recently, one intrepid fish went so far as to attack the research submarine *Alvin!*

Even without its sword, *xiphas gladius* is a formidable fish, attaining lengths of fifteen feet, with an average of six to nine feet. It is also a mysterious fish: its reproductive cycle is imperfectly understood, and babies are seldom landed. Swordfish spend most of the year in midocean, passing through shallower coastal waters from June through September.

Swordfish are caught one of two ways, by longline or harpoon. The former are hooked on lines up to a mile long, which are checked every forty-eight hours. Thus a longline swordfish could be dead for two days by the time it is hauled on the boat, and for up to ten days when it reaches the market. (Aficionados claim to be able to recognize a longline fish by a thin layer of lavender tissue just below the skin.) If you are lucky enough to live in an area where fishmongers make the distinction, harpooned swordfish is your best bet. Avoid swordfish with smooth, circular marks on the surface—the sure sign that the fish have been frozen, stacked like logs, and sawn with a circular blade into steaks. When buying swordfish, avoid steaks cut from too close to the tail or fins. These will be veined with white sinew and gristle, which remain tough even when cooked.

Swordfish is king of the steak fish, a tight-grained beauty with a firm flake and a flavor that is rich, buttery, and unique. It is well-served by such dry cooking methods as grilling, broiling, and baking. For broiling or grilling I cut swordfish into steaks no more than ½-inch thick. This enables the interior to be cooked without drying out the surface. Occasionally, you can find smoked swordfish, which is a delicacy in Portugal.

Swordfish with Lemongrass

SERVES 4

LEMONGRASS is a spear-shaped herb with a pungent citrus flavor, popular throughout Southeast Asia. Fresh lemongrass is available in Chinese and Southeast Asian markets; dried lemongrass (and this is an herb that dries well) is often sold at health food shops. (It is used for making tea.) There is no real substitute, although the zest of a lemon better approximates its flavor than the sour juice. Fish sauce is the Southeast Asian equivalent of soy sauce, made with fermented fish instead of soy beans. The sauce below can also be used for poultry or beef.

1½ pounds swordfish steaks

For the lemongrass sauce:
   4 stalks fresh lemongrass, or 2 tablespoons dried
   4 scallions
3–4 tablespoons Vietnamese or Thai fish sauce
2½ tablespoons honey
   1 teaspoon Vietnamese or Thai chili sauce, or Szechuan hot chili oil, or even Tabasco sauce
   Juice of ½ lemon, (about 2 tablespoons)

(1) Preheat the oven to 400 degrees. Cut the swordfish across the grain into ¼-inch-thick slices, and place in a glass or ceramic bowl. Lightly oil a baking dish just large enough to hold the fish in a single layer.

(2) Prepare the sauce. Cut the tips (top 3 inches) off the lemongrass stalks and discard. Finely chop the lemongrass and scallions, and combine with the remaining ingredients. Taste the sauce; you may need to add more lemon juice, fish sauce, or honey—it should be a little sweet, a little salty, a little hot, and very lemony. Pour the sauce over the fish, and marinate for 10 to 15 minutes, turning the steaks once or twice.

(3) Arrange the swordfish steaks in the baking dish and pour the sauce on top. Bake the steaks in the preheated oven for 15 minutes, or until the steaks flake easily when pressed. Prior to serving, scrape most of the lemongrass mixture off the fish (it is rather fibrous). Boiled rice makes a good accompaniment.

Variations: This recipe can also be prepared with hake, cod, tuna, halibut—in short, any fish but the most delicate sole.

Piccata of Swordfish

SERVES 4

THIS recipe was inspired by a dish I enjoyed at the Oyster Bar at Grand Central Station.

1½ **pounds swordfish**
   Salt and fresh black pepper
2 **lemons**
2–3 **tablespoons capers**
   6 **tablespoons clarified butter (see page 471), or 3 tablespoons butter and 3 tablespoons oil**

For the batter:
   3 **eggs**
   ½ **cup freshly grated Parmesan**
2–3 **tablespoons flour, plus ½ cup for dusting the fish**

(1) Cut the swordfish across the grain into ¼-inch medallions. Sprinkle lightly with salt and generously with pepper.

(2) Cut the ends off one of the lemons and carefully pare away the rind to expose the pulp. (The French call this *pêler à vif*, "to skin alive".) Cut the lemon widthwise into paper-thin slices, carefully removing any seeds. Rinse and drain the capers.

(3) Prepare the batter. Whisk the eggs, adding the cheese and enough flour to obtain a mixture with the consistency of heavy cream.

(4) Heat the clarified butter, or butter and oil, in a large skillet over medium heat. Dust the swordfish pieces with flour, then dip them in the batter. Pan-fry them in the butter for 1 to 2 minutes per side, or until the coating is golden brown and the fish feels firm when pressed. Transfer the picatta to warm plates or a platter. Deglaze the pan with juice from the second lemon, adding salt, pepper, and additional lemon juice to taste.

(5) Top each piccata with a few capers and thin lemon slices. Spoon a little lemon-butter sauce over each piece and serve at

once. A simply cooked, bright-green vegetable, like spinach or kale, would go well. So would a tart dry white wine, like a Gavi or Verdicchio.

Swordfish *Tabaka* (with a Spicy Orange Marinade)

SERVES 4

THE marriage of fruit with grilled meats is typical of Balkan cooking. *Tabaka*—a cinnamon-orange marinade—is a specialty of Georgia, in south-central Russia. The tabaka marinade is usually used for poultry, but it also goes well with meaty seafood like swordfish. For extra zing, we suggest brushing the cooked kebabs with umeboshi plum paste, a tart relish made from salted Japanese plums. The latter can be found at health food stores and Japanese markets.

1½ pounds swordfish steaks

For the marinade:
  2 cinnamon sticks
  Juice of 2 oranges
  Juice of 1 lime
  Juice of 1 lemon
  ½ cup dry white wine
  ½ cup vegetable oil
  1 clove garlic, minced
  1 small onion, diced
  1 1-inch piece fresh ginger root, thinly sliced
  1 tablespoon paprika
  1 teaspoon sugar
  ½ teaspoon salt and plenty of fresh black pepper
  Cayenne pepper and freshly grated nutmeg to taste
  2 tablespoons plum paste for serving (optional)

8 large bamboo skewers

(1) Skin the swordfish and cut it into 1½-inch cubes. (Do not buy the precut cubes available at some fish shops—they tend

to be tough, undesirable pieces of fish.) Combine the ingredients for the marinade in a nonaluminum bowl and marinate the fish 2 to 3 hours.

(2) Drain the swordfish and thread it on the skewers. Prepare the coals in your hibachi or grill, and grill the swordfish for 4 minutes per side, or until cooked, basting with marinade. Brush the kebabs with the plum paste just before serving. Swordfish tabaka goes well with rice pilaf and a buttery California Chardonnay.

CHERRIES

THESE luscious morsels are the most fleeting of summer fruits. They appear in their true glory at the end of June and are gone by mid-August. As with tomatoes and strawberries, cherries sold before their time are like vulgar imitations.

Cherries were popular in Colonial times. They were used to make a beverage called ratafia—sipped by diplomats to toast the ratification of treaties. Today, the U.S. grows more of these tiny fruits than any other country in the world. Traverse City, Michigan, is the self-proclaimed "Cherry Capital," but the bulk of the crop comes from Washington State, Oregon, and California.

But which cherry? There are over a hundred varieties to choose from. For the cook's purposes, cherries fall into two basic categories: sweet and tart. The former are ideal for eating raw, while the latter are used for cooking and preserving.

Bing cherries, supposedly named for a Chinese gardener who found the seedling on a trash heap, are the best-known sweet cherry, and the first to ripen. The Bing cherry is large, plump, and round, with a dark-red, almost mahogany-color skin and sweet flesh. Sour cherries, known as Morellas or Amerelles, are less easy to find.

Two famous spirits are made from cherries: kirsch and maraschino. The former, a cherry brandy, owes its nutty, almond flavor to the use of the pits as well as the fruit. Maraschino is a liqueur made from fermented cherries and honey.

Cherries gain 30 percent of their bulk the last two weeks on the stem, so the moment of picking is crucial. When buying cherries, look for plump, round fruits with firm, shiny skins. A dull surface, shriveled skin, or leaking stem indicate a cherry that is past its prime.

Tart cherries are best for cooking, but sweet cherries can be used if you add lemon juice and reduce the amount of sugar. A cherry pitter looks like a manual hole-punch, and can be purchased at any gourmet shop. One pound of stemmed, unpitted cherries equals three cups. It takes three to four pounds of whole cherries to make one quart stemmed, pitted fruit. Cherries can be preserved in a simple syrup (made by boiling 1½ cups sugar with 2 cups water). Split, stemmed, pitted cherries can be dried in a low oven (130 degrees for 12 hours): raisins never tasted so good!

Hungarian Tart Cherry Soup

SERVES 6

TART cherry soup is an Austro-Hungarian classic. Sour cherries are the traditional fruit, but the soup can be made with Bings or other sweet cherries, provided you reduce the sugar and substitute sour cream for the heavy cream.

> 2 pounds fresh sour cherries
> 1 cup sugar
> 1 large cinnamon stick
> 10 cloves and 10 allspice berries, wrapped in cheesecloth or perforated foil
> 2 strips lemon peel
> Pinch of salt

1 tablespoon arrowroot
½ cup heavy cream
¾ cup dry red wine

(1) Pit the cherries over a bowl, saving any juices. Combine the cherry juice with enough water to make 3 cups liquid, and place in a saucepan with the sugar and spices. Bring to a boil and add the cherries. Reduce the heat and simmer for 10 to 15 minutes, or until the cherries are tender. Remove the cinnamon stick, spice bag, and lemon peel.

(2) Dissolve the arrowroot in 2 tablespoons of the cream, and stir this paste into the remaining cream. Stir the cream and wine into the cherry mixture and boil for 1 minute. Chill the soup to room temperature, then refrigerate till cold. The recipe can be prepared to this stage up to 24 hours before serving.

Serve Hungarian tart cherry soup in chilled glass bowls. If you like, garnish with rosettes of whipped cream or sour cream.

Roast Duckling with Cherries

SERVES 4

ROAST duckling with cherries is a classic of French cuisine. The dish is traditionally made with sour cherries, but I rather like it with Bings.

2 4–5 pound ducklings (fresh, if possible)
½ lemon, plus 2 strips lemon zest
  Salt and fresh black pepper
2 cinnamon sticks

For the sauce:
  Giblets from the ducks
2 shallots
1 carrot, peeled
1 branch celery
1 clove garlic
2 cups brown stock (see recipe on page 473)
  Bouquet garni (see recipe on page 471)

For the cherries:
1½ pounds fresh cherries (2 cups pitted)
  ¼ cup sugar
  ¼ cup red wine vinegar
  ½ cup port
  1 stick cinnamon
  2 strips lemon peel

  1 tablespoon cornstarch or arrowroot
  2 tablespoons kirsch

(1) Preheat the oven to 450 degrees. Remove the giblets and wishbones from the ducks and any lumps of fat in the back. Drain off any liquid in the cavity and blot the ducks dry. Rub the skin with lemon and season the ducks with salt and pepper, outside and in. Place a cinnamon stick and some lemon zest inside each duck, and truss. Prick the skin (but not the meat) with a fork to release the fat. Set the duck in a roasting pan on a rack, and roast at 450 degrees for 30 minutes, then reduce the heat to 325 degrees. Cut the ducks in half lengthwise, using a cleaver or poultry shears. Discard the fat from the roasting pan, replace the ducks, cut side down, and roast for 1–1½ hours, or until the skin is golden brown and crisp.

(2) Meanwhile, prepare the sauce. Coarsely chop the giblets and vegetables. Add them to the roasting pan with the ducks, and roast for 45 minutes, or until well-browned. Place them in a saucepan with the stock and bouquet garni. Simmer the sauce for 30 minutes, or until 1 cup liquid remains.

(3) Meanwhile, pit the cherries—you should wind up with about 2 cups. Place the sugar in a small, heavy, non-tin-lined saucepan with 3 tablespoons water. Cook the sugar without stirring over high heat until it caramelizes (begins to brown). Remove the pan from the heat, add the vinegar, and stand back— the mixture will hiss like Mount Vesuvius! When it calms down, return the pan to the heat, and simmer, stirring with a whisk, until all the sugar is dissolved. Transfer the sugar mixture to a large saucepan, and add the cherries, port, cinnamon, and lemon peel. Cover the pan and gently simmer the cherries for 6 to 8

minutes, or until tender. Remove the cherries with a slotted spoon to a bowl. Boil the poaching liquid until only ½ cup remains.

(3) To finish the duck, strain the stock mixture into the cherry mixture. Bring it to a gentle boil, adding salt and pepper to taste. Dissolve the cornstarch in the kirsch, and whisk it into the sauce. When it returns to a boil, it will thicken. Drain the cooked cherries, and return them to the sauce. Correct the seasoning—it may be necessary to add a squeeze of lemon juice or a pinch of sugar. Place the duck halves on warm plates or a platter and spoon a little sauce on top. Serve the remaining sauce on the side. You'll want a fairly fruity wine with this dish: perhaps French Chambertin or Italian Amarone.

Kirschenknoedeln (Austrian Cherry Dumplings)

SERVES 4 TO 6

A few years ago, I had the pleasure of meeting Sophie Freud Lowenstein, granddaughter of Sigmund Freud and a psychotherapist in her own right. I was fascinated to hear about her grandfather, but we also talked of cooking. *Fruchtknoedeln,* fruit dumplings, were a childhood treat when Ms. Lowenstein lived in Vienna. The dough, which is made with potatoes, can be used with any stone fruit.

1 pound fresh sour cherries

For the potato dough:
2–3 boiling potatoes (a little less than 1 pound)
1 egg
⅓ teaspoon salt
Approximately ¾ cup flour, plus flour for your hands

To finish the dumplings:
  4 tablespoons butter
  ¼ cup sugar
  3 tablespoons fresh bread crumbs
  ⅛ teaspoon cinnamon (optional)

(1) Pit the cherries, leaving them as whole as possible. Cook the potatoes in their skins in gently boiling water for 6 to 8 minutes, or until soft but not mushy. Refresh them under cold water, drain, and cool.

(2) Prepare the dough. Peel the potatoes, and finely grate them or coarsely purée them through a ricer or a food mill. Beat the egg and salt in a bowl. Stir in the potatoes and enough flour to obtain a soft, malleable dough. (It should not, however, be sticky.) Cook a tiny piece of dough in boiling water—if it falls apart, add more flour. Let the dough rest for 15 to 20 minutes.

(3) Pinch off 1-inch pieces of dough, flatten with your thumb, and use them to envelop the cherries. If the dough sticks to your fingers, dip them in flour. Bring 4 quarts water to a rolling boil. Drop the dumplings in the water, lower the heat, and cook the dumplings at a gentle simmer for 5 minutes, or until they float to the surface. Remove them with a slotted spoon and drain on a dish towel. The recipe can be prepared to this stage up to 2 hours before serving.

(4) Just before serving, melt the butter in a large frying pan over medium heat. Stir in the sugar, bread crumbs, and cinnamon, if using, and cook until the bread crumbs begin to brown. Add the dumplings, swirling the pan to coat them with the crumb mixture. Cook the *Kirschenknoedeln* till thoroughly heated, and serve at once.

Wisconsin Cherry Pie

SERVES 6 TO 8

"MOST farms in the Midwest have fruit trees," writes my friend Darlene Peterson. "This pie was an annual treat and my favorite, made with sour cherries we picked ourselves." Reduce the sugar slightly if you must use sweet cherries.

1 1½-cup batch of your favorite pie dough (or see recipe on page 476)

3 cups fresh, pitted sour cherries (2½–3 pounds unpitted)
Approximately 1 cup sugar
2 tablespoons quick tapioca
⅛ teaspoon almond extract
2 tablespoons milk
2 tablespoons granulated sugar

1 8-inch pie pan

(1) Prepare the pie dough and chill for 30 minutes. Roll out two-thirds of the dough and use it to line the pie pan.

(2) Preheat the oven to 425 degrees. Gently mix the cherries, sugar, tapioca, and almond extract in a large bowl. Spoon this filling into the crust. Brush the edge of the bottom crust with milk. Roll out the remaining dough and use it to cover the pie, pressing the edges with your fingertips to join the top and bottom. Cut 5 or 6 slits in the top crust to allow the steam to escape. Brush the top crust with milk and sprinkle with the sugar.

(3) Bake the sour cherry pie for 35 to 45 minutes, or until the crust is golden brown and the filling is bubbly. Let cool to room temperature and serve.

STONE FRUITS

Little Jack Horner
Sat in a corner
Eating his Christmas pie
He stuck in his thumb
And pulled out a plum
And said, "What a good boy am I!"

NURSERY RHYME

LITTLE Jack Horner isn't the only one who likes plums. Or apricots, peaches, or nectarines. Our collective fondness for stone fruits is reflected in our colloquial speech: "a peach of a gal," "a plum of a job," "a precocious child" (the latter from the Latin word for apricot). But you don't need to be a linguist to appreciate a fragrant, ripe Georgia peach, a juicy plum, or a nectarine. Available from late spring to early fall, stone fruits reach their prime in July.

As the name suggests, the apricot is the first of the stone fruits to ripen. (Our word comes from the Latin *praecox,* "early ripener.") The Persians aptly named it "seed of the sun," and the Chinese believe the tree has oracular powers. Confucius completed his commentaries under an apricot tree; the sage Lao-Tzu was born under another. Considered a symbol of fidelity in the Near East, it is known by the lovely name of "moon of the faithful."

Unfortunately, apricots are among the most difficult fruits to enjoy ripe. When harvested prematurely, they never ripen completely, but when fully ripe, they are too fragile to transport. Your best bet is to find somone with an apricot tree; if you can't, select the softest, squishiest fruit you can find. The peachy, metallic fragrance is extraordinary.

Madame Récamier, the nineteenth-century French beauty, lay on her deathbed, and neither jewels nor her suitors' sighs could save her. She refused all food until someone brought her a dish of peaches and cream. They restored not only her appetite, but the lovely lady's will to live.

Peaches are a treat even when you're not on your deathbed! Few fruits are as wantonly luscious. The fuzz stings your tongue, the flavor explodes in your mouth, the juice dribbles sensuously down your chin.

Peaches come both white-fleshed and yellow: clingstone and freestone. Clingstone peaches are more flavorful but also more perishable. They are primarily for eating out of hand, as it's almost impossible to cut the fruit away from the pit and get neat slices for cooking.

Peaches are delicious with heavy cream and ice cream; their acidity also goes well with poultry. One of the best uses for the fruit is a *belini,* a cocktail made with puréed fresh peach and champagne.

The nectarine is a peach with a smooth skin and a flavor that suggests apricot and peach. Nectarines are said to have originated from mutant trees in China. Sometimes peach trees will bear nectarines, a reminder of their close parentage.

Plums are probably the most widespread stone fruit. There are hundreds of varieties, among them the greengage (the only plum to have a round seed); the large, green Wixton; and the prune plum (with its blue skin, yellow flesh, and easily removable stone).

Plums have long been associated with alcohol: the French make *eau de vie* from mirabelles (yellow, cherry-sized plums); the Yugoslavians favor *slivovitz* (plum brandy); and sloe gin is a cordial made with a tiny wild plum. Vacationers on Cape Cod and Martha's Vineyard use the tiny fruit of the beach plum for making jams and jellies (see recipe on page 466).

Plums, like peaches, come clingstone and freestone: eat the former and use the latter for cooking.

Ripe stone fruits should be yielding. If they fail the squeeze test, don't buy them. Another test of ripeness is smell: ripe stone fruit will be strongly perfumed. Apricots come into season first, then peaches and nectarines, and finally plums, which are available through September.

Fresh Apricot Mousse

SERVES 4

THIS fruit mousse owes its exceptional lightness to the fact that it does not contain gelatin. If the apricots aren't sufficiently sweet, add a little extra sugar to the poaching liquid. Similar mousses can be made from peaches or plums. My thanks for the recipe go to cooking teacher Ann Ayers.

> 1 pound fresh, ripe apricots
> Juice of 1–2 oranges (enough to make ½ cup)
> 2 eggs
> ⅓ cup sugar, or to taste
> Pinch of salt
> ½ teaspoon vanilla
> 2 tablespoons apricot brandy (or Grand Marnier)
> 1 cup heavy cream
> ¼ cup confectioners' sugar
> Fresh mint leaves for garnish (optional)

(1) Blanch the apricots in boiling water for 30 seconds, rinse under cold water, and remove the skins. Cut the apricots in half and remove the stones. Place the fruit in a shallow saucepan with the orange juice, and gently simmer over low heat for 10 minutes, or until the fruit is very soft. Purée the apricots with ¼ cup of the cooking liquid in a blender or food processor. Let cool.

(2) Using a mixer, beat the eggs at high speed for 2 minutes. Add the sugar and salt and continue beating for 6 to 8 minutes, or until the eggs are sufficiently stiff to fall from a raised whisk in a thick, silky ribbon. Gently fold in the apricot purée, followed by the vanilla and brandy.

(3) Beat the cream to stiff peaks, adding the confectioners' sugar as it thickens. Fold most of the cream into the apricot mixture, reserving ¼ cup for garnish. Spoon the mousse into wine glasses and chill for at least 2 hours. Pipe a rosette of whipped cream on each mousse, and garnish with a sprig of fresh mint.

Peaches Foster

SERVES 4

THIS recipe was born when another one failed: a chocolate torte I was planning to serve to forty people at a retreat group on Martha's Vineyard. Semisweet chocolate being unavailable, I tried using unsweetened: what emerged from the oven would have made macadam seem palatable. What do you do when you have no dessert, and only 10 minutes left till dessert time? You grab the nearest passable ingredients—peaches in this case—and improvise like crazy. The recipe below can be prepared in the kitchen or dining room.

- 4 large ripe peaches
- 4 tablespoons butter
  Approximately ¼ cup white sugar
- 3 tablespoons brown sugar
  Grated zest of 1 orange and 1 lemon
- 2 tablespoons peach brandy or schnapps
- 2 tablespoons dark rum
- 1 quart vanilla or peach ice cream

- 1 chafing dish (optional)

(1) Peel the peaches (blanch them in boiling water for 30 seconds first). Remove the stones, and cut each peach into 8 wedges.

(2) Melt the butter in a chafing dish or in a large skillet over high heat. Dip the peach slices in white sugar and sauté them in butter until golden brown and crusty. Transfer the peaches to a bowl with a slotted spoon.

(3) Add the brown sugar to the pan and cook until it is thick and bubbly. Add the citrus zest and spirits, and flambé if desired (see Note below). Boil this mixture until it is thick and syrupy. Add the peaches and simmer till warm.

(4) Serve peaches Foster over ice cream in individual bowls, or on plates.

NOTE: Flambéing has two purposes: to burn off alcohol (which has a harsh taste) and to impress your guests. The first can be accomplished simply by bringing the booze to a boil. For the second, you must bring the spirit in contact with an open flame. Alcohol must be warm (at body temperature) before it will ignite. Don't heat it too much, however, or the flammable alcohol will evaporate. To flambé over gas heat, add the liquid to the pan, warm for a few seconds, then tilt the edge of the pan toward the flames. To flambé with electric heat, add the liquid, warm for a few seconds, then hold a lit match over the pan. Be careful: alcohol sometimes ignites with an explosive whoosh. (Use baking soda to extinguish any accidents.)

Hot Peach Soufflé

SERVES 4

THIS hot peach soufflé is simplicity itself, consisting of fresh peach purée leavened with stiffly beaten egg whites. Apricot brandy or peach schnapps intensify the fruit flavor. If neither of

Plum *Kuchen*

SERVES 8

A *kuchen* is a Jewish fruit tart. The crust is made of *meurbe-teig,* a rich, crumbly dough that is often used to make cookies. Meurbeteig can be prepared ahead and frozen, but it should be made by hand, or it will be tough. The recipe comes from Dr. Carol Reich, a fine cook from New York.

For the meurbeteig:
  1 lemon
  3 cups flour
  1 cup butter
  2 egg yolks
  ¼ cup sugar

  1½ pounds fresh prune plums
  3–5 tablespoons sugar
  1½ teaspoons ground cinnamon

  1 9-inch springform pan

(1) Preheat the oven to 425 degrees. Prepare the meurbeteig. Finely grate the lemon zest, extract the lemon's juice, and reserve both. Cut the flour and butter together in a large bowl, using your fingers or a pastry cutter. (This is one of those times that a food processor will be of no help, as it tends to toughen the dough.) Work the butter and flour together until the mixture resembles gravel or coarse sand. Beat the egg yolks and ¼ cup cold water together and combine with the flour mixture. Add the sugar, lemon juice, and lemon zest last, continuing to mix by hand until there are no lumps of butter or flour remaining. The dough will be rough and somewhat sandy in texture.

(2) Press the dough into the bottom and sides of the spring-form pan. The dough should be about ½ inch thick on the bottom of the pan and about ¼ inch thick on the sides.

(3) Wash, quarter, and pit the plums. Press the fruit into the

dough in overlapping concentric circles. The plums should be firmly embedded in the meurbeteig crust.

(4) Combine the sugar and cinnamon, and sprinkle over the fruit. Bake the plum kuchen in the preheated oven for 30 to 35 minutes, or until the crust is golden brown and the fruit is bubbling hot. Serve plum kuchen at room temperature, with unsweetened whipped cream on the side.

AUGUST

The eighth was August, being richly arrayed,
In garments all of gold, down to the ground,
And he rode not, but led a lovely maid
By the lily hand, the which was crowned
With ears of corn, and full her hand was found.

EDMUND SPENSER

A U G U S T is vacation time. City dwellers flock to the coast or the mountains. In France, where people take their vacations seriously (a Frenchman at a cocktail party is apt to ask not "What do you do for a living?" but "Where do you go for vacation?"), Paris becomes a ghost town. The sun is bright, the weather is hot, although perhaps not quite so stifling as July.

August is named for the Roman statesman Gaius Octavianus Augustus. In Anglo-Saxon times, August 1 was Lammas Day (from the words "loaf" and "mass"), a holiday to welcome the harvest. On August 3, 1492, Christopher Columbus went a-sailing with three ships and 119 men: his discoveries introduced Europe to a host of new foods, including tomatoes, potatoes, peppers, turkey, and chocolate. August 15 is Assumption Day (commemorating the death of the Virgin), which Italians celebrate with a feast. August 22 is St. Philbert's Day, which traditionally marks the start of the filbert (hazelnut) season. Look for these tasty green nuts at specialty greengrocers.

August is a significant month for cooks and their equipment. August 19 marks the birth of Benjamin Thompson, a.k.a. Count Rumford, who invented the modern stove. And speaking of stoves, on August 23, the Romans celebrated Vulcanalia, the festival of the god of fire. August 24 is St. Bartholomew's Day, honoring a Christian martyr who was flayed alive in 44 A.D. Appropriately, Bartholomew is the patron saint of knives— the perfect gift for chefs. And on August 24, 1896, Cornelius Swartwout patented the waffle iron.

The Anglo-Saxons called August *Arn-Monath*, "harvest

month," and many fruits and vegetables are ready for picking. Corn attains sweetness unsurpassed during the rest of the year. This is the month for green tomatoes—ideal for frying and pickling. Summer squash is in season: look for pattypans, crooknecks, and marrows. Fruit lovers relish August raspberries, not to mention low-bush blueberries from Maine. And melons are particularly abundant.

Starting now and continuing through November, bluefish will be running off the northeast coast. Tuna and swordfish are plentiful, and lobsters are as inexpensive as they get. If you live near the shore, continue to look for periwinkles, mussels, and clams.

There is one place you don't want to be during the bright, sunny month of August: in the kitchen! Cold soups, salads, sushi and ceviche, and sorbets are ideal for summer feasting.

CORN

One for the squirrel,
One for the crow,
One for the cutworm,
And one to grow.

PILGRIM INSTRUCTIONS
FOR PLANTING CORN

As a Bay Stater, I'm mighty particular when it comes to corn. If I can't eat it within hours of harvesting, I would rather not eat it at all.

Corn is among the most perishable of vegetables. From the

moment it's picked, the sugar in the kernels undergoes an inex-
orable transformation into starch. For this reason, it's imperative
to enjoy it the same day (indeed the same afternoon) it is picked.
Mark Twain had the right idea about freshness, recommending
installing the boiling kettle right at the edge of the field.

Like peppers and tomatoes, corn is an American delicacy,
and has been cultivated in Central America for at least three
thousand years. Without it, the Pilgrims would never have sur-
vived their first rude winter in Plymouth.

For centuries, sweet corn on the cob was enjoyed solely by
the Indians, who grew it along the headwaters of the Susque-
hanna. It was discovered by white men on an expedition against
the Iroquois Indians in 1679. Benjamin Franklin called the
roasted ears "a delicacy beyond expression," and today it is a
favorite species for human consumption.

But which corn? Few vegetables are more botanically diverse.
There are varieties that grow two feet tall, and others that grow
twenty. The ears range in size from a few inches to two feet, with
sixteen kernels or five hundred. Midwesterners prefer yellow
corn; Southerners eat sweet, white "shoepeg" or "silver queen";
and we New Englanders favor "butter and sugar" corn, distinguished by its blend of yellow and white kernels.

When buying corn, look for ears with fresh, green husks and
clean, dry silk. But don't stop your investigations there. I always
strip back a little of the husk: the kernels should be firm, even-
sized, and plump with milky juices (it doesn't hurt to press one
with your fingernail). I favor ears with small kernels (they're
more tender), but not so small that they are undeveloped. Don't
worry if one end is marred by a worm hole (break it off and
discard it): the worms always go for the tenderest ears! The best
corn is sold from pickup trucks or farm stands that spring up
along country roads in August.

To cook corn—and do so as quickly as you can—bring
several quarts of water with a pinch of salt to a rolling boil. (I
also add a tablespoon of sugar if the corn is more than a day old.)
Add the husked corn to the water, and cook it for 2 to 3 minutes

once the water returns to a boil. The older or larger the kernels, the longer you will have to cook the corn—but never more than 5 to 6 minutes. Most people cook corn on the cob too long.

And serving? Rub the ears with butter (if you have lots of ears, use a pastry brush and melted butter) and sprinkle lightly with salt and pepper. I don't bother with pronged holders: eating with one's fingers appeals to the primeval caveman in all of us.

Enjoy the corn now, for the season will be over before you know it!

Corn Oysters

SERVES 2–4

CORN oysters were a popular New England snack in the nineteenth century. They take their name from their shape, which resembles a fried oyster. The recipe uses a technique called "milking" the corn: the rows of kernels are slit with a sharp knife, then scraped with the back of the knife to extract the milky pulp. (Corn was also "milked" to make puddings and custards.) The modern touch comes in using stiffly beaten egg whites to give the oysters a soufflélike consistency. This recipe comes from Boston's The Colony restaurant, which specializes in haute New England cuisine.

> 5–6 ears fresh sweet corn
> ¼ cup flour
> 2 eggs, separated
> Salt, fresh black pepper, cayenne pepper
> Pinch of cream of tartar
> 2 cups oil for frying
>
> 1 batch Spicy Tartar Sauce (see recipe on page 271)

(1) Working over a large bowl, "milk" two ears of corn (see above). You should wind up with ⅓ cup pulp. Slice the kernels

off the remaining ears of corn—you should wind up with ⅔ cup. Add them to the milked corn.

(2) Stir the flour into the corn mixture, followed by the egg yolks and seasonings. Add lots of cayenne pepper: the mixture should be highly seasoned. Beat the egg whites to stiff peaks, sprinkling in a pinch of salt and of cream of tartar after 10 seconds. Fold the stiffly beaten whites into the corn mixture.

(3) Heat the oil to 375 degrees in a shallow pan. Working with two spoons, form the batter into oyster-shaped fritters, and drop them into the hot fat. Fry the corn oysters, turning with a slotted spoon, for 1 minute, or until golden brown. Transfer them to paper towels to drain. Serve the corn oysters at once, on doily-lined plates, with ramekins of the tartar sauce for dipping.

Spicy Tartar Sauce

MAKES 1¼ CUPS

THIS recipe is prepared with homemade mayonnaise and homemade pickles at the Colony, but you could use good commercial brands.

1 cup mayonnaise (see recipe on page 477)
1 fresh jalapeño chili, seeded and minced (see Note on page 48)
2 tablespoons very finely chopped dill pickle
2 tablespoons drained, finely chopped capers
1 tablespoon finely chopped tarragon
1 tablespoon finely chopped parsley
1 tablespoon finely chopped chives
Approximately 1 tablespoon cider vinegar
Salt, fresh black pepper, and cayenne pepper

Whisk the flavorings into the mayonnaise, adding cider vinegar and seasonings to taste. The mixture should be piquant and highly seasoned.

Bay State Corn Chowder

SERVES 4 TO 6

CHOWDER originated in northern New England, where the early French settlers simmered fish in their *chaudières,* cast iron cauldrons. In landlocked areas, chowders were made from vegetables such as parsnips or corn. (For a richer chowder, use 1 cup light and 1 cup heavy cream, instead of the 2 cups light cream listed below.)

    5–6 ears fresh corn (enough for 2 cups kernels)
      3 tablespoons butter
      1 onion, finely diced
      1 rib celery, finely diced
      2 cups water or scalded milk
      2 potatoes, peeled and finely diced
      3 allspice berries
      3 whole cloves
      1 stick cinnamon
        Plenty of freshly grated nutmeg
    2–3 tablespoons brown sugar
        Salt and fresh black pepper
      2 cups light cream

Cut the corn kernels off the cobs with a sharp knife, and reserve. Melt the butter in a large pan, and sauté the onion and celery over medium heat for 3 to 4 minutes, or until soft. Add the water or milk, and the potatoes, spices, brown sugar, and seasonings, and gently simmer for 5 minutes, or until the potatoes are half cooked. Add the corn and cream, and continue simmering for 5 minutes, or until the vegetables are cooked. Correct the seasoning and sprinkle the chowder with freshly grated nutmeg before serving.

Corn Pudding

SERVES 4 TO 6

THE pudding is seldom a dish that gets epicurean hyperbole (no thanks to My-T-Fine). But puddings were popular in the nineteenth century, and they were not limited to desserts. Here's a corn pudding that's worthy of the most delicate French timbale.

> 5–6 ears fresh corn (enough to make 2 cups kernels)
> 1 cup heavy cream
> 3 egg yolks
> 1 tablespoon sugar (more or less, depending on the sweetness of the corn)
> Salt, fresh white pepper, freshly grated nutmeg
> 2 tablespoons butter, melted
>
> 4–6 ½-cup ramekins

(1) Cut the kernels off the corn. Whisk the cream with the yolks, sugar, and seasonings. Stir in the corn. Brush the ramekins with melted butter, chill, and brush with butter again. Spoon the mixture into the ramekins.

(2) Preheat the oven to 325 degrees. Place the ramekins in a small roasting pan with ½ inch boiling water. Loosely cover with foil, and bake the puddings for 30 to 40 minutes, or until the mixture is set. (When set, an inserted knife will come out clean.)

(3) Let the puddings stand for 15 minutes before unmolding. Run a sharp knife tip around the inside of each ramekin. Place a plate on top and invert. Gently shake the dish: the flan should slip out. Corn puddings are delicious served with poultry, veal, or fish.

C.D. Spach's Corn Dodgers

MAKES 12 TO 14 DODGERS, SERVING 3 TO 4

A dodger is a sort of griddlecake. The sweetness of the fresh corn and grainy richness of stone-ground cornmeal make a wonderful combination of flavors. C. D. Spach is a Virginia woodsman we know, and he spurns Yankee maple syrup for corn syrup, preferably an artisanal brand, like Roland's Pride, sold at roadside stands throughout the South.

- 1 cup all-purpose unbleached white flour
- 1 cup stone-ground cornmeal
- 1 tablespoon baking powder
- 1 tablespoon sugar
- Pinch of salt
- 2 eggs, beaten
- ¼ cup oil
- Approximately 1 cup buttermilk
- 2–3 ears fresh sweet corn
- 4 tablespoons butter

(1) Sift the dry ingredients in a bowl. Add the wet ingredients and beat just to mix. Cut the corn kernels off the cob, using a sharp knife, and stir them into the batter. (Note: The batter will thicken as it stands—it may be necessary to stir in a little more buttermilk.)

(2) Melt the butter in a large cast iron skillet over medium heat. Spoon the batter into the pan to make 3-inch pancakes. Fry each cake for 30 seconds per side, turning once with a spatula. Serve corn dodgers for breakfast with corn syrup and freshly brewed coffee. C. D. Spach recommends a side of Fried Green Tomatoes (see recipe on page 304).

LOBSTER

A greedy young spinster
ate, live, a lobster
and now every winter
when she sits dinner
as a kind of remonster
he pinches her inner.

WILLIAM GASS,
THE OMENSETTER'S LUCK

HENRY Fielding declared it an aphrodisiac. French novelist Gérard de Nerval walked one on a leash through the streets of Paris. Railroad tycoon Diamond Jim Brady supped on six or seven daily in the course of his gargantuan dinners. Lobster—delectable decapod, crimson king of the seas. Penny for pound, it's among the most costly sea creatures. It's also one of the most ferocious. Lobsters are shameless cannibals. Indeed, fishermen peg the claws less for their own safety than to protect the other lobsters.

Lobster hasn't always been a luxury food. The Pilgrims spurned it (perhaps because it was so readily available: the early settlers had but to wade into the water to gather bushelsful by hand). William Bradford, Governor of Salem, was shamefaced, indeed, when he could offer but "lobster and fresh water" to a new crew of colonists disembarking in 1623. The very name has humble origins: our word is a corruption of the Latin *locustra*, "locust." Fancy paying top dollar for a creature that's an overgrown insect!

Lobster's high price makes it a luxury, but like real estate, it costs less now than it will next year. Besides, someone should be able to tell our future grandchildren what the late, great lobster tasted like, since no one will be able to afford it in thirty or forty years!

The best time to buy lobster is during the summer months. The creatures move closer to shore, so they are easier—and cheaper—to catch. I prefer females: there's more meat in the tail, and sometimes you get a cache of bright orange roe. (This is also called coral—it's a delicacy.) To determine a lobster's sex, examine the first set of swimmerettes (tiny legs) on the underside at the juncture of the tail and body. A male's swimmerettes are stiff and bristly, the female's are feathery and soft.

Whatever the sex, make sure you buy lobster live and kicking. A good test for spunk is to invert the lobster: the tail should curl under, not droop, and the beast should wriggle violently. When a lobster dies, it loses its fluids, and its meat will taste dry and mealy. By the way, most precooked lobsters are crustaceans that died in the shop.

When possible, buy lobsters that are on ice, not in tanks: the latter absorb the water, which increases the price per pound. Lobsters don't feed in captivity, and although they can survive for months, the meat shrinks as they fast.

Every cookbook I have read maintains that a 10-pound lobster is as tender as a 2-pounder. I wonder if the authors ever ate one. You have to cook a 10-pounder longer to get it cooked in the center, and perforce, the meat at the edges gets rubbery. To my thinking, the best sizes are 1½–3 pounds—the former just right for one person, the latter just right for two. When buying larger lobsters, figure on 1½ pounds per person. Beware of "jelly-rolls," lobsters that have freshly molted. True, they are less expensive, but the meat is watery and bland.

The best way to cook lobster is to steam it in sea water. If you don't believe me, just visit one of the innumerable lobster "pounds" that dot the Maine coast. (The decapod is eaten at picnic tables outdoors, with melted butter as its sole accoutrement.) If sea water is unavailable, you can use the *court bouillon* on page 475, or lightly salted water.

A great deal has been written about the most humane way to kill a live lobster. I place the beast in a large pot with an inch of cold sea water. I put the pan on a high heat and leave it covered for at least 7 minutes. That way I am spared the final agony. (God will probably bring me back as a lobster.) Here are approximate cooking times for the various sizes:

1¼ pounds	8 to 10 minutes
1½ pounds	12 to 14 minutes
2 pounds	15 to 18 minutes
2½ pounds	19 to 24 minutes
for each additional pound	5 minutes

To tell when a lobster is cooked, lift up the carapace (the shell over the back of the body): the tomalley (the liver—the custardy green stuff) should be set but not too firm.

Americans tend to eat lobster simply: steamed, then dipped in melted butter. Europeans, who pay up to fifteen dollars a pound for their lobster, tend to stretch the meat with sauces, as in the recipes below.

Poor Man's Lobster Bisque

SERVES 4 TO 6

A bisque is a rich shellfish soup. But this recipe will please a pauper's purse, as it is made with lobster bodies (also called heads), which the fishmonger sells for a quarter apiece. (Better still, save and freeze the bodies left over from summertime lobster feasts.) If you're feeling lavish, add 1 to 2 cups diced lobster meat to the bisque at the end.

6–8 lobster bodies
  2 tablespoons flour
  3 tablespoons butter, softened
  1 carrot
  1 onion
  1 stalk celery
  1 clove garlic
  1 leek, furry root and green leaves discarded
  3 ripe tomatoes, or 1 14-ounce can imported plum tomatoes
3–4 tablespoons extra-virgin olive oil
  ¼ cup brandy
  ½ cup dry white wine
  3 tablespoons tomato paste
  5 cups fish stock or bottled clam broth, plus extra if necessary
  1 cup heavy cream
    Bouquet garni (see recipe on page 471)
    Salt, fresh black pepper, and cayenne peppper
1–2 cups diced, cooked lobster meat (optional)

(1) Using a cleaver, cut the lobster bodies in half. Remove the tomalley (the green lobster liver toward the rear of the head), and mix it with the flour and softened butter, using a whisk or fork. Reserve the lobster pieces and tomalley mixture. Finely chop the carrot, onion, celery, and garlic. Wash the leek (see page 123) and finely chop. Peel and seed the tomatoes (see page 304), and coarsely chop them.

(2) Heat the olive oil in a large pot and cook the carrot, onion, celery, and garlic over medium heat for 4 to 5 minutes, or until tender. Add the tomatoes, increase the heat to high, and cook for 1 minute. Add the brandy and wine, and bring to a boil. Add the remaining ingredients, except the lobster meat, and gently simmer for 40 to 50 minutes, or until very flavorful. (*Note:* If too much liquid boils away, add more stock.)

(3) Strain the bisque into a large pot, pressing hard to extract the liquid from the vegetables. Bring the soup to a gentle boil and whisk in the tomalley mixture. Simmer the soup for 2 to 3 minutes—it should thicken. Add salt and black pepper to taste, and plenty of cayenne—the bisque should be highly seasoned.

Stir in the lobster meat and serve. Lobster bisque, even for a poor man, deserves a good wine. I suggest an expensive white Burgundy or California Chardonnay!

Lobster Newburg

SERVES 2

THIS native American was invented by a gourmandizing sea captain, Ben Wenberg. His friend Charles Delmonico loved the dish and put it on the menu of his legendary New York restaurant. The story goes that Ben and Charles had a falling-out one day. By that time, Ben's creation had become a Delmonico's specialty, so Charles could hardly remove it from the menu. Instead he spitefully changed some of the letters around and lobster Wenberg became lobster Newburg.

1 1½- to 2-pound lobster
4 tablespoons butter
2 tablespoons flour
¼ cup Madeira
1 cup heavy cream
2 egg yolks
    A few drops lemon juice
1 teaspoon paprika
1 tablespoon Scotch or dry sherry
    Salt, fresh white pepper, and a pinch of cayenne pepper

(1) Steam the lobster in ½ inch water for 3 minutes. Reserve ½ cup of the steaming liquid. Cut the lobster in half lengthwise on a grooved cutting board, reserving the juices. Discard the papery sack at the front of the head, and the vein running down the tail. Scoop out the tomalley (the gray-green liver) and mix it with the reserved juices. Remove the meat from the claws and tail, and cut it into ½-inch pieces. Reserve the body-tail shell, and discard the empty claws.

(2) Melt 3 tablespoons of the butter in a sauté pan and cook the lobster pieces over low heat for 5 minutes, or until firm. Transfer the lobster to a platter and keep warm.

(3) Whisk in the flour and the remaining butter and cook for 1 minute to make a roux. Whisk in the ½ cup steaming liquid, Madeira, and heavy cream, and simmer for 5 minutes, or until the sauce is nicely thickened. Remove the pan from the heat.

(4) Whisk the egg yolks with the reserved tomalley and lobster juices. Gradually whisk this mixture into the sauce and return the pan to a low heat. Whisking steadily, heat the sauce to cook the yolks, but do not let boil, or the sauce will curdle. Whisk in the remaining ingredients and the diced lobster meat, and season to taste. Spoon the lobster Newburg back into the lobster shell or serve it on toast points. A Pouilly-Fumé or West Coast Sauvignon Blanc would be a good wine.

Lobster Thermidor

SERVES 2

THE year was 1794. In their zeal to establish a new order, French revolutionaries not only overturned the monarchy but also renamed the months of the year. July became Thermidor, the month in which the massacring Robespierre met his own death on the scaffold. One hundred years later, playwright Victorien Sardou launched a play called *Thermidor,* commemorating the last days of the French revolution. An enterprising restaurateur had the idea to create Lobster Thermidor, honoring the playwright. The play flopped and Sardou was forgotten, but Lobster Thermidor became a classic.

    1 1½- to 2-pound lobster
    ½ cup dry white wine
    3 tablespoons butter
    2 tablespoons minced shallots

1 tablespoon flour
½ cup heavy cream
2 teaspoons Dijon-style mustard
4 tablespoons freshly grated Parmesan
Salt, fresh white pepper, and cayenne pepper

(1) In a covered pot, steam the lobster in the white wine for 5 minutes. Reserve the liquid from the steaming. When the shellfish is cool enough to handle, cut it in ·half lengthwise on a grooved cutting board, reserving the juices. Discard the grey sack at the front of the lobster's head, and the dark vein running the length of the tail. Reserve the tomalley (the green lobster liver). Remove the claws and crack. Remove the lobster meat from the shell and cut into 1-inch pieces. Reserve the body-tail shell, and discard the empty claws.

(2) Melt 2 tablespoons of the butter in a frying pan and sauté the lobster meat for 3 to 4 minutes, or until cooked. Remove it from the pan and keep it warm. Add the shallots to the pan and sauté for 1 minute. Stir in the flour. Add ½ cup of the lobster steaming liquid, the lobster juices, tomalley, and cream. You should have a little more than 1 cup sauce. Simmer the sauce for 3 minutes, whisking vigorously. Whisk in the mustard and Parmesan, and salt, pepper, and cayenne to taste. Stir in the lobster meat, then spoon the mixture into the shells. The recipe can be prepared to this stage up to 2 hours before baking.

(3) Just before serving, dot the Lobster Thermidor with the remaining butter and bake in a preheated 400-degree oven for 10 minutes, or until it is thoroughly heated and the top is lightly browned. You'll want a wine of strength and refinement—I would suggest a Premier Cru Chablis.

BLUEFISH

THEY have "well been likened to an animated chopping-machine, the business of which is to cut to pieces and otherwise destroy as many fish as possible in a given space of time. . . . They move along like a pack of hungry wolves, destroying everything before them. Their trail is marked by fragments of fish and by the stain of the blood in the sea." Thus wrote Spencer F. Baird in a report to the United States Fish Commission in 1874. The species in question was not the Amazonian piranha, but the common North American bluefish.

The bluefish lives up to its reputation as "bulldog of the sea." The bulletlike head is filled with razor-sharp teeth; the body is lean and muscular; the disproportionately large tail drives the fish at prodigious speeds. It is estimated that bluefish eat twice their weight in other fish each day. Feeding schools have been known to chase their prey right out of the water.

Many people dislike bluefish, or think they dislike bluefish, because they have never tasted it fresh. And unless it is fresh, it is simply not worth eating. Bluefish is a highly predacious fish. It has strong digestive enzymes that cause the meat to spoil quickly. Like other fast swimmers, it contains lots of muscle hemoglobin (the dark strip running the length of the fillet), which makes the meat taste fishy. Even the blue-gray flesh, which partially lightens when cooked, has a way of turning people off.

That's the bad news. The good news is that when it is fresh, bluefish is as fine a morsel as ever graced a pisciphile's plate. Its flavor is delicate; its texture is soft; its long, moist flakes are deliciously meaty. There's more good news: bluefish contains a highly unsaturated fish oil that has been shown to reduce cholesterol and triglyceride levels, fatty plaque deposits on artery walls, and overall risk of heart attack.

Bluefish is abundant in the Atlantic from Florida to Cape Cod. The fish migrate north in the spring and summer, and south in the fall. They are at their peak in late summer. The price will let you know when bluefish are running in your area; in season they sell for as little as two dollars a pound. East Coasters are obviously at an advantage here, but airfreight makes it possible to find fresh bluefish in the Midwest.

When buying bluefish, look for whole fish with clear eyes, or fillets that are firm and shiny, not desiccated and drab. Juvenile bluefish are called *snappers* (their snapping teeth click like castanets); one-pound bluefish are called *choppers* (again for their table manners). Snappers and choppers tend to be milder than adult bluefish, and they are good for pan-frying or broiling.

Bluefish is best cooked by a dry method, like baking, broiling, or grilling. Being an oily fish, bluefish does well with acidic flavorings, such as tomato and lemon juice. Its forthright flavor will stand up to the most assertive spices, such as cumin, ginger, and soy sauce. Bluefish tends to taste less "fishy" served chilled the next day. Smoked, it can hold its own with sable or smoked salmon.

Bluefish Chowder with Chorizo and Saffron

SERVES 4

CHORIZO is a sausage flavored with cumin and chili—feel free to use linguiça (a spicy Portuguese sausage), hot Italian sausage, or even kielbasa in its place. This chowder is extremely versatile: add ½ pound more bluefish, cut back on the clam broth and cream, and it becomes a stew; add ½ cup flour and 3 eggs, and you can bake it in a crust as a pie.

1 pound skinless bluefish fillets
Generous pinch (about ⅛ teaspoon) of saffron
2–3 leeks, white part only (enough to make 1 cup chopped)
2 large potatoes
6 ounces chorizo
2–3 tablespoons extra-virgin olive oil
3 cups bottled clam broth, fish stock, or chicken stock
1 cup heavy cream
Salt and fresh black pepper

(1) Run your fingers over the fillets, feeling for bones, and remove any you may find with tweezers or needlenose pliers. Cut the fish into 2-inch pieces. Soak the saffron in ¼ cup hot water. Trim and wash the leeks (see page 123), and thinly slice. Peel the potatoes and cut them into ¼-inch slices. Cut the chorizo into ¼-inch slices. (Most chorizo is already cooked, but if yours is not, sauté the slices in 1 tablespoon oil over medium heat for 3 to 4 minutes, or until the fat is rendered and the sausage is cooked. Pour off the fat and reserve the sausage.)

(2) Add the olive oil and leeks to a large saucepan and sauté over medium heat for 3 to 4 minutes, or until the leeks are tender. Add the chorizo, potatoes, clam broth or stock, and saffron (and its soaking liquid), and bring the soup to a boil. Add the cream, bluefish, and salt and pepper, and simmer for 5 to 8 minutes, or until the potatoes are soft and the fish is cooked. Add additional salt and pepper to taste. Bluefish chowder calls for the sort of crisp, pleasantly acidic wines for which the Iberian Peninsula is famous. My vote would go to *vinho verde,* "green wine" from the north of Portugal.

Bluefish with Mustard Glaze

SERVES 4

BLUEFISH with mustard glaze is one of my summertime favorites. Like all good summer dishes, this one can be prepared in a jiffy. Some people (myself included) like a touch of sweetness with bluefish—if you are one, add a spoonful of honey to the glaze.

2 tablespoons mustard seeds
2 tablespoons dry white wine
1½ pounds skinless bluefish fillets
  Salt and fresh black pepper
1 tablespoon butter
⅓ cup Meaux-style (grainy) mustard
⅔ cup mayonnaise (see recipe on page 477 or use a good commercial brand)
  Juice of ½ lemon, or to taste

1 baking dish just large enough to hold the fish, buttered

(1) Soak the mustard seeds in the wine for 20 minutes.

(2) Run your fingers over the fish, feeling for bones. Extract any you find with tweezers or needlenose pliers. Cut the fish fillets into 4 equal portions and season with salt and pepper.

(3) Preheat the oven to 450 degrees and preheat the broiler. Prepare the mustard glaze. Drain the mustard seeds. Whisk the seeds, grainy mustard, and lemon juice into the mayonnaise, adding salt or pepper to taste. Make 4 mounds of glaze in the baking dish. Arrange the fish pieces on top. Spread the remaining glaze on top of the fish.

(4) Bake the bluefish for 10 to 15 minutes in the preheated oven, or until the fish flakes easily. Place the pan under the broiler for 1 minute, or until the glaze is puffed and browned. A Greco di Tufo from southern Italy would be a good wine.

Bluefish with Moroccan Spices

SERVES 4

THE fragrant flavors of cumin, coriander, turmeric, and ginger are characteristic of the cooking of Morocco. This robust sauce goes well with dark-fleshed fish, like kingfish, jack, and mackerel.

1½ pounds skinless bluefish fillets

For the spice mixture:
  2 teaspoons ground cumin
  1 scant teaspoon ground coriander
  1 scant teaspoon turmeric
  ¼ teaspoon cinnamon
  1 teaspoon salt
  Fresh black pepper and pinch of cayenne pepper

For the tomato sauce:
  1 medium onion
  2 cloves garlic
2–3 fresh ripe tomatoes, or 4–6 canned tomatoes (about 1 cup chopped)
  3 tablespoons extra-virgin olive oil
  Juice of ½ lemon, or to taste
  3 tablespoons chopped fresh cilantro or flat-leaf parsley for garnish

  1 12-inch baking dish (or one just large enough to hold the fish), lightly oiled

(1) Preheat the oven to 400 degrees. Run your fingers over the fish fillets, feeling for bones, and remove any you find, using needlenose pliers or tweezers. Combine the ingredients of the spice mixture in a small bowl. Rub half the spice mixture into the fish.

(2) Prepare the tomato sauce. Thinly slice the onion and garlic. Peel and seed the tomato, as described on page 304, and coarsely chop. You should wind up with approximately 1 cup. Heat the olive oil in a non–cast iron skillet. Add the onions and cook over medium heat for 3 to 4 minutes, or until soft and golden, adding the garlic and remaining spice mixture after 2 minutes. Add the chopped tomato and cook for 3 minutes or until most of the tomato liquid has evaporated. Add salt, pepper, lemon juice, and any of the other spices to taste: the sauce should be aromatic and spicy. Spoon half the sauce into the baking dish, place the fish on top, and spoon the remaining sauce over the fish. The recipe can be prepared to this stage up to 4 hours ahead.

(3) Loosely cover the fish with oiled foil and bake it in the preheated oven for 15 to 20 minutes, or until the sauce is bubbly and the fish flakes easily when pressed. Sprinkle the cilantro or parsley on top and serve at once.

Couscous—a grainlike starch made from semolina—would make an excellent accompaniment.

Bluefish Teriyaki

SERVES 4

THE Oriental ingredients in this recipe—ginger, soy sauce, sesame oil—help cut the inherent oiliness of the fish. Mirin, sweetened rice wine, is available in any Japanese market. In its absence, substitute white wine sweetened with a little sugar. The fish can be braised in the oven, but it is even better cooked on the grill. The recipe is also delicious made with salmon.

1½ **pounds bluefish fillets**
2 **tablespoons toasted sesame seeds**

For the marinade:
4 **tablespoons soy sauce**
3 **tablespoons mirin**
3 **tablespoons sesame oil**
2 **tablespoons maple syrup**
1 **teaspoon Asian chili sauce (optional)**
2 **strips lemon zest (remove them with a vegetable peeler)**
  Juice of ½ lemon
1 **clove garlic, sliced**
3 **scallions, chopped**
1 **1-inch piece ginger root, sliced**

(1) Remove the skin from the fish by pressing it between the knife and the cutting board and sliding the knife the length of fish. Cut away or pull out any bones, and cut the fish on the diagonal into ½-inch-thick medallions. Combine the ingredients

for the marinade, adjusting the proportions to suit your taste. Marinate the fish for 4 to 8 hours, turning it several times.

(2) To braise the fish, place it in a lightly oiled baking dish with the marinade on top. Loosely cover it with foil and bake it in a preheated 400-degree oven for 20 minutes, or until the fish flakes easily, spooning the marinade on top as the fish bakes.

To grill the fish, drain it and place it on an oiled, preheated grill. Grill it for 1 to 2 minutes per side, basting it liberally with marinade. (*Note:* It helps to have a wide spatula for turning the fish.) To prevent the fish from crumbling, you may wish to wrap it in foil. Perforate the foil with a fork to allow the smoke flavor to penetrate it. Once the first side is cooked and inverted, open the foil and spoon the marinade on top.

(3) Sprinkle the fish with sesame seeds. Serve bluefish teriyaki with white rice. An Alsatian or Californian Gewürztraminer would make a good wine.

SQUASH

THIS time of year I am beleaguered by zucchini. Oh, they mean well enough, those green-thumbed friends who leave basketfuls of squash at my doorstep. Mother Nature has gone haywire, and as I am the cook, I'm the one to whom they bring zucchini the size of melons and baseball bats. It's enough to make you look forward to winter, when vegetable gardens are covered with snow!

But if August brings unmanageable quantities of zucchini, it also brings such once-a-year delicacies as crookneck and pattypan squash. There are hundreds of squash varieties, all indigenous to the Americas. Summer varieties differ from winter squash in that they are eaten when botanically immature—that is, when the skin is still paper-thin and the seeds are undeveloped. The flavor diminishes as the size increases. Zucchini growers, beware! Below are some of the varieties we can look forward to in the upcoming weeks.

Crookneck: This bright-yellow squash is six to eight inches long, with bumpy skin covering a bulbous base tapering to a slender, curving neck.

Italian Marrow: If ever a vegetable looked phallic, it is the light-green Italian marrow. Imagine a pale zucchini that is stretched like Pinocchio's nose, and you've got the right idea. An inch or two in diameter, Italian marrows have been known to grow three to four feet in length.

Pattypan: The alternative names tell a lot about this one. It is also called *bush scallop* (on account of its scalloped edges) or *custard marrow* (because it looks like an inverted flan). The pattypan is a hockey puck-shaped squash with scalloped edges and pale green or yellow skin. Its rotund shape makes it ideal for stuffing.

Scallopini: This squash resembles a pattypan, but it is deeper and more cylindrical. Its light-green rind is often speckled like that of a zucchini.

Zucchini: Most people are familiar with the dark-green variety, but more and more markets are carrying yellow or even white zucchini. This cucumber-shaped squash tastes best when it is small.

Spicy Summer Squash Salad

SERVES 4

THIS unusual salad features zucchini and crookneck squash cut into the smallest dice possible (such a fine dice is called a *brunoise*). The cilantro adds a Mexican accent—if you don't like this pungent herb, substitute flat-leaf parsley or fresh basil.

1 small green zucchini
1 small yellow zucchini or crookneck squash
1 ear of corn (optional)
1 fresh or pickled jalapeño chili
4 tablespoons chopped fresh cilantro
3 scallions
1 head radicchio or butter lettuce (for garnish)

For the dressing:
　　Juice of 1 lime, or to taste
1–2 teaspoons red wine vinegar or pickled jalapeño chili juice
　　2 tablespoons extra-virgin olive oil, or to taste
　　Salt and fresh black pepper to taste
4–5 Szechuan peppercorns, crushed in a mortar and pestle or
　　under a skillet

(1) Wash the squash and cut off the ends. Cut each squash into ⅛-inch dice. (To do so, make a series of lengthwise parallel slices, rotate the squash 90 degrees, and make a second set of parallel cuts, then cut the squash widthwise into ⅛-inch slices.) Cut the corn kernels off the cob, if using. Cook the kernels for 1 minute in boiling water, refresh under cold water, and drain. Cut the chili in half (see Note on page 48) and discard the seeds, unless you like your food really spicy, in which case keep them. Mince the chili as finely as possible. Finely chop the cilantro and scallions. Wash and dry the lettuce leaves, leaving them whole.

(2) Combine the ingredients for the dressing in a large bowl, and whisk. Add the vegetables and herbs, and mix well. The salad should be tart and spicy—add additional lime juice, oil, or salt and pepper as necessary. Just before serving, spoon the salad into lettuce leaf cups. Serve at once.

My Grammie Ethel's Squash Pancakes

SERVES 4

GRAMMIE Ethel favors pattypans, but you could use any summer squash.

> 3–4 small pattypan or other summer squash (1 pound in all)
> 1 small onion or 2 scallions
> 1 egg, beaten
>   Salt, fresh black pepper, and a little freshly grated nutmeg
> ¼–½ cup flour
> 4–6 tablespoons unsalted butter
>   Sour cream and chopped fresh chives for garnish

(1) Grate the squash on the coarse side of a hand grater or using the shredding disk of a food processor. Chop the onion very finely. Combine the vegetables in a bowl with the egg and seasonings. Stir in enough flour to make a thickish batter.

(2) Heat the butter in a large skillet over medium heat. Spoon the batter into 3-inch pancakes and fry them for 3 minutes per side, or until golden brown. Blot the pancakes on paper towels and serve at once, topped with sour cream and chives.

Crookneck Squash *Aillade* (with Garlic and Herbs)

SERVES 4

HERE'S a quick, tasty way to prepare any summer squash. This *aillade* makes a perfect vegetable for fish. If rosemary is unavailable fresh, use another herb: what's important here is freshness.

1 medium-size or 2 small crookneck squash or zucchini
3 tablespoons extra-virgin oil oil
1 clove garlic, minced
4 tablespoons finely chopped flat-leaf parsley
3 tablespoons finely chopped chives or scallions
1 tablespoon finely chopped rosemary (or tarragon or other fresh herb)
Squeeze of fresh lemon
Salt and fresh black pepper

(1) Cut the squash into ⅛-inch slices, discarding the ends.

(2) Just before serving, heat the oil in a wok or large frying pan over high heat. Add the garlic and herbs, and sauté for 10 seconds. Add the squash and cook, stirring constantly, for 1 minute, or until tender. Stir in the lemon juice, and salt and pepper to taste. The virtue of this dish is its spontaneity: serve at once.

Fried Zucchini Sticks with Blue Cheese Dipping Sauce

SERVES 6

SOMETIMES the best-tasting recipes are those that are the simplest. Consider these fried zucchini sticks, a specialty of the London Chop House in Detroit. Fried zucchini sticks can also be served with the mustard sauce on page 470.

3–4 small zucchini (1½ pounds)
2 eggs
1 cup milk
1½ cups flour
2 tablespoons paprika
½ teaspoon salt
Fresh black pepper and cayenne pepper
1 quart oil for frying

1 batch Blue Cheese Dipping Sauce (see recipe on page 293)

(1) Wash the zucchini and cut off the ends. Cut the zucchini lengthwise into ¼-inch strips. (*Note:* The zucchini can be cut by hand, on a mandoline, or in a food processor fitted with a french fry disk.)

(2) Combine the eggs and milk, and beat thoroughly. In a large bowl or paper bag, combine the flour, paprika, and salt, and black pepper and cayenne to taste.

(3) Heat the oil to 350 degrees in a wok or electric skillet. Dip the zucchini strips in the egg mixture and transfer to a strainer to drain. Toss the sticks with the seasoned flour, shaking off the excess. Fry the strips for 2 to 3 minutes, or until golden brown, working in several batches to avoid overcrowding the pan. Serve at once with the dipping sauce.

Blue Cheese Dipping Sauce

MAKES ABOUT 1 CUP

2 ounces Maytag, Saga, or other blue cheese
½ cup sour cream
¼ cup light cream, or to taste
Fresh black pepper and perhaps a little salt

Combine the ingredients in a blender or food processor, and purée until smooth.

MELONS

WHEN I was growing up, Baltimore was pretty much a backwater. We still had a "melon man," who rode a horse-drawn wagon piled high with enormous, ripe watermelons. Occasionally, my father would stop to purchase one—at that time, I was more interested in sneaking a lump of sugar to the horse. Those are the sweetest melons I ever tasted, especially when seasoned with twenty-five years of nostalgia!

Melons belong to the cucumber family, and have been cultivated since the time of the Pharaohs. Certain stones on Mount Carmel are called "Elijah's melons"—legend has it that the owner of the land refused to supply food for the prophet, so as punishment his melons were turned into stone. Melons were enormously popular during the Renaissance: Ronsard praised them in his odes; Montaigne was "excessively fond" of them; and in 1583, no less a personage than the dean of the College of Doctors of Lyons published a "Succinct Treatise on Melons," outlining fifty different ways of eating the fruit, such as in fritters, soups, and compotes.

Although all melons belong to the same species, there are hundreds of different varieties. When it comes to cross-pollination, melons are positively promiscuous! Below are some of the types you are apt to find at market.

Boule d'Or: As the name suggests (in French it means "golden ball"), this one looks like a gold-hued honeydew. The taste is also similar to that of a honeydew.

Canary: an elongated yellow melon with a ridged rind. More pungent than a honeydew.

Cantaloupe: named for Cantalupo, a papal garden near Tivoli, where the variety was developed. A true cantaloupe has a fragrant orange flesh and deeply ridged rind. What most of us call cantaloupe is actually a muskmelon.

Casaba: a large, onion-shaped melon with a yellow, deeply ridged rind. Similar in taste to a canary.

Cranshaw: a large, roundish melon whose smooth, yellow rind is dappled with green. Cranshaws ripen rather later than most melons—they are available into November.

Honeydew: This spherical fruit, with its smooth, cream-colored rind, is one of our most popular melons. Given its honeylike sweetness, the name is particularly apt.

Muskmelon: similar to the cantaloupe, but smaller, with a netted rind and shallow ridges. Muskmelons are sweeter than cantaloupes.

Watermelon: Mark Twain, who was not one to mince words, called it "chief of this world's luxuries . . . When one has tasted it, he knows what angels eat." Watermelons can be round or oval, ranging in length from eight to twenty-four inches. The flesh can be bright red, pale pink, or even yellow. Farmers test the ripeness of a watermelon by thumping: as long as it sounds metallic, it isn't ripe.

Melons lack the starch reserves of other fruits, and consequently they don't ripen or become sweeter once picked. (They will, however, become softer.) Therefore, the melon should be left on the vine till the last possible moment. When the sugar within reaches its highest level, the melon will break cleanly away from the stem. Other tests for ripeness include pressing the "button" or "eye" (the stem end): it should be slightly yielding. A ripe melon emits a perfumed scent. Avoid melons with soft or dark spots. When possible, avoid melons with part of the stem left on: they were probably cut off the vine before ripe.

The best way to enjoy melon is simply: halved, seeded, and eaten with a spoon. Melon and prosciutto ham is a classic combination; so is a melon half-filled with port. Melon also does well in chilled soups and salads. The hollowed shell of a watermelon can be sculpted into an ornamental bowl or basket—fill it with fruit salad.

Spicy Melon Relish

MAKES 3 CUPS

ONE of the most enjoyable new trends on the restaurant scene is the resurrection of the American diner. Our youthful chefs are rediscovering such homey dishes as mashed potatoes and meatloaf. This spicy melon relish comes from the very exemplar of the species—the Blue Diner in Boston. It goes well with fish. Then again, I like to eat it straight with a spoon!

1 ripe cantaloupe
1 ripe honeydew melon
1 cucumber
1 small purple onion
1 jalapeño chili, or to taste
4 tablespoons chopped cilantro or flat-leaf parsley
   Juice of 1–2 limes, or to taste

(1) Cut the melons in quarters and scrape out the seeds. Cut away the rind and chop the melon flesh into ¼-inch dice. You will need 1 cup of each melon (use any excess in a fruit salad). Peel and seed the cucumber and cut into ¼-inch dice. Finely chop the onion. Seed and mince the chili (see page 48 for a note on handling chilies).

(2) Not more than 2 hours before serving, combine the ingredients, adding lime juice and minced chili to taste. The relish should be somewhat sweet from the melon, but also a little sour and spicy. This relish does not keep particularly well, so prepare it in small batches.

Chilled Melon Soup

SERVES 6

HERE'S a nice soup to refresh you in hot weather. Use the ripest melons you can find, and feel free to substitute other varieties.

1 medium-size, ripe cantaloupe (approximately 2 cups cubed melon)
1 medium-size, ripe honeydew (approximately 3 cups cubed melon)
2 cups freshly squeezed orange juice
   Juice of 1 lemon
   Juice of 1 lime
2 tablespoons honey, or to taste

1 spice bundle of 2 cloves, 2 allspice berries, and 1 stick of
  cinnamon
1 cup light cream

For the garnish:
½ cup sour cream
6 sprigs fresh mint

(1) Peel and seed the melons, and coarsely dice the flesh. Combine the diced melon, fruit juices, honey, and spices in a large saucepan, and simmer over medium heat for 10 to 15 minutes, or until the melon is very soft. Allow the soup to cool to room temperature, discard the spice bundle, and purée the soup in a blender or food processor. Chill the soup over ice or in the refrigerator. The recipe can be prepared to this stage up to 2 days before serving.

(2) Just before serving, whisk the light cream into the soup. Serve the melon soup in chilled glass bowls. Garnish with a spoonful of sour cream and a sprig of mint.

Watermelon Preserves

MAKES 4 TO 5 CUPS

WATERMELON preserves are popular in central Europe, where they are eaten for dessert. They're also great for spooning over ice cream or spreading on toast.

2 pounds watermelon rind
1 lemon
2 pounds sugar
½ cup water
1 cinnamon stick
1 vanilla bean, split

(1) Cut the dark skin and any pink flesh off the rind, until only the pale-green part remains. Cut it into ½-inch cubes. Cut the lemon into thin slices and coarsely chop, removing and discarding the seeds.

(2) Place the watermelon rind in a saucepan with cold water to cover. Bring it to a boil. Drain, cover with cold water, and bring to a boil again. Repeat this again, but this time simmer the rind for 15 minutes. Drain.

(3) Return the watermelon rind to the pan and add the remaining ingredients. Cook over low heat, stirring from time to time, for 30 to 40 minutes, or until the sugar reaches the soft-ball state (239 degrees on a candy thermometer). Spoon the watermelon preserves into sterile canning jars. The preserves will keep for 6 to 8 months.

Drunken Watermelon

SERVES 16

DRUNKEN watermelon is great for summertime parties. The idea comes from an old high school buddy, Nick Hall.

1 large watermelon
½ bottle gold tequila

Cut two or three 1-inch holes in the top of the watermelon. Pour in as much tequila as the melon will absorb and replace the plugs. Let the flavors ripen for 2 to 3 hours. Cut the watermelon into slices and serve.

NOTE: Warn your guests that they are not eating innocent watermelon. This is one of the few desserts I know that can lead to intoxication!

SEPTEMBER

By all these lovely tokens
September days are here,
With summer's best of weather
And autumn's best of cheer.

HELEN HUNT JACKSON

SEPTEMBER is the harvest month. The Anglo-Saxons called it *Gerst-Monath*, "barley month," for this was when they reaped barley. In agrarian cultures, this was and still is a period of frenetic activity: grapes must be picked and pressed, corn gathered and dried, fruits and vegetables turned into preserves. The farmer works overtime in September; fortunately, the harvest moon is high in the sky to illuminate his nocturnal toil.

Jews celebrate their most sacred holidays in September: Rosh Hashanah and Yom Kippur. Rosh Hashanah, the Jewish New Year, marks the completion of the harvest cycle. The New Year is rung in with a trumpetlike blast of the *shofer,* the ram's horn. It is customary to eat apples dipped in honey to invoke a sweet New Year. Yom Kippur is a day of atonement for past sins, a time of rigorous fasting, confession, and repentance. Jews symbolically purge the evil that would harm the prosperity of the coming year.

September 14 is Holy Rood Day, on which Christians exalt the cross on which Christ was crucified. In England it was customary for young people to go "a-nutting" this day, gathering freshly fallen walnuts. September 29 is Michaelmas Day, honoring St. Michael and all the angels. Traditionally, one eats goose at the Michaelmas Feast. A Renaissance poet put it this way:

At Christmas a capon,
At Michaelmas, a goose.
And somewhat else at New Yere's tide
For fear the thread flies loose!

The autumn equinox occurs in September—from here on, in the Northern Hemisphere, the days will be shorter than the nights. School resumes for students, and people generally become more serious about their pursuits.

September is a beneficent month for cooks. We are confronted with an embarrassment of vegetable riches. Tomatoes, those hothouse horrors of winter, come to juicy, vine-ripened fruition. Peppers are plentiful for picking; so are grapes, apples, pomegranates, and figs. Bluefish begin their migration southward; tuna and squid are abundant. Wild September delicacies include beach plums and rose hips.

The harvest is all too short, however, so we take measures to preserve Nature's bounties. Fruits wind up in jam sessions; vegetables are pickled and relished. As the weather turns cool, we begin to hunger for heartier fare: soups, stews, and homemade breads. A harvest spirit invades all of us—we return to the pleasures of cooking.

TOMATOES

FOR ten months a year, the tomato is a hothouse horror: a tough-skinned, juiceless, anemic orb with about as much flavor as the cellophane it's wrapped in. September brings us the vine-ripened variety—soft, juicy, and bursting with flavor. We frantically consume enough salads and tomato sauce to last us the rest of the winter.

The origin of the term *tomato* takes us through a linguistic labyrinth. The fruit was a native of Mexico and Peru: the Aztecs called it *xtomatle.* The Spanish explorers named it *manzana,* "apple," for its roundness reminded them of the fruit. Southern

Italians called it *pomo d'oro,* "golden apple," because the first variety introduced to Europe was yellow. Mistaking its place of origin, Northern Italians dubbed it *pomo dei mori,* "Moorish apple." To the French, this sounded like *pomme d'amour,* "love apple," and in the eighteenth century, tomatoes were thought to be aphrodisiac.

Southern Europeans took to tomatoes; Northern Europeans didn't. The English botanist Gerard declared them "corrupt" in his famous *Herball.* In 1830, a daredevil named Robert Johnson ate a raw tomato on the steps of the Salem, New Jersey, courthouse; the horrified spectators predicted he would be dead before morning. Fortunately, Johnson didn't die, writes food historian James Trager, and the tomato became one of the most popular fruits in America.

For fruit it is, botanically speaking—it's a berry in the nightshade family. Legally it's a vegetable, however, decreed so by no less an authority than the United States Supreme Court. (Because it is used like a vegetable, went the argument, it must be considered one for the purposes of trade.) And speaking of the tomato's uses, the most unusual one we know of is as a poultice, placed by Egyptians over the eye to relieve the sting of an infection. The tomato works by sympathetic magic: being red, it soothes that part of the eye which is bloodshot.

The best place to find vine-ripened tomatoes is on a tomato plant in a garden—yours or your neighbors. Pluck them off the bush, sprinkle with salt, and take a big bite, as you would of an apple. Lacking a garden, your next best bet is to drive to a country farm stand. Ripe tomatoes are bright red and squishy. Don't worry about lumps or blemishes. Red-green tomatoes will ripen (put them in a paper bag with an apple—the ethylene gas exuded by the apple helps speed up the ripening process), but they will never be as luscious as vine-ripened fruit. Popular varieties include the large *beefsteak tomato* (plump and juicy), the pear-shaped *plum tomato* (popular with Italians), the diminutive *cherry tomato* (excellent for stuffing), and the exotic *yellow tomato* (which comes in a variety of sizes and is all the rage in California). By the way, don't overlook hard, green tomatoes: they are excellent for pickling and pan-frying.

PEELING AND SEEDING TOMATOES

TO peel tomatoes, cut out the stem end with a sharp paring knife, and cut a small X on the bottom. Plunge the tomato into rapidly boiling water for 20 to 30 seconds, rinse it under cold water, then pull the skin off with your fingers. To seed tomatoes, cut them in half widthwise and hold them, cut side down, in the palm of your hand. Squeeze each half gently over a bowl or garbage disposal to wring out the seeds and watery juices.

The easiest way to enjoy tomatoes is not cooked at all but sliced and drizzled with olive oil and vinegar as a salad. (Add a sprinkling of fresh thyme or tarragon.) If you cook them, do it briefly: I simmer tomato sauce for 10 to 15 minutes—longer, and you loose the fresh taste.

Fried Green Tomatoes

SERVES 4

ONE of the joys of tomato season is that you can find not only vine-ripened red tomatoes but unripe green ones. The latter, of course, are delicious in chutneys, pickled, and fried. It is all right for a little pink to be showing, but the tomatoes should be basically green, or you won't get the right acidity. The following is an old Southern recipe, and it is delicious with ham or fish.

2 large green tomatoes
¼ cup flour
¼ cup stone-ground cornmeal

½ teaspoon paprika
   Plenty of salt and fresh black pepper
4–5 tablespoons butter, bacon fat, or oil for frying

Wash the tomatoes and cut them widthwise into ¼-inch slices. Thoroughly mix the flour, cornmeal, and seasonings in a shallow bowl. Melt the butter or bacon fat in a large skillet over medium heat. Dip each tomato slice in seasoned flour on both sides, shaking it over the bowl to knock off the excess. Fry the tomato slices for 3 to 4 minutes per side, or until golden brown. Serve at once.

Tomato Vinaigrette with Dill

MAKES 1 CUP

THE French would call this uncooked sauce a *coulis* and it is wonderful with poached fish, grilled fowl, and fritters of all persuasions. If dill is unavailable, substitute another fresh herb. If vine-ripened tomatoes are unavailable, use imported canned plum tomatoes.

3 ripe tomatoes
4 tablespoons extra-virgin olive oil
2 tablespoons balsamic or red wine vinegar, or to taste
   Salt and fresh black peper
3 tablespoons chopped scallions
3 tablespoons chopped dill

Peel and seed the tomatoes as described on page 304. Place the tomatoes in a blender or food processor with the oil, vinegar, salt, and pepper, and process until smooth. Stir in the chopped herbs and adjust the seasonings to taste.

A Simple Salad of Tomatoes, Mozzarella, and Basil

SERVES 4

HERE'S another dish that's simplicity itself, but I wouldn't trade it for all the aspic in Paris. The key here is the raw materials: vine-ripened tomatoes, day-old mozzarella, and basil plucked a few hours before from the garden. Of the three, the mozarella will be hardest to locate: if you find it in a pan of water or still dripping with whey, you'll know you've got the right stuff. (Fresh buffalo milk mozzarella from Italy has also become increasingly available at gourmet shops.) The salad is so fresh, we don't even bother mixing the ingredients for the dressing.

> 2 or 3 vine-ripened tomatoes
> 1 *fresh* mozzarella or buffalo milk mozzarella
> 1 bunch fresh basil
> 3–4 tablespoons extra-virgin olive oil
> 1–2 tablespoons balsamic vinegar
> Salt and coarsely ground fresh black pepper

(1) Cut the tomatoes and mozzarella into thin slices. Pluck the basil leaves off the stems. Arrange the tomato and mozzarella slices on a platter, one overlapping the other, a basil leaf in between each. You are aiming for a zebra-stripe effect. The recipe can be prepared to this stage up to 30 minutes before serving.

(2) Just before serving, drizzle the olive oil over the salad, followed by the vinegar, and salt and pepper to taste. This simple salad makes a wonderful appetizer; on many a warm night, I've made it my entire meal.

Cherry Tomatoes with Herbed Cheese

MAKES 30 TO 40 PIECES

HERE'S an hors d'oeuvre that's pretty to look at and tasty to serve. The herbed cheese is a homemade version of French boursin, and it costs a fraction of the price. But don't stop with cherry tomatoes—the herbed cheese can be piped into snow pea pods or mushroom caps, or onto rounds of cucumber.

30–40 red or yellow cherry tomatoes

For the homemade boursin:
- **⅓ pound cream cheese, at room temperature**
- **½ cup unsalted butter, at room temperature**
- **3 tablespoons minced scallions**
- **3 tablespoons minced fresh parsley**
- **3 tablespoons minced fresh herbs, including basil, dill, thyme, oregano, and/or tarragon**
- **1 small clove garlic, minced**
- **Salt and fresh black pepper**

30–40 tiny sprigs fresh tarragon or dill

1 piping bag fitted with a ¼-inch star tip

(1) Remove the stems from the tomatoes and cut off the rounded bottoms (about ¼-inch). Hollow out each tomato, using a paring knife, paper clip, or tiny melon baller. Arrange the tomatoes, stem side down (this will keep them from rolling away), on a platter.

(2) Cream the cheese and butter in the food processor, or in a bowl with a whisk. Beat in the herbs and spices. Let the mixture stand for 15 minutes, so the flavors have a chance to blend and ripen. Using the piping bag, pipe the herbed cheese into the tomatoes. Top each rosette of cheese with a sprig of tarragon or dill.

Tabooli Tomatoes

SERVES 6

THIS recipe combines two favorite warm-weather dishes: tabooli and tomato salad. Tabooli, of course, is a Middle Eastern salad made of bulghur (cracked wheat), lemon, and mint. Bulghur will be found at any health food store or Middle Eastern market. The tiny center leaves from a head of romaine lettuce or Belgian endive make a nifty garnish.

For the tabooli:
   1 cup bulghur
3–4 tablespoons fresh-squeezed lemon juice
   3 tablespoons extra-virgin olive oil
   ½ cup finely chopped fresh parsley
   ¼ cup finely chopped fresh mint
   3 tablespoons finely chopped scallion
      Salt and fresh black pepper

   6 ripe tomatoes
      Salt

   6 small leaves of Belgian endive or romaine (optional)

(1) At least 6 hours before serving (and preferably the night before), place the bulghur in a large bowl with cold water to cover by at least 3 inches. Let stand until the grains are soft and swelled to several times their original bulk. Thoroughly drain the bulghur in a strainer, pressing to extract excess water.

(2) Cut the caps (the stem end) off the tomatoes, and if necessary, cut a tiny slice off the bottom so the tomatoes stand upright. Hollow out each tomato, using a paring knife or melon baller. Lightly sprinkle the insides of the tomatoes with salt and invert them over a cake rack. This will draw out excess moisture.

(3) Prepare the tabooli. Place the soaked bulghur in a large bowl and mix in the flavorings, adding salt, lemon juice, or oil as necessary. The mixture should be piquant and highly seasoned. Shake the moisture out of the tomato halves. Spoon in

the tabooli. Garnish each tomato with an upright leaf of Belgian endive or romaine lettuce. Tabooli tomatoes make an excellent first course for brunch.

TUNA

MY Grammie Sarah wasn't much of a cook, but there was one dish she excelled at: tuna fish salad. I should know—for the first five years of my life, tuna fish sandwiches were my chief source of protein!

Imagine my astonishment when I finally encountered real tuna. The place was Palermo, Sicily, where I happened to arrive on the opening day of tuna season. Card tables had been erected on countless street corners, each sagging beneath the weight of fish the size of calves. No innocuous canned tuna were these, but briny Leviathans, so wide of girth you'd be hard-pressed to wrap your arms around one. And the color! The fish was as blood-red as beef. Dubious, I bought a steak and, according to the instructions of the vendor, grilled it over charcoal, basting it with a sprig of rosemary dipped in olive oil. One taste of its rich beefy flavor and I was hooked. Grammie Sarah never knew what she was missing!

The tuna is a member of the mackerel family, the largest attaining fifteen hundred pounds. The fish has been immensely popular for most of human history. Tuna bones have turned up in Paleolithic middens; its image appeared on Byzantine coins; and according to fish authority A. J. McClane, the cities of Tunis, Tripoli, and Syracuse began as "tinnoscopes," tuna observation centers manned by fishermen who would follow the tuna migrations from towers on the coastal cliffs.

Tuna spawn in the Bahamas and fatten up on herring and squid as they migrate north in late spring. Tuna season opens in

June, but the fish are at their best when fished from New England waters in late summer and early fall.

There are six major species of tuna, each with its own unique color, texture, and flavor. Below are the ones you are apt to find at market.

Albacore: This is the fish that provides white meat tuna in cans. It is also delicious poached, cut in steaks, and grilled.

Bluefin: This is the largest tuna, averaging three to six feet in length, weighing an average of four hundred to six hundred pounds. Its dark, decisively flavored flesh makes it the preferred tuna for sushi: raw, it bears a striking resemblance to beef.

Bonito: A smallish fish, the bonito has a silvery body and steel-blue back, with slanting dark-blue stripes. The dark flesh has a strong flavor, and cannot be labeled "tuna" by the American canning industry.

Yellowfin: Another smallish tuna, this fish averages twenty to thirty pounds. Yellowfin is a fine eating fish, with meat that is darker than that of albacore but lighter than that of bluefin.

In Japan and the Mediterranean, tuna is butchered as methodically as beef is in the United States. As a general rule, the lighter the meat, the more delicate the flavor. The belly, with its generous marbling, is particularly esteemed. (This is the *toro* beloved by sushi buffs, and the *ventresca* favored by Italians.) When buying tuna, avoid pieces with excessive tendon or veins of dark meat (rich in myoglobin, which tastes bitter when cooked). The Portuguese soak the darker cuts of tuna in brine to remove the blood (see recipe on the next page).

Atum de Escabeche
(Madeira-style Tuna)

SERVES 4

MADEIRA is the peak of a submarine mountain, an island off the coast of Africa whose precipitous slopes rise nearly a mile above sea level. The island is best-known for its fortified wine, but it is an enchanting place to visit, a wild mass of craggy cliffs and tropical forests, of terraced hillsides and tiny fishing villages connected by roads with dizzying hairpin turns. Tuna is one of the island's principal fish. It is lightly brined to remove the blood, then simmered with aromatic vegetables and served chilled. The result has the firm flake of canned tuna but is infinitely more flavorful. This recipe was inspired by one in A. J. McClane's *Encyclopedia of Fish*.

> **2 pounds fresh bluefin tuna**
> **4 tablespoons sea salt**
>
> *For cooking the tuna:*
> **1 small onion, quartered**
> **2 cloves garlic, peeled**
> **1 carrot, peeled and cut into 1-inch pieces**
> **1 branch celery, cut into 1-inch pieces**
> **Juice of ½ lemon**
> **2–3 tablespoons excellent extra-virgin olive oil**

(1) Cut the tuna into 2-inch chunks. Combine the salt and 2 cups water in a lidded jar, and shake until thoroughly mixed. Marinate the tuna pieces in this mixture for 1 hour, and drain.

(2) Place the tuna, vegetables, lemon juice, and oil in a saucepan with water to cover. Bring the liquid to a boil, reduce the heat, cover the pan, and gently simmer the tuna for 30 to 40 minutes. Let cool to room temperature, then chill the tuna in its poaching liquid for at least 4 hours, or overnight.

(3) To serve, remove the tuna from the broth, scraping off any gelatin. It is delicious as is, on sandwiches or in salads. For

a fancier presentation, mound the tuna on lettuce leaves and top with sliced hot red peppers, capers, and Tomato Vinaigrette with Dill or Joe's Mustard Sauce (see recipes on pages 305 and 469).

Basque Tuna

SERVES 4

I first tasted this dish in St. Jean de Luz, a fishing village/resort on the Atlantic coast in southwestern France. The occasion was the annual tuna festival, a day of wild celebrations to mark the start of the tuna fishing season at the end of June. The quays along the harbor were lined with boisterous crowds at vast communal tables. The kitchens were manned by members of local soccer or *pelote* (a game like jai alai) teams, and the heady scent of fresh-cooked tuna was everywhere. This dish is delicious with any firm steak fish, like swordfish, whiting, or halibut.

   4 fresh 6-ounce tuna steaks cut ½- to ¾-inch thick.
   1 large clove garlic

For the Basque tomato sauce:
3–4 tablespoons extra-virgin olive oil
   1 small onion, diced (about ½ cup)
   1 clove garlic, minced
   1 red bell pepper (roast it if you wish—see instructions on
      page 318), cored, seeded, and diced
   1 green bell pepper, prepared in the same way as the red pepper
   1 very small chili pepper (or to taste), seeded and minced, or a
      generous pinch of cayenne papper
   2 ounces prosciutto or other uncooked ham, cut into ⅛-inch
      slices, then ¼-inch dice
   4 fresh tomatoes, peeled, seeded, and coarsely chopped, or 1 cup
      peeled, seeded, good imported canned tomatoes
   1 teaspoon each chopped fresh basil and oregano, or ⅓ teaspoon
      each dried
      Salt, fresh black pepper, and cayenne pepper

1 heavy metal baking dish just large enough to hold the fish
2 tablespoons olive oil to oil the dish

(1) Using the tip of a paring knife, make tiny slits in the fish steaks, and insert slivers of garlic. Place the unoiled baking dish in the oven and preheat it to 400 degrees.

(2) Meanwhile, prepare the Basque tomato sauce. Heat the olive oil in a saucepan. Add the onions, garlic, peppers, chili, and ham, and sauté over medium heat for 3 minutes, or until the onions are soft. Add the tomatoes and increase the heat to high. Cook the tomatoes for 3 minutes, or until most of the liquid has evaporated. Stir in the herbs, and salt, black pepper, and cayenne to taste—the sauce should be very highly seasoned. (*Note:* The Basque tomato sauce can be prepared up to 24 hours before you bake the fish.)

(3) Just before serving, add the 2 tablespoons olive oil to the preheated baking dish. Sprinkle the fish steaks with salt and pepper, and add them as well. Sear the steaks on one side in the oven for 1 minute, then turn to sear the other side. Spoon the Basque tomato sauce over the tuna, and bake for 10 minutes, or until the fish is cooked (it will flake when pressed). Serve Basque tuna with sharp, dry wine, like a Gaillac or rosé from Provence.

Tuna Steaks with
Pumpkin-Seed Sauce

SERVES 4

THIS sauce is a variation on a *pipan*, a Mexican pumpkin-seed sauce. The *pasilla* is a long, dark-green, mildly piquant chili. If unavailable, use a poblano or even a jalapeño. (Instructions on roasting and peeling peppers are found on page 318.) In this recipe the fish is grilled, but it could also be broiled or baked. (For that matter, the marinade is delicious with chicken.) The

½-inch thickness of the slices allows the steaks to be cooked through without drying out the exterior.

4 6-ounce skinless tuna steaks, cut ½ inch thick

For the marinade/sauce:
½ **cup raw pumpkin seeds**
1 **pasilla chili**
1 **bunch fresh cilantro (about 1 cup leaves)**
4 **scallions**
1 **very small onion**
½ **teaspoon cumin seed**
  Juice of 1 lemon
  Juice of 1 lime, or to taste
  Juice of 1 orange
2 **tablespoons tequila**
  Salt

(1) Cook the pumpkin seeds in a dry skillet over medium heat, stirring constantly, for 1 minute, or until the seeds swell and begin to pop and brown. Do not overcook, however, or the seeds will become bitter. Roast the chili, scrape off the burnt skin, and cut in half lengthwise to discard the seeds (see page 48 for a note on handling chilies). Remove the coarse stems from the cilantro; reserve 8 to 10 whole sprigs for garnish. Purée the ingredients for the marinade/sauce in a blender, adding salt and lime juice to taste. Marinate the tuna steaks with half the sauce in a shallow dish for at least 2 to 3 hours.

(2) Preheat the grill. Cook the steaks for 2 minutes per side, or until the fish flakes easily when pressed. To serve, place a spoonful of the remaining sauce on top of each steak, and garnish with sprigs of cilantro.

John Silberman's
Pan-blackened Tuna

SERVES 4

IF one were to pick a single dish to represent the fiery glory of Cajun cooking, it would have to be pan-blackened fish. Pioneered by Paul Prudhomme, this unusual cooking method consists of cooking a spice-encrusted fish fillet in a superhot ungreased skillet. The spices form a fragrant crust, leaving the inside moist and tender. Pan-blackening generates a great deal of smoke, so if you do not have a strong exhaust fan, you may wish to try the procedure outdoors, heating the frying pan on a barbecue grill. John Silberman runs the Cajun Yankee restaurant in Cambridge.

> 4 6-ounce skinless tuna steaks, cut ½ inch thick
> ½ cup clarified butter (see page 471)

For the spice mixture:
> 1 tablespoon salt
> 1 tablespon garlic powder
> 1 tablespoon onion powder
> 1 tablespoon dried oregano
> 1 tablespoon paprika
> 2 teaspoons freshly ground black pepper
> 2 teaspoons freshly ground white pepper
> 2 teaspoons dried thyme
> 1 teaspoon cayenne pepper

> 1 lemon, cut into 8 wedges

(1) Trim the fish to remove any skin or darkened pieces of flesh. Combine the ingredients for the spice mixture. Preheat a dry cast iron skillet over a high heat for 5 minutes.

(2) Spoon 1 tablespoon clarified butter onto each fish steak and spread it out with your fingers. Sprinkle the steak with the spice mixture—it should be generously coated, although not too

thickly encrusted. Invert the steaks and sprinkle with the remaining butter and spice mixture (*Note:* You may not need to use all the spice mixture in the recipe.)

(3) Place the steaks in the superhot skillet and cook them for 1–1½ minutes per side. Don't be disconcerted by all the smoke. The fish should be singed on the exterior, but not quite burnt.

Transfer the pan-blackened fish to plates or a platter and garnish with lemon wedges. Cold beer makes a welcome refresher.

PEPPERS

EVERY revolution has victors and vanquished; one of the winners of "American nouvelle cuisine" was the bell pepper. When I was growing up, the only available variety was the green bell; as often as not it arrived raw and indigestible, or hopelessly overcooked. Today, bell peppers come in a rainbow of hues: red, brown, purple, and—my unabashed favorite—yellow. They turn up at the finest restaurants roasted, grilled, marinated, puréed, served with goat cheese and even lobster.

What accounts for the sudden rise in the pepper's prestige? Undoubtedly, our heightened interest in ethnic cuisine has helped. Peppers figure prominently in the cooking of Spain, Italy, Eastern Europe, and the American Southwest. Then there's the increased availability of new species, such as brown and purple peppers from Holland. Finally, America's young chefs learned the age-old technique of roasting pepper to remove the skins, and there's nothing like roasting for bringing out a pepper's natural sweetness. Peppers are even good for you: a medium red pepper contains 3320 units of vitamin A and 148 milligrams of vitamin C.

Bell peppers are members of the Capsicum family, whose

more fiery members include jalapeño chilies. (*Capsicum* derives from the Latin word *caspa*, "box," an apt description of some of the larger varieties.) The term *pepper* is a misnomer, coined by Columbus after he tasted one of the more fiery varieties and mistook it for the *piper nigrum*, the peppercorn. (This was less a mistake than wishful thinking—the goal of Columbus's voyage was to find a quicker and less expensive route to that source of spices, India. The pepper is native to the Americas: European explorers introduced the milder varieties to Europe and the fiery ones to Asia.

As peppers ripen, they turn from green to red. This is the reason green peppers are generally found at the market before red ones. Once picked they do not change color. To confuse matters further, the yellow, purple, and brown peppers are special hybrids. The purple and brown ones taste like green peppers, and lose their vivid hue when cooked. Most of the colorful peppers come from Holland, but American farmers are beginning to cultivate them here.

In addition to sweet bell peppers, here are some of the other varieties you will find at this time of year.

Bull's Horn: Long and curved, like the horn of a bull, this pepper is popular with Italians. (Italian toughs like to wear models of this one around their neck.) Most are mild, but some have bite. They are delicious roasted and layered with olive oil.

Cubanelle: Bright yellow to pale green in color, this one looks like an elongated bell pepper. The flavor is mild and sweet.

Japanese Green Pepper: This long, slender, wrinkly skinned pepper tapers to a sharp, curved point. It is quite spicy by bell pepper standards, but not quite as fiery as a chili.

Lamuyo: Another European import, this one is larger and longer than a bell pepper, but more slender in overall shape. It is available in a variety of colors and has a thick and meaty flesh.

Pimiento: This sweet, heart-shaped, dark-red pepper usually winds up in olives, but it is also delectable fresh. Its thick walls make it ideal for roasting. The best pimientos are the ones the size of a lemon.

All varieties are at their best in autumn. Look for firm, glossy peppers that feel heavy and crisp. As a general rule, the thinner the skin or the longer and skinnier the shape, the hotter a pepper will be. Thick-skinned peppers tend to be more sweet. Peppers are wind-pollinated, by the way, so individuals from the some bush can vary in their degree of piquancy.

ROASTING PEPPERS

My favorite way to enjoy peppers is roasted and peeled. As the skin chars, the pepper acquires a velvety softness and distinctive smoky flavor.

Roast peppers are the one food you are allowed to burn. Cook them at the highest heat directly on the burner. (This works equally well for gas and electric burners.) Roast the peppers, turning with tongs, for 4 to 6 minutes, or until the skins are completely charred. Extinguish the heat, and wrap the peppers in moist paper towels for 5 to 10 minutes. The moisture will steam off the skin. Alternatively, you can put the peppers in a sealed paper bag. (*Note:* The procedure is messy—I try to roast peppers the day before the cleaning service comes!)

Peppers can also be roasted on the grill or under the broiler, but you must use the maximum heat. These methods are less desirable, because they tend to cook the pepper as well as char the skin.

To peel peppers, scrape off the blistered skin with your fingers, a blunt knife, or a kitchen brush. It's easiest to work under running water, but blot the peppers to remove the excess water. Core and seed before using.

To core a bell pepper, cut a little circle around the stem. Grasp the stem firmly, jam it into the pepper, then pull it out: the core and seeds should be attached. If any seeds or membranes remain, scrape them out with a spoon.

A Colorful Salad of Yellow Peppers and Green Beans

SERVES 4

THIS salad may be simplicity itself, but it's also a visual knockout. If you live in a big city, you may be able to find *haricots verts,* those lovely skinny French stringbeans. Otherwise, select the slenderest beans you can find.

> 2 large yellow bell peppers
> 1 pound slender green beans
> Salt
>
> *For the herb vinaigrette:*
> 1 teaspoon Dijon-style mustard
> 1 tablespoon balsamic vinegar
> ⅛ teaspoon salt
> Fresh black pepper to taste
> 1 tablespoon chopped fresh herbs (dill, tarragon, oregano, and/ or basil)
> 3–4 tablespoons extra-virgin olive oil

(1) Core and seed the peppers, and cut each one lengthwise into ¼-inch strips. Snap the ends off the beans and remove any strings. Blanch the pepper strips in rapidly boiling salted water for 15 seconds, then transfer them with a slotted spoon to a strainer and refresh under cold water. Cook the green beans in rapidly boiling salted water for 2 to 3 minutes, or until crispy-tender. Refresh under cold water and drain.

(2) Prepare the vinaigrette. Place the mustard, vinegar, salt, pepper, and herbs in the bottom of a salad bowl, and whisk them into a smooth paste. Gradually whisk in the oil—the sauce should thicken. Add the beans and peppers and toss to mix.

Red Pepper Vinaigrette

MAKES 1 CUP

THIS redolent sauce is just the thing for grilled shrimp, breast of chicken, or veal. Vinaigrettes can also be made with yellow bell peppers or cubanelles.

> 2 large red bell peppers
> ½ cup extra-virgin olive oil
> 3 tablespoons red wine vinegar, or to taste
> 1 pinch saffron, soaked in 1 tablespoon hot water (optional)
> Salt, fresh black pepper, and cayenne pepper

Roast and peel the peppers as described on page 318. Discard the seeds. Place the peppers in a blender or food processor with the oil, vinegar, and seasonings to taste, and purée until smooth.

Salad of Goat Cheese and Roasted Peppers

SERVES 4

THIS colorful salad can be made with a variety of bell peppers: my favorites are yellow and red. Use a soft mild goat cheese, like monterey chèvre or montrachet.

> 2 large red bell peppers
> 2 large yellow bell peppers

For the saffron vinaigrette:
> ¼ teaspoon saffron
> ½ teaspoon Dijon-style mustard
> 1 tablespoon red wine vinegar
> Salt
> Juice of ½ lemon

4 tablespoons extra-virgin olive oil
Freshly ground black pepper

8 ounces soft mild goat cheese
2 tablespoons slivered fresh basil leaves
¼ cup calamata olives

4 large salad plates

(1) Roast the peppers as described on page 318. Peel, core, and seed each. Cut each pepper in four.

(2) Prepare the vinaigrette. Infuse the saffron in 1 teaspoon hot water for 5 minutes. Combine the mustard, vinegar, salt, and lemon juice, and whisk until the salt is dissolved. Gradually whisk in the saffron (with its liquid), oil, and salt and pepper to taste.

(3) To assemble the salad, arrange 2 strips red pepper and 2 strips yellow pepper on the left side of each plate, alternating colors. Cut the goat cheese into ¼-inch slices, and arrange 4 to 5 slices, each overlapping the next, on the right side of the plate. Spoon the vinaigrette over the peppers and cheese. Garnish the center of each plate with basil leaves and olives.

Variations: Use poached shrimp or scallops instead of olives.

Piperade Basquaise
(Basque-style Peppers and Eggs)

SERVES 4 AS AN APPETIZER, 2 OR 3 AS A LIGHT ENTRÉE

THE Basque country lies in the Pyrénées mountains, straddling the border of France and Spain. The narrow roads and high mountain passes have kept the region remote from the rest of France. The cuisine favors spicy mixtures of onions, olive oil, and peppers. A *piperade* is a sort of omelette, and the recipe below comes from a lovely country inn called Arraya.

1 green bell pepper
1 red bell pepper
1 yellow bell pepper (optional)
2 ripe tomatoes
3 tablespoons olive oil
1 medium onion, coarsely chopped
1 small clove garlic, minced
1 bay leaf
2 tablespoons chopped fresh parsley
  Generous pinch of thyme
  Salt and fresh black pepper
½ teaspoon sugar, or to taste
8 strips thick-sliced bacon
4 eggs

(1) Roast and peel the peppers as described on page 318. Remove the stems and seeds, and cut the peppers into strips.

(2) Blanch and peel the tomatoes. Cut the tomatoes in half widthwise and squeeze them to remove the water and seeds. Coarsely chop.

(3) Heat the olive oil in a large pan. Add the onions and cook over a low heat for 2 minutes. Add the garlic and continue cooking for 3 to 4 minutes, or until the onions are golden brown. Add the tomatoes, peppers, bay leaf, and 1 tablespoon of the parsley, and cook the mixture over low heat for 20 minutes. Remove the bay leaf and season the mixture to taste with salt and pepper, adding sugar as necessary to counteract the acidity of the tomatoes. In a separate pan, fry the bacon.

(4) Just before serving, beat the eggs till smooth. Remove the pepper mixture from the heat and stir in the eggs. Return the pan to the heat for 30 to 60 seconds, or until the eggs are cooked, stirring constantly. Do not overcook—the mixture should be creamy, not scrambled. Spoon the piperade onto a platter and garnish with the bacon and the remaining tablespoon parsley. Serve with crusty French bread.

GRAPES

BRILLAT-SAVARIN tells the story of a wine lover who was offered some grapes for dessert. " 'Thank you, no,' he said, pushing the plate away. 'I am not accustomed to taking my wine in pills!' " In our haste to become a nation of wine buffs, we laud grapes for wine-making while ignoring their virtues for eating. And good for eating they are at this time of year, fresh in from the vineyard, bursting with sugar.

Grapes are among man's most venerable fruits. Grape seeds have been found at neolithic sites across Europe. Vines grew in the hanging gardens of Babylon and in the shadow of the pyramids. Under Richard the Lionhearted, grape theft was punishable by dismemberment. ("Whosoever takes a bunch of grapes from another's vineyard will pay five sous or will lose an ear," proclaimed Richard.) As for the New World, wild grapes grew here in such abundance that when Viking mariner Leif the Lucky landed here in 1000 A.D., he named the place Vinland, "Land of the Vine."

There are some ten thousand grape varieties in the world, eight thousand cultivated in Europe. The latter all belong to a single species: *Vitis vinifera,* the wine grape. The discovery of America introduced forty new species, among them the *Niagara* and the *scuppernong.* The Colonists called the fruit of these wild vines *fox grapes,* an appropriate description of their wild, musky flavor. In the nineteenth century, New York State growers crossed European wine grapes with American vines to produce such popular varieties as the *Delaware, Catawba,* and *Concord.* Today, most of the American varieties, which are eating grapes, are grown east of the Rockies, while the European varieties, used mainly for wine-making, are grown on the West Coast.

That is not to say that wine grapes don't make fine eating. One has but to visit a vineyard at harvest time to realize how sweet, how juicy, how incredibly flavorful wine grapes can be. Wine grapes tend to have small berries and large seeds, however, which is why one seldom sees them at produce stands. A French grape-picker in Burgundy taught me the best way to enjoy them: hold the bunch in the palm of your hand over your head, your thumb extended as though you were hitchhiking. Gently squeeze the grapes and the juice will trickle down your thumb into your mouth!

MAJOR TABLE GRAPE VARIETIES

Vinifera (Wine Grapes)

Muscat: Small and round; comes both purple and white; perfumed and intensely sweet; good for eating as well as wine-making (California: September–October)

Red Seedless: Medium-size; red to purple; mild-flavored and somewhat acidic (California: July–October)

Ribier: Large and round; thick, jet black skin; mild and sweet, but not super-juicy (California: July–February)

Thompson Seedless: Medium-size and slightly elongated; pale green; thin-skinned and tender; mild but nicely acidic; an excellent table grape (California: June–November)

Tokay: Large and elongated; red when ripe; tough, thick skin; mild and sweet (California: August–January)

Euvitis (Eating Grapes)

Catawba: Medium-size and oval; red-purple; slip-off skins; sweet, full, "foxy" flavor (New York and Ohio: September–November)

Concord: Small and round; deep blue (almost black) with light dusting on skin; slip-off skins; very sweet and nicely acidic; a poor traveler (use immediately); often made into jam or jelly (East Coast: September–October)

Delaware: Small; pale red; sweet and very juicy (East Coast: August–September)

Niagara: Large and egg-shaped; pale amber; slip-off skins; sweet and juicy (East Coast: September–October)

When buying grapes, look for bunches with full, round berries. The grapes should be slightly yielding but not squishy, and firmly attached to the capstem.

The fruit is only part of the grape story, for the leaves of young vines are delicious pickled or baked. Grape leaves also make an attractive liner for a cheese tray or dish of fresh berries. Grape-seed oil, made in France, is delicious for dressing salads.

Grape Gazpacho

SERVES 4

THIS refreshing dish comes from Malaga on the Andalusian coast. It's a chilled soup made with grapes and olive oil. The almonds and soaked bread reflect a Moorish influence. (The term *gazpacho* comes from the Arabic word for "soaked bread.")

¾ pound (3 cups) Thompson seedless grapes
3 slices Italian bread
3 ounces (½ cup) blanched almonds
2 or 3 cloves garlic (or to taste), peeled
Plenty of salt and fresh black pepper
¼ cup Spanish olive oil
2–3 tablespoons wine vinegar

(1) Remove the stems from the grapes. Cut one-third of the grapes in half. Remove the crusts from the bread and place the bread in a shallow bowl with cold water to cover, about 2 cups. Soak the bread until soft.

(2) Place the whole grapes in a blender with the almonds, garlic, salt, pepper, and ¼ cup cold water. Blend until smooth. Add the bread and soaking water, and blend until smooth. With the motor running, blend in the oil and vinegar, adding more of either ingredient or salt and pepper as necessary, to obtain a rich flavor. (The sweetness of the grapes should be balanced by the acidity of the garlic and vinegar.)

Ladle the soup into chilled bowls and garnish with the grape halves.

Fillets of Sole with Curry and Grapes

SERVES 4

THIS recipe is a contemporary adaptation of classical French *sole Véronique*. To jazz up the original, we've added candied ginger and curry. Bottled clam broth is an excellent substitute for fish stock, but you must cut back on the salt. The recipe would also be delicious with monkfish or salmon.

1½ **pounds fillet of sole, monkfish, or salmon**
½ **pound ribier or red seedless grapes**
2–3 **shallots (2 tablespoons chopped)**
2–3 **pieces candied ginger (2 tablespoons slivered)**
  Salt and fresh black pepper
½ **cup dry white wine**
3 **tablespoons butter**
2 **teaspoons high-quality curry powder**
1 **tablespoon flour**
1 **cup fish stock (see recipe on page 474) or clam broth**
¼ **cup heavy cream**
  A few drops fresh lemon juice
  Sprigs of fresh cilantro for garnish

(1) Cut the sole fillets in half lengthwise. Run your fingers over the fish, feeling for bones: trim off any bones with a paring knife or extract them with pliers. Tie each half fillet into a loose

knot. If you are using monkfish or salmon, cut the fillets into diagonal ¼-inch-thick escallopes.

(2) Preheat the oven to 400 degrees. Cut the grapes in half and seed them if necessary. Finely chop the shallots. Cut the candied ginger into thin slivers. Lightly butter a baking dish just large enough to hold the fish. Sprinkle the fish with salt and pepper, add the wine, and loosely cover the dish with foil or parchment paper. The recipe can be prepared to this stage up to 2 hours before baking.

(3) Place the fish in the oven and bake it for 20 minutes, or until cooked. (The flesh will flake easily when pressed with your finger.) Meanwhile, prepare the sauce. Melt the butter in a sauce-pan. Add the shallots and cook over medium heat for 10 seconds. Whisk in the curry powder and flour, and continue cooking for 10 seconds. Remove the pan from the heat, and add the fish stock or clam broth, and the cream. Bring the sauce to a boil, whisking vigorously. Gently simmer the sauce for 10 minutes, or until a little less than 1 cup liquid remains. Add the ginger.

(4) When the fish is cooked, transfer it to a warm platter. Add the grapes and 3 to 4 tablespoons of the fish poaching liquid to the sauce. Boil the sauce for 2 to 3 minutes, or until it thickly coats the back of a wooden spoon. Add the lemon juice and correct the seasoning with salt, pepper, and, perhaps, additional curry.

To serve, spoon the sauce over the fish. Decorate the fish with a sprig of cilantro. Rice pilaf would make a good accompaniment, as would a spicy Alsatian wine, like a Riesling or Gewürztraminer.

Grapes with Almond Bean Curd

SERVES 4 TO 6

THIS recipe was inspired by a classic Chinese dessert: *hsing jen tou fu,* almond bean curd. The "bean curd" is actually a sort of almond-flavored jello.

1 pound mixed grapes (a variety of shapes, colors, and flavors)

For the almond bean curd:
1 envelope gelatin
⅓ cup sugar
½ cup evaporated milk
1 generous teaspoon almond extract

For the syrup:
4 cups water
1 cup sugar
1 tablespoon cognac, or to taste
1 tablespoon Grand Marnier, or to taste

1 8-inch cake pan lined with parchment or wax paper

(1) Remove the grapes from the stems. Seed them by inserting the loop end of a sterilized bobby pin through the stem hole or by cutting them in half. Place ¼ cup cold water in a small bowl and sprinkle the gelatin on top. Let it stand for 5 minutes, or until spongy. Have the cake pan ready.

(2) Combine 2 cups water with the ⅓ cup sugar in a saucepan. Bring the mixture to a boil, and remove the pan from the heat. Whisk in the gelatin, followed by the evaporated milk and almond extract. Pour the mixture into the cake pan and chill for 4 hours, or until the gelatin is set.

(3) Meanwhile, make the syrup. Combine 4 cups water with the 1 cup sugar, and bring to a rolling boil. Add the cognac and Grand Marnier to taste, and chill this mixture thoroughly.

(4) Unmold the almond bean curd onto a cutting board. (You may need to dip the cake pan in boiling water for a few seconds.) Cut the curd into 1-inch diamonds. Add these to the chilled syrup with the grapes. Present the dessert in a large glass bowl, ladling the servings into individual bowls.

Mustalevria
(Grape Must Pudding)

SERVES 4

MUSTALEVRIA is a Greek dessert made with must, freshly pressed grape juice used for making wine. In the old days, most rural Greek families made their own wine, so the must was readily available at harvest time. The recipe below uses the juice of freshly pressed Concord grapes.

    1 pound Concord grapes
    ¼ cup slivered almonds
    2 cinnamon sticks
    ½ teaspoon anise seed
   10 cardamom pods
    5 cloves
    5 allspice berries
    2 strips lemon zest
    2 strips orange zest
    4 tablespoons sugar, or to taste
    2 tablespoons cornstarch

(1) Wash the grapes and remove the stems. Crush the grapes, using a potato masher in a deep pot. Strain the juice: you should have a little more than 2 cups of juice. Chop the almonds and toast them in a hot (400-degree) oven or under the broiler until golden brown. Tie the spices and citrus zest in cheesecloth or wrap them loosely in foil (perforate the foil with a fork to release the flavor).

(2) Place the sugar and grape juice in a large saucepan (non-aluminum or non–cast iron), reserving 2 tablespoons juice. Add the spice bundle, cover the pan, and gently simmer the juice for 20 minutes, or until well-flavored. Remove the spice bundle. Dissolve the cornstarch in the 2 tablespoons reserved grape juice, and whisk this mixture into the simmered grape juice. Gently bring the juice to a boil, whisking vigorously. Remove the pan

from the heat, let the *mustalevria* cool slightly, spoon it into champagne coupes or ramekins, and wipe clean their rims.

(3) Chill for at least 3 hours or overnight. Sprinkle each dish of mustalevria with toasted almonds before serving.

APPLES

Eat an apple going to bed,
Make a doctor beg his bread.

OLD NORWEGIAN SAYING

THE greatest pleasure of autumn for me is the harvest of a new crop of apples. Oh, I know that the fruit is available year-round, flown in from France or shipped from Australia. But these apples have as much in common with the tree-picked fruit as black-and-white television does with the movies. To bite into a crisp Spy or Gravenstein, so crisp it makes your teeth squeak, is one of the world's great gastronomic pleasures.

No other fruit has played such a key role in the course of human history. An apple (a golden one given by Paris to Helen) caused the fall of Troy. A falling apple, so the legend goes, inspired Newton to discover the laws of physics; William Tell, as punishment for protesting tyranny, was forced to shoot one off his son's head.

From the end of August to the middle of November, each passing week brings new apple varieties to market: Gravensteins giving way to McIntoshes giving way to Romes, Staymans, and Baldwins. You may not find these varieties at the supermarket, but if you are willing to seek them out at farm stands, you'll be amazed by the ever-changing selection. The start of the apple season brings us another delicacy: freshly pressed cider, and it too will vary—now honey-sweet, now bracingly tart—as different apples come into season.

There are in the world more than ten thousand varieties of apples; unfortunately, fewer and fewer are available each year. Below are some of the most important varieties, with their characteristics for eating and cooking.

APPLE VARIETIES AND AVAILABILITY

August

Gravenstein: red and yellow-green skin; firm and tart; good for baking, pies, and sauces.

September

Cortland: red and green skin; crisp, juicy, and pleasantly tart. Cortlands are good eating and all-purpose cooking apples. Slow to discolor, they are excellent for salads.

Golden Delicious: large; pale-yellow skin; crisp and very sweet. Good for eating and all-purpose cooking, but it quickly shrivels with age.

Jonathan: The red-and-yellow-skinned Jonathan is an all-purpose fruit. Its sweet-sour flavor and spicy aftertaste make it excellent for eating; the crisp, firm flesh holds its shape when baked and in pies.

McCoun: The small, red-green McCoun is one of America's best eating apples—firm and tart like a Grannie Smith, but sweet like a Red Delicious. Available primarily in New England, it is excellent for salads and apple sauce. Enjoy it while you can: the season is short, and it does not keep well.

McIntosh: the primary apple of New England; red or red-green skin; soft, white flesh with a sweet, perfumed flavor. Just off the tree, the McIntosh is a good eating apple, but it quickly becomes soft and insipid. Best used for sauce or apple butter.

Red Delicious: This large, red apple is America's best seller, its flesh crisp and white, its flavor mild and sweet. Better for eating than cooking.

October

Empire: A cross between the red delicious and McIntosh, the red-and-yellow-skinned empire is sweet, spicy, and juicy. Good for eating and all-purpose cooking.

Northern Spy: pale green with red striping; mild, creamy flesh with a pleasant, semi-tart taste. A good eating apple, and excellent for baking, pies, and sauces.

Rhode Island Greening: bright-green skin; tart and juicy; fair for eating, but good in pies and sauces.

Rome Beauty: a large, deep red apple, with a mild, sweet flavor. Fair for eating, but it holds its shape well for baking and pies.

Grannie Smith: Originally from Australia, the Grannie Smith is widely grown in California and Washington. Green skin, delectably firm, tart flesh. One of my favorite eating apples, and excellent for all sorts of cooking and salads.

Stayman: dark-red skin; rich, juicy, sweet-tart flesh. Good for eating and pies.

York Imperial: red skin with yellow-green streaking; firm pale flesh; mild sweet-tart flavor. Chiefly used for pies and apple sauce.

November

Baldwin: Large, red apple with green streaking; tart and aromatic—a welcome addition to the November larder; good for munching and excellent baked, sautéed, and in pies.

Winesap: One of our oldest varieties, and one of the best. Its thick, red skin covers a crunchy, white flesh; as the name suggests, the winesap has a tart, winey aftertaste. Excellent for eating and cooking.

Apple Butter with Calvados

MAKES 5 TO 6 PINTS

CALVADOS (accent on the first syllable) is an apple brandy distilled from cider; its name came from the Spanish galleon *Calvador,* which was shipwrecked on the Norman coast at the time of the Spanish Armada. The American equivalent of calvados is applejack, but it is a harsher, coarser beverage.

This recipe was inspired by one in an old *Farmer's Almanac.* It uses a sweetener popular in the nineteenth century—apple molasses, made by boiling down cider to a thick, sweet syrup. The result is an apple butter less sugary than commercial brands but nonetheless very tasty.

  1 **gallon apple cider**
10 **pounds cooking apples**
 ½ **cup brown sugar, or to taste**
 ½ **cup honey**
 ½ **cup molasses**
  3 **cinnamon sticks**
    Juice and zest of 2 lemons (remove the latter with a vegetable peeler)
 ½ **cup calvados or applejack**

  6 **1-pint canning jars**

(1) Pour the cider into a heavy stockpot, and boil it until reduced by half. Meanwhile, core and seed the apples, but leave the skins on. (They are loaded with pectin, which helps the apple butter thicken.) Add the apples to the reduced cider and simmer until soft. Remove the apples and put them through a food mill, or force them through a strainer with a wooden spoon, back into the apple cider.

(2) Add the remaining ingredients. Simmer the apple butter over a low, low flame for 3 hours, or until the mixture is thick and flavorful. (You will need to stir the apple butter from time to time, to keep it from burning on the bottom.) You can also cook it in a large roasting pan in a 350-degree oven. A traditional test for doneness is to spoon a little apple butter onto a plate. When

the juice no longer runs, the apple butter is ready. Add additional brown sugar if necessary, but don't make the butter too sweet.

(3) Sterilize the canning jars in boiling water. Spoon in the apple butter and seal. Apple butter will easily keep six months, and makes a lovely present for the holidays.

Veal Chops *Vallée d'Auge*

SERVES 4

THE Vallée d'Auge, in Normandy, is a district famous for its calvados. The hard cider used in this recipe should be very dry, like English Bulmer's or Woodpecker. If unavailable, use ¾ cup sweet cider and ¾ cup dry white wine.

> 4 veal chops (approximately 2 pounds)
> Salt and fresh white pepper
> 2 shallots
> 3 tablespoons butter
> 1 Jonathan or Cortland apple
> 1 tablespoon flour
> 2 tablespoons calvados, plus a few extra drops if desired
> 1½ cups hard cider
> ½ cup heavy cream

> *For the garnish:*
> 4 Jonathan or Cortland apples
> 4 tablespoons butter
> Approximately 1 cup sugar

(1) Trim the fat off the chops, and sprinkle with salt and pepper. Finely chop the shallots. Peel, core, and finely chop the first apple. Melt the butter in a nonaluminum sauté pan and brown the chops on both sides over high heat. Remove the chops from the pan and set aside. Add the shallots and apple to the pan and sauté over medium heat for 2 to 3 minutes, or until soft. Stir in the flour. Return the veal chops to the pan, add the 2 table-spoons calvados, and flambé. Stir in the dry cider and bring to a

boil, scraping the bottom of the pan to dissolve the congealed meat juices.

(2) Gently simmer the veal for 20 minutes, or until tender, adding the cream halfway through. Transfer the veal to a platter and keep warm. Boil the sauce until a generous cup of liquid remains. Add salt, pepper, and perhaps a few drops more calvados.

(3) Meanwhile, prepare the garnish. Peel and core the remaining 4 apples and cut them into quarters or eighths. Melt the butter in a large frying pan. Dip the apple wedges in sugar, and sauté over a high heat, turning frequently. The apples should be caramelized on all sides.

To serve, arrange the veal chops on a platter or individual plates and strain the sauce over them. Arrange the caramelized apples around the veal. Hard cider would be a good beverage. So would a tart white wine, like a Muscadet.

Grated Apple Pie

SERVES 8 TO 10

THIS apple pie owes its incredible richness to the fact that the apples are grated rather than sliced, so you can pack more into the crust. Use any good cooking apple (Baldwins or Cortlands work well), and leave the skins on for extra flavor. The recipe comes to us from a fine Midwestern cook named Rosemary Mack.

1 1½-cup batch basic pie dough (see recipe on page 476), or use your favorite dough

For the topping:
¼ cup brown sugar
¼ cup flour
   Pinch of salt
4 tablespoons cold butter

For the filling:
  6 large cooking apples (2½ pounds)
  ¼ cup white sugar, or more to taste
  ¼ cup brown sugar
  ½ teaspoon cinnamon
    Generous pinch each freshly grated nutmeg, powdered cloves,
      ground allspice, and salt
  1 tablespoon cornstarch
  1 teaspoon vanilla
    Grated zest and juice of 1 lemon

  1 10-inch pie pan

(1) Prepare the pastry dough, and chill for 30 minutes. Roll out the dough on a lightly floured surface and use it to line the pie pan.

(2) Preheat the oven to 375 degrees. Prepare the topping. Combine the brown sugar, flour, and salt in a food processor or bowl, and cut in the butter. Set aside. Prepare the filling. Core the apples and quarter them. Using the julienning or grating disk of a food processor or the coarse face of a hand grater, grate the apple quarters, skins and all. Remove any large pieces of skin; small pieces will add extra flavor. Stir in the remaining ingredients, adding additional sugar, if necessary, to taste.

(3) Spoon the filling into the crust. Sprinkle the topping over the filling. Bake the pie in the preheated oven for 40 minutes, or until the filling is bubbling and the topping is dappled with brown. Let cool to room temperature before serving, or serve warm with vanilla ice cream.

Caramelized Apple Pancake

SERVES 6 TO 8 UNDER NORMAL CIRCUMSTANCES,
BUT I HAVE BEEN KNOWN TO EAT A WHOLE ONE BY MYSELF

THIS apple dessert is part pie, part crêpe, part caramel apple, and 100 percent delicious. The recipe comes from my downstairs neighbor, Ellen Caldwell, who perfumes our building with exquisite smells from her kitchen. Use a firm tart green apple, like a Grannie Smith.

 2 tart green apples
 4 tablespoons butter for sautéing
 3 eggs
 ½ cup milk
 ½ cup flour
 ½ cup butter, melted
 ¼ cup white sugar
 ¼ cup brown sugar
 2 teaspoons cinnamon
  Juice of ½ lemon

 1 10-inch ovenproof teflon or well-seasoned cast iron frying pan

(1) Preheat the oven to 500 degrees. (The high temperature is necessary to caramelize the apples). Peel and core the apples and cut them into thin (⅛-inch) slices. Melt the 4 tablespoons butter in the frying pan over high heat. Add the apples, and sauté for 3 to 4 minutes, or until the slices are soft.

(2) Meanwhile, combine the eggs, milk, and flour in a bowl, and whisk to mix. Pour this mixture over the apples, place the pan in the oven, and bake for 10 to 12 minutes, or until the edges of the pancake are puffed and lightly browned.

(3) Pour the ½ cup melted butter over the pancake. Combine the sugar with the cinnamon and sprinkle on top. Return the pancake to the oven for 5 minutes, or until the sugar and butter have caramelized. Squeeze the lemon juice on top and cut the pancake into wedges. Serve warm.

OCTOBER

O suns and skies and clouds of June,
And flowers of June together,
Ye cannot rival for one hour
October's bright blue weather.

HELEN HUNT JACKSON

O CTOBER is a month loved by landscape painters and leaf-peepers. We are treated to a fireworks display of leaves turning from green to crimson to golden. New England's autumnal forests blaze like the burning bush of the Bible. Farm stands come alive with gaily colored squash.

October was the eighth month of the old Roman calendar, *octo* being Latin for "eight," In northern Europe October was known as *Wyn-Monath,* "wine month," for this was the time of year for treading grapes into wine. It was also called *Winter-Fullith.* Winter was said to begin with the first full moon of October. In medieval iconography, October is portrayed as a farmer sowing grains of winter wheat.

October fills the more melancholy among us with feelings of foreboding. The riotous hues of fall foliage gradually give way to the skeletal bare branches of winter.

The baring of field and forest makes us mindful of the end of the life cycle. October 31 was the last day of the Celtic calendar. For Christians it became Halloween, also called the Eve of All Saints or All Hallows. Great fires were once kindled at home and outdoors to warm the souls of the dead. Other activities included cracking walnuts and bobbing for apples. Today we light jack-o'-lanterns, not All Hallows' bonfires, and the medieval belief in hobgoblins survives in our costumed young trick-or-treaters.

A Jewish holiday called Sukkot—also known as the Feast of Booths—is celebrated in October. In the days when the Hebrews were an agrarian people, the demands of the harvest were so pressing that farmers slept in hastily erected shelters in the fields.

Modern Jews observe the holiday by constructing a *sukkah,* a booth of canvas or wood, decked with a roof of branches—the sky must shine through the leaves. For seven days the family eats all its meals in the sukkah, and harvest fruits, like figs, squash, and pomegranates, are traditionally served.

October brings many fall crops to the market: a profusion of apples and pears, and squashes of every hue and dimension. Pomegranates come to us from the warmer climates; we look forward to persimmons and quinces. In many states hunting season opens in October—for the next few months game enthusiasts are treated to fresh venison, pheasant, and dove. On the East Coast fishermen can harvest bay scallops now that the warm summer months are over. These diminutive creatures are the sweetest shellfish we know of.

October marks the start of football season. Armchair athletes take to their cars and celebrate with tailgate picnics. Those of us with wood stoves or fireplaces must split and stack wood, and there's no better way to work up an appetite. October, then, is a month of transition. Our thoughts move inward, even as we reap the last of the fruits of the harvest.

POMEGRANATES

The pomegranate opens
A hundred sons

S o mused a Chinese poet about the scarlet fruit called the pomegranate. In many cultures this multiseeded fruit is a symbol of fertility. (The name comes from the Latin *pomum,* "apple," and *granatum,* "full of seeds.") In Turkey, for example, young women dash the fruit to the ground: the number of seeds that fall out foretell how many children they will have.

In Greek mythology the pomegranate is responsible for winter. Persephone, daughter of the Harvest Goddess, Demeter, was abducted by Pluto to Hades. Enraged, her mother cursed the earth, withering crops and killing cattle. After many entreaties from gods and men, Zeus gave Demeter leave to fetch her daughter back to Mount Olympus. Unfortunately, the maiden had eaten six pomegranate seeds, so she was obliged to spend six months of the year in Hades. Demeter, rejoicing at her daughter's return, gave the world six months of spring and summer. When Persephone is absent, the mother's lament takes the form of autumn and winter.

The pomegranate looks like a leathery red ball filled with ruby-colored seeds the size of currants. It is prized in hot climates, where its refreshing juice makes an ideal thirst-quencher. The pomegranate has a unique flavor: it is tart, like the cranberry; perfumed, like rose water; and as refreshing as freshly squeezed orange juice. The taste is only half the pleasure: the fleshy grains are delightful to chew, each one bursting like a bead of salmon caviar. Yes, you can swallow the seeds.

When buying pomegranates, look for large, round fruits with an unblemished red or pink skin. Choose a fruit that feels heavy in the hand, avoiding those with soft spots or split skins.

EXTRACTING THE JUICE AND SEEDS

IN cooking, as in life, few good things come easy. This is true for the pomegranate, with its leathery skin, bitter pith, and tightly packed seeds. To extract the seeds, use a knife to score the skin, and cut or break the fruit in half, working over a bowl to catch the juice. Use your hands to break the halves into sections, and flake these into individual seeds.

To extract the juice, simply cut the pomegranate in half, and press each half on a citrus reamer. One pomegranate yields approximately ⅓ cup juice.

Mohamarra
(Pomegranate-Walnut Pâté)

MAKES 3 CUPS

MOHAMARRA is an Armenian dish, a spicy dip made from pomegranates, walnuts, and peppers. It is scooped up and eaten on wedges of pita bread. The version below uses a formidable dose of hot peppers—if you don't have an iron gullet, feel free to add less. (Aleppo is the brand of hot peppers preferred by Armenians—it is available at most Middle Eastern grocery stores.) The recipe comes from Julia Zerounian, a fine cook from Soviet Armenia.

  1 large pomegranate (enough for ⅓ cup juice)
  1 cup walnuts
  2 tablespoons red pepper flakes
  2 large red bell peppers
  Juice of 1–2 lemons
⅓–½ cup fresh bread crumbs
  1 tablespoon ground cumin
  3 tablespoons pine nuts, plus 2 tablespoons for garnish
  Approximately ¼ cup extra-virgin olive oil
  Salt and fresh black pepper

  Sprigs of flat-leaf parsley for garnish
  Wedges of pita for serving

(1) Juice the pomegranate on a citrus reamer: you should have ⅓ cup juice. Finely chop the walnuts. (You can use the food processor, but run the machine in spurts and don't overgrind, or you'll wind up with an oily mess.) Soak the pepper flakes in 2 tablespoons warm water. Core and seed the bell peppers and very finely chop (almost purée) in the food processor. Juice the lemons.

(2) Combine the ingredients in the food processor or a mixing bowl, adding just enough olive oil to hold everything together. Add salt and pepper to taste. Serve the mohamarra in a bowl or mounded on a platter, with wedges of pita bread for

serving. Use the remaining pine nuts and parsley sprigs for garnish.

NOTE: This pâté, delicious as it is, has a rather strange color. You may wish to cover the top with parsley.

Pomegranate Salad Waldorf

SERVES 4

WALDORF salad was created by Oscar Tschirky (of veal fame) to honor the opening of the famous Waldorf Hotel in 1893. In this version, pomegranate seeds replace the traditional celery, and pomegranate juice is used to enliven the dressing.

2 pomegranates
1 large, crisp, tart apple
1 ripe pear
Juice of ½ lemon
½ cup pecans
2 tablespoons chopped fresh chives or scallions

For the dressing:
Pomegranate juice from above
3 tablespoons mayonnaise (see recipe on page 477 or use a good commercial brand)
2 teaspoons balsamic vinegar
1 tablespoon walnut or hazelnut oil (or olive oil)
Salt and fresh black pepper
A small amount of honey, if necessary

(1) Break 1 pomegranate into individual grains. Cut the other pomegranate in half and extract the juice with a reamer. Peel and core the apple and pear, and cut them into ½-inch dice. Sprinkle the fruit with lemon juice to prevent it from discoloring. Lightly toast the pecans on a baking sheet in a preheated 400-degree oven.

(2) Prepare the dressing. Place the mayonnaise in a salad

bowl, and gradually whisk in the remaining ingredients. Add salt and pepper to taste, and, if the dressing is too tart, a little honey. Add the fruit and nuts, and gently toss to coat the individual pieces with dressing.

Chicken with Pomegranate Sauce

SERVES 4

THIS dish is a specialty of the Caucasus, a mountainous region in southeast Russia, where people live to be over 100. Traditionally the walnuts are ground, but I like to leave them in small pieces to give the sauce more texture. A whole chicken, cut into 8 pieces, can be substituted for the chicken breasts. I highly recommend Sonia Uvezian's *Cooking from the Caucasus* (Harcourt, Brace, and Jovanovich) to anyone who wants to learn more about the soulful cooking of this region.

    4 whole boneless chicken breasts
    3 pomegranates
    ¾ cup shelled walnuts
    1 small onion, or 2 shallots
      Salt and fresh black pepper
      Flour for dredging
    3 tablespoons butter
      Juice of 1 lemon, or to taste
    1 cup chicken stock (see recipe on page 472)
    ½ teaspoon cinnamon
      Pinch of ground coriander
    ½ teaspoon sugar

(1) Cut each breast in half and trim off any fat or sinew. Cut 2 of the pomegranates in half and press out the juice with a reamer. Break the third pomegranate open and extract the seeds, working over a bowl to catch the juices. You should have approximately ⅔ cup pomegranate juice and ⅔–1 cup seeds. Finely chop or grind the walnuts. Finely chop the onion or shallots. Preheat the oven to 350 degrees.

(2) Season the chicken breasts with salt and fresh black pepper. Dredge them in flour, shaking off the excess. Meanwhile, heat the butter in a frying pan that is not cast iron or aluminum. Lightly brown the chicken breasts on both sides over high heat, and transfer to a baking dish. Lower the heat to medium, and cook the onions or shallots for 3 minutes, or until soft, adding the walnuts halfway through.

(3) Deglaze the pan with the lemon juice. Add the pomegranate juice, stock, cinnamon, coriander, sugar, and a little salt and pepper. Simmer for a minute and correct the seasoning with salt, pepper, sugar, and perhaps a squeeze of lemon. The sauce should be balanced between sweet and sour. Reduce the sauce to coating consistency.

(4) Drain any collected juices from the chicken breasts, cover with sauce, and bake in the preheated oven for 15 minutes, or until the chicken is cooked through. Sprinkle the chicken with the remaining pomegranate seeds, and serve at once.

SCALLOPS

Give me my scallop-shell of quiet,
My staff of faith to walk upon,
My scrip of joy, immortal diet,
My bottle of salvation,
My gown of glory, hope's true gage,
And thus I'll take my pilgrimage.

SIR WALTER RALEIGH,
''HIS PILGRIMAGE''

THE scallop is the only bivalve to have a patron saint. Considering the rigors of gathering this fan-shaped shellfish, the scallop fishermen need one. Imagine donning waist-high boots, wading in icy water up to your hips, and raking up hundreds of pounds of scallops as a numbing November wind whips the sea around you. And that's the easy part! The hard part is shucking the scallops: prying open the razor-sharp shells with your bare fingers and inserting a knife to cut the adductor, the muscle that holds the shells together. It is only this meaty muscle that we eat. To obtain a single pound of meat, the fisherman must haul and shuck ten pounds of scallops. Which helps explain why this shellfish is among the most costly of the fishmonger's wares.

The association of scallops and religion is a venerable one, dating from the martyrdom of St. James, the apostle who brought Christianity to Spain. The saint was put to death in Judea in 44 A.D., and his corpse was put to sea in a boat. According to the legend, a steed swam out, recovered the body, and miraculously returned it to Santiago de Campostela in Spain. The horse and rider emerged from the sea covered with round, ribbed scallop shells. Santiago became an important destination for pilgrims during the Middle Ages; worshipers would return to Paris, London, or Cologne decked with scallop shells—a testimony to their pilgrimage. The French name for scallop, appropriately enough, is *coquille St. Jacques,* "St. James shell."

Religion aside, scallops are remarkable creatures, and among the rare bivalves that can see. Their shells are rimmed with iridescent green eyes (forty to fifty of them) that can detect light and motion, but not form. Scallops are hermaphroditic, and Europeans consider their firm, pink roe a delicacy. They are also speedy critters: when threatened, they snap shut their shells, firing jets of water to shoot themselves away.

The meat is sweet and fine-textured. I, for one, would just as soon eat scallops as lobster. There are two major types: sea scallops and bay scallops. The former are four to six inches across, and yield nuggets of meat the size of a walnut. Bay scallops are found in shallow waters from Cape Cod to the Gulf of Mexico. The edible part is no bigger than your thumbnail, but it's incredibly sweet and delicate.

Unlike other bivalves, scallops cannot hold their shells

closed; they quickly die out of the water. Consequently, scallops are usually shelled at sea. Sometimes commercial distributors soak their scallops in fresh water to make the muscles heavier and moister. This improves the appearance of the shellfish but only at the expense of flavor. A downright fraudulent practice is that of stamping out scallop-shaped pieces from the wings of ray or skate. Ersatz scallops are recognizable by a suspicious uniformity in size and shape. Another check for duplicity is the consistent lack of the small, crescent shaped muscle on the side (see below).

When buying scallops, look for whole, plump muscles, with a clean, pleasantly briny smell. Sea scallops are available year-round, and are at their best during the summer. Bay scallop season ranges from mid-October to March. Freezing makes scallops look watery and opaque; another telltale sign is lots of milky liquid at the bottom of the tray. As is true with most seafood, freezing is worse for the texture than the taste.

Like most shellfish, scallops are most tender when raw. Their cooking time should be measured in seconds, not minutes. (Indeed, in Latin America scallops are marinated and enjoyed raw in a dish called ceviche.) Scallops are well-suited to sautéing, broiling, frying, and baking. In this country the term *coquilles St. Jacques* indicates scallops baked in their shells in cream sauce and surrounded by a border of decoratively swirled mashed potatoes. Whichever cooking method you use, don't skimp on the butter: the scallop itself has very little fat. The scallop's firm texture and lack of bones make it excellent for mousses and pâtés.

Scallops have a small, opaque, crescent-shaped muscle on one side, which should be removed before cooking. (It's noticeably tougher than the rest of the shellfish.) Simply pull it off with your fingers. I call this technique "circumsizing," a term which is not yet universally accepted! Not every scallop will have such an appendage (they fall off during shucking), but be suspicious if all are removed. When buying scallops, figure on one-half pound per person.

Carpaccio of Scallops and Tuna

SERVES 4 AS AN APPETIZER

THIS colorful dish was a specialty of Louis LeRoy, a Breton chef with whom I happily apprenticed one summer. Think of it, if you will, as a French rendition of ceviche. The important thing about the herbs is freshness—feel free to make substitutions for the ones called for below.

    ½ **pound fresh sea scallops**
    ½ **pound fresh tuna**
    2 **tablespoons drained green peppercorns**
    2 **tablespoons finely chopped flat-leaf parsley**
    1 **tablespoon finely chopped fresh tarragon or basil**
    1 **tablespoon finely chopped fresh chives**
    1 **tablespoon finely minced shallots or scallions**
    3 **tablespoons extra-virgin olive oil**
      Juice of 1–2 lemons
      Salt and a little fresh black pepper

(1) Cut the scallops across the grain into the thinnest possible slices. Cut the tuna the same way. (If necessary, flatten the slices with the side of a cleaver—they should be thin enough to read through!) Use the fish to carpet four chilled dinner plates, one side white and one side red. (For a whimsical touch, you could use the two colors of seafood to decorate the plates like the yin-yang symbol.)

(2) Crush the peppercorns with the side of a knife. Finely chop all the herbs. Sprinkle the fish with the herbs and peppercorns. The recipe can be prepared to this stage up to 1 hour before serving.

(3) Just before serving, sprinkle the fish with the olive oil, lemon juice, salt, and pepper. Gently pat the fish with your fingers to work in the flavors, adding lemon juice or salt to taste.

Scallops with Lemon and Rosemary, Wrapped and Broiled in Pancetta

SERVES 8 AS AN APPETIZER

THIS recipe is simplicity itself, but I know of no better way to serve scallops. Pancetta is Italian bacon, cured with the same spices as prosciutto. If unavailable, substitute a good smoked bacon.

> 1 **pound sea scallops**
> 3 **tablespoons extra-virgin olive oil**
> 4 **strips lemon peel**
> 2 **sprigs rosemary**
> 20 **coarse grinds of pepper**
> 6–8 **ounces thinly sliced pancetta**
>
> **Toothpicks**

(1) "Circumcise" the scallops—that is, remove and discard the half moon–shaped muscle on the side. Cut the larger scallops in half, so all are the same size. Combine the scallops, oil, lemon peel, rosemary, and pepper in a glass bowl and marinate for 2 hours. Cut the pancetta into 2-inch pieces.

(2) Drain the scallops, discarding the lemon peel and rosemary. Wrap each scallop with pancetta and secure with a toothpick. Just before serving, preheat the broiler, and broil the scallops for 1 to 2 minutes per side, or until the pancetta is crisp and the scallops are firm. Blot the excess fat on paper towels and drain. Serve immediately.

Bay Scallops with Ginger, Scallions, and Garlic

SERVES 3 TO 4

THIS dish is a Cantonese specialty. Have all your ingredients chopped and measured ahead. The actual cooking time is measured in seconds, not minutes. Snow peas can be added to the dish for extra color.

- 1 pound bay scallops
- 1 2-inch piece fresh ginger root
- 4 scallions
- 2 cloves garlic

For the sauce:
- 3 tablespoons chicken stock or water
- 2 teaspoons soy sauce
- 2 teaspoons rice wine or sherry
- 1 teaspoon sesame oil
- Juice of ½ lemon, or to taste
- ½ teaspoon sugar
- Salt and fresh black pepper to taste
- 1 teaspoon cornstarch

2 tablespoons peanut oil for frying

(1) "Circumcise" the scallops—that is, remove the small, opaque muscle on the side of each scallop. Cut the ginger diagonally into ¼-inch slices. Finely chop the scallions. Mince the garlic. Combine the ingredients for the sauce in a small bowl, and stir in the cornstarch to make a thin paste. The recipe can be prepared up to 6 hours ahead to this stage.

(2) Just before serving, place a wok over a high flame. Add the peanut oil, heat it for 10 seconds, and swirl the wok to coat the inside with oil. Add the ginger, scallions, and garlic, and fry for 20 seconds. Add the scallops and stir-fry for 30 seconds, or until the scallops are almost cooked. Stir the sauce to redissolve the cornstarch, then add it to the scallops. Cook for 30 seconds,

or until the sauce has thickened and the scallops are cooked. Correct the seasoning, adding salt or lemon juice to taste. Serve at once—a Chardonnay from California or Burgundy would make a nice accompaniment.

NOTE: The ginger is added as a flavoring. Warn your guests that they are not actually meant to eat the whole slices.

Scallop Mousselines with Saffron Butter Sauce

MAKES 12 ½-CUP MOUSSELINES, WHICH
WILL SERVE 12 AS AN APPETIZER, 6 AS A
FIRST COURSE, OR 4 AS A MAIN COURSE

MOUSSELINES are the lightest fish mousses—made exclusively with egg whites and cream. In the following recipe, scallop mousselines are baked in lettuce-lined ramekins and served with an orange-hued saffron sauce—the result is as colorful as a Van Gogh painting. It is important to use fresh seafood: previously frozen makes watery mousselines. The mousse mixture can be made entirely in the food processor, but run the machine in short spurts when adding the cream to prevent it from separating.

1 pound fresh bay scallops or sea scallops
½ pound fresh fillet of sole or other mild white fish
  Salt, fresh white pepper, cayenne pepper, and freshly grated nutmeg
  Juice of ½ lemon, or to taste
3 egg whites, plus 1 extra if necessary
1 large head Boston or Bibb lettuce
½–⅔ cup heavy cream

1 batch Saffron Butter Sauce (see recipe on page 355)

12 ½-cup ramekins or timbale molds
2–3 tablespoons butter, melted, for buttering the ramekins

(1) Cut any large scallops in half. It is not necessary to "circumcise" them (see above recipe). Run your fingers over the fish, feeling for bones—remove any you find. Cut the fish into ½-inch pieces. Purée the scallops and fish in a food processor. Leave the processor running, and add the seasonings, lemon juice, and, one by one, the egg whites. Purée until smooth. Place the purée, processor bowl and all, in the freezer for 15 minutes—the cream is less likely to separate if the mixture is very well chilled.

(2) Meanwhile, break apart the lettuce leaves and wash, trying to keep the leaves intact. Cook the leaves in rapidly boiling, lightly salted water for 30 seconds, then refresh under cold water and drain. Thickly brush the ramekins with the melted butter, chill, and brush again. Line each ramekin with a lettuce leaf, letting the excess hang over the edge. Bring 1 quart water to a boil.

(3) Finish the mousseline mixture. Place the bowl back on the processor. Add ½ cup cream in a thin stream, running the processor in short spurts. Take a hazelnut-sized bit of mousseline mixture on the end of a spoon and drop it in the boiling water. Cook for 30 seconds, then taste it—if the mousseline seems rubbery, add more cream. If it falls apart, add more egg white. Correct the seasonings. Keep testing the mixture as necessary, adding cream or seasonings, but running the machine as little as possible. When you are satisfied with the results, spoon the mousseline mixture into the ramekins, folding the excess lettuce leaf back over the top. The recipe can be prepared to this stage up to 8 hours before baking.

(4) Preheat the oven to 350 degrees. Bring 1 quart water to a boil. Set the ramekins in a roasting pan with ½ inch boiling water. (This is called a water bath, and it provides a moist, gentle heat for cooking the mousselines.) Cover the ramekins with a sheet of buttered foil, and bake them for 25 to 35 minutes, or until the mousseline mixture is cooked. (It will feel firm and springy, and an inserted skewer will come out clean.) Prepare the saffron butter sauce, adding any liquid from the mousselines.

(5) To serve, invert the mousselines onto a small dish, and

slide them onto a platter or warm plates. Spoon the sauce around them, and serve at once. (For another nice presentation, cut each mousseline in half, spread the halves to form a V, and spoon the sauce in the middle.)

Scallop mousseline is a refined dish—serve your best Meursault, Montrachet, or California Chardonnay.

Saffron Butter Sauce

MAKES 1 CUP

THIS colorful sauce is a cousin of *beurre blanc,* white butter sauce from the Loire Valley. It goes well with most types of seafood.

    1 cup dry white wine
    ¼ cup white wine vinegar or rice vinegar
    3 tablespoons very finely chopped shallots (about 3 shallots)
    ⅛ teaspoon saffron
    ¼ cup heavy cream
    ¾ cup cold unsalted butter, cut into ½-inch pieces
     Salt, fresh white pepper, and cayenne pepper

Combine the wine, vinegar, shallots, and saffron in a heavy nonaluminum saucepan. Boil these ingredients until only ¼ cup liquid remains. Add the cream and continue boiling until only ¼ cup liquid remains. Working over high heat, whisk in the butter, piece by piece, followed by seasonings to taste. The sauce can boil while you are adding the butter, but do not let it boil once all the butter is in. Keep the saffron butter sauce on a warm corner of the stove, or on a cake rack over a pan of hot water. If the sauce curdles, try whisking it in a thin stream into 2 to 3 tablespoons cold heavy cream.

GAME

GROWING up in a nice Jewish home in the Baltimore suburbs, I did not have much exposure to game. It wasn't till I moved to Paris that I saw—and tasted—my first pheasant, boar, and venison. I was living around the corner from the open air rue Cler market. Come autumn, my walk to work took me past antlered deer, bristling wild boars, gaudily plumed pheasants, and warmly furred hares hanging on racks in front of the meat markets. It was as if an assassin had gone on a rampage at the local zoo, and I was the first person to arrive at the scene of the crime. Fortunately, gourmandise is a stronger force than squeamishness: although I don't enjoy killing game, I relish eating it.

Game can be divided into three categories: large game, small game, and birds. The first covers deer, elk, moose, and bear. Small game takes in rabbit, hare, racoon, and other furry animals. Game birds include, in descending order of size, wild turkey, goose, duck, pheasant, partridge, grouse, squab, dove, thrush (the alouette of the French children's song), and, the most delicious of them all, woodcock. The latter is eaten entrails and all, traditionally with a napkin over one's head to keep it from spattering. (It is rather messy.)

The best book I know of on game cookery is Jane Hibler's *Fair Game: A Hunter's Cookbook* (a volume in the Great American Cooking Schools series, published by Irena Chalmers). Jane is married to an inveterate hunter: it was at her home that I first sampled elk steaks (they tasted like beef, only more so), moose stroganoff, and burgers made of venison.

Game used to be the province of hunters but more and more is available at butcher shops and specialty markets. Two kinds of game are available today: beasts bagged by the hunter, and domesticated game, which is raised like cattle or poultry. The former has a richer flavor but can generally not be sold: to enjoy it, you must be a hunter yourself, or have a hunter friend. Domestic game is becoming increasingly popular: in addition to quail, pheasant, partridge, and venison, you can now get farm-raised boar, antelope, llama, and even hippopotamus!

Game lacks the benefit of a regular food supply and a vitamin-enriched diet. As a result, the meat is leaner than that of domestic animals. (Venison contains 2 percent fat, for example, while beef contains up to 14 percent.) Consequently, game must be bolstered with additional fat, or it will be unpalatably dry.

Because game is constantly on the move, it is tougher than penned up cattle or poultry. Marinating before cooking helps tenderize the muscle fibers. The marinade should contain an acid, like wine or vinegar, to break down muscle fibers, and a fat, like olive or walnut oil, to help the flavorings penetrate more quickly.

Tuscan Roast Pheasant

SERVES 4

HERE'S a delicious *fagiano arrosto* from Il Toscano, a stylish Italian restaurant on Beacon Hill. Pancetta is Italian bacon—it's cured like prosciutto, and it's available at Italian markets and gourmet shops. Try to use fresh herbs: if unavailable, use half the quantities called for of dry.

    2 fresh pheasants
    5 ounces thinly sliced pancetta (or bacon)
    1 tablespoon chopped fresh rosemary
    1 tablespoon chopped fresh thyme (1 ounce of herbs in all)
  2–3 cloves garlic
      Salt and fresh black pepper
   ¾ cup dry white wine
    3 tablespoons butter
    3 tablespoons cognac

(1) Prepare the pheasants for roasting. Normally they are sold ready to cook, but sometimes you will need to pull out the tiny pin feathers around the wings and legs. Do this with a tweezers or the edge of a paring knife. Remove any lumps of fat from the cavity. Preheat the oven to 350 degrees.

(2) Prepare the stuffing. Finely chop the pancetta, herbs, and garlic, and combine. Spoon the stuffing into the cavity, and truss the birds with string. Season the outsides with salt and pepper. Place the pheasants on their sides on a rack in a roasting pan. Roast them in the oven, turning the birds from one side to the other every 15 minutes. (The breast should remain down to prevent it from drying out.) After 30 minutes add the wine to the pan, and continue roasting and turning the birds for another 10 to 15 minutes. Increase the heat to 450 degrees (to brown the skin), and cook the pheasant for 5 minutes per side. The pheasants can can be prepared up to 1 hour ahead to this stage and kept warm.

(3) Remove the birds from the oven and cut each one in half. Place the halves, cut side down, in a large sauté pan, with any stuffing that falls out and the pan juices. Add the butter, and cook the birds over high heat for 3 to 4 minutes, or until no traces of pink remain in the meat. Add the cognac and flambé (see Note on page 258).

(4) Serve the pheasant at once, spooning the pan juices and stuffing on top. Wild rice would make a fine accompaniment. Choose a wonderful Italian wine, like a Gattinara or Barolo.

Blackened Venison with Citrus Sour Cream

SERVES 4

THIS dish is a nice example of the marriage of two cuisines. The mellow sour cream sauce tones down the pepper used for pan-blackening. The pan must be very hot to char the surface of the meat, leaving the center moist and tender. (The dish can also be made with beef tenderloin.) The recipe comes from the Boston French restaurant L'Espalier.

1½ pounds venison loin
2 tablespoons whole white peppercorns
1 tablespoon sea salt

For the sauce:
Juice of 3 oranges
Juice of 1–2 lemons
Pinch of cayenne pepper
¾ cup sour cream
Salt and fresh white pepper

2 tablespoons clarified butter (see page 471)
8 sprigs of fresh cilantro for garnish

(1) Cut the venison into medallions (small, ½-inch thick steaks). Coarsely grind the peppercorns and salt in a spice mill, in a mortar and pestle, or under a skillet.

(2) Prepare the sauce. Combine the citrus juices and cayenne pepper in a nonaluminum saucepan. Boil them over high heat until only 3 tablespoons liquid remain. Remove the pan from the heat, and stir in the sour cream, and salt and pepper to taste.

(3) Just before serving, heat a heavy skillet over high heat for 3 minutes. Dust the venison medallions with the pepper mixture. Add the clarified butter to the pan, heat it almost to smoking, then add the medallions. Cook for 1 minute per side: the meat should be charred and crisp on the outside and rare within. Place the venison medallions on warm dinner plates and spoon the sauce on top. Garnish each medallion with a sprig of coriander leaf.

Blackened venison would go well with the Parsnip Pancakes on page 54. For wine I would recommend a red Burgundy like Volnay or Chambertin.

Venison Hash

FOOD, like fashion, has its rising and plunging hemlines. Consider that homey specialty of the greasy spoon, hash. Hash was originally invented as a way to use up leftovers. (Our word comes from the French *hâcher,* "to chop.") More recently, hash has become the darling of "new" American restaurants, selling for as much as twelve dollars an order. Good hash is like an impressionist painting: a marriage of individual flavors into a harmonious, brightly hued whole. The following recipe calls for venison (it's a great hunter's breakfast), but beef or lamb will give you equally delectable results.

For the hash:

   Enough cooked venison (or beef or lamb) to make 1½ cups diced meat
2 large baking potatoes
2 tablespoons butter
2 tablespoons olive oil
1 small red bell pepper, cored, seeded, and diced (about ½ cup)
1 small green bell pepper, cored, seeded, and diced (about ½ cup)
2 ribs celery, diced (about ½ cup)
2–3 scallions, diced (about ½ cup)
   Approximately 1 cup chicken stock (see recipe on page 472), beef stock, or water
1 scant teaspoon Tabasco sauce, or to taste
1 scant tablespoon Worcestershire sauce, or to taste
3 tablespoons chopped fresh parsley or other herbs
   Salt and fresh black pepper

4 fresh extra-large eggs
   Butter for frying eggs

(1) Cut the meat into cubes just shy of a ½ inch in length. Cut the potatoes the same way. Place the potatoes in water to cover, bring to a boil, and simmer for 5 minutes, or until the cubes are almost tender. Drain.

(2) Heat the butter and oil in a large skillet. Add the peppers,

celery, and scallions, and sauté over medium heat for 3 minutes, or until the vegetables are tender. Add the potatoes, venison, stock or water, and flavorings, and increase the heat to high. Cook the hash, stirring from time to time, until most of the liquid has evaporated. If the meat is not sufficiently tender, add more stock or water, and boil most of it away. Let the hash brown and crisp in the pan before serving.

(3) Correct the seasoning, adding additional salt, pepper, Tabasco sauce, and Worcestershire sauce to taste. Melt the butter in another skillet. Fry the eggs (you can also poach them). Spoon the hash onto warm plates, topping each serving with a fried egg. There are lots of possibilities for beverages: mimosas, bloody marys, stout, ale, or even strong black coffee.

Rabbit with Pearl Onions and White Wine

SERVES 4

HERE'S a dish from our northern neighbors in Canada. The taste of rabbit is usually likened to a cross between chicken and veal. Fresh rabbit can usually be found at an Italian market. Our thanks for the recipe go to Guy and Kathy Viens.

1 3–4 pound rabbit
Salt and fresh black pepper

For the marinade:
1 onion
3 cloves garlic
2 cups Riesling or other white wine
¼ cup wine vinegar
2 tablespoons paprika
3 cloves
Bouquet garni (see recipe on page 471)
2 tablespoons soy sauce

For cooking:
¼ pound salt pork
2 tablespoons olive oil
1 cup flour for dredging the rabbit
4 tablespoons brandy or cognac
24 pearl onions
2 tablespoons butter, at room temperature
2 tablespoons flour for thickening the sauce

(1) Cut the rabbit into serving pieces and sprinkle liberally with salt and pepper. Prepare the marinade. Finely chop the onion and garlic. Combine the ingredients for the marinade in a nonaluminum bowl, add the rabbit pieces, and marinate overnight.

(2) Blanch the salt pork, drain, and dice. Heat the olive oil in a large skillet and brown the salt pork. Meanwhile, remove the rabbit from the marinade, pat it dry, and dust with flour, reserving the marinade. Discard all but 4 tablespoons fat from the frying pan. Sauté the rabbit pieces over medium heat until browned on all sides, and flambé with the brandy or cognac (see Note on page 258). Scrape the bottom of the pan with a spatula to dissolve any congealed meat juices. Peel the baby onions.

(3) Add the reserved marinade to the rabbit. Cover the pan and simmer the rabbit for 30 minutes. Uncover the pan, add the onions, and continue simmering for 30 to 40 minutes, or until the rabbit is tender. Remove the bouquet garni and discard.

(4) Prepare a kneaded butter (*beurre manie*). Using a fork, mix the 2 tablespoons butter and flour. Whisk the mixture into the sauce, and simmer for 2 to 3 minutes—the sauce will thicken. Correct the seasonings, adding salt and pepper to taste.

Serve the rabbit with an Alsatian Riesling and the Scalloped Jerusalem Artichokes on page 443.

Curried Game

SERVES 4

THIS recipe comes to us from a lodge in Nairobi. It is suitable for any sort of big game, from venison to zebra. The yogurt and lemon juice in the marinade help break down tough muscle fibers. The game can be grilled, broiled, or pan-fried.

1½ pounds venison, moose, or elk steaks

For the marinade:
- 2 medium onions
- 2 cloves garlic
- 1 ½-inch piece fresh ginger root
- 1 cup unflavored yogurt
  Juice of 1 lemon, or to taste
- 1 teaspoon ground turmeric
- ½ teaspoon ground coriander
- ¼ teaspoon ground cinnamon
- ½ teaspoon salt, or to taste
- 20 grinds of black pepper

- 2 teaspoons flour
- 3 tablespoons oil
- 2 tablespoons butter

(1) Cut the game into steaks ¾-inch thick. Finely chop the onions and garlic. Grate the ginger. Combine the ingredients for the marinade, adding additional salt or lemon juice to taste. Marinate the game for at least 2 hours, preferably overnight.

(2) Just before serving, remove the steaks from the marinade, blot them dry, and season with salt and pepper. Whisk the flour into the marinade, place it in a saucepan over a medium flame, and heat to a gentle simmer. Season the sauce to taste. Heat the oil and butter in a large skillet over a medium-high flame. Fry the steaks for 2 minutes per side, or until cooked to taste, and spoon the sauce on top.

Serve curried game with rice pilaf and a sturdy green, like

the Fried Kale with Sesame on page 69 or the Collard Greens with Spicy Relish on page 72. For a beverage try a Gewürztraminer from Alsace or a pilsner-style beer.

WINTER SQUASH

THIS one looks like a Turkish turban emblazoned with golden insignias. That one looks like a space monster, its blue-green skin gnarled and warty. Others resemble tom-toms, bananas, or overgrown acorns. Winter squash has arrived, turning our farm stands into autumn-colored menageries.

Squash is one of the numerous foods the New World gave to Europe. (Other contributions include turkey, cranberries, chocolate, potatoes, and corn.) Our word is an abbreviation of the Narraganset Indian word *askutasquash*. People tend to take squash for granted; children push it, uneaten, to the edge of their plates. The first European settlers felt differently, however: winter squash was among the few vegetables available during those long, harsh winters.

Winter squash differs from summer squash in that it is eaten when fully ripe. The thick, protective rind must be removed, as must the seeds, which are completely developed. (Roasted, the latter make a great high-protein snack.) Below are some of the many varieties that come to market in the fall.

Buttercup Squash: Looks like a dark-green pumpkin. The orange flesh is good for pies.

Butternut Squash: One of the most common winter squashes, the butternut resembles a giant, misshapen light bulb. The rind is tan, the flesh is orange, with fine-grained seeds in the long end. Excellent for steaming and purées.

Delicata Squash (sometimes called *sweet potato squash*): Looks like a swollen cucumber, with alternating lengthwise stripes and shallow ridges. The color ranges from yellow to green, with lengthwise pinkish stripes.

Gourd: Includes numerous squashes with bumpy, yellow to pale-green skin. Gourds are nonedible, but they do make nice table ornaments.

Hubbard Squash: A mammoth of the vegetable kingdom, the hubbard squash looks like a creature from *Return of the Jedi*. It is pointed at both ends, blue-green in color, and covered with thick, warty skin. A typical hubbard weighs ten to twelve pounds; an axe is the best tool for cutting it. (It is usually sold already peeled and sectioned.) Incidentally, the squash is named for one Elizabeth Hubbard of Marblehead, Massachusetts, who gave one to a botanically minded friend in 1842.

Spaghetti Squash: This fall squash is remarkable for its mild-flavored flesh, which forms perfect spaghetti strands when scraped with a fork. Shaped like a watermelon, with a bright yellow rind, spaghetti squash measures six to twelve inches in length.

Turk's Turban (also called *turban squash*): As the name suggests, this orange and green squash has a turbanlike base surmounted by a wide, round crown. Turban squash is good for baking.

Winter squash is extremely versatile: it can be steamed, boiled, stuffed, or baked, and made into soups, purées, gratins, and desserts. It is well-served by such autumnal flavorings as maple syrup, brown sugar, ginger, and nutmeg. It also goes well with turkey, sausage, and pork.

Sherried Winter Squash Soup

SERVES 8

USE one of the less sweet varieties, like hubbard, turban, or butternut. Roasted squash seeds make a delicious garnish (see roasted pumpkin seed recipe on page 399), as would a spoonful of fig chutney (see page 59).

4 **pounds winter squash**
2 **carrots**
2 **branches celery**
1 **small onion**
1 **leek, trimmed and washed**
4 **tablespoons butter**
1 **sweet potato**
6–7 **cups chicken stock (see recipe on page 472)**
Bouquet garni (see recipe on page 471)
¼ **teaspoon ground coriander**
¼ **teaspoon ground sage**
Freshly grated nutmeg
Salt and fresh black pepper
Approximately 1 cup heavy cream
¼ **cup cream sherry**

(1) Cut the squash in half and remove the seeds. If using butternut or turban squash, place them on a lightly buttered baking sheet, cut side down. If using hubbard squash, butter the cut side and loosely wrap it in foil. Bake the squash in a pre-heated 350-degree oven for 1 hour or till tender. *Note*: The recipe can be prepared ahead to this stage, or feel free to use leftover cooked squash.

(2) When squash is done, finely chop the carrots, celery, onion, and leek. Melt the butter in a large saucepan, and cook the vegetables over medium heat for 4 to 5 minutes, or until tender but not browned. Meanwhile, scrape the cooked squash out of the skin. Peel and dice the sweet potato. Add the stock to the large saucepan along with the squash, sweet potato, bouquet garni, and seasonings. Gently simmer these ingredients for 30 to 40 minutes, or until all are very tender. Remove and discard the bouquet garni.

(3) Purée the soup in batches in a blender (a blender works better than a food processor). Return it to the pan, and add enough cream to obtain a liquidy consistency, and salt and pepper to taste. Just before serving, bring the soup to a boil, and whisk in sherry to taste off the heat. Ladle the soup into bowls; garnish each with roasted squash seeds, a spoonful of chutney, or finely chopped parsley.

Gratin of Squash and Sweet Potatoes

SERVES 6

THIS savory gratin has become a favorite of mine for holiday dinners. As the gratin bakes, a crisp, golden-brown crust forms on top. This crust is the best part, but you have to work to scrape it away from the sides of the pan. (This is how gratins got their name—the French word for "to scratch" or "to scrape" is *gratter*.)

½ **pound peeled winter squash, like butternut or hubbard**
½ **pound sweet potatoes or yams**
3–4 **tablespoons freshly grated Gruyère**
3–4 **tablespoons freshly grated Parmesan**
2 **scallions**
2 **sprigs parsley**
½ **cup sour cream**
Salt, fresh black pepper, and freshly grated nutmeg
2 **tablespoons butter**

1 **10-inch gratin dish or shallow baking dish, thickly buttered**

(1) Preheat the oven to 400 degrees. Cut the squash and sweet potatoes into 1-inch pieces. Cook them in a steamer till tender and cool. Grate the cheese. Cut the roots off the scallions and the stems off the parsley and finely chop.

(2) Combine the vegetables, cheese, scallions, parsley, sour cream, and seasonings in a bowl, and mix with a fork. Don't mash the squash too much—the mixture should be coarse and chunky. Correct the seasoning. Spoon the mixture into the buttered gratin dish and dot the top with butter. The recipe can be prepared to this stage a day in advance and stored in the refrigerator.

(3) Just before serving, cook the gratin in the preheated oven for 10 minutes, or until the mixture is hot and the top is lightly browned and bubbly. The gratin is an excellent accompaniment for Mama Spach's "Wedding" Turkey on page 383.

Winter Squash Timbales

SERVES 6

A timbale is a drum-shaped molded custard. The one below can be made with any orange-fleshed squash, not to mention with other winter vegetables, like celeriac or broccoli. (For a colorful presentation, make three batches of filling: one with squash, one with celeriac, and one with broccoli, and spoon them into the molds in layers.) Timbale molds look like miniature buckets; you can also use ramekins or custard cups.

¾ pound dense, orange-fleshed squash, like butternut or turban
3 tablespoons butter
2 eggs
2 egg yolks
2 teaspoons honey or maple syrup
2 teaspoons brown sugar, or to taste
    A few drops fresh lemon juice
    Salt and fresh black pepper
    Freshly grated nutmeg
¾ cup heavy cream

6 ½-cup timbale molds

(1) Cut the rind off the squash and cut the flesh into 1-inch pieces. Steam the squash for 10 to 15 minutes, or until soft. Meanwhile, melt the butter and use it to brush the insides of the molds. Chill the molds briefly, then brush again with butter. Preheat the oven to 350 degrees.

(2) Purée the squash in a food processor (or force it through a strainer): you should have 1½ cups purée. Work in the eggs, egg yolks, and flavorings, adjusting the latter to the natural sweetness of the squash. Work in the cream, running the processor in short bursts. Be careful—overpuréeing will cause the cream to separate. (Or alternatively, work the cream in with a wooden spoon.) Spoon the filling into the buttered molds, and place the molds in a roasting pan with ½ inch boiling water.

(3) Bake the squash timbales for 20 to 30 minutes, or until

the filling is set. (The top will feel springy when pressed, and an inserted skewer will come out clean.) The timbales can be held in a pan of hot water for up to 30 minutes. To serve, invert the molds onto a platter or plates. Squash timbales make an attractive accompaniment to holiday turkey.

Spaghetti Squash with Mezithra Cheese and Brown Butter

SERVES 4

SPAGHETTI with mezithra cheese and brown butter is a traditional pasta dish in Greece. Mezithra is a tangy Greek cheese made from sheep's or goat's milk. You want an aged version suitable for grating—it is available at most Greek markets. (If mezithra is unavailable, use freshly grated Romano.) Brown butter is made by lightly burning fresh butter: remove the pan from the heat the moment the tiny particles of milk solids turn brown.

1 medium spaghetti squash
6 tablespoons unsalted butter
4 tablespoons finely chopped scallion
6 tablespoons finely grated mezithra cheese
Fresh black pepper

(1) Cut the spaghetti squash in half and remove the seeds. Bake it cut side down on a lightly buttered baking sheet in a preheated 350-degree oven for 30 to 40 minutes, or until tender.

(2) Scrape the inside of the squash with a fork to separate the flesh into spaghettilike strands. Mound these on a serving platter. Cook the butter in a saucepan or skillet over high heat for 1 to 2 minutes, or until it begins to brown. Add the scallions and cook for 10 seconds. Pour the brown butter over the spaghetti squash, and sprinkle with mezithra cheese and pepper. You probably won't need salt, as the cheese is quite salty, but add it if necessary.

PEARS

PITY the pear. Its cousin, the apple, got all the lead roles in history. But in Colonial America, pears rivaled apples: they were used to make wine, sauce, preserves, and even a sort of hard cider. We're pleased to report that this bulbous fruit is currently making a comeback.

There are over three thousand varieties of pears around the world, many developed during the nineteenth century. Pears can be grouped in two classes: the soft-fleshed European varieties and the hard-fleshed Oriental. Soft pears include the Comice, Bartlett, and Anjou, while hard-fleshed types include the Seckel and Asian. Below are some of the varieties most widely sold in the United States.

Comice (also called *red pear*): This splendid fruit is the aristocrat of peardom. Its bright-red skin covers a fine white flesh that's as fragrant and pleasing as perfume. (There is also a green-skinned variety.) Most of our Comice pears come from the Hood River Valley in Oregon, where they are handpicked and lovingly nurtured. An excellent eating fruit, the Comice pear is also good for desserts.

Bartlett: America's Bartlett pear is none other than the popular Williams pear of Europe. It was brought to this country from England in the eighteenth century by a farmer named Brewer, but it was named for his neighbor, Enoch Bartlett. Bartlett (1779–1860) was a merchant in Dorchester, Massachusetts, who promoted the pear under his own name and eventually bought Brewer's orchard. The Bartlett is the most widely grown pear in the United States. A yellow-skinned pear (sometimes with a red blush), it is fragrant and exceptionally juicy. Its flavor has the honied sweetness of muscatel wine.

Anjou: The Anjou pear, named for a town in the Loire Valley, is a large, plump fruit with a short neck and yellow-green skin. The smooth-textured flesh has spicy, almost winy aftertaste.

Bosc: Recognizable by its long, tapering neck and russet skin, the Bosc pear is mildly acidic and tasty. The texture is slightly grainy.

Seckel: This diminutive pear turns up at the end of September, and is all but gone by Thanksgiving. Named for the Philadelphia farmer who first grew it, it resembles the hard-fleshed pears grown in Asia. Seckels are small, long-necked pears, russet or green-brown in color. The flesh is snappy and crisp, with a grainy, almost sandy consistency. Seckel pears are excellent for salads and canning.

Asian: The Asian pear is round like an apple, and its green-brown skin is speckled with russet. The celery-crisp texture is its chief virtue, as the flavor is rather bland.

Anjou and Bosc pears are available most of the year; Comice and Seckel only in the fall. The harvest starts in early October: look for Bartlett pears first, then Seckels, and last of all Comice. Most pears are picked underripe: let them ripen at room temperature until fragrant and palpably soft.

Pears are delectable not only in desserts, but also in soups and with poultry or vegetables. Harder varieties, like Seckels or Boscs, are excellent in salads. Pears for pies should be soft and ripe: if you don't have time to let a green pear ripen, poach it till tender in a simple syrup (made by bringing equal parts sugar and water to a boil). Another way to enjoy pears is with cheese, particularly Brie and chèvre.

Brandied Seckel Pears

MAKES 4 TO 6 PINTS

SECKEL pears rank among the most ephemeral of fall fruits. The recipe below and the one that follows are two delicious ways to give them an extended shelf-life. Our thanks to Marcia Walsh for the recipes. Jars of brandied or pickled pears make wonderful gifts for the holidays.

The heady brandied pears below are a good accompaniment for cold meats. The following recipe can be halved if desired.

    4 pounds whole Seckel pears
    2 cups sugar
    1 lemon
  4–6 cinnamon sticks
1½–2 cups brandy

    4–6 1-pint canning jars

(1) The pears must be free of any blemishes or bruises. Wash and set aside. Combine the sugar and 4 cups water in a saucepan large enough to hold all the pears. Place the pan over a low heat to dissolve the sugar, bring to a simmer, and add the pears. Simmer for 10 minutes, remove from the heat, and allow the pears to cool in the syrup.

(2) Meanwhile, slice the lemon into sixths and sterilize the canning jars. (If you have enough room in your refrigerator to store all the jars and want to skip this step you can, but be sure to simmer all the ingredients in the syrup and brandy mixture before putting the pears in jars.) Put a slice of lemon and a cinnamon stick in each jar. Add the cooled pears, alternating stem and blossom ends. (About 10 to 12 pears should fit in each jar.)

(3) Measure the poaching syrup and return to the saucepan. Add ¼ cup brandy for every cup of syrup. Bring the syrup and brandy mixture to a simmer and ladle into the filled jars, leaving ¼ inch of headroom. Seal and process the jars (gently simmer them) in a hot water bath for 15 minutes, cool, and store at room temperature. Allow the pears to mellow at least 3 months before eating them.

Pickled Seckel Pears

MAKES 4 TO 6 PINTS

THESE sweet-and-sour pears are the whole-fruit equivalent of chutney. Enjoy them with baked or cold ham or as an interesting addition to salads. Use only fruit that is free of bruises and blemishes.

    4 pounds Seckel pears
    4 cinnamon sticks
    ½ teaspoon whole cloves
    1½ cups sugar
    1 cup brown sugar
    1 cup cider vinegar

    4–6 1-pint canning jars

(1) Sterilize the canning jars and prepare a water bath. If you do not have a canning pot, you can keep the pickled pears stored in the refrigerator. Wash the pears and place them in a large pot of simmering water, and cook for 2 to 3 minutes. Remove the pears and reserve the cooking liquid. Combine 4 cups of the liquid with the remaining ingredients and heat over a low flame for 5 minutes, or until the sugars have melted. Return the pears to the pot and simmer for 6 to 8 minutes, or until the pears are just tender.

(2) Pack the pears into the canning jars, alternating the blossom and stem ends. Bring the pickling syrup to a boil, remove the spices, and ladle in the syrup, leaving ¼ inch headroom. Wipe the lids of the jars, seal, and process (gently simmer in a pan of hot water) for 15 minutes. Store in a cool, dry place and refrigerate after opening.

Ragout of Duckling with Pears

SERVES 4

I first tasted this dish at the La Varenne cooking school in Paris. It can be made with either whole duck or thighs (left over from pan-frying the breasts). The best pears for this dish are Comice; they should be slightly underripe. *Poire William* is pear brandy—if unavailable, substitute cognac.

       1 5-pound duck
         Salt and fresh black pepper
       4 slightly underripe pears
     3–4 tablespoons brown sugar
       1 tablespoon butter
     ¼ cup wine vinegar
       1 cup duck or veal stock
     ½ teaspoon cornstarch
     1–2 tablespoons Poire William, or cognac

(1) Cut the duck into quarters—two leg sections, two breast-wing sections—discarding any lumps of fat. Lightly score the skin to release the fat. Season the pieces with salt and pepper.

(2) Heat a large frying pan and add the duck pieces, skin side down. Cook the meat over a medium heat for 10 minutes, turning the pieces so they brown thoroughly on all sides. Pour off excess fat as it accumulates in the pan. Reduce the heat and gently sauté the duck pieces for 20 minutes, or until cooked. Transfer the duck to a warm platter and discard all but 2 table-spoons fat.

(3) Peel, halve, and core the pears, and rub them with lemon to keep them from discoloring. Place the pears in the pan, and brown them in the duck fat. Discard the fat from the frying pan, and add the brown sugar and the butter; cook over high heat for 20 to 30 seconds, or until the sugar bubbles and caramelizes. Add the vinegar (stand back—it will hiss and sputter), and stir it with a whisk until the sugar and pan juices are completely dissolved. Add the stock and simmer for 10 minutes, or until the pears are tender; the point of a paring knife will pass easily

through the fruit when it is done. Taste the sauce for seasoning, adding more salt and pepper as necessary. The ragout can be prepared ahead of time to this point, and reheated or frozen.

(4) To finish the ragout, warm the duck in the sauce and arrange the duck and pears on a warm platter. Dissolve the cornstarch in the Poire William or cognac, and whisk the mixture into the pan juices. Simmer the sauce for 30 seconds, then pour it over the duck and pears. Chefs with a penchant for showmanship can warm a few additional tablespoons Poire William in a small saucepan and ignite it, then dim the lights and pour the flaming liquor over the platter.

Ripe Pears with Brandied Goat Cheese

SERVES 4

THIS recipe takes its inspiration from *fromageon*, a traditional dessert in Gascony consisting of goat cheese, sugar, and Armagnac. Armagnac is the brandy of the region, and it owes its brash character to the fact that it is distilled only once. (Cognac, France's other great brandy, is distilled twice.) Use a soft, mild goat cheese like Monterey chèvre or Montrachet.

 2 very ripe pears
 ½ lemon
 ¼ pound soft mild goat cheese, at room temperature
 2 tablespoons sugar, or to taste
 1 tablespoon Armagnac or cognac, or to taste
   Fresh mint leaves or slivered maraschino cherries for garnish

   Piping bag fitted with ½-inch star tip (optional)

(1) Peel the pears and cut them lengthwise in quarters. Cut out the core with a melon baller or paring knife. Rub the pears with lemon juice to prevent them from discoloring.

(2) Not more than 10 minutes before you plan to serve it,

prepare the fromageon (cheese mixture). Soften the cheese by mashing it with a fork or wooden spoon. Whisk in the sugar and Armagnac and beat until smooth. Using a piping bag fitted with a star tip, pipe swirls of goat cheese mixture along the top of each pear. Alternatively, place a spoonful of cheese mixture on top of each pear. Arrange the pears, like the spokes of a wheel, on a round platter, crowning each with a mint leaf or some slivered cherries. Serve at once.

NOTE: The sugar has a tendency to make the cheese melt, so it is important that you serve the pears right away.

NOVEMBER

No warmth, no cheerfulness, no healthful ease—
No comfortable feel in any member—
No shade, no shine, no butterflies, no bees,
No fruits, no flowers, no leaves, no birds,
November!

THOMAS HOOD

W E L L , that's one way to look at the eleventh month of the year. But November can bring a welcome respite from the restless activity of summer, as we give way to a mood of repose and rumination. We shift our psychic energy from the out-of-doors to the interiors of our homes and hearts.

Many people consider November the gloomiest month of the year; Londoners called it "the month of blue devils and suicides." It is a time, in the words of an eighteenth-century bishop, "when the little witches drown themselves, and the great ones sell themselves to the devil." November opens with a rather morbid holiday, All Souls Day, honoring the souls of the faithful who died the preceding year. In ancient Naples it was customary to open the charnel houses, adorn the bones of the departed with robes and flowers, and admire them by torchlight.

November is for most Americans inextricably tied to Thanksgiving. But let's get a few things straight: the Pilgrims didn't eat turkey and cranberries at their first Thanksgiving. The holiday originated in the 1760s, not as a harvest feast, but as a day honoring our forefathers. It was held on December 22 (the anniversary of the Mayflower landing) and it featured such "poor fare" as eels, clams, codfish, venison, succotash, and whortleberry pudding. In 1777 the Continental Congress proclaimed December 18 a "Day of Thanksgiving" for the surrender of the British Army. George Washington moved the holiday to November 26, to give thanks for the adoption of the Constitution. The turkey and cranberries came later, as did the official date, the fourth Thursday in November.

Other November holidays include Punky Night (November 1), when the children in Somerset, England, hollowed out "mangel-wurzels" (beets), carved them with faces, and illuminated them with candles. The English celebrated Guy Fawkes day on November 5, burning effigies of a conspirator who planned to blow up the Houses of Parliament. On November 11 the Romans held the Festival of Bacchus, honoring the first of the season's wine. This day was also sacred to St. Martin, the Patron of Innkeepers and Reformed Drinkers.

The Anglo-Saxons called November *Blot-Monath,* "blood month," mindful of the annual slaughter of livestock. In rural France, this is the season for slaying the pig, which is transformed into sausages, pâtés, and other porcine delicacies. In America, some 45 million turkeys are dispatched to satisfy the demand for Thanksgiving. In Florida, stone crab season starts in November, and in the Northeast, cod is particularly toothsome. Other November delicacies include fennel, quinces, pumpkins, and cranberries.

The fields might be barren, the weather cold, but we can always drink and be merry. November 15 at 12:01 A.M. signals the official release of Beaujolais Nouveau, the "new" Beaujolais. In England it is customary to ring in Martinmas (November 11) with a cup of ale. A medieval songwriter summed up the cozy comfort of November:

> *What though Winter has begun,*
> *To push down the summer sun,*
> *To our fire we can betake,*
> *And enjoy the crackling brake,*
> *Never heeding Winter's face.*

TURKEY

IF I were a turkey, I would dread the month of November. Forty-five million birds will meet their maker in the weeks leading up to Thanksgiving. (Add 13 million turkeys for Christmas and 9 million for Easter, and you've got a barnyard massacre!) Americans like turkey so much, we eat some 70 million birds a year.

Our national bird is the eagle, of course, but it might well have been the turkey. (Benjamin Franklin thought it "a much more respectable bird, and withall a true original native of America.") The bird was already domesticated when the Spanish reached Mexico in 1518. The Aztecs ate it daily, with a sauce made from unsweetened chocolate and chilis. (The preparation survives as Mexican *mole*.) Europeans, usually finicky about New World foods, adopted it with gusto: a German cookbook published in the sixteenth century listed twenty turkey recipes alone.

How did a native American bird come to be called "turkey"? There are almost as many explanations as there are individual recipes. Food historian Reay Tannahill cites the "Turkie merchants," English traders who specialized in Eastern Mediterranean wares. (In the sixteenth century, Near Eastern goods had the same cachet that French or Californian products do today.) The traders encountered the bird in Seville (where it had been brought by New World explorers) and introduced it to England as the "turkey bird." The French used a similar marketing technique, naming the bird *dinde* (short for *poule d'Inde,* "Indian hen.").

New Englanders called salt cod "Cape Cod turkey," and "Irish turkey" was a euphemism for corned beef and cabbage. "To talk turkey" meant to speak plainly (there's no mistaking a turkey's gobble). As for the expression "cold turkey," an addict's goose bumps resemble the skin of an uncooked tom.

Contrary to popular prejudice, tom turkeys are no tougher than hens, just larger—weighing up to thirty pounds, versus fifteen pounds for a hen. On the average, one pound of raw turkey yields four to five ounces cooked meat, or enough for one serving. Large turkeys are harder to handle and take longer to cook, but they yield more meat—and servings—per pound. Thus, a six-pound turkey will feed four or five people, but a twenty-five-pound turkey feeds up to fifty. Waverly Root had a fondness for large birds, observing, "Turkey, like wine, should be served in magnums."

This time of year many Americans will be confronted by a bewildering selection of turkeys: fresh or frozen, grain-fed, free-ranging, self-basting, Grade A, B, or C. Self-basting birds are injected with broth or margarine, and while succulent, they offend the purist. I favor fresh, organic, grain-fed birds: due to the lack of chemicals, the meat may seem tough, but the flavor is incomparable.

COOKING TURKEY

In the past ten years, I have tried dozens of methods for cooking turkey: high heat for a short time (to sear in the juices); low heat for a long time (to prevent the meat from drying out); in a roasting pan, under an aluminum foil tent; even wrapped in a wool blanket. (The latter was suggested by some cooking friends from Oregon.) I have tried basting the bird with booze, cloaking it in butter-soaked cheesecloth, sliding bacon and truffles under the skin. Last year, I cooked the bird in a smoker: it was one of the best turkeys I ever had. But my favorite method is stuffing the bird under the skin with butter and herbs, and browning it at high heat, then cooking it in a moderate oven, as described in the recipe below.

Mama Spach's Wedding Turkey (Roasted with Boursin Butter Beneath the Skin)

SERVES 10 TO 12

MY friend Ted "Mama" Spach makes a superb roast turkey, which I first tasted at his wedding. The turkey is roasted at a high heat to brown the skin, then cooked in a covered pan at a moderate heat to keep the meat moist and tender. And instead of basting the outside of the bird with butter (the skin, after all, is impermeable), Ted places butter and herbs beneath the skin, where the mixture can actually baste the meat. What results is turkey that's as succulent as gravy, the skin crisp, the meat fall-off-the-bone tender. Don't wait till Thanksgiving to try it.

1 10–12 pound turkey
  Salt and fresh black pepper
1 small apple, quartered
1 carrot, cut into 1-inch pieces
1 branch celery, cut into 1-inch pieces

For the stuffing:
4 tablespoons unsalted butter
4 ounces Boursin cheese or cream cheese
4–5 tablespoons finely chopped fresh herbs, including thyme, sage, basil, parsley, and/or chives (*Note:* You can also use dried herbs, at least for the thyme and sage, but cut back on the quantities)
2 tablespoons Madeira or cognac
  Salt and fresh black pepper

1 batch Madeira Gravy (see recipe on page 384)

1 large roasting pan with a snugly fitting lid (or plenty of foil)

(1) Wash the turkey and pat dry. Season the cavity. Stuff the turkey with the apple, carrot, and celery. Truss the bird with string.

(2) Preheat the oven to 425 degrees. Prepare the under-the-skin stuffing. Cream the butter with the cheese, and beat in the

herbs, Madeira or cognac, and seasonings to taste. Starting at the front cavity, work your hand under the skin, over the breast, up the thighs, down the legs. The idea here is to create a thin pocket between the skin and the meat. Then spread the butter mixture under the skin, all over the bird, concentrating on the breast and thighs. Sprinkle the outside of the turkey with additional salt and pepper. The recipe can be prepared to this stage and refrigerated for a day, but let the turkey warm for 30 minutes at room temperature before roasting.

(3) Place the turkey, breast up, on a rack in the roasting pan. Roast it at 425 degrees for 20 minutes, or until the skin is nicely browned. Cover the pan and reduce the heat to 350 degrees. Roast the turkey for approximately 3 hours (20 minutes per pound), or until cooked. (To test for doneness, wiggle a leg: the bone should move easily in the hip joint.) Pour the pan juices into a bowl or measuring cup. To crisp the skin, increase the heat to 425 degrees and roast the bird, uncovered, for 5 to 10 minutes. Meanwhile, make the gravy below. Let the turkey stand for at least 10 minutes before carving. It's just as good cold the next day as hot right out of the oven.

Madeira Gravy

MAKES 2 CUPS

HERE'S an old-fashioned gravy to serve with the turkey. To defat the turkey juices, pour them into a deep bowl or measuring cup, and let stand for 10 minutes. The fat will float to the top. If you have time, chill the juices in the freezer. The fat will congeal and can be scraped off with a spoon. (Save it for the chopped turkey liver—see recipe below.) If you are in a hurry, use a bulb baster to draw off the clear broth from the bottom, leaving the fat in the bowl, or use a gravy boat with a bottom spout.

Reserved juices from roasting the turkey (you should have about
  2 cups)
2 tablespoons butter
2 tablespoons flour
⅓ cup heavy cream
3 tablespoons Madeira

(1) Defat the turkey juices: you should wind up with 1½ cups. (If you have more, boil it down; if you have less, use more cream.)

(2) Melt the butter in a saucepan. Whisk in the flour to make a roux, and cook over medium heat, whisking frequently, till lightly browned. Remove the pan from the heat and strain in the turkey juices, followed by the cream and Madeira. Return the pan to the heat and simmer the gravy for 3 minutes, adding salt and pepper to taste, and perhaps an additional splash of Madeira.

Chopped Turkey Liver in the Style of a Jewish Grandmother

SERVES 2 TO 4

TURKEY liver has a richer flavor than chicken liver. This "pâté" features the flavorings my grandmother uses for her fabulous chopped liver. Unless you are using an enormous turkey, you may wish to stretch the pâté with chicken liver. Saltines or matzoh make the best crackers for spreading.

1 turkey liver, plus enough chicken liver to equal ½ pound
1 small onion
1–2 hard-cooked eggs
2 tablespoons turkey fat (see gravy recipe above), chicken fat, or
  butter for frying, plus 2 tablespoons for the pâté
  Salt and fresh black pepper

(1) Trim any sinews or green spots off the livers and blot dry. Finely chop the onion. Shell and finely chop, or coarsely grate, the eggs. Heat the turkey fat in a small skillet. Sprinkle the livers with salt and pepper, and fry over high heat for 1 to 2 minutes per side, or until the livers are cooked but still very pink in the center. Transfer the livers to a strainer to drain. Lower the heat and fry the onion for 2 to 3 minutes, or until very tender and ever so slightly browned. Drain in the strainer as well.

(2) Coarsely chop the liver and onion together: my grandmother uses a hand-cranked meat grinder, but a food processor, run in spurts, will work fine. Beat in the eggs, salt and pepper to taste, and enough turkey fat to make a soft, creamy pâté. Chill the liver for at least 1 hour, but let it stand for 15 minutes at room temperature before serving. Some people like to decorate their chopped liver with sieved or chopped hard-cooked egg.

Turkey Stock and Turkey Noodle Soup

MAKES APPROXIMATELY 8 CUPS, WHICH WILL SERVE 8

As you can see, nothing goes to waste in my house. Turkey noodle soup, made the day after Thanksgiving with the leftover carcass, is something I look forward to all year. Why, I've even been known to beg for the bones when I am at someone else's house for dinner! The trick to this, like any stock, is to cook it at the gentlest simmer, conscientiously skimming off any fat. If the stock is allowed to boil, the fat will homogenize with the broth, making the latter cloudy and oily.

To make turkey stock:
  The carcass from a 10 to 12 pound turkey (adjust the
    quantities up or down if your turkey is larger or smaller)
  1 large onion
  1 parsnip (optional)

2 large carrots
2 branches celery
2 cloves garlic
  Bouquet garni (see recipe on page 471)
1 tablespoon tomato paste (optional)

To turn the stock into broth and soup:
2–3 teaspoons salt, or to taste
  Fresh black pepper
1 pound of your favorite soup noodles

(1) Remove any pieces of skin or fat from the carcass, and place the bones in a large stockpot. Cut the onion in quarters, leaving the skin on. Cut the parsnip, carrots, and celery into 1-inch chunks. Peel the garlic. Add the vegetables to the pot. Tie the herbs and spices in a piece of cheese cloth, or wrap them in foil, which you perforate with a fork. Add the bouquet garni and tomato paste to the pot, with enough cold water to completely cover the bones.

(2) Place the pot over high heat and bring the stock to a boil. Skim off the foam that forms on the surface, and reduce the heat. Gently simmer the stock to 2 to 3 hours, frequently skimming to remove fat and foam, adding cold water as necessary to keep the bones submerged. At the end of 3 hours, the stock should have an intense turkey flavor. Strain it into a large bowl, pressing the bones and vegetables with a spoon to extract every last bit of flavor. Let the stock cool to room temperature before refrigerating. Skim off any fat that remains on the surface. The broth will keep for 4 to 5 days in the refrigerator and can be frozen. It is delicious in any recipe that calls for chicken stock.

(3) To make turkey broth, season the stock with salt and pepper. To make turkey noodle soup, cook the noodles *al dente* in a separate pot of water. (Cooking the noodles right in the broth will make it cloudy.) Add them to the turkey broth and serve at once. When I was a kid, we used to add drops of ketchup to noodle soup to make a smiling face.

FENNEL

FENNEL is a mathematical vegetable. It is one of the three thousand members of the carrot family, and one of the forty plants which sixteenth-century herbalist Thomas Tusser declared indispensable to an herb garden. It was also, according to Waverly Root, one of the nine holy herbs of the Anglo-Saxons, one of the ingredients in Chinese five-spice powder, and one of the four "hot" seeds in the age of Chaucer. Not bad for a plant that the *Larousse Gastronomique* dismisses as "little appreciated in France."

Fennel is one of our most venerable and versatile foods: the bulbous base is cooked as a vegetable, the stalks are cut up in salads, the leaves are used as an herb and for fuel, while the seeds turn up in liqueurs. The Romans pickled it; the Berbers add it to their fiery spice paste; and the *Larousse Gastronomique* not withstanding, a Marseillaise bouillabaisse would be humble fish soup without it.

Fennel is one of those "what-the-heck-is-it" plants, a round base crowned with celerylike stalks, dill-like leaves, and a flowering crown like Queen Anne's lace. The base and stalks taste like anisey celery; the leaves and seeds are licoricey. Many people associate fennel with a strong, almost medicinal flavor: it is actually quite mild, especially when cooked.

Its virtues don't stop there. In Shakespeare's day, the eating of fennel and eel was thought to provoke sexual license. ("He plays at quoits well, and eats conger and fennel," observed Falstaff to Poins.) According to the seventeenth-century physician Nicholas Culpeper, "a decoction of the leaves and root is good for serpent bites." More recently, nineteenth-century chef Alexis Soyer attributed to it the power to restore eyesight.

The Greek word for fennel was marathon: the famous battle-field was called Marathon because it was overgrown with wild fennel. Phedippides, the messenger who ran twenty-six miles to Athens to announce the victory in 490 B.C. (he spoke and promptly expired), gave the plant's name to the popular road race. Our word *fennel* comes from the Latin *faeniculum,* "little hay."

Fennel is available—irregularly—throughout the year. In Boston we find it in late fall, and again in spring. On the West Coast it turns up during the summer. Given its capricious supply, I rarely plan menus around it, but buy it whenever I can. Fennel can often be found in Italian markets, where it goes by the name of *finocchio.* There are two basic types: a slender, flowering type grown for the leaves and the seeds, and the bulbous, or Florentine, variety, which is eaten as a vegetable. Fennel is sometimes referred to as sweet anise, but the latter—also licorice-flavored—is a different plant. When buying fennel, look for compact bulbs: spreading leaves indicate overripeness—the center will be woody. The cut edges should appear fresh, and the base should be free of brown spots.

Fennel Salad in White, Green, and Black

SERVES 4

THIS autumn salad is a shameless attempt to use every trendy ingredient of the eighties: niçoise olives, walnut oil and balsamic vinegar, even buffalo milk mozzarella.

1 large or two small bulbs fennel
¼ pound green beans
1 buffalo milk or fresh mozzarella
⅔ cup niçoise or black olives, drained

For the dressing:
  2 tablespoons balsamic vinegar
    Juice of ½ lemon or orange
    Salt and fresh black pepper
  4 tablespoons walnut or hazelnut oil
  1 tablespoon finely chopped fennel leaves

(1) Cut the stems off the fennel. Remove the leaves and reserve for garnish. Cut the stems into ¼-inch slices—you want approximately ⅔ cup. Cut the bulbous base lengthwise, through the flat side, into very thin strips. Arrange these strips on a round platter or round plates like the spokes of a wheel, leaving a 2-inch hub at the center.

(2) Snap the ends off the green beans, and cut the beans into 2-inch lengths. Cook them in rapidly boiling salted water for 1 minute, or until crispy-tender. Rinse under cold water and drain. Cut the mozzarella into ½-inch cubes.

(3) Prepare the dressing. Place the vinegar, lemon or orange juice, and seasonings in a bowl. Gradually whisk in the oil and chopped fennel leaves, adding salt and pepper to taste. Spoon half the dressing over the fennel strips. Toss the sliced fennel stems, green beans, mozzarella, and olives in the remaining dressing and spoon this mixture into the center of the platter. Decorate the fennel slices with feathery sprigs of the leaves.

A Rich Stew of Fennel, Mussels, and Saffron

SERVES 4 TO 6

PART stew and part chowder, this dish makes a lavish first course. Leave a few mussels in the shell for a garnish: the black shell against the golden broth is stunning.

  1 large bulb fennel
3–4 pounds mussels
  1 small onion

   Bouquet garni (see recipe on page 471)
¾ cup dry white wine
 2 leeks (about ½ cup chopped), furry root ends and dark green
   leaves removed
 3 tablespoons butter
 2 tablespoons Pernod or anisette
 2 cups bottled clam broth or fish stock
⅛ teaspoon saffron
 1 cup heavy cream
   Salt, fresh black pepper, and cayenne pepper

(1) Cut the stalks off the fennel. Cut one stalk into ¼-inch slices and add it to the pot for steaming the mussels. Reserve a few of the feathery leaves for garnish. (Save the remaining stalks for use in a soup or salad.) Cut the bulb in half lengthwise, make a V-shaped cut to remove the hard part of the core, and cut the fennel widthwise into ¼-inch slices.

(2) Scrub the mussels, pulling out the tuftlike strings at the hinge, discarding any with cracked shells or shells that fail to close when tapped. Chop the onion. Combine the mussels, onion, bouquet garni, wine, and fennel stems in a large pot with a tight-fitting cover. Steam the mussels over high heat for 4 to 5 minutes, or until the shells just open, stirring once or twice. Remove from the heat and let cool.

(3) Meanwhile, cut the leeks in half lengthwise, wash thoroughly, and finely chop. Melt the butter in a large saucepan, and cook the leeks and sliced fennel over a medium heat for 3 to 4 minutes, or until crispy-tender, but do not let brown. Add the Pernod or anisette, clam broth or stock, and saffron, and gently simmer the soup for 5 minutes, or until the vegetables are tender.

(4) Meanwhile, remove most of the mussels from the shells (leave a few in for garnish). Strain the mussel broth into the stew, discarding the silty dregs. The recipe can be prepared to this stage up to 24 hours before serving.

(5) Just before serving, add the mussels, cream, and seasonings to the stew. Simmer for a minute or two to heat the mussels. Correct the seasonings and don't stint on the cayenne—the stew should be quite spicy.

Serve fennel and mussel stew in warm bowls, using the fennel leaves and reserved mussels in their shells for garnish. This dish deserves a Grand Cru Chablis.

Fennel-Potato Galette

SERVES 3 TO 4

A galette is a crisp potato pancake. The interesting twist here is the addition of grated fennel. Do not soak or wash the potatoes, as the starch in them is needed to hold the pancake together.

    1 bulb fennel
    Salt
    1 large potato
4–6 tablespoons butter
    Fresh black pepper

(1) Coarsely grate or finely julienne the fennel. Cook it in rapidly boiling, lightly salted water for 30 seconds. Refresh under cold water and drain.

(2) Coarsely grate or finely julienne the potato, and mix it with the fennel. Melt half the butter in a heavy 10-inch nonstick frying pan over medium heat. Add the fennel-potato mixture and pat it with a spatula into a pancake. Cook the galette for 5 to 7 minutes per side, lowering the heat after 2 minutes, to prevent the bottom from burning. Shake the pan every few minutes to prevent the pancake from sticking. Sprinkle both sides with salt and pepper.

(3) Flip the pancake by flicking the pan with your wrist. (If you're a chicken, place a large plate over the pan, invert the pancake onto the plate, then slide it back into the pan to finish cooking.) Sprinkle with salt and fresh black pepper to taste.

PUMPKINS

Peter, Peter, Pumpkin Eater,
Had a wife and couldn't keep her.
Put her in a pumpkin shell
And there he kept her very well.

NURSERY RHYME

PUMPKINS have been put to some pretty peculiar uses. Cinderella rode to the ball in a pumpkin coach drawn by field mice. Henry David Thoreau declared he would rather sit on a pumpkin he had all to himself than be crowded on a velvet cushion. The early settlers of New Haven placed dried pumpkin shells on the heads of hirsute colonists to guide the barber's scissors (whence the epithet "pumpkin head"). Yankee farmers still use the expression "softer than a stewed pumpkin" to describe something that is mawkishly sentimental.

We think there are better ends for this orange, round, autumn harbinger. In this country pumpkins are most often used as pie filling and served at Thanksgiving. In other parts of the world, pumpkins are simmered in soups, baked with meats, and served in ravioli or with pasta. A mere hundred years ago in this country, you could have enjoyed pumpkin butter, pumpkin pickles, pumpkin french fries, and even pumpkin beer.

When selecting pumpkins for cooking, leave the monsters for youthful surgeons to carve into jack-o'-lanterns. The smaller pumpkins—six to eight inches across—are the best ones for eating. Connoisseurs argue the merits of the Sweet Sugar, Winter Luxury, Connecticut Field, and Big Cheese, varieties grown here in New England. But any pumpkin that is plump and unblemished, that feels heavy for its size and resounds with a dull thud when thumped, will be excellent for eating. There is very little waste in a pumpkin. The seeds can be washed, dried, and roasted for nutritious munching. The bright orange flesh is excellent in soups, casseroles, and desserts.

MAKING PURÉE

CUT the pumpkin in half and scrape out the fibrous material in the center. (An ice cream scoop works admirably.) Place the halves, cut side down, on a greased baking sheet, and bake in a 350-degree oven for 45 minutes, or until the flesh is tender. Scoop the pulp from the skin, and purée it in a food processor or force through a vegetable mill or sieve. Fresh pumpkin purée can be stored in the freezer for up to two months.

Pumpkin Spice Muffins

MAKES 12 TO 15 MUFFINS

PUMPKIN spice muffins are the breakfast equivalent of that dessert classic, pumpkin pie. Adjust the spice quantities to suit your particular taste.

1 cup fresh pumpkin purée (see above)
⅔ cup sultanas (golden raisins) or regular raisins
2 eggs
1 cup sugar
½ teaspoon salt
½ teaspoon each cinnamon, ginger, and nutmeg
¼ teaspoon each ground allspice and ground cloves
2 cups all-purpose flour
1 scant tablespoon baking powder

1 teaspoon baking soda
½ cup vegetable oil

Muffin tins to hold 12–15 large muffins, thoroughly buttered or greased with shortening

(1) Prepare the pumpkin purée following the instructions above. Pour ½ cup boiling water over the raisins and let them soften for 15 minutes. Meanwhile, beat the eggs in a mixer with the sugar, salt, and spices. Gradually beat in the pumpkin purée. Sift the flour with the baking powder and baking soda, and gradually add it to the batter. Last of all beat in the oil and the raisins with their liquid. Preheat the oven to 400 degrees.

(2) Ladle the batter into the tins, filling each depression two-thirds full. Bake the muffins for 20 to 30 minutes, or until they are puffed and firm and an inserted skewer comes out clean. Serve pumpkin spice muffins warm, with butter, for breakfast or brunch.

Pumpkin Bolognaise Sauce

MAKES 4 TO 5 CUPS SAUCE, ENOUGH TO SERVE 6 TO 8

NEWCOMERS to Al Forno in Providence, Rhode Island, are surprised to find one wall of the popular restaurant decorated with hundreds of dried pumpkin stalks. The unusual decor bears witness to owner-chef George Germon's obsession with this orange-skinned vegetable. Germon and his wife, Johanna, visited an Italian town called Ferrara, famed for its pumpkin ravioli. Since that time, George and Johanna have used pumpkin in every imaginable dish, including the following bolognaise sauce. Germon recommends using a sugar pumpkin, which is sweeter than the standard jack-o'-lantern variety.

½ **small pumpkin (about 10 ounces), seeds removed**

For the sauce:
- 1 medium onion (enough for ¾ cup chopped)
- 2 cloves garlic
- 1 carrot
- 1½ teaspoons grated fresh ginger
- 8 ounces lean pork, ground or very finely chopped
- 8 ounces veal, ground or very finely chopped
- 4 tablespoons virgin olive oil
- 3 tablespoons unsalted butter
- ½ cup dry white wine
- ½ cup chicken stock
- ½ cup heavy cream
- 1 35-ounce can imported plum tomatoes, seeded
- Salt, cracked fresh black pepper, and freshly grated nutmeg.

(1) Preheat the oven to 375 degrees. Place the pumpkin, cut side down, on an oiled baking sheet. Cover with foil, and bake the pumpkin for 30 minutes, or until tender.

(2) Meanwhile, prepare the sauce. Finely chop the onion, garlic, and carrot. Grate the ginger. Grind the pork and veal. Heat the oil and butter in a large, heavy-bottomed saucepan. Add the vegetables and ginger, and cook over low heat for 10 minutes, or until the vegetables are tender but not browned. Add the pork and veal, increase the heat to high, and cook the meat, stirring constantly, until all trace of pink disappears. Add the wine and stock, and boil until only ½ cup liquid remains. Add the cream and boil until only ¾ cup liquid remains. Add the tomatoes with the can juices, and salt, pepper, and nutmeg to taste, and gently simmer the sauce, stirring frequently, for 30 minutes.

(2) Scoop the flesh of the baked pumpkin from the shell and coarsely chop it. Add it to the sauce, and simmer for an additional 30 minutes, or until the pumpkin pieces just begin to disintegrate. Correct the seasoning with salt, pepper, and nutmeg.

Serve pumpkin bolognaise sauce over buttered spaghetti, sprinkled with cracked pepper, fresh nutmeg, and freshly grated Parmesan. A Barolo or Amarone, red wines from northern Italy, would make a splendid beverage.

Pumpkin Ice Cream

MAKES 1 QUART

HERE'S an unusual dessert for people who are tired of pumpkin pie. If you are making fresh pumpkin purée, a 2–3 pound pumpkin will yield the necessary 2 cups. *Crème anglaise* is French custard sauce—it makes an exceptionally smooth, rich ice cream.

For the crème anglaise:
- 2 cups milk
- 1 vanilla bean
- 6 egg yolks
- 1 cup sugar

- 2 cups fresh pumpkin purée (see page 394), or 15-ounce can
- 2 tablespoons molasses
- ½ teaspoon each cinnamon and freshly grated ginger
- ¼ teaspoon each allspice and freshly grated nutmeg
- ⅛ teaspoon each ground cloves and ground cardamom
- 1 cup heavy cream

Ice cream machine, ice, coarse salt

(1) Prepare the crème anglaise. Over medium heat, scald the milk with the split vanilla bean. Whisk the egg yolks with the sugar in a large mixing bowl. Remove the vanilla bean (you can rinse it off and use it again), and gradually whisk the milk into the yolk mixture. Return the mixture to medium heat, and stirring constantly with a wooden spoon, cook until the foam subsides, the raw egg yolk smell disappears, and the mixture thickens to the consistency of heavy cream. Do not let the custard boil, or it will curdle. Strain it back into a bowl

(2) Whisk in the pumpkin purée, then the molasses, then the spices. Add more or less to suit your taste. When the mixture is cool, fold in the cream. Churn the mixture in your ice cream machine, following the manufacturer's instructions, until the ice cream is frozen. Serve pumpkin ice cream in chilled bowls with a sprinkling of dark rum on top.

Pumpkin Cheesecake

SERVES 10 TO 12

THIS dish was an experiment in cooking class one day, and it promptly became my favorite way to eat cheesecake. Leaving the cheesecake to cool in the oven prevents the top from cracking.

For the crust:

8 ounces cinnamon-flavored graham crackers or gingersnap cookies (1½ cups crumbs)
½ cup butter, melted

For the filling:

24 ounces cream cheese, at room temperature
1¼ cups sugar
5 eggs
2 cups pumpkin purée (see page 394)
3 tablespoons rum
2 teaspoons vanilla extract
1 teaspoon cinnamon
½ teaspoon freshly grated ginger
¼ teaspoon freshly grated nutmeg
⅛ teaspoon each ground cloves, cardamom, and allspice

For the topping:

2 cups sour cream
⅓ cup sugar
3 tablespoons rum

1 10-inch springform pan

(1) Crush the cookies to fine crumbs in the food processor or with a rolling pin. Mix in the melted butter, and press the crust into the bottom and along the sides of the springform pan. Chill for 30 minutes. Preheat the oven to 325 degrees.

(2) Meanwhile, beat the cream cheese and sugar together in a mixer (or by hand) until smooth. Beat in the eggs, one by one, until the mixture is light and fluffy. Combine the pumpkin purée with the rum, vanilla, and spices, and beat until smooth. Beat

the pumpkin mixture into the cream cheese mixture. Pour the filling into the crust and bake for 1¼ hours or until set.

(3) Whisk the sour cream, sugar, and rum together until light and smooth. Spoon this mixture on top of the cheesecake, turn off the oven, and let the cake cool in the oven. Chill the pumpkin cheesecake for at least 6 hours, and up to 48, before serving.

Roast Pumpkin Seeds

PEPITAS, hulled pumpkin seeds, are a delicacy in Mexico. In our country, doctors used to prescribe whole pumpkin seeds as a diuretic and remedy for tapeworm. The only hard part about roasting pumpkin seeds is cleaning off the stringy, orange pulp. Even that's not so bad if you have fellow jack-o'-lantern carvers to help.

Seeds from a fresh pumpkin
Vegetable oil
Salt, fresh black pepper, and cayenne pepper

(1) Separate the pumpkin seeds from the fibrous orange flesh. Wash the seeds three times in warm water, and drain in a colander. Spread the seeds on paper towels to dry.

(2) Preheat the oven to 400 degrees. Toss the seeds with vegetable oil, 3 to 4 tablespoons oil per cup of seeds. Arrange the seeds in a single layer on a baking sheet, and sprinkle liberally with salt and pepper. Bake the seeds for 10 to 15 minutes, or until golden brown, turning frequently with a spatula.

Roast pumpkin seeds make an excellent snack.

CRANBERRIES

BOGS yield all sorts of strange things: mummified Vikings in Scandinavia, odd bits of clothing from medieval plague victims, peat for roasting the barley used to make whiskey in the Highlands of Scotland. But my favorite bogs are the ones that produce cranberries in eastern Massachusetts. Half of the nation's cranberries grow here, and this time of year the cranberry bogs are ablaze with billions of bright scarlet berries.

Cranberries are a uniquely American food. The Indians mixed them with venison and fat to make a sturdy ration called pemmican. The Pilgrims ate them with maple syrup during that first hungry winter in Plymouth. The blossom of the cranberry resembles a sand crane's profile—hence the term *crane berry,* which was shortened to cranberry. But despite their appeal to both Indians and Pilgrims, it wasn't till the establishment of the first cane plantations in the Caribbean, and the increased availability of sugar, that the cranberry achieved its current popularity.

In the old days, cranberries were laboriously raked from the low bushes with long-toothed scoops called "combs." Today the bogs are flooded with water, and the berries float to the top, where they are gathered with a machine that resembles an oversized vacuum cleaner.

The cranberry season starts in late September and continues through early November—the later the harvest, the darker the berry. Due to their high acidity cranberries keep well (up to ten days in the refrigerator) and can be frozen almost indefinitely. You'll also be relieved to know that cranberries, because of their high vitamin C content, are an excellent defense against scurvy.

Chilled Cranberry Soup

SERVES 4 TO 5

CHERRY soup (*hideg meggyleves*) is one of the glories of Hungarian cooking. We used similar flavorings but substituted cranberries for cherries in the recipe below. Stick cinnamon has a better flavor than the ground spice and will leave only its flavor, and not a silty deposit, behind.

        1 12-ounce bag cranberries
1¼–1½ cups sugar
        2 cinnamon sticks
        2 allspice berries
        2 whole cloves
        4 black peppercorns
        1 tablespoon cornstarch
        ¼ cup heavy cream
        ¾ cup dry red wine, or to taste

(1) Pick through the cranberries, discarding any stems. Combine 3 cups water, 1¼ cups sugar, and the spices in a large saucepan, and bring to a boil. Reduce the heat and add the cranberries. Gently simmer the soup for 30 minutes, or until the cranberries are tender and the liquid is well flavored. If necessary, add additional sugar to taste.

(2) Mix the cornstarch with 2 tablespoons cold water to make a paste. Whisk this mixture into the soup, and boil for 1 minute: the soup should thicken slightly. Let the soup cool to room temperature, then refrigerate until chilled. The recipe can be prepared to this stage up to 2 days before serving.

(3) Just before serving, stir in the heavy cream and wine. I like to leave the spices in, but feel free to remove them. Serve cold cranberry soup in chilled glass bowls. If you like, you can garnish each bowl with a dollop of sour cream.

Gingered Cranberry Sauce

MAKES 2 CUPS

CRANBERRY sauce takes quite literally 10 minutes to make; once you know how easy it is, you'll be embarrassed you ever bought the canned stuff.

    1 pound fresh cranberries, washed and picked clean
    ½ cup sugar, or to taste
    3 strips lemon zest (remove it with a vegetable peeler)
    2 cinnamon sticks
    1 ½-inch piece fresh ginger root, thinly sliced
    ¼ cup apple cider
    ¼ cup ginger brandy (or orange juice or more cider)

(1) Combine all the ingredients in a large saucepan. Bring to a boil, reduce the heat, and simmer for 10 minutes, or until cooked to taste. Let cool before refrigerating, and chill for at least 1 hour before serving.

Gingered cranberry sauce will keep for up to 3 weeks in the refrigerator. For extra flavor, I leave the lemon, cinnamon, and ginger right in the sauce until serving.

Cranberry Conserves

MAKES 4 CUPS

LINDA Wong is a longtime friend and a fine cook. Currants are tiny raisins originally grown in the Greek city of Corinth, hence their name. This spicy relish goes well with duck, turkey, and pork.

    4 cups fresh cranberries (1 pound)
    1 small, unpeeled, thin-skinned orange
    ½ cup currants

    1 cup dark brown sugar
    ¾ cup cider vinegar
    2 sticks cinnamon
    4 whole cloves
    ¼ teaspoon salt
      Juice and grated zest of 1 lemon
    ½ cup coarsely chopped walnuts or pecans

Wash the cranberries and pick out any stems. Remove the seeds from the orange and finely chop in the food processor or by hand. Combine all the ingredients, except the walnuts or pecans, in a heavy saucepan. Bring the relish to a boil, reduce the heat, and simmer for 10 to 12 minutes, or just until the cranberries begin to pop. Skim off the foam and remove from the heat. Stir in the walnuts. Refrigerate for at least 2 hours, preferably overnight.

Cranberry Linzer Torte

SERVES 8

A chef I trained with in Paris used to say, "There's no such thing as a 'new' dish, just variations on old ones." So it is with the cranberry linzer torte below. A quick cranberry marmalade replaces the traditional raspberry jam. The crust is pretty much the same as any you would find in Linz, Austria, the town where this nutty dessert was developed. My thanks to Chris Kauth, who collaborated on the recipe.

For the cranberry marmalade:
    1½ 12-ounce packages of cranberries (3 cups)
      1 orange
      1 apple
      4 tablespoons butter
    ⅔–1 cup sugar, or to taste
      1 cinnamon stick

For the dough:
  1½ cups walnuts (about 6 ounces)
  1½ cups almonds (about 6 ounces)
  1½ cups sugar
  2 tablespoons powdered cocoa
  1 tablespoon cinnamon
  1 teaspoon each grated lemon peel and grated orange peel
  ¼ teaspoon allspice
  ¼ teaspoon fresh nutmeg
     Pinch of salt
  3 cups flour
  1¼ cups cold unsalted butter, cut into ½-inch pieces
  2 eggs
  1–3 egg yolks

     Wax paper or parchment paper
     10- or 11-inch tart pan with a removable bottom

(1) Prepare the cranberry marmalade. Pick through the cranberries, removing any stems. Peel, seed, and finely chop the orange. Peel, core, and finely chop the apple. Melt the butter in a large sauté pan, and add all the ingredients for the marmalade. Cook over medium heat for 5 to 6 minutes, or until the cranberries are tender, adding sugar as necessary to compensate for the tartness of the berries. Remove the cinnamon stick, transfer the marmalade to a bowl, and chill

(2) Prepare the dough. Place the nuts, sugar, and flavorings in the food processor, and grind the nuts to a powder. (Run the machine in short bursts, and don't overprocess or the nuts will become paste.) Add the flour and mix. Cut in the butter. Add the whole eggs and 1 yolk, and run the processor in bursts until the dough comes together in a smooth ball. (*Note:* If the dough fails to come together after 2 minutes, add an additional egg yolk or two.) Divide the dough in two (one part should be somewhat larger than the other), wrap, and chill for 1 hour.

(3) Preheat the oven to 400 degrees. Roll out the larger half of the dough between two sheets of parchment or waxed paper into a circle 2 inches larger than the tart pan. Peel off the top paper, invert the dough onto the pan, and peel off the remaining paper. Press the dough into the sides and bottom of the pan.

Spoon in the cranberry marmalade. Roll out the remaining dough between two sheets of parchment paper. Peel off the top sheet, cut the dough into 1-inch strips, and use these to make a lattice on top.

(4) Bake the linzer torte in the preheated oven for 1 hour, or until the crust is lightly browned. Remove the torte from the oven and let cool to room temperature. Some people like to serve linzer torte with a ruff of whipped cream, but I think it's gilding the lily.

 Cranberry Bread

SERVES 8

THIS cranberry bread is fairly straightforward—I like to have it with tea.

    2 cups fresh cranberries
    ½ cup pecans
      Grated zest of 1 orange
      Juice of 2–3 oranges, including the one used for grating (¾ cup
      juice altogether)
    2 cups flour
    ½ teaspoon salt
    ½ teaspoon cinnamon
    ¼ teaspoon freshly grated nutmeg
      Pinch each of ground cloves and allspice
    1 teaspoon baking powder
    1 teaspoon baking soda
    1 cup light brown sugar
    4 tablespoons butter, melted
    1 egg, beaten

    1 9 × 5 × 4–inch loaf pan, about 2 tablespoons melted butter,
      and a little flour

(1) Preheat the oven to 350 degrees. Pick through the cranberries, removing any stems. Coarsely chop the nuts. Brush the pan with melted butter, chill, brush it again with butter, and lightly dust it with flour.

(2) Sift the flour into a bowl, followed by the salt, spices, and leavenings. Stir in the brown sugar. Add the butter, egg, orange juice, and orange zest, and stir until thoroughly mixed. Fold in the pecans and cranberries. Spoon the batter into the loaf pan and bake it for 60 minutes, or until the loaf sounds hollow when tapped and an inserted skewer comes out clean. Unmold the bread onto a cake rack and cool for 15 minutes. You can serve the cranberry bread now, but it will taste better if wrapped in plastic and "ripened" (stored) overnight before serving.

QUINCES

They dined on mince, and slices of quince,
Which they ate with a runcible spoon;
And hand in hand, on the edge of the sand,
They danced by the light of the moon . . .

EDWARD LEAR,
''THE OWL AND THE PUSSY-CAT''

HAVE you ever tasted a quince? If you sampled it raw, you'd remember it: one taste is enough to strip the enamel off your teeth and deposit it in the back of your throat. For quince in its natural state is astringent and bitter. But subject it to heat and mellow it with sugar, and it becomes an epicure's morsel.

The quince looks like a yellow pear: elongated at one end, flat at the other. The rind is often covered with downy fuzz. The flesh is yellowish but turns pink when cooked. The flavor suggests apple and pear, with overtones of guava.

Scholars believe the famed golden apples of the Hesperides were actually quinces. Young Greek men gave quinces to their sweethearts; maidens ate them on their wedding night. Quince jelly was a princely gift in the Middle Ages: the grateful burghers of Orleans gave some to Joan of Arc when she lifted the English siege. The Portuguese excelled at making quince preserves: the Portuguese word for quince is *marmelo,* the origin of our term *marmalade.* Rich in pectin, quinces are indeed excellent for making jellies.

I often wonder who buys the quinces that flood our markets this time of year. Arabs and Armenians use them for making desserts and fruit leathers. North Africans find their tartness a welcome addition to fish. The acidity of the quince counteracts greasiness and Germans often serve it with pork.

Aficionados maintain that quinces taste best when harvested after the first frost. Look for smooth, round, unblemished fruits with an apple-pineapple-banana smell. They are always rock hard—a boon to fledgling jugglers, who can drop them without fear of bruising them. In their natural state, quinces are covered with a soft, downy fuzz. This should be rubbed off with a damp cloth. Unlike apples and pears, quinces must be cooked a long time before becoming palatable.

Lamb Stew with Quinces

SERVES 4 TO 6

IN most recipes, quinces are used to make preserves or desserts. This one combines the tartness of the fruit with lamb and saffron. The dish can also be made with seafood, in which case it becomes a Tunisian fish stew.

```
    2 pounds lamb (leg or stew meat)
  2–3 quinces (1½ pounds)
    3 carrots
    2 potatoes
    1 onion
  ½ cup raisins
  ¼ teaspoon saffron
    Salt and fresh black pepper
    6 tablespoons olive oil
    2 teaspoons paprika
    Cayenne pepper
```

(1) Cut the lamb into 1-inch chunks. Peel and core the quinces, and cut them into 1-inch pieces. Peel the carrots and potatoes, and cut them into 1-inch pieces. Finely chop the onion. Place the raisins and saffron in a bowl and add 1 cup boiling water.

(2) Heat 2–3 tablespoons olive oil in a large pan. Season the lamb with salt and pepper. Brown the lamb on all sides over high heat, and transfer it to a platter. Discard the fat and add the remaining olive oil to the pan. Sauté the onion and quince over medium heat for 3 to 4 minutes, or until the onion is tender but not browned. Stir in the paprika and cook for 15 seconds. Add the raisins and saffron with their liquid, the meat, and water to cover, and bring the stew to a boil.

(3) Reduce the heat and gently simmer for 35 to 45 minutes, or until the lamb is tender, adding water as necessary. The carrots and potatoes should be added halfway through. When the meat and vegetables are tender, correct the seasoning with salt, black pepper, and a little cayenne.

Serve the lamb stew with quinces over rice or couscous. A Gewürztraminer would make a nice beverage, but so would a pilsner-style beer.

Quince Compote

SERVES 4

RICH in pectin, a vegetable jelling agent, quinces are ideal for making compotes and marmalades. Rose water and orange flower water are perfumey flavorings popular in the Near East. They are available in Middle Eastern markets, or you can substitute Grand Marnier or kirsch.

2–3 quinces (about 1 pound)
    1 cup sugar, or to taste
    3 cardamom pods
    2 cloves

1 cinnamon stick
2 strips lemon zest, plus the juice of a whole lemon
½ teaspoon rose water or orange flower water

(1) Peel the quinces, cut them in half lengthwise, and cut out the core. Cut the halves into 1-inch pieces. Place them in a heavy saucepan with the remaining ingredients and water barely to cover (about ¾ cup).

(2) Cook the quinces over low heat for 30 to 40 minutes, or until the pieces of quince are soft. It may be necessary to add additional water to prevent the quinces from drying out during cooking. The compote should be sweet and tart: add more sugar, lemon juice, and rose water as necessary. Remove the whole spices and serve the compote chilled or at room temperature.

Armenian-style Baked Quinces

SERVES 6 TO 8

THIS traditional Armenian recipe transforms the cantankerous quince into a dessert of sugarplum sweetness. The recipe comes from Carol Zeytoonjian, a fine Armenian cook who lives in Arlington, Massachusetts.

12 quinces
1½ cups sugar
½ cup fresh lemon juice
24 whole cloves
3 cinnamon sticks
2–4 tablespoons unsalted butter

(1) Wash the quinces but do not peel. Cut each quince in half, then cut each half into 3 to 4 lengthwise slices (each should be 1-inch wide). Cut out the cores.

(2) Combine the sugar and 1 cup water in a large saucepan and boil for 10 minutes. Add the lemon juice, cloves, and cinnamon, and boil for a few minutes more. Add one-third of the

quinces to the syrup and gently simmer for 10 minutes, or until semisoft, then remove from syrup. Repeat until all the quince has been cooked.

(3) Preheat the oven to 350 degrees. Lightly butter a 9- × 13-inch glass baking dish. Arrange the quince slices in the dish in neat rows. Strain the syrup over the fruit. The recipe can be prepared to this stage up to 2 days before serving.

(4) Before serving, dot the quinces with butter and bake in the preheated oven for 1 hour, or until the fruit is pink and very tender. Serve the baked quinces warm, with whipped cream or vanilla ice cream.

BEAUJOLAIS NOUVEAU

As a rule, wine buffs are a decorous lot, forever fussing with their tasting notes and decanters. But once a year, they kick up their heels for an oenophilic version of Mardi Gras. The party begins on November 15 at precisely 12:01 A.M., for the stroke of the clock signals the official release of *Beaujolais nouveau,* the "new" Beaujolais. (Say "new-voh" Beaujolais—but "new-vell" cuisine.)

The Beaujolais is a forty-five-mile expanse of rolling hills, two-lane roads, and steepled villages, sandwiched between the distinguished wine districts of Burgundy and the Côtes du Rhône. It's a land of wine—not the sort you age for decades and sip in a hushed room, but a light, fruity, straightforward red you drink because you're thirsty. Beaujolais is made from the gamay grape, a viticultural oddball that prospers in the region's stony soil. Some Beaujolais, particularly that from the villages of Brouilly, Morgon, and Fleurie, is capable of extended bottle age.

But the bulk of Beaujolais wine is meant to be drunk the same year it's made.

The most famous Beaujolais, however, is barely wine at all. Only six weeks have elapsed since the grapes were picked, pressed, fermented, filtered, and bottled. This is the infamous Beaujolais nouveau, also called *primeur*. Each year, on November 15, the wine makers are allowed to release the fledgling wine and oenophiles go to absurd lengths to be the first on the block to drink it. Beaujolais nouveau has been chauffeured in a limo to Paris, jetted on the Concorde to New York, and even parachuted into London. A restaurant in Boston went so far as to serve a Beaujolais breakfast at 7 A.M.!

Beaujolais nouveau is, well, youthful stuff—purple in color, grapey in smell, light (9 percent alcohol), rough, and fruity. Wine growers love it—they can turn their inventory over in a few weeks—and it acounts for a third of the 140 million bottles of wine made in the region each year. As a serious wine, Beaujolais nouveau is of dubious merit, but it sure is fun to drink. Its youth and fruitiness make it ideal for cooking, as attest the recipes below.

Coq au Beaujolais

SERVES 4

HERE'S an interesting variation on classic coq au vin. The bird will be more flavorful if you marinate it overnight.

1 3- to 4-pound chicken

For the marinade:
1 onion
2 carrots
2 branches celery
1 clove garlic
Bouquet garni (see recipe on page 471)
1 tablespoon olive oil
1 bottle Beaujolais nouveau

To cook the chicken:
¼ pound slab or thick-sliced bacon
 Salt and fresh black pepper
2 tablespoons flour

For the garnish:
½ pound baby onions
½ pound mushrooms
¼ cup chopped fresh parsley

(1) Cut the chicken into 8 pieces (2 legs, 2 thighs, 2 breast pieces, and 2 wing pieces with some of the breast attached). Finely chop all the vegetables for the marinade. Combine all the ingredients for the marinade in a nonmetal pan, and marinate the chicken overnight. Reserve a little wine to add at the end. (*Note:* If you don't have time to marinate the chicken overnight, proceed to Step 2—you'll still get excellent results.)

(2) Drain the marinated chicken in a colander, reserving the wine. Pat the chicken pieces dry with a paper towel. Cut the bacon into ¼-inch slivers. Over medium heat, lightly brown the bacon pieces in a sauté pan large enough to hold the chicken. Transfer the bacon to paper towels to drain. Pour off all but 2 tablespoons bacon fat. Season the chicken with salt and pepper, and brown on all sides, starting skin side down. Transfer the chicken to a platter. Pour off all but 3 tablespoons fat.

(3) Add the marinade vegetables to the pan, and cook over medium heat for 3 minutes, or until soft. Return the chicken to the pan and stir in the flour. Add the reserved marinade and bring to a boil, scraping the bottom of the pan with a spatula to dissolve congealed meat juices. Reduce the heat, and gently simmer the chicken for 30 to 40 minutes, or until tender, adding a little salt and pepper.

(4) Meanwhile, prepare the garnish. Peel the onions. Cook them in lightly salted boiling water for 4 to 5 minutes, or until tender. Refresh under cold water and drain. Wash and stem the mushrooms, cutting large ones into halves or quarters. Cook them in ¼ inch water in a covered pot for 2 minutes, or until tender, then drain.

(5) To finish the coq au Beaujolais: Add a splash of wine to the chicken and simmer for a few minutes to "refresh" the sauce. Correct the seasoning. Transfer the chicken pieces to a serving platter and arrange the bacon, mushrooms, and onions on top. Skim any grease off the sauce with a spoon, and strain the sauce over the chicken. Sprinkle on the fresh parsley and serve at once. Coq au Beaujolais improves with age, but always be sure to freshen up the sauce by adding a little more wine before serving.

Eggs *en Meurette* (in Beaujolais Wine Sauce)

SERVES 4 AS A LIGHT LUNCH OR 8 AS AN APPETIZER

EGGS poached in red wine are a traditional Burgundian appetizer. Be forewarned: the eggs will look terrible, but the dish is truly delicious. It's important to use fresh eggs, as old ones will fall apart during poaching. If possible, avoid using canned stock as the dish will be unpalatably salty.

1 bottle Beaujolais nouveau
8 extra-large eggs, as fresh as possible
4 tablespoons very finely chpped shallots
1 cup brown stock (see page 473)
  Bouquet garni (see recipe on page 471)
1 clove garlic, peeled and cut in half
2 tablespoons butter
2 tablespoons flour
  Salt and fresh black pepper
1 teaspoon sugar (optional)

1 loaf French bread
3 tablespoons butter, melted
¼ pound lean slab or thick-sliced bacon
½ pound baby onions
½ pound fresh mushrooms
¼ cup fresh chopped parsley

(1) Poach the eggs. Bring the wine to a rapid boil in a deep, narrow pot. Working in batches of three, crack the eggs into bubbling spots in the boiling wine. (The swirling motion of the bubbles helps the white envelop the yolk.) Reduce the heat to a simmer, and cook the eggs for 3 minutes, or to taste. Transfer the eggs with a slotted spoon to a bowl of cold water. (This prevents the eggs from overcooking.) The eggs can be poached up to 4 hours before serving and kept in water.

(2) Prepare the sauce. Strain the poaching wine, and combine it with the shallots in a heavy nonaluminum saucepan. Boil until reduced by half. Add the stock, bouquet garni, and garlic, and continue boiling until only 1½ cups liquid remain. Melt the butter in a 1-quart saucepan. Whisk in the flour, and cook for 2 minutes over medium heat to make a roux. Working off the heat, add the reduced wine mixture to the roux. Return the pan to the heat, and simmer the sauce, whisking vigorously, for 2 to 3 minutes. Add salt and pepper to taste, and a little sugar if the sauce is too tart. The sauce can be made up to 4 hours before serving.

(3) Prepare the garnish. Preheat the oven to 400 degrees. Cut the French bread into 8 diagonal slices, each ½ inch thick. Brush both sides with butter, and bake the bread in the preheated oven for 8 to 10 minutes per side, or until golden brown. Cut the bacon into ¼-inch slivers and lightly brown over medium heat. Drain the bacon on paper towels.

(4) Peel the onions. Cook them in lightly salted boiling water for 4 to 5 minutes, or until tender. Refresh under cold water and drain. Wash and stem the mushrooms, cutting large ones into halves or quarters. Cook them in ¼ inch water in a covered pot for 2 minutes or until tender, then drain. Add the bacon, onions, and mushrooms to the sauce.

(5) To assemble the eggs *en meurette,* gently warm the sauce, adding salt and pepper as necessary. Trim any scraggly bits off the poached eggs, and warm them in a pan of gently simmering water. Arrange the bread slices on a platter. Transfer the eggs with a slotted spoon to paper towels to drain. Place one egg on

each slice of toast. Spoon the sauce over the eggs, and sprinkle with fresh chopped parsley.

Beaujolais Nouveau Granité

SERVES 8

GRANITÉS are the simplest dessert in the world to make, consisting of frozen sweetened wine. (The term comes from the Italian *granita,* "small seed," an apt description of the tiny ice crystals that make up this grainy sherbet.) Granités are ideal for serving midmeal to refresh the palate. Few gustatory experiences can match the sensation of these delicately sweetened wine crystals melting on the tongue.

½ bottle Beaujolais nouveau
⅓–½ cup sugar, or to taste

Combine the wine, 1 cup cold water, and the sugar in a bowl, and whisk until the sugar is completely dissolved. Freeze the mixture in a shallow bowl overnight. To serve, scrape the iced wine into snowflakelike crystals with a fork. Serve in chilled goblets, and hurry—the wine melts quickly!

DECEMBER

By all rights, December should be a grim time of year for gourmets: the streams are frozen, the fields are bare, and produce is rare and expensive. Nonetheless, this wintery month has its halcyon days for eaters. Cooks welcome the holidays with a burst of extravagance: party hors d'oeuvres, cookies, and fruitcakes. In the spirit of gift-giving, epicures treat their friends to such delicacies as foie gras, caviar, and smoked salmon. Jews enjoy latkes and doughnuts during Hanukkah, while Christians look forward to roast goose, mince pies, and plum puddings on Christmas.

December is also the month in which the winter solstice occurs. Long before the triumph of the Jewish Maccabees or the birth of Christ, pagan peoples celebrated this calendrical turning point by worshiping trees and kindling fires, acknowledging the importance of light during the darkest month of the year.

And Hanukkah, the Festival of Light, does just that. It honors the triumph of the Maccabees, a small band of Jews, over an invading army of Syrians. When the Jews recaptured the Temple, they found only enough holy oil to light the Eternal Flame for twenty-four hours. A messenger was dispatched to obtain more oil from a distant city. Miraculously, the tiny cruet of oil burned for the eight days it took the messenger to return. To commemorate this miracle, Jews light Hanukkah candles for eight days and eat foods fried in oil.

The most famous December holiday is Christmas, of course, yet many Christmas traditions originated in the pagan worship of winter solstice. The Vikings ignited huge bonfires to ward off the darkness—the source of the Yule log burned on Christmas day. The Anglo-Saxons toasted the solstice with *guil,* a sort of beer, which gave us the words *yule* and *ale.* The Druids took advantage of this barren period to clear their sacred tree, the oak, of a parasitic vine called mistletoe. Boughs of evergreen trees were hung over the hearth as a reminder of nature's fecundity amid winter's dearth—the forerunner of the modern Christmas tree. The holiday revels found their origin in the Roman festival Saturnalia, celebrated by boisterous public processions.

Other December holidays include the feast of St. Nicholas, patron of Russia (he died on December 6, 342 A.D.), and of St. Lucy, who had her eyes plucked out and given to a suitor who lamented he was haunted by their loveliness. December 27 is the day of St. John, who downed a goblet of poisoned wine—and lived—to prove the efficacy of his religion. It is said that drinking a glass of wine on St. John's Day will protect you from poisoning during the coming year.

December produce includes fiery horseradish, gnarled celery root, and tuberlike Jerusalem artichokes. Farmers in France and Italy take to the woods with their pigs, hunting the costliest of fungi: truffles. Fishermen may shun the high seas, but icy estuaries yield the year's most succulent oysters. Fresh geese and turkeys give up the ghost to be reincarnated at Christmas dinner.

The days may seem short, the evenings endless, but the solstice is the turning point. From now on till Midsummer's Eve, the days will brighten and lengthen. Even in the heart of darkness, the promise of light and the gift of holiday cheer are with us.

CAVIAR

Caviar comes from virgin sturgeon;
Virgin sturgeon's one fine fish.
Virgin sturgeon needs no urgin';
That's why caviar's my dish.

FROM A SONG SUNG
BY CHARLIE DREW

ITS suppliers resort to James Bondian tactics to smuggle it from behind the Iron Curtain. Its devotees spend astronomical sums for portions that would fit inside a nutshell. It is sold by the gram, and is best enjoyed at the end of a tiny spoon. No, I'm not talking about cocaine, but about a substance that is every bit as expensive, rare, and addictive: caviar!

Caviar, simply defined, is lightly salted fish eggs. In addition to being a renowned delicacy, it is reputed to be a tonic, an aphrodisiac, and even a remedy for hangovers. (The word comes from the Persian *chav-jar,* "cake of strength.") The fish species, the size of the eggs, and the amount of salt determine the quality —and price—of the caviar. The better the eggs, the less salt is used. Low-salt caviar is called *malassol,* from the Russian words for "little salt."

True caviar comes from the sturgeon, a large, whiskered, prehistoric-looking fish that dwells chiefly in the Caspian Sea. There are three species of sturgeon and the caviar of each is unique. *Beluga* eggs are the largest (about the size of buckshot), ranging from grey to jet black in hue. The rareness of the roe, not to mention its delicate flavor, make it the most expensive, costing up to thirty-five dollars an ounce. *Osetra* is a medium-sized caviar, distinguished by a thin golden-brown coating of fat. Aficionados prefer its rich, nutty flavor to the delicacy of beluga. *Sevruga* is the most common sturgeon caviar, and the soft small grains have the strongest fish flavor. In the process of straining, salting, and grading caviar, some eggs are invariably broken. These are collected and packed together to make a marmalade-like mass called *pressed caviar,* which is rich in flavor and relatively low in price.

The skyrocketing prices of Caspian caviar and a renewed interest in American foods have spurred a caviar renaissance in this country. In the United States, sturgeon are found in Alaska, Oregon, the Great Lakes, tributaries of the Mississippi, and even the Hudson. American caviar is of sevruga quality, with a less delicate taste than that of the Caspian product. An ounce costs eight to ten dollars.

Excellent caviars are also made from the roe of the salmon, whitefish, and lumpfish. *Salmon caviar* has the largest grain (about the size of a pea), with an inviting orange hue, semicrunchy shell, and soft, gooey center. *Whitefish caviar* have tiny eggs with a relatively low fat content—their crunchy consistency makes them an ideal garnish for freshly cooked pasta. *Lumpfish caviar* from Iceland is the most plebeian, having a strong, salty fish flavor. The eggs are dyed red or black, and should be rinsed in a sieve under cold running water to remove the excess dye.

Two other roes are of interest to the lover of fish eggs. The first is *tobiko*—iridescent red flying-fish roe—a popular item at sushi bars. Tobiko has a crunchy consistency similar to that of golden whitefish caviar. The second is carp roe, which is used in *taramasalata,* a Greek dip made with lemon juice and olive oil. Taramasalata is available at Greek markets—it is delicious spread on sesame breadsticks or wedges of toasted pita bread.

Caviar will probably be the most expensive food you ever invest in: buy it from a reputable shop that turns over its inventory frequently. Good caviar is recognizable by its bright, plump, whole grains, and should smell like the seashore, not a fish store.

Unpasteurized caviar is the best, but it is extremely perishable: buy it the day you plan to serve it, and store it on ice.

Sturgeon caviar should be served in ice: the ambitious can make a hole in a block of ice just large enough to hold a tin of caviar. Freeze a block of ice in a bowl, and place an empty can the size of the caviar tin on top of it. Fill the can with boiling water. Repeat until the heat has melted a suitably-sized depression.

The better the caviar, the more simply it should be savored. I like to eat beluga and osetra right out of the can with a spoon. Do not use silver (it reacts with the brine); epicures favor spoons made of ivory or horn, but white plastic spoons do fine, too. The ultimate splurge is to eat sturgeon caviar rolled up in a slice of smoked salmon.

One to two ounces of caviar make a reasonable serving. The appropriate beverage is iced vodka or champagne.

To eat beluga or osetra any way but raw would be a sacrilege, but the lesser caviars lend elegance to pasta, omelets, or crêpes. Don't cook the caviar over direct heat: add it to a hot sauce or dish. That way, you will preserve its pristine texture.

The classic garnishes for caviar include capers, onions, hard cooked eggs, sour cream, and toast points. The capers should be rinsed to remove excess brine; the onions should be finely chopped, wrapped in a dish towel, and run under cold water to rid them of their eye-stinging pungency; the egg whites and yolks can be pushed through a sieve separately to give them the tufted appearance of mimosa flowers. To make toast points, lightly brush bread slices with melted butter on both sides, and bake them in a preheated 400-degree oven for 10 minutes per side, or until lightly browned.

Scrambled Eggs in the Shells with Beluga

SERVES 2 AS A LIGHT APPETIZER

THIS dish was invented by Michel Guérard, a founding father of French nouvelle cuisine. It helps to have an egg topper —a ringlike device with metal teeth, used for cutting the tops off soft-boiled eggs. Egg toppers are available at cookware shops, but the shells can also be cut with a knife. A less expensive grade of caviar can be substituted. The recipe can be multiplied at will.

  2 extra-large eggs
  2 tablespoons butter
  2 tablespoons heavy cream
  2 teaspoons finely chopped fresh chives
    Fresh black pepper and a little salt
  1 ounce beluga caviar

  2 egg cups

(1) Using an egg topper or a sharp serrated knife, cut off the top ½ inch of the eggshell. Take care not to crack the shell, as it will be used for serving the eggs. Pour the eggs into a bowl and carefully rinse the shells and caps.

(2) Melt the butter in a saucepan over a pan of gently simmering water. Beat the eggs with the cream, chives, and seasonings. Pour the eggs in the saucepan and gently cook them, stirring with a whisk. French scrambled eggs are more like hollandaise sauce: they should be very loose and creamy.

(3) Spoon the scrambled eggs back into the shells, leaving ½ inch for the caviar. Spoon in the beluga. Place the eggshell caps on top, and serve the eggs at once in egg cups.

NOTE: Parisian restaurateur Michel Pasquet serves these caviar-filled eggs in a dish of flaming vodka.

Fettuccine with
Caviar and Vodka Sauce

SERVES 3 TO 4

IN this dish we use salmon roe and golden whitefish caviar, the former for its salty succulence, the latter for its crunchy consistency. *Parmigiano-reggiano* is the best Parmesan cheese: its name should be stamped on the rind. The vodka makes a dubious contribution to the sauce but makes great sipping while you cook.

For the sauce:
1½ cups heavy cream
   1 small clove garlic, peeled but left whole
   2 strips lemon zest (removed with a vegetable peeler)
   4 tablespoons butter
   3 tablespoons sour cream
   2 tablespoons vodka
   2 tablespoons very finely chopped chives or scallions
     Fresh black pepper

   1 pound fresh egg fettuccine
     Salt
   1 tablespoon oil
   4 tablespoons freshly grated Parmigiano-reggiano cheese, plus
     additional cheese for serving
   2 ounces golden whitefish caviar
   2 ounces salmon roe

(1) Prepare the sauce. Combine the cream, garlic, and lemon zest in a heavy saucepan, and boil, stirring occasionally, until only half the mixture remains. Remove the pan from the heat and discard the garlic and zest. Whisk in the butter, then the remaining ingredients for the sauce.

(2) Cook the fettuccine with the oil for 2 minutes, or to taste, in 4 quarts rapidly boiling, lightly salted water. Do not overcook: the noodles should remain *al dente*. Drain the pasta and place in a large bowl. Add the sauce, cheese, and golden whitefish caviar,

and gently toss to mix. Garnish each serving with some of the salmon roe. (It is more delicate than the whitefish and has a tendency to burst if tossed with the pasta.) Serve additional cheese on the side for sprinkling.

Checkerboard of Caviar Eggs

MAKES 16 HALVES

THIS recipe features a new twist on a cocktail party standby, deviled eggs topped with caviar. The checkerboard effect is achieved by using black lumpfish roe, red salmon caviar, and yellow roe from whitefish. The eggs are cut in half widthwise, not lengthwise, to make them manageable to eat with your fingers. The lumpfish roe should be thoroughly rinsed to remove the black dye.

8 eggs

For the filling:
4 tablespoons mayonnaise (see page 477) or sour cream
4 tablespoons cream cheese, at room temperature
2 tablespoons smoked whitefish or cooked shrimp (or mustard, if you don't like smoked fish)
2 tablespoons very finely chopped scallions
A few drops lemon juice
Fresh black pepper

1 ounce black lumpfish caviar
1 ounce salmon roe or red lumpfish caviar
1 ounce golden whitefish caviar

1 piping bag with ½-inch star tip

(1) Place the eggs with cold water to cover in a pan. Bring the water to a boil, reduce the heat, and gently simmer the eggs for exactly 11 minutes. (More than 11 minutes and you will get

a green ring around the yolk.) Run the eggs under cold water and shell them immediately.

(2) Cut a ⅛-inch slice off the end of each egg, so that the halves will sit stably. Cut each egg in half widthwise and carefully remove the yolk with a spoon. Purée the egg yolks in a food processor with the ingredients for the filling. (Alternatively, mash the ingredients to a smooth paste with a fork.) Not more than 1 hour before serving, pipe the filling into the egg halves in neat rosettes.

(3) Place the lumpfish caviar in a strainer, rinse it under cold running water, and drain. Using a fork, place small mounds of black caviar on some of the eggs, red on some, and yellow on some. To achieve a checkerboard effect, arrange the eggs in rows, alternating color.

TRUFFLES

He who says "truffle" pronounces a word that awakens erotic and gastronomic memories in the skirted sex and gastronomic and erotic memories in the bearded sex.

BRILLAT-SAVARIN

SINCE Roman times, these dark, round fungi have been attributed with aphrodisiac powers. The price alone (several hundred dollars a pound) limits one's serving of truffles to none but one's most intimate friends.

The Romans believed that truffles grew wherever lightning struck the earth. We now know that truffles grow beneath oak trees, but we still haven't figured out how to cultivate them. Truffle season starts in November, and gathering them requires the olfactory acuity of specially trained pigs or dogs that can sniff where they grow underground. The truffle hardly looks like an epicure's morsel—it is a lumpy ball the size of a walnut, with a dusty, leathery skin. The penetrating aroma is unlike anything else in the world. Adjectives like "earthy, musky," come to mind, but the experience can't really be described in words.

There are two sorts of truffles: black and white. The former come from the Périgord region in southwest France. The latter come from the Piedmont in northern Italy. Black truffles have a sharper flavor; the white ones (actually a dusky tan) are more pungent—they smell like dirty gym socks. Fresh truffles are available in late November and December. But most of the harvest is canned for use throughout the year.

Ten years ago, the only way to enjoy fresh truffles in the U.S. was to smuggle them in. Today, fresh truffles can be purchased at luxury gourmet shops or from restaurateurs who buy them in bulk. Store white truffles in the refrigerator, buried in rice. Store black truffles in cognac or goose fat to cover.

There are three sorts of canned truffles: whole, pieces, and peelings. The second and third cost a fraction of whole truffles and are fine for adding to scrambled eggs and pasta. White truffles are also available in paste form for spreading on toast or *crostini*. But remember, canned truffles are as similar to fresh ones as "sink stoppers" (canned mushrooms) are to fresh.

Truffles are served with relatively bland foods—pasta, risotto, scrambled eggs—which absorb, not compete with, their flavor. Black truffles are generally consumed cooked, and white ones raw, cut into paper-thin slices on a special cutter. They can also be baked in puff pastry and roasted over charcoal in foil.

Truffle Omelet

SERVES 2

THE neutral flavor of eggs makes them ideal for serving with truffles. The trick to making good omelets is to vigorously shake the pan while cooking.

1 tablespoon chopped fresh black truffle
4 eggs
4 tablespoons heavy cream
   Salt and fresh black pepper
5 tablespoons butter

1 or 2 8-inch omelet pans

(1) Finely chop the truffle. Beat it with the eggs and cream and refrigerate for at least 2 hours, preferably overnight. (This gives the eggs time to absorb the truffle flavor.)

(2) Add salt and pepper to the egg mixture, and beat with a whisk for 3 minutes. Melt half the butter in the omelet pan over high heat. When the foam subsides, add half the omelet mixture. Stir the omelet with a fork, shaking the pan, until the eggs start to thicken. Immediately start swirling the pan over the heat to prevent the omelet from sticking. Cook for 1½–2 minutes, or until the eggs are set, but still very moist, then remove the pan from the heat. Hit the handle to slide the omelet to the far side of the pan, and flip it onto a plate. Prepare the other omelet the same way.

With truffled omelets, serve crusty French bread and a Batard-Montrachet (a fine white wine from Burgundy).

Harlequin Pasta (Fettuccine with White and Black Truffles)

SERVES 3 TO 4 AS AN APPETIZER

HERE'S, a dish with which to celebrate making a killing in the commodities market. (You'll need it to buy the ingredients.) The black truffle is optional, but it does look nice against the white sauce.

> 1 small black truffle (1 ounce)
> 1 small white truffle (1 ounce)
> 1 cup heavy cream
> 6 tablespoons butter
> ½ cup freshly grated Parmigiano-reggiano cheese (see headnote on page 425)
> Salt and fresh black pepper
> 1 pound fresh fettuccine

(1) Bring 4 quarts lightly salted water to a boil for cooking the pasta. Meanwhile, cut the black truffle and half the white one into paper-thin slices. Combine them with the cream in a heavy saucepan, and simmer until reduced by half. Working over a low heat, whisk in the butter, half the cheese, and salt and pepper to taste.

(2) Just before serving, boil the pasta for 1 to 2 minutes, or until cooked to taste, and drain. Pour the cream sauce over the pasta and toss. Shave the remaining white truffle over the pasta and serve at once, passing the remaining cheese on the side. For wine you could try a Barolo or well-aged St. Emilion.

OYSTERS

Do you remember your first time? Your heart was aflutter with nervousness; you struggled to work up your courage. It was soft, wet, squishy, sensual, and very, very nice. No, I'm not talking abut sex, but about something that is eminently sexy. I speak of a wintertime seafood delicacy: *ostrea edulis,* the oyster.

Are oysters really aphrodisiac? Casanova consumed fifty a day. (His preferred method was slurping them off the lips of his lover.) There is the story of the young bride who, concerned about her husband's shyness, paid a visit to her neighborhood fishmonger. "Just make sure he eats these," the man told her, shucking a dozen extra-large oysters. "How did it go?" the fish man asked, when the woman returned the next day. "Not bad," she replied with a blush, "but half of them failed to work!" There may be more to the shellfish's generative powers than its suggestively squishy texture. Pound for milligram, oysters contain more zinc than any other food, and zinc has been linked by scientists to reduced prostate trouble and the production of semen and hormones.

America's waters are blessed with a bounty of oysters: briny *Cotuits* from Cape Cod, succulent *Chincoteagues* from the Chesapeake Bay, fleshy *Apalachicolas* from Florida, and tiny *Olympias* from the Pacific Northwest. The most exciting new oyster to reach the U.S. is the *belon,* a flat-shelled oyster with a sharp, almost iodine tang. (Originally from France, belons are now being "farmed" in the Damariscotta River in Maine.) The best place to taste oysters from all over the country is the Oyster Bar and Restaurant at Grand Central Station in New York.

Oysters ship and store surprisingly well. (The ancient Romans enjoyed oysters from the British Isles, shipped overland in ice-filled carts.) Buy them from a fishmonger, and buy only those whose shells are tightly closed. (The one exception here is the belon, whose shells gap naturally.) Once home, scrub the shells under cold running water, and store the oysters on ice (or in the coldest section of the refrigerator) until you are ready to eat them. Do not store oysters in a sealed plastic bag, or they will suffocate.

Contrary to popular belief, oysters are not dangerous to eat during the non-*R* months. May through August is their breeding season, however, and during this time, oysters will often taste flabby or milky.

SHUCKING OYSTERS

THE preferred implement for shucking oysters is a short, stiff-bladed knife. (A church key can opener will work in a pinch.) If you are right-handed, grasp the oyster firmly in your left hand, the "hinge" or narrow part of the shell facing out. (It doesn't hurt to protect your hand with a garden glove or pot-holder.) Hold the knife at the hinge of the oyster and wriggle the tip of the blade under the top shell. Now give the knife a firm twist, and the top shell will pop open. Slip the blade along the underside of the top shell to cut the adductor muscle, and dis-card. Slide the knife under the oyster to loosen it from the bottom shell, and you are ready to eat. For the cook's convenience, at this time of year most fish stores sell shucked oysters by the pint.

The best way to enjoy oysters is on the half shell, with a squeeze of lemon juice or a dab of cocktail sauce (the latter enlivened with fresh horseradish—see page 439). The French like to dip oysters in a *mignonette,* vinegar flavored with shallots and cracked black peppercorns. A tart white wine, like Muscadet, is the right drink, or for a Dickensian touch, a pint of ale.

Oysters are also delectable poached, broiled, baked, fried, and even grilled (lay the half shells right on the grill and lower the cover). One word of caution: do not overcook, or the oysters will be as chewy as erasers. The cooking time should be mea-sured in seconds instead of minutes.

Cajun Fried Oysters

MAKES APPROXIMATELY 24 OYSTERS,
WHICH WILL SERVE 4 TO 6

FIVE years ago, few people had even heard of Cajun cooking, much less tasted it. Then a portly chef named Paul Prudhomme spread the gastronomic gospel, and all America became believers.

For the spice powder:
- 1 tablespoon salt
- 1 tablespoon filé gumbo
- 1 tablespoon paprika
- ½ teaspoon cayenne pepper
- ½ teaspoon white pepper
- ½ teaspoon black pepper
- ½ teaspoon garlic powder
- ½ teaspoon onion powder
- ½ teaspoon dried thyme

- 1 quart shucked oysters (do not discard liquor)
- 2 cups flour
- 2 eggs
- 1 cup milk
- 2–3 cups oil for frying

- 1 batch Cajun mayonnaise (see recipe below)

(1) Combine the ingredients for the spice mixture. Toss the oysters with 1 tablespoon of the spice mixture. Combine the remaining spice mixture with the flour. Beat the reserved oyster liquor (discarding any grit or sand), eggs, and milk together in a large bowl.

(2) Heat the oil to 350 degrees in a wok or electric frying pan. Dip the oysters in the milk mixture, then the seasoned flour, then the milk mixture again, then again the seasoned flour, shaking off the excess. Fry the oysters for 1 to 2 minutes, or until golden brown. Drain on paper towels and serve the oysters with lemon wedges and toothpicks, with Cajun mayonnaise for dipping.

Cajun Mayonnaise

MAKES 1 CUP

1 egg yolk
2 tablespoons Dijon-style mustard
1 tablespoon paprika
1 tablespoon ketchup
1 tablespoon prepared horseradish
1 tablespoon Worcestershire sauce
½ teaspoon Pickapepper sauce or Tabasco sauce
½ teaspoon sugar
½ cup vegetable oil
2 tablespoons chopped fresh parsley
Salt and freshly ground black pepper

Place the first 8 ingredients in a bowl and whisk them together thoroughly. Gradually whisk in the oil, followed by the chopped parsley, then the salt and pepper to taste. Alternatively, the ingredients can be combined in a food processor.

Oyster Chowder with Jerusalem Artichokes and Spinach

SERVES 6

THIS hearty chowder makes a perfect post-holiday meal. If Jerusalem artichokes are unavailable, substitute parsnips or more potatoes.

1 pint fresh shucked oysters with liquor
4 strips lean bacon (about 3 ounces)
3–4 shallots (3–4 tablespoons minced)
1 stalk celery
½ pound Jerusalem artichokes
1 large potato
5 ounces (½ package) fresh spinach
4 tablespoons butter
1 tablespoon flour
4 cups bottled clam broth or fish stock (see recipe on page 474)

1 cup heavy cream
Salt and fresh black pepper

(1) Strain the oysters and reserve the liquor. Cut the bacon into ¼-inch slivers. Mince the shallots. Wash the celery and cut it into ¼-inch slices. Peel the Jerusalem artichokes and potato and cut them into ½-inch cubes. Stem the spinach and wash.

(2) Sauté the bacon in a large saucepan over medium heat for 3 minutes, or until lightly browned but not too crisp. Transfer the bacon to a bowl, and discard the fat. Add the butter, shallots, and celery to the pan, and cook over medium heat for 2 to 3 minutes, or until the vegetables are soft but not brown. Stir in the flour. Stir in the clam broth, or fish stock, and oyster liquor and bring the chowder to a boil. Add the Jerusalem artichokes and potatoes, and gently simmer for 10 minutes, or until the vegetables are tender. Add the cream, and salt and pepper to taste. The chowder can be prepared to this stage up to 24 hours before serving.

(3) Just before serving, add the oysters and simmer the chowder for 2 minutes, or until the oysters are cooked—but just barely. Stir in the spinach—the heat from the chowder should be sufficient to cook it, but if not, simmer the soup for a few seconds more. Correct the seasoning.

Serve the oyster chowder in warm bowls. A Sancerre from the Loire Valley, a sauvignon blanc from California, or English ale would make a fitting beverage.

***

Oyster Soufflé with Bacon and Saffron

SERVES 4 AS AN APPETIZER, 2 TO 3 AS A MAIN COURSE

LIKE so many new dishes, this soufflé came into being when I had unexpected company and no time to shop. You can use preshucked oysters: during the winter months, I always keep a pint on hand in the refrigerator; they will keep up to 10 days.

½ pint fresh shucked oysters with liquor
   Approximately ¾ cup milk
 4 strips bacon
 1 leek, or 2–3 scallions
⅛ teaspoon saffron
2–3 tablespoons butter
¼ cup bread crumbs
 3 tablespoons flour
 4 egg yolks
   Salt, fresh black pepper, and cayenne pepper
 6 egg whites
   Pinch of cream of tartar

 1 5-cup soufflé dish, and approximately 2 tablespoons melted
   butter

(1) Strain the oysters, reserving the liquor. Add enough milk to the liquor to make 1 cup. Cut the bacon into ¼-inch slivers. Wash and finely chop the white part of the leek or scallions. Place the saffron in 1 tablespoon hot water to soak. Brush the soufflé dish with melted butter, chill it, and thoroughly brush again. Line the dish with the bread crumbs, discarding the excess.

(2) Sauté the bacon pieces in a 1-quart saucepan for 1 minute. Add the leeks or scallions, and continue cooking for 2 minutes, or until the bacon pieces are lightly browned. Pour off the bacon grease and add enough butter to make 3 tablespoons fat. Stir in the flour and cook for 1 minute to make a roux. Remove the pan from the heat, add the milk and saffron, and return the pan to the heat. Bring the mixture to a boil, stirring constantly. Whisk in the egg yolks, one by one, followed by the oysters. (The mixture should thicken: if it doesn't, bring it back to a simmer.) Add seasonings to taste: the mixture should be very highly seasoned.

(3) Preheat the oven to 400 degrees. Beat the egg whites to stiff peaks, adding a pinch of salt and cream of tartar after 10 seconds. Heat the base mixture almost to boiling. Add ¼ of the whites to the base mixture and stir vigorously. Fold the base mixture into the remaining whites, working as gently as possible. (Don't worry if there are a few clumps of white, don't overdo it:

overfolding will deflate the soufflé.) Spoon the mixture into the soufflé dish and smooth the top with a wet knife or spatula. *Note:* If the whites are properly beaten, the soufflé can be prepared to this stage up to 2 hours before baking.

(4) Bake the soufflé in the preheated oven for 20 minutes, or until cooked to taste. (I like mine a little gooey in the center.) To test for doneness, gently tap the dish—if the soufflé wobbles, it is still wet in the center. Serve at once: people wait for soufflés, not the other way around. A Muscadet or tart sauvignon blanc would make a suitable wine.

AUTUMN ROOTS

ROOT vegetables are the foot soldiers of the legions of the vegetable kingdom. Uncouth. Ungainly. Unglamourous. Uncomplaining. And uncommonly delicious. Tomatoes and other sun worshipers have long passed out of season, and the sturdy root vegetables will sustain us through the cold winter months ahead. Starting in December and continuing through March, these stalwart soldiers will be on parade at the market. Herewith, a look a three of my favorites: horseradish, celeriac, and Jerusalem artichokes.

Armoracia rusticana, better known as horseradish, is hardly for impulse shoppers. This gnarly root looks less like an edible vegetable than a Neanderthal's fossilized femur and is available from late fall to early spring. In its natural form it smells innocent enough, but grated it burns like tear gas. My family loves it—the hotter the better—and whenever we eat gefilte fish, we compete to see who can eat the most horseradish sauce.

Horseradish is a member of the mustard family. It owes its pungency to volatile mustard oils that form when exposed to air. The fiery root is most popular in Central Europe and Scandinavia. The English favor horseradish sauce as a condiment for roast beef. When cooked, horseradish loses some of its bite, becoming sweet, like a parsnip or turnip.

Mirror, mirror, on the wall, who's the fairest of them all? Certainly not celeriac! This knobby root is as warty and wrinkled as the wickedest Halloween witch. But strip away its tattered cloak, and you'll find a heart that's soft as velvet and white as a bridal veil.

Celeriac (also called celery root) is a cousin of commonplace celery. You don't eat the stalks, which are stringy and spindly, but the root is an epicure's morsel. Celeriac is best known in the form of *celerie rémoulade,* a mayonnaise-based salad served as part of a French *hors-d'oeuvres variés* platter. But its earthy, celery-flavored flesh also makes a lovely purée; soups, mashed potatoes, even potato pancakes benefit by its presence. Celery root comes in season late fall and is available most of the winter. Choose the smaller roots: the large ones tend to be woody and often hollow inside.

The Jerusalem artichoke—also called sunchoke—is a paradoxical creature. This small, lumpy tuber is neither from Jerusalem, nor is it an artichoke. It belongs to the same family as the sunflower, which in Italian is called *girasole.* Native to the New World, it reached England in the seventeeth century—an age when most luxury items were imported from the Near East. Girasole sounds like Jerusalem, and the earthy flavor of the tuber does, indeed, resemble that of an artichoke, which is how this cousin of the sunflower came to acquire its name. When buying Jerusalem artichokes, look for the large, relatively smooth tubers: the knobby ones are difficult to peel. Refrigerated, they will keep for up to a week.

Jerusalem artichokes can be boiled, steamed, deep-fried, stir-fried, and baked in their skins like potatoes. The earthy artichoke flavor goes well with game and in salads, soups, and casseroles.

Volcanic Horseradish Sauce

MAKES 2 CUPS

THIS homemade horseradish sauce is as fiery as molten lava. The merest whiff will remind you of a sixties protest march, when the smell of tear gas hung in the air. Our thanks to Rick Spencer of the Bernerhof Inn for the recipe.

    2–3 horseradish roots (enough to make 2 cups grated)
    ½ cup white wine vinegar
    3–4 tablespoons dry white wine

Peel the horseradish with a paring knife. Grate the roots, using the fine shredding side of a grater, or finely chop in the food processor. Mix in the vinegar and wine, adjusting the proportions to taste. Horseradish sauce should be stored in glass jars in the refrigerator and will keep for 2 to 3 months.

NOTE: To make volcanic cocktail sauce, mix equal parts horseradish sauce and ketchup.

Horseradish–Cheddar Cheese Dip

MAKES 1½ CUPS

THIS fiery dip will clear the sinuses of anyone who partakes. I like to serve it with Italian sesame breadsticks.

    2–3 tablespoons freshly grated horseradish or Volcanic
       Horseradish Sauce (see recipe above)
    ½ pound medium or sharp white Cheddar cheese
    ¼ pound cream cheese
    3–4 tablespoons heavy cream

    Salt and fresh black pepper

Peel and and grate the horseradish. Cut the cheese into ½-inch cubes. Combine the first three ingredients in the food processor and purée until smooth (it helps to have the cheeses at room temperature). Add enough cream to obtain a dipping consistency, running the machine in spurts. (Overpuréeing will cause the cream to separate.) Add salt, pepper, and, if you can stand it, additional horseradish to taste. Let the dip "ripen" for 1 hour before serving.

Cream of Celeriac Soup

SERVES 4 TO 6

NOTHING matches the velvety smoothness of cream of celeriac soup. The root is sprinkled with lemon juice to prevent it from discoloring.

> 1–1½ pounds celeriac (celery root)
>   Juice of ½ lemon
> 1–2 leeks, roots and dark green leaves discarded
> 1–2 parsnips or carrots
>   4 tablespoons butter
>   Bouquet garni (see recipe on page 471)
>   4 cups chicken stock (see recipe on page 472)
>   Salt, fresh black pepper, cayenne pepper, and freshly grated nutmeg
>   3 celery stalks
>   1 cup heavy cream

(1) Peel the celery root with a paring knife and cut it into 1-inch pieces. Sprinkle with lemon juice. Wash the leeks and finely chop. Peel and chop the parsnips or carrots. Melt the butter in a large saucepan and cook the leeks, parsnips, and celery root over medium heat for 4 to 5 minutes, or until the leeks are tender but not brown. Add the bouquet garni, stock, and seasonings to taste. Simmer the soup for 30 to 40 minutes, or until the celery root is very soft.

(2) Meanwhile, wash the celery stalks, and remove the

strings from the rounded side with a vegetable peeler. Cut the stalks into ¼-inch slices. Cook the slices in rapidly boiling salted water for 2 minutes, or until tender. Refresh under cold water and drain.

(3) When the celery root is tender, remove the bouquet garni and purée the soup in a blender or food processor. Return the soup to the pan and stir in the cream. Correct the seasoning. Just before serving, garnish the cream of celeriac soup with the diced celery.

Purée of Celeriac and Parsnips

SERVES 4 TO 6

THIS rich purée goes well with beef, game, and chicken. The parsnips add a touch of sweetness—omit them if you wish. The vegetables can be puréed in the food processor, but once the cream is added, run the machine in short spurts—overprocessing can cause the cream to separate.

            1 celeriac (1–1¼ pounds)
            ½ lemon
            ½ pound parsnips
              Salt
            2 stalks celery
          4–6 tablespoons heavy cream
          2–3 tablespoons butter
              Fresh white pepper and freshly grated nutmeg

(1) Peel the celeriac with a paring knife and rub the flesh with cut lemon. Peel the parsnips. Cut the celeriac and parsnips into ½-inch dice. Place the vegetables in a saucepan with salt and cold water to cover. Bring the water to a boil, and simmer for 10 minutes, or until the vegetables are very tender. Drain and purée the vegetables in a food processor or through a sieve, adding enough cream to obtain a smooth, moist consistency.

(2) Meanwhile, peel the celery stalks with a vegetable peeler

to remove the annoying strings. Cut the celery into a ¼-inch dice. Cook the celery pieces in rapidly boiling, lightly salted water for 2 minutes, or until crispy-tender. Refresh the celery under cold water and drain.

(3) Just before serving, heat the purée and stir in the butter and seasonings to taste. Mound the purée on plates or in a serving bowl, and garnish the top with the diced celery stalks.

Jerusalem Artichoke Chips

SERVES 4

HERE'S a variation on the plebeian potato chip that's as tasty as it is unexpected. For deep-frying I like to use an electric skillet or wok. My thanks to Elizabeth Lowe for the recipe.

1 pound large Jerusalem artichokes
1 quart peanut or corn oil for deep-frying
Salt

(1) Peel the Jerusalem artichokes. Cut them lengthwise into ¹⁄₁₆-inch slices, using a mandoline or food processor fitted with a slicing blade. Blot the slices dry with paper towels. Heat the oil to 375 degrees.

(2) Fry the chips in the oil for 30 seconds, or until golden brown, working in several batches to avoid overcrowding the pan. Lift the cooked chips out of the oil with a skimmer and set them on paper towels to drain. Sprinkle with salt and serve at once.

Scalloped Jerusalem Artichokes

SERVES 6

HERE'S a good recipe for people who have never tasted Jerusalem artichokes. For a richer flavor, you could add a handful of slivered smoked ham. Scalloped Jerusalem artichokes make an excellent accompaniment to meat and poultry entrées.

> 1 pound Jerusalem artichokes
> 1 large baking potato
> ½ cup sour cream or heavy cream
> ½ cup grated Gruyère, Parmesan, or white Cheddar cheese
> Salt, fresh white pepper, and freshly grated nutmeg
> 2–3 tablespoons butter

> **1 8-inch ovenproof gratin or baking dish, thickly buttered**

(1) Peel the Jerusalem artichokes, and place in a pot with cold, lightly salted water to cover. Bring the chokes to a boil, reduce the heat, and simmer for 5 minutes, or until tender. Refresh the chokes under cold water and drain. Peel the potato, cut it into ½-inch cubes, and boil, refresh, and drain the same way.

(2) Preheat the oven to 400 degrees. Place the Jerusalem artichokes and potato in a mixing bowl. Using a wooden spoon, beat in the cream, cheese, and seasonings. (*Note:* The mixture should be highly seasoned and it should remain a little lumpy.) Spoon the mixture into the baking dish, and dot the top with pieces of butter. The recipe can be prepared to this stage up to 48 hours before baking.

(3) Bake the scalloped Jerusalem artichokes in the preheated oven for 15 minutes, or until the top begins to brown and the filling is thoroughly heated. Serve at once.

POTATOES

One potato, two potato, three potato, four,
Five potato, six potato, seven potato, more . . .

CHILDREN'S RHYME

IN 1885, a young Dutch artist named Vincent Van Gogh painted his first masterpiece. It portrayed five peasants seated at a rough table in the dim light of an oil lamp, eating a humble meal of potatoes. No food is quite as sustaining as what the French aptly call the "earth apple."

Whole volumes have been written on the history of the potato: its origins in the Andes mountains, where it was a mainstay of the Indian diet; its export to Spain in the sixteenth century, where it was quickly adopted for use in ships' stores. Northern Europeans were less enthusiastic. Believed to cause leprosy, the potato was actually banned in Burgundy in 1619. "None for me!" cried the French gastronome Brillat-Savarin. "I appreciate the potato only as a protection against famine." Even in that role it performed poorly in Ireland in the mid-nineteenth century, when a massive failure of the potato crop caused widespread famine and waves of immigration to the United States.

Still, the spud had its champions, among them an eighteenth-century French pharmacist named Antoine Augustin Parmentier. He presented Louis XVI with a bouquet of potato flowers, saying, "If one tenth of the land in France were planted with potatoes, there would never be a shortage of food." He spent fifty years promoting this useful vegetable, writing ninety-five books and pamphlets. Voltaire wrote of his efforts: "They merit the ovation of all who love mankind."

The potato is, today, the world's largest vegetable crop. It ranks fourth as a food crop after corn, wheat, and rice. It is incredibly versatile: it can be baked, boiled, mashed, fried, and even ground into flour. Its mild taste makes it an excellent foil for other flavors, and few foods are more economical or filling.

There are hundreds of potato varieties (160 in the U.S. alone), which can be grouped into four broad categories.

Red: Red potatoes have thin skins ranging in color from pink to ruby red. The flesh is crisp, white, delicate in flavor, and excellent for boiling. Red potatoes mature quickly; they are often harvested early and served as new potatoes. Some popular varieties include the Red Rose, Red Pontiac, and Red La Soda.

Russet or Idaho: These are the standard baking potato—large, sturdy, and thick-skinned. They are high in starch, which gives them a light, fluffy texture when mashed or baked. Varieties include the Russet Burbank, Green Mountain, Irish Cobble, Norgold, and Butte.

White or Light-skinned (also known as *Irish*): These potatoes are light-colored and thin-skinned, with delicate yellow or white flesh. They are often sold as new potatoes. White potatoes are all-purpose spuds, good for boiling, sautéing, and salads. Varieties include Finnish Wax, Yukon Gold, German Fingerling, and Kennebec.

Blue: If there's such a thing as "potato chic," it's the exotic blue potato. The skin is grayish blue; the flesh has an inky tinge, too. Blue spuds are available at specialty produce shops: they are best enjoyed steamed or boiled with butter. Varieties include the Blue Carib and All Blue.

Potatoes come in two grades: U.S. Extra Number 1 and U.S. Number 1. The former are superior, the latter more widespread. Potatoes should be smooth, clean, shallow-eyed, and unblemished. Avoid spuds with sprouts, soft or wet spots, holes, or greenish skins. (The latter are underripe and will be bitter.)

Store potatoes in a cool, dark, slightly moist place, like the cellar, but not near the furnace. Do not keep potatoes and onions or garlic together: they will become moldy.

Potatoes are available year-round, of course. But their comforting bulk is especially welcome in the cold, lean month of December.

Latkes (Potato Pancakes)

MAKES 15 PANCAKES, TO SERVE 4 OR 5

LATKES are potato pancakes traditionally served at Hanukkah. The recipe comes from my friend and fellow food writer, Faye Levy.

> 4 boiling potatoes (about 1¼ pounds)
> 1 medium onion (about ½ pound)
> 1 egg
> 1 teaspoon salt
> ¼ teaspoon white pepper
> 2 tablespoons all-purpose flour
> ½ teaspoon baking powder
> ½–1 cup vegetable oil for frying

> **Applesauce, quince compote (see page 408), or sour cream for serving**

(1) Grate the potatoes and onions, using the grating disk of a food processor or the large holes of a grater. Transfer them to a colander. Squeeze the mixture to press out as much liquid as possible. Place the potatoes and onions in a bowl and stir in the egg, salt, pepper, flour, and baking powder.

(2) Heat ½ cup oil in a deep, heavy 10- to 12-inch frying pan or electric skillet. Drop 2 generous tablespoons of the potato mixture into the pan to make pancakes. Use the back of a spoon to flatten the mixture so that each cake is 3 inches in diameter. Fry the latkes over medium heat for 4 to 5 minutes per side, or until golden brown and crisp, turning carefully to prevent the oil from spattering. Drain the pancakes on paper towels and keep them warm in the oven.

(3) Stir the potato mixture before frying each new batch. If

all the oil is absorbed, add more to the pan. Latkes should be served hot with applesauce, quince compote, or sour cream on the side.

Roesti (Swiss Potato Pancakes)

ROESTI (pronounced "*ruhr*-schtee") are Swiss potato pancakes. They are unique in that they are made from cooked, not raw, potatoes; the spuds must be boiled the day before and chilled for 24 hours before grating. Roesti makes a fine vegetable accompaniment. Topped with a fried egg, or melted cheese and ham, it becomes a main course for brunch, lunch, or a light supper. The recipe below makes one serving and can be multiplied as desired.

> 1 large baking potato
> 1–2 scallions (optional)
>   Salt and fresh black pepper
> 3 tablespoons clarified butter (see recipe on page 471), or 1½ tablespoons butter and 1½ tablespoons oil
>
> *For garnish (optional):*
> 1 egg
>   Butter or oil for frying
> *or:*
> 2 ounces Emmenthaler or Gruyère, grated
> 1 ounce smoked ham, cut into thin slivers

(1) Place the potato in a pot with cold water to cover. Bring the water to a boil, reduce the heat, and simmer the potato for 15 to 20 minutes, or until cooked (it will be easy to pierce with a skewer). Run cold water over the potato to cool it, then refrigerate for at leat 24 hours. The recipe can be made up to 4 days ahead to this stage.

(2) Peel the potato and coarsely grate with a hand grater or food processor. Finely chop the scallions and add them to the potato with salt and pepper to taste. Heat the clarified butter in

a 6-inch cast iron or nonstick skillet over a high flame. Add the potato mixture, lower the heat, and using the back of a spatula, presss the potato into a cake. Shake the pan from time to time to prevent the pancake from sticking. Cook the roesti for 5 to 6 minutes per side, turning the pancake by flipping. (If you are afraid to flip it, place a plate over the skillet, invert the pancake onto the plate, then slide it back into the skillet.) The secret to preparing roesti is temperature control. The potato must go into hot fat, or it will stick, but it must be cooked over a low flame or it will burn.

(3) Prepare the garnish. Fry the egg sunny-side up, and slide it onto the roesti. Or sprinkle the grated cheese and slivered ham on top, and run the roesti under the broiler till the cheese is melted and bubbly. Serve at once.

Feather-light Potato Pancakes

MAKES 12 TO 14 2-INCH PANCAKES

I first tasted these ethereal potato pancakes at a French restaurant in Boston called L'Espalier. I savored them a second time in Miami, at the stylish Grand Bay Café. I was determined that the next time I had them, it would be in the privacy of my own home where I could eat as many as I desired. L'Espalier owner Moncef Meddeb serves them with *crème fraîche* and osetra caviar, but I assure you they are quite delectable plain.

> 1 pound red potatoes
> ⅓ cup flour
> 2 teaspoons cornstarch
> 1 whole egg
> 3 egg yolks
> ½ cup milk
> Salt, fresh black pepper, and cayenne pepper
> ½ cup clarified butter (see page 471)

(1) Boil the potatoes in their skins until soft. Cool and remove the skins. Purée the potatoes in a food processor. Run the blade in bursts and process as little as possible. Add the remaining ingredients except the clarified butter, and process until smooth.

(2) Heat some of the butter in a heavy skillet over a medium flame. Spoon mounds of batter into the pan to form 2-inch pancakes. Fry the pancakes for 30 seconds per side or until lightly browned. Serve with a small dollop of sour cream or *crème fraîche* and caviar, or with the Apple Butter with Calvados on page 333.

Jack Tar Potatoes

SERVES 4 OVERLY GENEROUSLY,
8 AS A SIDE DISH TO A LARGE ENTRÉE

THESE stuffed baked potatoes were a specialty of the late 3900 Restaurant in Baltimore, where I had my first taste of "gourmet" cooking. The best potato for this dish is the russet, which has a fine, firm, dry consistency.

    4 large russet baking potatoes
    6 strips bacon, cut into ¼-inch slivers
    6 tablespoons butter
    4 tablespoons finely chopped scallions
    ¼ pound grated white cheddar cheese
    ½ cup sour cream
      Salt and fresh black pepper
      Paprika for sprinkling

(1) Scrub the potatoes, and bake in a preheated 400-degree oven for 40 minutes, or until tender. Cut each potato in half and carefully scrape out the flesh.

(2) Meanwhile, fry the bacon over medium heat until the pieces are crisp but not brown. Pour off the fat. Add the bacon

pieces to the mashed potatoes with 4 tablespoons of the butter, and the scallions, cheese, sour cream, and seasonings. Toss until the ingredients are well mixed, but do not mash them too finely —the filling should have a coarse texture. Spoon the filling into the potato skins, mounding it toward the center. Top each potato with a pat of butter and sprinkle with paprika. The potatoes can be prepared to this stage up to 24 hours before serving.

(3) Just before serving, heat the Jack Tar potatoes in a pre-heated 400-degree oven for 10 to 15 minutes, or until heated through and through.

Rumbledethumps
(Potatoes and Cabbage with Butter and Cheese)

SERVES 6

THIS dish certainly wins a prize for the most intriguing nomenclature. *Rumbledethumps* are Scottish soul food, a hardy dish of cabbage and mashed potatoes that is guaranteed to take the chill off an autumn night. The recipe comes from the Scottish Lion Inn in the Mount Washington Valley.

> 4 baking potatoes
> 1 small or ½ large green cabbage
> Salt
> 6 tablespoons unsalted butter
> 2 tablespoons chopped fresh chives or scallions
> Fresh black pepper
> ½–1 cup milk
> 1–1½ cups grated Cheddar
>
> 1 earthenware or glass baking dish, thickly buttered

(1) Peel the potatoes and cut them into ½-inch pieces. Core the cabbage and coarsely chop. Place the potatoes and cabbage

in separate pans with lightly salted water to cover. Bring to a boil, reduce the heat, and simmer until each vegetable is very tender. Drain.

(2) Preheat the oven to 350 degrees. Mash the potatoes with the butter, chives or scallions, salt, and pepper, adding enough milk to give the mixture the consistency of soft ice cream. Mix in the cabbage and reseason to taste. Add the cabbage mixture to the baking dish. Sprinkle the grated Cheddar on top. The recipe can be prepared to this stage up to 24 hours before baking.

(3) Bake the rumbledethumps in the preheated oven for 20 to 30 minutes, or until the cheese is melted and bubbly, and the cabbage mixture is thoroughly heated.

PERSIMMONS

LONG after the summer and fall fruits have passed out of season, we look forward to eating persimmons. These heart-shaped, bright-orange, lacquer-skinned fruits come to market after the first frost. An unripe persimmon is harshly astringent: the merest nibble will make you understand the virtue of patience.

If you've ever wondered what tannin is (wine buffs use the term), take a bite of an unripe persimmon. Your lips will pucker, your throat will constrict, and your tongue will feel like a chalk-covered blackboard. No wonder the first Europeans to encounter it didn't rush to bring the tree back to Europe. But when a persimmon is ripe (squishy soft), it is downright delectable: its texture is as creamy as custard, its flavor reminiscent of dates. (Indeed, it is sometimes called the date plum.) Persimmon makes a refreshing dessert and an unusual accompaniment to pork.

Persimmons are native to China, but the Japanese were the

first to cultivate them extensively. Most languages use the Japanese name, *kaki,* but our word is a corruption of the Algonquin Indian word *pessemin.* There are several hundred varieties: the most commonly sold in this country are the *hachiya* and the *fuyu.* The former is the size of a juice orange; the latter—the only variety that can be eaten when not fully ripe—is the size of a plum. There is also a native American persimmon, which is found chiefly in Indiana. It seldom exceeds the size of a walnut and grows semiwild in most places.

Persimmons appear at the market in late October and are available through January or February. Most are sold in a hard, underripe state and must be allowed to ripen at home. Buy fruits with unblemished orange skin, avoiding any with patches of yellow. Store unripe persimmons, stem side up, in a sealed plastic bag or box at room temperature for three to six days. (To speed up the ripening process, add a banana.) The fruit is ready to eat when squishy soft.

The easiest way to eat a persimmon is to cut out the stem and scrape out the pulp with a spoon. The fruit freezes well: semithawed, it makes an easy, unusual sherbet. To obtain the pulp, push it through a nonaluminum sieve. (Tannin reacts with aluminum.) Traditional American recipes include persimmon pudding, cake, and nut breads. In the recipes below, we leave the fruit in its natural state.

Persimmon Chutney

MAKES 4 CUPS

THIS recipe comes from the restaurant Jasper, on Boston's waterfront. The persimmons must be extremely ripe, soft, and squishy. (The chef ripens his persimmons in a cool, dark corner of his basement.) Persimmon chutney goes particularly well with smoked ham.

3–4 persimmons (about 1–1½ pounds—enough to make 2 cups
    pulp)
3–4 limes (enough for ½ cup juice)
  1 2-inch piece fresh ginger root
  2 ripe apples or pears
  1 small red bell pepper
  ½ cup sugar, or to taste
  ¼ cup golden raisins
  ¼ cup black raisins or currants
    Salt, fresh black pepper, and cayenne pepper
    Splash of vinegar (optional)

(1) Squeeze the pulp out of the persimmons: you should
have about 2 cups. Grate the zest of half the limes. Squeeze the
limes to obtain ½ cup juice. Cut the ginger root into a fine
julienne (matchsticklike slivers). Peel and core the apples or
pears and cut into ½-inch dice. Core and seed the bell pepper
and cut into ½-inch dice.

(2) Combine the lime juice, zest, ginger, and sugar in a large
saucepan, and bring the mixture to a boil. Add the apples or
pears, bell pepper, and raisins, and simmer the mixture for 5
minutes, or until the apple is soft. Increase the heat to high,
and stir in the persimmon pulp. Simmer for 2 minutes. Add
salt, black pepper, and cayenne pepper to taste—the mixture
should be quite spicy. If necessary, add additional sugar, lime
juice, or a splash of vinegar—the chutney should be both sour
and sweet.

(3) Store persimmon chutney in clean jars until you are
ready to use it. Refrigerated, it will keep for up to 1 month. It
goes well with baked ham, smoked turkey, and cold roasts, such
as pork and veal.

Iced Persimmons with Kirsch

SERVES 1

THIS recipe comes from the august *Larousse Gastronomique*.
It makes a quick dessert, and can even be served as a *trou nor-*

mande, a sorbetlike midmeal refresher. For each serving you will need the following:

    1 small, cold, very ripe persimmon
    2 teaspoons kirsch, or to taste
    2 teaspoons sugar, or to taste
      Squeeze of lemon juice

(1) Cut a hole in the fruit around the stem end. Make holes in the pulp with a fork, taking care not to puncture the skin. Spoon the kirsch, sugar, and lemon juice inside the persimmon, and serve it on crushed ice.

Persimmon Ice Cream

MAKES 5 CUPS

ICE cream in autumn? We New Englanders think it's fine any time of the year. (We should know—we have the highest per capita consumption in the United States.) Persimmon ice cream makes an unusual fall treat—try serving it for dessert at Thanksgiving. The persimmons must be squishy soft.

    3–4 large, ripe persimmons (enough to make 2 cups pulp)
      2 cups heavy cream
        Approximately 1 cup sugar
      1 teaspoon vanilla
      1 teaspoon grated lemon rind
        Juice of 1–2 lemons

(1) Scoop out the persimmons and purée the pulp with a fork. Scald the cream with most of the sugar. Stir in the persimmon and flavorings, adding additional sugar as necessary. Chill the mixture for 2 hours.

(2) Freeze the mixture in an ice cream churn, following the instructions of your particular machine. This ice cream is rather perishable, so serve it as soon as possible.

Persimmon Mousse

SERVES 6

HERE'S an unusual fruit mousse for winter. If you don't like Marsala, substitute additional lemon juice.

3–4 ripe persimmons (enough to make 2 cups pulp)
1 envelope unflavored gelatin
3 tablespoons Marsala wine
1 cup milk
½–⅔ cup sugar
3 egg yolks
1 teaspoon vanilla
Juice of ½ lemon, or to taste
¾ cup heavy cream
1 cup gingersnap cookies
6 candied violets, fresh mint leaves, or hazelnuts for garnish

6 martini glasses or wine glasses for serving

(1) Remove the stems from the persimmons, and cut the fruit into 1-inch pieces. Purée the fruit, skins and all, through a food mill or strainer: you should have 1½–2 cups purée. Place the Marsala in a small bowl and sprinkle the gelatin on top to soften. Place the bowl in a shallow pan of simmering water to melt the gelatin.

(2) Prepare a *crème anglaise* (custard sauce). Scald the milk in a heavy saucepan. Whisk the sugar with the yolks in a large bowl. Whisk the hot milk into the egg mixture. Return the egg mixture to the saucepan, and cook it over medium heat, stirring with a wooden spoon, for 2 to 3 minutes, or until the foam subsides, the yolks lose their eggy smell, and the mixture thickens to the consistency of heavy cream. It should thickly coat the back of the wooden spoon. Do not let it boil, however, or it will curdle. Strain the sauce back into the large bowl. Whisk in the melted gelatin, followed by the puréed persimmon, vanilla, and lemon juice to taste. (Feel free to also add a little more Marsala, if necessary.)

(3) Chill the persimmon mixture over a pan of ice or in the

refrigerator, stirring frequently with a rubber spatula. Whip the cream to stiff peaks. Coarsely crush the gingersnap cookies. When the persimmon mixture is on the verge of gelling, fold in most of the whipped cream, reserving a few tablespoons for garnish. Spoon a third of the mousse mixture into the glasses, add half the gingersnap crumbs, add more mousse, the remaining crumbs, and finally the remaining mousse. Pipe rosettes of whipped cream in the center of each glass and garnish with candied violets. Chill the mousses for at least 4 hours, preferably overnight.

CHESTNUTS

"AMARYLLIS was fond of this fruit; but Amaryllis was only a shepherdess, and her beauty did not prevent her from having rather rustic tastes." Thus wrote the flamboyant, nineteenth-century chef Alexis Soyer about that autumn harbinger, the chestnut. This humble nut has been a-roasting for most of human history. Easy to gather (it falls to the ground when ripe), it was, indeed, the provender of the poor.

The nut leads a double life, however. The rich dote on *marrons glacés,* candied chestnuts sold in jars, which cost a king's ransom. Gourmet shops sell a whole line of luxury chestnut products: purées, creams, whole nuts in water or syrup. Penny per pound, chestnuts aren't particularly thrifty, and even when price is no object, they require enormous time and energy to shell.

The chestnut may be named for Castana, a city in Thessaly, where the tree was said to grow in abundance. Castanets, clicked by Spanish dancers, are rounded like chestnuts (*castana* in Spanish), which is where they got their name.

Few foods are more fleeting than chestnuts. They appear just in time for Thanksgiving and are gone by the end of January. During the season, they are an integral part of any big city landscape, sold on street corners by vendors who roast them over coals. I remember when you could buy a whole bag in New York and still have change from a dollar. These days, a handful of chestnuts sells for $2.50, and half of them are moldy. Then again, nutrition is only part of their value: the roasted shells are excellent for warming your fingers!

A chestnut blight at the turn of the century destroyed America's crop. Most of the chestnuts sold here are imported from Italy, so it is important to buy them from a shop with a rapid turnover. When buying chestnuts, look for nuts that feel dense and heavy. A shriveled skin or peeling or blistering end are indicative of mold. A tiny hole in the shell betokens the presence of unwelcome visitors—worms. Because of their high water content, chestnuts are very perishable: keep them covered and refrigerated until ready to use.

ROASTING CHESTNUTS
FOR EATING

THE simplest way to enjoy fresh chestnuts is roasted in the oven. The first step is to make a ¼-inch slash in the rounded side of the shell with the tip of a paring knife. (This allows the steam to escape, preventing the nuts from exploding.) Cook the nuts on a baking sheet in a 400-degree oven for 15 to 20 minutes, or until tender. Alternatively, they can be roasted on top of a wood stove, or in a long-handled skillet in the fire. Let each guest peel his own—remind him to remove the fibrous brown membrane as well as the shell. Serve roasted chestnuts with eggnog or by themselves as an hors d'oeuvre.

TO PEEL CHESTNUTS
FOR COOKING

SLASH the chestnuts as described above and roast them on a baking sheet in a preheated 400-degree oven for 5 minutes. Remove the nuts and peel off the shells, starting at the spot where they blister. It helps to use a small paring knife, cutting the shell at each end of the nut. The hotter the nut, the easier it is to remove the shells: after five or six, you will probably need to return the nuts to the oven. Be sure to remove the brown membrane under the shell, and to cut off any moldy or wormy parts.

Chestnut Soup with Amaretto

SERVES 6 TO 8

I make chestnut soup but once a year. After I've finished peeling all those chestnuts, I vow never to do it again. By the time chestnuts are back in season, my craving for the soup has returned, and, to the necessary degree, so has my patience. A splash of Amaretto or hazelnut liqueur reinforces the nutty flavor of the chestnuts.

> 2 pounds fresh chestnuts
> 2 carrots
> 2 parsnips
> 1 small onion
> 1 small clove garlic
> 2–3 scallions
> 3 stalks celery, or 1 small celery root
> 4 tablespoons butter
> 5 cups brown stock or chicken stock (see pages 472 and 473)
> Bouquet garni (see recipe on page 471)
> Salt, fresh black pepper, cayenne pepper, and freshly grated nutmeg

1 cup heavy cream
3–4 tablespoons Amaretto or hazelnut liqueur (like Frangelico)
2–3 teaspoons brown sugar (optional)

(1) Preheat the oven to 400 degrees. Make a gash in the rounded side of each chestnut and roast for 5 minutes. Peel off the shell and inner skin as described above.

(2) Peel the carrots, parsnips, onion, and garlic. Finely chop all the vegetables. Melt the butter in a large saucepan over medium heat. Add the vegetables, and cook for 5 minutes, or until soft but not brown. Add the chestnuts and remaining ingredients, except for the cream and liqueur. Gently simmer the soup for 40 minutes, or until the chestnuts are very soft.

(3) Remove the bouquet garni and purée the soup in a blender or food processor. Return the soup to the saucepan, adding the Amaretto or hazelnut liqueur, and two-thirds of the cream. Add salt, black pepper, cayenne pepper, and nutmeg to taste: the soup should be very flavorful. If a sweeter flavor is desired, add a spoonful or two of brown sugar.

(4) To serve, ladle the chestnut soup into warm bowls. Pour a little of the remaining cream in each bowl and marble it into the soup, using a paring knife to stir. Chestnut soup is extremely rich—the rest of the meal should be relatively simple.

Hungarian Chestnut Stuffing

SERVES 6

THIS recipe, a Hungarian dish, comes from Budapest-born Alex Lichtman. Mr. Lichtman—who just turned eighty and is still going strong—ran a famous bakery, called Mrs. Herbst's, on New York's Upper East Side.

2 large, crusty rolls
1 pound unshelled chestnuts
1 medium onion
1 clove garlic
3 tablespoons chicken fat or butter
6 ounces chicken or turkey livers
2 eggs
  Juice of ½ lemon
2 tablespoons brandy
1 tablespoon sweet paprika
3 tablespoons finely chopped parsley
  Salt and fresh black pepper

1 9-inch gratin dish or baking dish, thickly greased with chicken fat or butter

(1) Place the rolls in a bowl with cold water to cover, and let soak for 10 minutes. Boil or roast the chestnuts for 20 minutes, gashing the rounded side, and peel as described on pages 457–458. Coarsely chop half the chestnuts and reserve. Purée the remaining chestnuts in a food processor while still warm. Leave the purée in the machine. Finely chop the onion and mince the garlic. Preheat the oven to 375 degrees.

(2) Melt the chicken fat in a medium frying pan over low heat. Add the onions, garlic, and livers, and sauté for 10 minutes, or until the onions are soft but not browned. Remove the pan from the heat. Squeeze as much water as possible from the rolls. Add the rolls, liver mixture, eggs, brandy, lemon juice, paprika, parsley, and seasonings to the chestnut purée, and process for 1 to 2 minutes, or until smooth. Correct the seasoning and stir in the coarsely chopped chestnuts by hand.

(*3*) Spoon the stuffing into the prepared pan and bake for 30 to 40 minutes, or until the mixture is firm and the edges are crisp. Hungarian chestnut stuffing is a great accompaniment for holiday turkey or goose.

Hungarian Chestnut Purée

SERVES 6

MENTION chestnuts to a Hungarian and his eyes will light up. The dish of which he is dreaming is *gestenye puré,* fresh chestnuts puréed with rum, squeezed into squiggly strands, and topped with clouds of whipped cream. The following recipe is labor-intensive, but well worth the trouble.

  1½ **pounds fresh chestnuts**
   ½ **cup sugar, or to taste**
   1 **vanilla bean, split**
4–6 **tablespoons light rum**
   1 **cup heavy cream**
   3 **tablespoons confectioners' sugar**
    Freshly grated nutmeg

(*1*) Use the tip of a paring knife to make a small gash in the rounded side of each chestnut. Heat the nuts on a baking sheet in a preheated 400-degree oven for 3 to 4 minutes, or until the shells blister. Remove the nuts from the oven, a few at a time, and peel off the shells and papery brown skin. Some people prefer to boil the chestnuts to loosen the shells.

(*2*) Place the chestnuts in a large saucepan with the sugar, vanilla bean, and water to cover. Gradually bring the liquid to a boil, and simmer for 20 to 30 minutes, or until the nuts are very tender. Remove the vanilla bean and purée the nuts in a food processor, adding 3 tablespoons of the rum (or to taste) and enough cooking liquid to obtain a soft, smooth purée. The purée should be wet enough to pipe, but dry enough to hold its shape.

(*3*) Beat the cream to stiff peaks in a chilled bowl, adding the confectioners' sugar and remaining rum. Force the chestnut purée through a ricer into 6 serving bowls, or pipe it into squiggles, using a piping bag fitted with a small star tip. Pipe rosettes of whipped cream on top, and crown with a sprinkle of nutmeg. The purée is sweet and very rich, so serve strong black coffee as an accompaniment.

Chestnut Cheesecake

SERVES 8 TO 10

HERE's an unusual cheesecake flavored with chestnuts and rum. Fresh chestnuts produce a superior flavor, but if you are in a hurry, acceptable results can be obtained with canned chestnut purée. (A good brand is Clément Faugier, but be sure you buy the *purée*, not the *crème*.)

For the crust:
  6 ounces gingersnap cookies (1 cup crumbs)
  ¼ cup butter, melted

For the chestnut purée:
  1½ pounds fresh chestnuts (or 1 1-pound can of purée)
  ½ cup sugar
  1 vanilla bean, split

To finish the filling:
  24 ounces cream cheese, at room temperature
  1½ cups sugar, or to taste
  5 eggs
  ¼ cup dark rum
  2 teaspoons vanilla extract

For the topping:
  2 cups sour cream
  ⅓ cup sugar
  3 tablespoons light rum

  1 9-inch springform pan, thoroughly buttered

(*1*) Crush the cookies to fine crumbs in the food processor or with a rolling pin. Mix in the melted butter, and press the crust into the bottom and along the sides of the springform pan. Chill for 30 minutes.

(*2*) Meanwhile, cook the chestnuts. Score, roast, and peel the chestnuts as described on pages 457–458. Place the nuts in a saucepan with the sugar, vanilla bean, and cold water to cover. Gradually bring the liquid to a boil, and simmer for 15 to 20 minutes, or until the chestnuts are very tender. Remove the vanilla bean and purée the nuts in a food processor, adding enough cooking liquid to obtain a soft, smooth purée. Preheat the oven to 325 degrees.

(*3*) Beat the cream cheese and sugar together in a mixer (or by hand) until smooth. Beat in the eggs, one by one, until the mixture is light and fluffy. Add the chestnut purée, dark rum, and vanilla extract, and beat until smooth. Pour the filling into the crust and bake at 325 degrees for 1 to 1¼ hours or until the filling is set.

(*4*) Whisk the sour cream, sugar, and light rum together until light and smooth. Spoon this mixture on top of the cheesecake, turn off the oven, and let the cake cool in the oven. Chill chestnut cheesecake for at least 4 hours, preferably overnight, before serving.

A SEASONAL MISCELLANY

Cream of Fava Bean Soup

SERVES 8 TO 10

SOMETIMES the best dishes are those that are the most simple. Like this cream of fava bean soup that was served to me at the Quinta do Bom Retiro, a hillside "château" in Portugal's magnificent Douro River valley. (The Douro is where the grapes for port are grown.) The fava beans were fresh from the garden, picked and shucked that afternoon. The soup was simmered on a wood-fired stove, and after dinner we sipped 1929 port!

1½ pounds fresh fava beans
1 leek, furry root and green leaves discarded
5 tablespoons olive oil (try to use an imported Portuguese or Spanish oil), plus extra if necessary
4 cups chicken stock (see recipe on page 472)
Bouquet garni (see recipe on page 471)
Salt, fresh black pepper, cayenne pepper, and freshly grated nutmeg
1 cup heavy cream
3 tablespoons finely slivered fresh mint

(1) Shell the fava beans. Wash and chop the leek. Heat 3 tablespoons oil in a large saucepan and cook the leeks over medium heat until soft but not brown. Add the remaining ingredients, minus the mint. Gently simmer the soup for 30 minutes, or until the beans are very soft. Reserve ½ cup whole beans for garnish. Discard the bouquet garni. Purée the remaining beans

with the broth in a blender, food processor, or through a vegetable mill. (If using a processor, purée the beans first, gradually adding the liquid.) For an extra-fine texture, put the soup through a fine-meshed china cap strainer. The recipe can be prepared to this stage up to 24 hours before serving.

(2) Reheat the soup over a low flame. Correct the seasoning, adding salt, black pepper, cayenne, nutmeg, and additional olive oil to taste. Serve cream of fava in warm bowls, garnishing each with a few whole fava beans and a sprinkle of fresh mint.

Fresh Figs with Prosciutto and Melon

SERVES 6 AS AN APPETIZER

KADOTA figs have purple skins and a delicate white flesh within. If good melon is unavailable, feel free to substitute fresh berries or other fruit. This recipe comes from the Upstairs at the Pudding restaurant in Cambridge, Massachusetts.

12 fresh kadota figs
1 tablespoon finely chopped fresh thyme leaves
¼ cup honey
12 very thin slices of prosciutto ham
1 ripe melon of any kind

(1) Take 6 of the figs and slice each fig into 4 even wedges. (Reserve the remainder.) Sprinkle the wedges lightly with thyme. Thin the honey with ¼ cup warm water, and in it dip the prosciutto slices. Cut the prosciutto widthwise into 1-inch strips and use them to wrap up the thyme-coated fig slices. Cut the melon into thin slices.

(2) Just before serving, cut each of the remaining figs into 4 wedges, and arrange them on chilled salad plates with the ham-wrapped figs and melon slices.

Martha's Vineyard
Beach Plum Jam

MAKES 10 CUPS JAM

HERE'S a delicacy for anyone who is lucky enough to be at the beach in September. Beach plums look like small red grapes, and they're found in profusion on shoulder-high bushes along the littoral zone from the Carolinas to Maine. The best plums for jam making are those sweet enough to eat by themselves.

2 quarts freshly picked beach plums
6 cups sugar
  Juice of ½ lemon
1 3-ounce package liquid pectin
¼ cup Cointreau

10 1-cup canning jars

(1) Gently simmer the beach plums in enough water to cover three-quarters of them (about 2 cups) for 5 to 10 minutes, or until soft. Strain the plums and reserve the liquid (approximately 3 cups). Put the plums through a food mill or sieve: you should wind up with 3 cups pulp.

(2) Combine the pulp and liquid in a heavy, nonaluminum saucepan, and heat almost to boiling. Stir in the sugar and lemon juice. Bring the mixture to a rolling boil, and cook for 1 minute. Remove the pan from the heat, and stir in the pectin, followed by the Cointreau. Ladle the hot jam into hot sterilized jars, and cover.

(3) Put the jars in a large pot with enough water to cover by 2 inches. Boil for 10 minutes. Let cool to room temperature.

Beach plum jam is a labor of love. Be sure to sign each label.

Rose Hip Jam

MAKES 2 CUPS

I got my first taste of rose hip jam in Budapest. I liked its tart, herbal, citrusy flavor so much, I carried a jar of it all over Europe. I needn't have gone so far, because rose hips grow like weeds on Nantucket, Martha's Vineyard, indeed all along the Atlantic coast. The sea rose has delicate purple flowers, while the "hip" is a bright orange-red berry with a hard shiny skin and bristly stem. This jam is even more a labor of love than beach plum jam (it takes 2 quarts of rose hips to make 2 cups of jam), but it is well worth the effort.

> **2 quarts freshly picked rose hips**
> **½–1 cup sugar**
> **A few drops lemon juice (optional)**
>
> **2 1-cup canning jars**

(1) Combine the rose hips and 3 to 4 cups water (almost to cover) in a large, heavy pan. Simmer the rose hips for 20 to 30 minutes or until soft. Strain off the liquid and reserve. Purée the rose hips in a food mill: you should wind up with 1 to 2 cups.

(2) Place the rose hip purée in a heavy pan, adding ¼ cup of the reserved cooking liquid and ½ cup sugar for every cup of purée. Gently simmer the jam for 5 minutes, or until thick, adding water, sugar, or even a few drops lemon juice to taste. Spoon the jam into warm sterile jars and cover.

(3) Put the jars in a large pot with enough water to cover by 2 inches. Boil for 10 minutes. Let cool to room temperature. Rose hip jam will keep for 3 to 6 months.

Turnip-Green Soup

SERVES 4

IN the fall, my neighborhood hosts a farmers' market at which it is possible to buy turnips and beets and other root vegetables with the leaves still attached. Turnip greens have a peppery flavor, not unlike that of mustard greens—added judiciously, they are excellent in salads. They also make delicious soup, as I discovered one evening when I had a hankering for escarole soup, but no escarole on the premises.

   1 bunch turnip greens, beet greens, or escarole (enough to make 2 cups greens)
   1 small onion or leek
   1 large potato
3–4 strips bacon (optional)
   3 tablespoons butter
   4 cups chicken stock or broth (see recipe on page 472)
     Salt and fresh black pepper
   1 egg (optional)
6–8 tablespoons of freshly grated Parmesan

(1) Trim the thick stems off the turnip leaves, and thoroughly wash the leaves in cold water. Spin them dry in a salad spinner, and cut into ½-inch ribbons. Finely chop the onion or leek. Peel and cut the potato into ¼-inch slices. Cut the bacon into ¼-inch slivers.

(2) Melt the butter in a large saucepan. Cook the onion or leek over low heat for 3 minutes, or until soft but not brown. Add the stock or broth, turnip greens, potatoes, and salt and pepper to taste, and simmer the soup for 8 to 10 minutes, or until the vegetables are tender.

(3) Meanwhile, sauté the bacon pieces over medium heat until golden brown. Transfer them with a slotted spoon to a paper towel to drain. Just before serving, add the bacon to the soup. If an egg-drop effect is desired, beat an egg, and pour it in a thin stream into the rapidly boiling soup, stirring vigorously. Correct the seasoning with salt and pepper. Serve the Parmesan on the side for sprinkling on the soup.

Stone Crabs with Joe's Mustard Sauce

THE RECIPE BELOW SERVES 1 AND
CAN BE MULTIPLIED AT WILL

THE stone crab wasn't very popular until Joe Weiss, founder of the famous Joe's Stone Crab restaurant in Miami, had the idea to serve it chilled. (Chilling firms up its otherwise watery flesh.) The stone crab season starts in November—the claws are always sold cooked.

    5 jumbo stone crab claws (1½ pounds claws per person)
    ½ lemon, cut in wedges
    ¼ cup melted butter
      Joe's Mustard Sauce (see recipe on page 470)

(1) Keep the crabs on ice until ready to serve. To crack the claws, place them on a cutting board and cover with a dish towel. (The towel keeps bits of meat and shell from spattering.) Crack the shell with a wide-headed mallet, starting at the knuckle, working toward the claw. Serve the claws on ice, with lemon wedges, and melted butter or Joe's Mustard Sauce for dipping.

Joe's Mustard Sauce

MAKES 1½ CUPS

YOU wouldn't believe what I had to go through to get this coveted recipe. Often imitated, never duplicated, Joe's mustard sauce is almost as famous as the stone crabs themselves.

3 tablespoons Coleman's dry English mustard
1 cup mayonnaise (see recipe on page 477 or use a good commercial brand)
2 teaspoons Worcestershire sauce
1 teaspoon A-1 sauce
2 tablespoons light cream
⅛ teaspoon salt

Combine the ingredients and whisk until smooth.

BASIC RECIPES

Bouquet Garni

A bouquet garni is an herb bundle used for flavoring soups, stews, and sauces. Traditionally the herbs are tied in cheesecloth, but I never seem to have cheesecloth on hand, so I use aluminum foil, which I perforate with a fork. The wrapping keeps the herbs together, and spares your guests the potential discomfort of choking on a whole peppercorn or bay leaf.

> 1 bay leaf
> 1 sprig thyme, or ½ teaspoon dried thyme
> 1 large sprig parsley
> 10 black peppercorns
> 2 allspice berries (optional)
> 1 clove (optional)
> Cheese cloth or aluminum foil

Tightly wrap the ingredients in a square of cheesecloth or aluminum foil. If using foil, perforate it with a fork to release the flavors. Always remember to remove and discard the bouquet garni before serving the dish.

Clarified Butter

MAKES ABOUT ¾ CUP

CLARIFIED butter is ideal for sautéing, because it can be heated to a higher temperature without burning than ordinary butter. This is made possible by removing milk solids and other impurities.

1 cup butter

Melt the butter in a small saucepan. Using a spoon, skim off the white foam on the surface—this is made up of milk solids, which burn when the butter is heated. The golden liquid underneath is clarified butter, ready to be spooned out with a small ladle. At the bottom is a thin layer of water. To remove it, refrigerate the pan until the butter resolidifies. Crack through it with a spoon and pour out the milky white liquid at the bottom. Clarified butter will keep for several weeks.

NOTE: An alternative to clarified butter is to use equal parts vegetable oil and butter for pan-frying. The oil raises the temperature at which butter begins to burn.

Chicken Stock

MAKES 8 CUPS

STOCK is the cornerstone of fine cooking. It's easy and economical to prepare, and it makes your whole house smell nice. I'm not much of a partisan of canned stock or bouillon cubes: both taste unnaturally salty. The stock can be frozen in 1-cup containers for convenient use in the future.

   3–4 **pounds chicken bones, chicken or turkey carcass, chicken necks, etc.**
   1 **large onion**
   2 **carrots**
   2 **stalks celery**
   1 **leek, furry root and dark green leaves discarded**
   2 **cloves garlic, peeled**
   Bouquet garni (see recipe on page 471)

(1) Remove any fat from the chicken bones. If using necks, pull off the skin. Place the bones, vegetables, and bouquet garni in a large (at least 6-quart) stockpot with enough cold water to cover (approximately 3 quarts).

(2) Bring the stock to a boil over a high heat: the pot should not be covered. Skim off any foam or fat that rises to the surface. Reduce the heat and gently simmer the stock for 3 hours, adding cold water as necessary to keep the bones covered.

(3) Skim the stock frequently, using a shallow ladle, not a slotted spoon. It is important to remove all the impurities, or the stock will be cloudy. For the same reason, it is important that the stock be gently simmered, not boiled.

(4) At the end of 3 hours, you should have a golden full-flavored broth. Strain it into 1- or 2-cup containers and let it cool to room temperature. Do not refrigerate stock until it has come to room temperature. (A hot stock or sauce in a cold refrigerator is a breeding ground for bacterial action.) Stock will keep for 3 to 4 days in the refrigerator, and 2 to 3 months in the freezer. To use frozen stock, simply melt it in a saucepan or add it directly to the soup or stew.

Veal Stock

SUBSTITUTE veal bones for chicken bones. Try to use bones with some meat on them, such as neck or back bones. For extra flavor, add a pound or two of veal shin.

Brown Stock

BROWN stock can be made with chicken, duck, turkey, veal, or beef bones. Roast the bones in a 400-degree oven for 1½ hours, or until thoroughly browned, adding the vegetables halfway through, so they brown too. (Leave the skin on the onion for color.)

Transfer the bones and vegetables with a slotted spoon to the stockpot, and discard the fat. Place the roasting pan over high heat and deglaze it with 1 cup dry white wine. (To deglaze, scrape the bottom of the pan with a spatula to loosen congealed meat juices.) Add the wine to the stockpot. Add 3 tablespoons tomato paste, and proceed as described above.

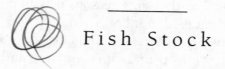

Fish Stock

MAKES 4 CUPS

FISH stock resembles chicken and veal stock, but it is cooked for a much shorter time. The best bones to use are those of firm white fish, like Dover sole or halibut. Do not use the bones of dark-fleshed fish, like mackerel or bluefish—the flavor will be too strong. Fish stock keeps a few days in the refrigerator, and 6 to 8 weeks in the freezer.

2 pounds "frames" or heads from fine-flavored white fish
3 tablespoons butter
1 onion, finely chopped
1 small leek, finely chopped
2 stalks celery, finely chopped
1 clove garlic, minced
Bouquet garni (see recipe on page 471)

(1) Remove the gills and wash the fish frames thoroughly to eliminate all traces of blood. Using a cleaver, cut the frames into 4-inch pieces.

(2) Melt the butter in a large (at least 4-quart) pot and sauté the chopped vegetables and the minced garlic over medium heat for 3 to 4 minutes, or until soft. Add the fish bodies, increase the heat to high, and cook for 1 to 2 minutes, or until the fish starts

to turn opaque. Add cold water to cover (approximately 1 quart) and the bouquet garni.

(3) Bring the stock to a boil and skim off the white foam that forms on the surface. Reduce the heat and gently simmer the stock for 20 minutes, skimming often to remove any impurities. Strain the stock and discard the bones. If the flavor of the stock is not concentrated enough, continue boiling the stock *without* the bones, until it is reduced to the taste and consistency you desire. Let cool to room temperature before refrigerating.

Court Bouillon

MAKES 4 CUPS

COURT bouillon means "quick broth," literally, for it only takes 10 minutes to make. It is used for poaching shellfish.

1 carrot, diced
1 onion, diced
1 stalk celery, diced
1 small leek (green tops discarded), washed and chopped
2 strips lemon zest
Juice of 1 lemon
1 teaspoon black or green peppercorns
Bouquet garni (see recipe on page 471)
1 teaspoon salt
2 cups dry white wine

Combine the ingredients in a large, nonaluminum saucepan. Add 2 cups water and simmer the ingredients for 20 minutes. You are now ready to poach the shellfish in this mixture.

Basic Pie Dough

THE following dough is my version of French *pâte briseé* (short pastry), and it is good for all manner of pies and tarts. It takes 30 seconds to make in the food processor—I actually prefer the consistency of machine-made dough. Note that I use a "special" flour, made by adding one part cake flour to every two parts all-purpose flour: this helps reduce toughness and shrinkage in the dough.

Steve's Special Flour

2 cups all-purpose flour
1 cup cake flour

Combine the flours and mix thoroughly with a whisk.

NOTE: Provided that you respect the two-to-one ratio, the recipe can be expanded or reduced to suit your needs. I make a large batch of special pastry flour ahead of time and keep it on hand in my kitchen.

Basic Pie Dough

Special Flour	1 cup	1½ cups	2 cups
Butter	4 tablespoons	6 tablespoons	8 tablespoons
Salt	½ scant tsp.	¾ scant tsp.	1 scant tsp.
Egg yolks	1	1	2
Heavy cream	2–3 tablespoons	4–5 tablespoons	5–7 tablespoons
Yield	1 8-inch tart	1 10-inch tart	1 12-inch tart

(1) Cut the butter into ½-inch cubes (it should be very cold), and place it with the flour and salt in a food processor fitted with a chopping blade. Run the machine for 30 seconds, or until the butter is completely cut up and the mixture feels sandy and even-textured. Add the egg yolk and cream, and run the machine in short bursts for 30 seconds, or just until the dough comes together into a compact mass. (*Note:* It may be necessary to add a little more cream.) Gather the dough into a ball and chill for at least 30 minutes before rolling.

Mayonnaise

MAKES 1½ CUPS

HOMEMADE mayonnaise is quick to make, and it's far superior to store-bought. The trick lies in having all the ingredients at room temperature and in adding the oil in a slow, thin stream.

> 1 **extra-large egg (run it under warm water to bring it to room temperature)**
> 1 **heaping teaspoon Dijon-style mustard**
> **Approximately ¼ teaspoon salt**
> 1½ **cups vegetable oil**
> **Juice of ½ lemon, or to taste (or an equal amount of wine vinegar)**
> **Fresh white pepper and cayenne pepper**

Food Processor Method:
(1) Place 1 whole egg, the mustard, and the salt in the food processor, and run the machine for 1 minute. Add the oil in a thin stream, followed by the lemon juice and seasonings. Correct the seasoning with additional salt, pepper, cayenne, and lemon juice—mayonnaise should be very flavorful.

Hand Method:
(1) When making mayonnaise by hand, we use only the yolk and 1 cup oil. Place the egg yolk, the mustard, and the salt in a

heavy glass bowl. Whisk these ingredients together until the individual grains of salt are dissolved. Whisk in the oil in a very thin stream. When the sauce begins to thicken (after 3 to 4 tablespoons of oil), you can add the oil more quickly. Once all the oil has been added, the sauce should be as thick as pudding.

(2) Whisk in the lemon juice, which will thin and lighten the sauce, followed by the white pepper and cayenne pepper. Correct the seasoning with additional salt, pepper, cayenne, and lemon juice—mayonnaise should be very flavorful.

Coconut Milk

MAKES 2 TO 3 CUPS

COCONUT milk is used in Asia the way heavy cream is used in the West. The procedure is rather involved, so most people—even Asians—use canned unsweetened coconut milk. Here's how you make it from scratch.

1 large, fresh coconut (approximately 2 cups grated meat)
3 cups boiling water
Cheesecloth

(1) Crack open the coconut (save the liquid inside for drinking) and place the coconut pieces in a 250-degree oven for 5 to 10 minutes, or until the flesh comes away from the shell. Remove the shell and brown skin. (I find that a vegetable peeler works best for removing the latter). Grate the coconut in a food processor or by hand.

(2) Place the coconut in a large bowl and pour the boiling water over it. Allow it to cool to lukewarm, and then knead firmly with your hands for 3 to 4 minutes. Strain the coconut mixture through a piece of cheesecloth, squeezing out as much liquid as possible. The liquid you obtain is coconut milk.

BIBLIOGRAPHY

Books about Holidays, the Months, and the Calendar

Evans, Ivor H., ed. *Brewer's Dictionary of Phrase and Fable*. New York: Harper & Row, 1981.

Frazer, James. *The New Golden Bough*. New York: Signet, 1959.

Gaster, Theodor H. *Festivals of the Jewish Year*. New York: Morrow Quill Paperbacks, 1978.

Haley, Pat. *The Nine Seasons' Cookbook*. Dublin, New Hampshire: Yankee Books, 1986.

General Books about Food

Bailey, Adrian. *Cook's Ingredients*. New York: William Morrow & Co., 1980.

Beard, James. *The New James Beard*. New York: Alfred A. Knopf, 1981.

Castelot, André. *L'Histoire à Table*. Paris: Prisma, 1962.

Hodgson, Moira. *The New York Times Gourmet Shopper*. New York: Times Books, 1983.

Mariani, John F. *The Dictionary of American Food and Drink*. New York: Ticknor & Fields, 1983.

McGee, Harold. *On Food and Cooking*. New York: Charles Scribners, 1984.

Raichlen, Steven. *A Taste of the Mountains Cooking School Cookbook*. New York: Poseidon Press, 1986.

Root, Waverly. *Food*. New York: Simon & Schuster, 1980.

Selden, Gary. *Aphrodesia*. New York: E. P. Dutton, 1979.

Soyer, Alexis. *The Pantropheon*. New York: Paddington Press, 1977.

Tannahill, Reay. *Food in History*. New York: Stein & Day, 1973.

Trager, James. *Foodbook*. New York: Grossman, 1970.

Willan, Anne. *Great Cooks and Their Recipes*. New York: McGraw-Hill, 1977.

Fish and Seafood

Maine Department of Sea and Shore Fisheries. *The State of Maine's Best Seafood Recipes.* Augusta: Statehouse.

Davidson, Alan. *North Atlantic Seafood.* London: Macmillan, 1979.

McClane, A. J. *The Encyclopedia of Fish Cookery.* New York: Holt, Rinehart, & Winston, 1977.

Fruits and Vegetables

Bianchini, Francesco, and Corbetta, Francesco. *The Complete Book of Fruits and Vegetables.* New York: Crown Publishers, 1975.

Brennan, Georgeanne, Cronin, Isaac, and Glenn, Charlotte. *The New American Vegetable Cookbook.* Berkeley: Aris Books, 1985.

Greene, Bert. *Greene on Greens.* New York: Workman Publishing, 1984.

Jagendorf, M. A. *Folk Wines, Cordials, and Brandies.* New York: Vanguard Press, 1963.

Leibenstein, Margaret. *The Edible Mushroom.* New York: Fawcett Columbine, 1986.

Meyers, Perla. *The Seasonal Kitchen.* New York: Vintage Books, 1975.

Morash, Marian. *The Victory Garden Cookbook.* New York: Alfred A. Knopf, 1982.

Radecka, Helen. *The Fruit and Nut Book.* New York: McGraw-Hill, 1984.

Schneider, Elizabeth. *Uncommon Fruits and Vegetables: A Commonsense Guide.* Cambridge: Harper & Row, 1986.

Woodier, Olwen. *The Apple Cookbook.* Pownal, Vermont: Garden Way Publishing, 1984.

Ethnic Cuisines

Prudhomme, Paul. *Chef Paul Prudhomme's Louisiana Kitchen.* New York: William Morrow & Co., 1984.

Rozin, Elisabeth. *Ethnic Cuisine: The Flavor Principle Cookbook.* Brattleboro: Stephen Greene Press, 1983.

Shosteck, Patti. *A Lexicon of Jewish Cooking.* Chicago: Contemporary Books, 1981.

Steinberg, Rafael. *Pacific and Southeast Asian Cooking*. New York: Time-Life Books, 1970.

Willan, Anne. *French Regional Cooking*. New York: William Morrow & Co., 1981.

Books about Individual Foods

Del Conte, Anna. *Portrait of Pasta*. New York: Paddington Press, 1976.

Jones, Evan. *The World of Cheese*. New York: Alfred A. Knopf, 1977.

Kolpas, Norman. *The Chocolate Lover's Companion*. New York: Quick Fox, 1977.

Marquis, Vivienne, and Haskell, Patricia. *The Cheese Book*. New York: Simon & Schuster, 1964.

INDEX